GURDJIEFF'S

TRANSFORMATIONAL

PSYCHOLOGY

The Art of Compassionate Self-Study

Gurdjieff's Transformational Psychology: The Art of Compassionate Self-Study

Published by Present Moment Press, Sebastopol, CA, 95472

For permissions, ordering and interest in online groups please contact dr.russellschreiber@gmail.com.

Cover Design by Darcy Sinclair
Book Layout by Anthony Blake

Printed in the United States of America

Library of Congress Cataloging-In-Publication Data
Gurdjieff's Transformational Psychology: The Art of Compassionate Self-Study/Russell Schreiber
ISBN 978-1-54397-452-2

GURDJIEFF'S TRANSFORMATIONAL PSYCHOLOGY

The Art of Compassionate Self-Study

RUSSELL SCHREIBER

Dedicated to Annie Lou Staveley.
She opened the communication pathways between separate Gurdjieff groups and modeled for all of us that this is a collaborative endeavor.

"Faith," "Love," and "Hope"

Faith of consciousness is freedom
Faith of feeling is weakness
Faith of body is stupidity

Love of consciousness evokes the same in response
Love of feeling evokes the opposite
Love of body depends only on type and polarity

Hope of consciousness is strength
Hope of feeling is slavery
Hope of body is disease

—George Ivanovich Gurdjieff

ACKNOWLEDGMENTS

I give the greatest thanks to my parents and grandparents, who, though only with me for a short time, taught me how to love. Without that teaching, what would I have been? Through their caring for me, I received what I needed to learn about compassion.

My great thanks goes to Mr. Gurdjieff. I realize that I would never have had the opportunity to live a meaningful life had it not been for the inspiration I received from his profound legacy: his writings, the Movements, and the example of his life and efforts. I wish to thank my teachers Willem A. Nyland, Annie Lou Staveley, and Dr. John Lester, and all those who supported them in their Work. Annie Lou Staveley and also George and Mary Cornelius are special to me in that they began the process of dissolving the barriers between different lineages of teaching the Work. I feel a debt to John Bennett, whose ability to make the most complex concepts understandable, has been a gift to me. All of these individuals have been guiding lights for me, and each has given me so much that I will always be grateful for.

I wish to thank all my friends, group members, and all those who I have worked with over the years and have added so much to my life. Without their attention to inner work, their efforts at Movements, participation in workdays, and their efforts to keep the Work alive, my life would have indeed been poorer. Phil Cain and Marcia Paul have been especially important.

My heartfelt thanks go to Anthony Blake, whose work, editing, and layout made this book possible. He warned me at the beginning that I did not know what I was getting into, and he was supremely correct. He has helped me to both distill and fill out needed aspects of these ideas. His vast knowledge and understanding of Gurdjieff's Work, and Bennett's ideas and writing, have provided me with countless insights into what is needed in this Work at this time.

I am thankful for Linda Moore's friendship and her expert editing contribution. She has worked tirelessly to clarify the writing and help me to think deeply about ideas and concepts that are at once simple and complex. Anthony and Linda have helped to me to explicate the many different facets of psychology and the Work that are so intertwined.

I wish to absolve of responsibility for any mistakes or errors of judgment all those friends who helped me in the publication of this book. Any omissions or errors within this book are solely my own.

Thanks to my wife, Elizabeth Schreiber, who has been a constant source of support and a catalyst for helping me write what is important and meaningful. She is a continual fund of knowledge and inspiration for me. Her love of psychology, love of our children, and all the children and others she serves, love of our four dogs, and her creative nature are a constant source of energy and inspiration for me. My writing had to finally pass her scrutiny, where she pushed me to be certain and clear about what I wished to say. It was Elizabeth who prompted me to begin this process of filling out and continuing Gurdjieff's psychological journey. I admire her continual commitment to bringing psychology and the Work together.

Thanks to Darcy Sinclair and her wonderful direction and help with the cover and elegant physical presentation of this book.

Finally, I must thank all those who I do not know that are responsible for creating, developing, and preserving the concepts, methods, practices, information, and the Movements that provide us all with the possibility of inner growth. Without their efforts, the legacy that Gurdjieff passed on to us would not still be available.

CONTENTS

PART II: SELF-STUDY

PART III: THE ELUSIVE "I"

PART IV: PSYCHOLOGICAL INVESTIGATIONS

PART V: NEW MATERIAL AND REFLECTIONS

INTRODUCTION

My life has been a quest for truthful self-knowledge and to answer the question of why I exist. The search to find answers to these questions led me to the transformative psychological practices of George I. Gurdjieff and these are the focus of this book.

I arrived in Berkeley, California, in December 1964 to attend the University of California. The Free Speech Movement that signaled a major change in the consciousness of young people throughout the world was just beginning. Berkeley was the epicenter of that energy, an energy that involved drug experimentation, protests against the Vietnam War and more importantly a revolution in consciousness and spiritual awakening. My major at the university changed a number of times until I settled on psychology. I wanted to understand my own life and vaguely realized that psychology was the key. However, the study of psychology at the university level proved disappointing to me. It revolved around a set of theories perpetrated by old white men who were overly intellectual and emotionally undernourished.

By the time I finally received my undergraduate degree in psychology in 1970, I was so disappointed with what passed for the study of human psychology that I became a carpenter. The study of psychology at the university had been purely an intellectual pursuit. It was not experiential and I never felt I learned anything practical about my own inner workings. On the other hand, carpentry was an excellent choice for me. I developed real skills and had experiences that balanced out the lopsided over-development of my mind due to many years of formal education. I never gave up my study of psychology, but continued it through a process of self-study that I discovered during my last few years in college. When I finally felt I had enough life experience, self-knowledge, and practical skill, I returned to graduate school and became a psychologist.

During the last few years of college, I discovered the ideas and practices of Gurdjieff. His system for human development differed dramatically from the mainstream current of psychology. The methods were practical, experiential, and transformative. The study of psychology became for me the study of myself. The "Work," as Gurdjieff's system is called, emphasizes that the responsibility for real change in oneself—psychological transformation—lies with the individual, rather than mediated through someone else such as a therapist. The emphasis of psychotherapy focuses on a difficulty or dysfunction that has become so pronounced that the client seeks help with the problem, and it depends heavily on the therapist's directing the client's progress and helping him learn about himself.

GURDJIEFF

Whereas my formal education in psychology at college had left me confused, empty and provided no real understanding of myself, Gurdjieff's presentation had just the opposite effect. When I came in touch with the Gurdjieff Work, it felt as if I had walked by a gigantic magnet and every part of me — my thoughts, emotions and my body — was magnetized and pulled towards it. I felt for the first time that I was being fed real ideas, concepts, practices, and everything was experiential and not just intellectual. I started to understand myself and what I was experiencing.

Whereas everything that I had learned in college felt purely subjective and liable to change at any moment, the Work was different. It illuminated and made understandable many experiences that I already had and I sensed that this knowledge and understanding came from a very high level — beyond Gurdjieff as an individual man — from a center of knowledge and understanding that existed outside of any particular time or culture. My reaction to what Gurdjieff presented created in me the need to know more and a craving for personal transformation.

The first step in the Gurdjieff Work was to learn how to find the truth about myself. Gurdjieff placed the responsibility of finding this truth squarely on my shoulders. It was not a matter of believing his ideas or following a guru, but depended on my own self-study and the knowledge gained through that study. Gurdjieff's method, which actually consists of many practices, begins with learning to study and observe oneself objectively. Ultimately, this method promised to lead me to find the aim and purpose of my life.

Gurdjieff was a contemporary of Freud and Jung, but is rarely, if ever, mentioned in histories of psychology. He was born in approximately 1877 in Alexandropol (now Gyumri), Armenia, then part of the Russian Empire. A great many biographers have written about his childhood, his search, and his teachings.

By the time he was in his early twenties, Gurdjieff had decided to devote his life to answering the questions of the purpose of life on the earth and the aim of human existence, and the nearly unbridgeable gaps between the vastness of human potential and humanity's limited development thus far. How was it that people's great potential had failed to materialize? How did it happen that, time after time, people repeatedly engaged in destroying each other's existence? War, throughout history, results in the wholesale decimation of all the advances of a particular civilization.

He could not find the answers from intellectual authorities, in the Church, or in books; and thus he was driven to his own practical research. His search took him to centers of esoteric learning in the Near and Far East. He found schools where the psychological history of the human species had been preserved, along with practices that could restore human beings to their essential humanity. What he learned seemed so crucial that he was compelled to bring these teachings to the West. In the early twentieth century, he began by establishing groups in Russia to disseminate what he had found. Today, his work has spread around the world.

Gurdjieff found answers to his questions about the human predicament. His answers were inner psychological answers, not external ones (economic, social, or biological). He found it was the inner psychological state of people, their state of consciousness, that determines the way people interact with one another and develop cultural behavior, including the periodic need to engage in war. He determined that people's inner psychological state had become distorted, and in turn, their culture then perpetuated its own distortions, resulting in a unique dilemma. Humans had developed an ambiguous state of consciousness that was neither fully awake nor completely asleep, and they lived in this waking-sleeping state, believing they were fully awake. Gurdjieff created conditions to help people experience and understand the reasons for their "abnormal" state of consciousness and its terrible consequences. He developed methods to enable them to verify their inadequate state of consciousness and to improve it.

Gurdjieff's Work was made difficult by two facts. First, from the time he began teaching, the world was in turmoil. It began with the Russian Revolution, spanned two World Wars, and the birth of the nuclear age in Hiroshima. Second, the very people he would depend on to disseminate his ideas and methods were themselves not fully awake, but were also in the state of waking-sleep.

His attempts to communicate also included the role of creative artist. In Russia he worked on a ballet which, though never completed, was the possible stimulus for his later compositions in music and dance. He collaborated with Russian composer Thomas de Hartmann on hundreds of pieces for piano used for the unique form of "sacred gymnastics," now known as the Movements. He let it be known that he would like to be called a "teacher of dancing." He was also an author. His first book appeared in 1933, but he was displeased with it and it was soon withdrawn.

During the 1920s and 30s Gurdjieff worked on his magnum opus, *All and Everything*, ten books in three series. The first series was a mythical account of the history and malaise of human life entitled, *Beelzebub's Tales to his Grandson*. The second was a somewhat allegorical account of his friends and travels called *Meetings with Remarkable Men*. The third, a kind of "confession," was *Life is Real, then Only When "I Am."*

With the one exception of the book he withdrew, none of Gurdjieff's writings were published during his lifetime. P.D. Ouspensky, a major pupil of Gurdjieff's, published an account of the early groups in Russia under the title, *In Search of the Miraculous* (initially it had the much better title, *Fragments of an Unknown Teaching*) in 1949. Gurdjieff confirmed that this was an accurate account. In 1950, the year after his death, Gurdjieff's first series, *Beelzebub's Tales to His Grandson* was in print. The two books are in stark contrast. Ouspensky was a journalist and wrote clearly and engagingly. Gurdjieff did almost the opposite, writing a complex, mythological, comic and strenuous critique of the whole of the modern world spanning thousands of years.

In this book I make considerable use of both *In Search of the Miraculous* and *Beelzebub's Tales to His Grandson*. A significant place is also given to the ideas of another of Gurdjieff's leading pupils, A. R. Orage, whose ideas on psychological transformation were written up by C. Daly King in what he called *The Oragean Version*. And I use explanations from several of John G. Bennett's books, another English pupil of Gurdjieff's and by Rodney Collin, a pupil of Ouspensky's.

Gurdjieff continually experimented with the transmission and application of his transformative practices. This constant evolution can be seen in the accounts of his early work and lectures, then his work at his institute at the Château le Prieuré at Fontainebleau-Avon, and finally in his later group work. His writings also show constant evolution. I surmise that the reasons for his changes in exposition and application were that he was searching to find and refine the most effective means to transmit the teachings he had assembled so that his followers could make correct use of them.

Gurdjieff had noticed that his teachings were often too narrowly interpreted. Different groups, sometimes in different countries, fixated on a particular aspect of the Work to the exclusion of other important parts. For example, a group might fixate on self-observation and make that aspect of Work the centerpiece of their efforts. This is a common fault we all share when we find one method useful and then repeat it while dismissing other methods that might be equally important and effective. This is especially significant if the aim of Gurdjieff's legacy is the harmonious development of men and women.

PSYCHOLOGY

My background is in psychodynamic and somatic psychology. Psychodynamic work focuses on the intrapsychic and unconscious conflicts within an individual and their relationship to human experience and behavior. The overarching belief is that through increasing a person's insight, psychological integration and healing can occur. Somatic psychology is an interdisciplinary field that involves the study of the body, somatic experience, and the embodied self. It includes therapeutic and holistic approaches to the body. Both these areas of psychology resonate with the processes of self-study that characterize Gurdjieff's methods. In addition, I have practiced Gurdjieff's methods, worked with groups, taught the Gurdjieff Movements, and been involved in the Work for over forty years. In exploring Gurdjieff's methodology, I will bring in what I consider relevant and supportive psychological concepts and practices. This is an experiential book in that what I will present is meant to be worked with and not simply remain ideas written on a page.

If Gurdjieff focuses attention on the individual and their work on themselves, then I can also say that mainstream psychology primarily focuses on "relational units," by which I mean, the dyad of therapist and client. The therapist-client dyad emphasizes the leadership of the therapist in healing a problem that the client brings in. The emphasis is to reduce the client's suffering and increase his or her insight. The therapist is tasked with observing the client and guiding him toward health and out of suffering. This is a psychology of relieving suffering and helping the client to function better or at least attain their previous level of functioning.

Those familiar with the practice of mainstream psychology may notice that finding the aim and purpose of one's life through self-study and self-observation is not its primary focus. Both in research and therapy, current psychology remains concerned with understanding and making adjustments in personal and interpersonal behavior, with the aim of better functioning. By contrast, Gurdjieff's method aims for transformation of the inner life of a person rather than simply adjustment—it is a spiritual psychology concerned with actualizing inner potential.

Psychologists today often use the words "soul" and "spirit." Perhaps they begin to recognize there is something more important in human psychology than adjustment or correction of behavior. Some psychologists may even recognize that a part of every man and woman—usually a part buried under their ordinary consciousness—cries out for greater connection, self-understanding and development.

An integral human capacity that connects Gurdjieffian psychology and mainstream psychology is the development of self-compassion. Both psychologies have inadvertently neglected the development of self-compassion — the root of empathy and understanding of oneself— alongside the development of consciousness and insight. When self-compassion is left out, we miss a vital catalyst in the transformation and creation of inner life. But, you may ask what is self-compassion?

Compassion is a word having two parts, *com* meaning "together," plus *pati* meaning "to suffer." The general definition comes from the Old French and implies a deep awareness of the suffering of another coupled with the wish to relieve it. Every normal person has at moments felt compassion for another person or animal. And yet, we rarely experience this emotion in relation to ourselves. "Self-compassion" as used in this inquiry means the ability to observe and accept the truth of myself, allowing myself to be affected by what I find while maintaining an attitude of kindness and interest in understanding my behavior and experience. Self-compassion does not occur automatically, but has to be learned and practiced during the process of acquiring experience and knowledge of ourselves whether it is through psychotherapy, religion, a spiritual practice, or the Gurdjieff Work.

Without self-compassion, real emotional growth may be stymied. This is due to a little recognized psychological process that occurs when we try to evolve psychologically. Modern psychology alludes to this process when it refers to the "shadow" side of consciousness. As we gain more knowledge and understanding of ourselves, there is often the simultaneous growth of an interior psychological "judge" that offsets and resists inner evolution. This judge occurs in the shadows (we are unconscious of it) and can derail us. Such a shadow process can lead to the fundamentalist thinking so evident in many religions where the world is seen in extremely black and white terms. In this way, religions originally designed to expand human consciousness end up narrowing consciousness. In my practice as a psychologist and my experience working with Gurdjieff's system, I have witnessed the negative effects of this inner judge on myself and others and how it curtails emotional growth. I have found an antidote to these negative effects in the practice of self-compassion.

WE BELIEVE WE ARE AWAKE

Periodically, in the many forms of therapy—cognitive behavioral, analytical, object relational, depth psychology, or Jungian psychology—the questioning of a patient's beliefs becomes the focus of therapy. Beliefs determine our values, desires, behavior, vocations, relationships, etc. Psychologists become experts at dissecting, interpreting, and relating a client's suffering to his or her beliefs. By gradually understanding belief structures, a client may be able understand the causes of their suffering. But what about the therapist's beliefs?

Rarely, if ever, does the therapist look at his own beliefs and assumptions, particularly about whether the client in front of him is awake, and more importantly, whether he himself is awake. The unexamined belief of both therapist and client that they are awake is never examined. Is their belief correct? Are they awake? If we look carefully at certain terms used in psychological parlance, such as "transference," "countertransference," and "projection," they are actually clues that unconscious mechanisms operate in the midst of this "conscious" therapy. It is possible that client and therapist are engaged in a waking-sleeping level of consciousness, one moment asleep and dreaming and the next moment awake. It is here that Gurdjieff's understanding illuminates what is actually taking place in our lived experience and obligates us to examine what we believe to be our awake state of consciousness.

What does it mean to be awake? For the purposes of this inquiry we require a definition. It is not sufficient to say or believe that we are awake, nor can awake be defined as "not asleep." The meaning of awake as used here is as follows: Being awake is a state of consciousness in which a person is aware of where he is, what he is doing, his inner and outer condition (including thoughts, emotions, movements, and sensations), and as he does something, or simply is, there is a part within him that is clearly experiencing his existence and aware of being alive in the present moment.

Gurdjieff developed practices that allow people to verify their waking-sleeping state, break free from their sleep and experience an actual awakened state. Although Gurdjieff could clearly see the connection between the destructive tendencies of civilizations and the waking-sleeping consciousness of their inhabitants, waking them up would prove to be very problematic.

To wish to wake up, one must notice that he or she might not be fully awake; for this to occur, one must see this sleeping aspect of their "conscious" state repeatedly. Becoming aware of the sleeping nature of one's consciousness can only be accomplished through self-study—that is, through correctly conducted self-observation. When a person sees through the veil of sleep and gathers proof that he is asleep most of the time, then the wish to escape from this waking-sleeping state may take hold. The Work is a vehicle for helping people become fully alive, wake up out of their semi-sleep, gain their own independent knowledge, and find the purpose of their own and humanity's existence.

Gurdjieff's Work is not meditation. Although quiet inner exercises are a distinct group of practices within the Work, such inner exercises are more active than meditation and require our active participation. The practice of objective self-study is to be done in the midst of ordinary life because it is here that one must learn to wake up.

This book in many ways is a reference book of topics that I have found to be fundamental for the study of oneself and the process of acknowledging my "sleep" and beginning to awaken. The book is structured so that the ideas proceed from basic concepts and exercises to subjects that are more complex, with the most sophisticated subjects and practices at the end of the book. My purpose in covering such a wide range of topics is to encourage you, the reader, to become interested in your own self-study and to explore areas of personal interest that you may not have previously recognized. The Gurdjieff Work is not about following another person's path. It requires that you become a researcher of yourself, seeking to understand how and why you are trapped in your own unique waking-sleeping state.

Bringing together Gurdjieff's great legacy with its unique gifts for humanity and useful supporting material from current psychological practice is complex and will take some time. I ask you to "bear with me" as I explore ideas, practices and my own experiences to put flesh on the bones of these transformative practices.

Russell Schreiber
Sebastopol, California
July 2013

PART I

A PSYCHOLOGY OF TRANSFORMATION

Chapter 1

ATTENTION

As you read this sentence, you are making use of an extremely important ability: your capacity to pay attention. Attention is an instinctive function that is indicative of our degree of health. Our capacity to pay attention is diminished when we are ill, tired, or feeling stressed. If we suffer a head injury or a stroke, our attention may be permanently affected. Our relationship to this wonderful human capacity of attention is similar to using a magnificent tool of which most of us have almost no understanding.

In this chapter, we are going to explore many aspects of attention. Primarily, we will explore attention as a capacity we use to gain self-knowledge. It is impossible to understand anything without using attention. But the degree of attention each of us has does not represent a finished product. As we shall find out, its functioning varies from moment to moment. Attention can also be improved, and at the end of this chapter we will look at some exercises to learn about attention and how to develop it.

Life's Journey

I am certain that I am not alone in imagining my life as a journey that began at my birth and will end at my death. However, modern life tends to shield us from experiencing the terror of our approaching death and realizing the time-limited nature of this journey. In many ways, the pace and demands of modern life anesthetize us to death's inevitability by the infinite distractions it makes available. A single lifetime is actually very short, as most people over the age of fifty soon realize. Of course, these questions probably arose for us as early as our teenage years. We questioned why people acted the way they did and what the meaning of life was, but these questions were soon forgotten.

When we see that the purpose of our individual existence remains an enigma to us, we have to "invent meaning." We learn to value making a living, having children, getting material things, enjoying ourselves; but, while doing so, we learn to ignore the other critical questions of life and also those facing humanity. Our many activities give us some relief from the gnawing fact of our approaching demise.

Most people are on this journey without any idea of where they are headed; they do not want to look up and out or wonder where all this is leading them. Our so-called "consciousness," — that supposedly alert, cognitive state where we are aware of our situation and ourselves— remains preoccupied with interests we have accidentally found or have gravitated toward because of our subjectivities and personalities. The majority of people in Western society desire to have *more*: more money, more material goods, more happiness and security, more sexual satisfaction, more fulfilling jobs, and so on. These desires easily fill up our lives and become habitual, just as the ability to appreciate life in the present moment seems to be decreasing. Most of our aims are future-oriented. Our activities primarily revolve around providing safety and security for our bodies and our psyches. The need to be safe distracts us from living in the present moment. Activities as diverse as mountain climbing, hobbies, making money, addictions of every sort, TV, the Internet, etc., all can distract us from the present moment and the important questions of life.

The fact that we are asleep to our primary underlying motivation— the need to feel safe and secure—limits our understanding of ourselves. Our need for security is similar to the air we breathe or the ocean for sea creatures; it is so pervasive that unless our cocoon of safety is penetrated, we do not even notice how it pushes us around. Our inability to notice this constant, underlying need for safety is in the nature of our distracted consciousness—we cannot notice it because of our lack of self-awareness at any given moment. We remain in a semiconscious state, unaware of our motivations. It is important to realize that an understanding of our *actual* state of consciousness is fundamental to any real understanding of ourselves. Let us examine this more closely.

Know Thyself

In the forecourt of the Temple of Apollo at Delphi were inscribed the words, *gnothi seauton*, know thyself. Gurdjieff bases the possibility of human evolution on this ancient idea: to know myself, to be aware of myself, to understand myself. The knowledge referred to here is not superficial knowledge, but rather self-knowledge that can elucidate the profound meaning of my life. This is a knowledge and understanding I have to find for myself. Teachers, friends, and therapists can help me, but the real—and invisible—work is done within me. This immediately raises a profound question: How can I know that what I find out about myself is trustworthy? How do I learn about myself objectively so that I can rely on the facts I find? What characterizes this objective knowledge and how is it different than the superficial knowledge that typifies my current knowledge?

For most of us, knowledge about ourselves is scanty and superficial. We may know, for example, that we were born to certain parents in a certain country. We went to a certain school. We had such and such friends. We like the way certain people look and act. We like a certain-shaped body in our sexual companions, and their faces must look a certain way. Why this is so, we have no idea, and for the most part, we remain uninterested. It is as if we are blind to our inner lives. We just want things to go well and to feel good. We don't want to be depressed, scared, anxious, insecure, or frustrated. We live out our lives moving toward what we have come to like and away from what we dislike. What is beyond like and dislike? Almost always, we remain uninterested in what this might be.

This lack of interest in our psychological state presents a difficult problem for those who want to evolve. Our dilemma, as Gurdjieff found, is that most of us *do not notice* we are asleep and *uninterested* in our lives. I am referring to our ordinary state. Have you ever noticed that most of the time you cannot remember any details about what you did even three days ago? I am placing the emphasis here on the word "details." Most of us can remember we were at work, at school, or traveling. But the details of our experience—the impression of ourselves doing something and realizing we were present—climbing into the car, having the feeling of air on our faces at a particular moment, knowing how hot it was, being conscious of how we felt, what we were thinking—all that is simply gone. It remains unremembered because although we experienced it, it was not recorded by us in a useful way. We were not present. There was no "I" there to record it, only the mechanism of ourselves going through the motions.

Of course, our lives are punctuated by events we enjoy, but other important experiences are lost to us. Furthermore, most parts of us are not interested in learning more about ourselves, about what sort of consciousness we usually have. This was Gurdjieff's quandary. How can human beings be made aware of the fact that they are not conscious and might still become conscious, if they already believe they are conscious and thus remain uninterested in making any effort?

I have found the following analogy useful in understanding my condition. Imagine a young fish swimming in a foul, polluted area of a river near a factory that dumps chemicals into the water continuously. The water she swims in is not fresh, yet it is the only water she knows. Because of her limited experience, she is uninterested in finding fresher water, since most of her time is spent just looking for things to eat and trying to avoid predators. Such is the state of consciousness of most people. They are not aware of the precariousness of their situation and the limited nature of the consciousness they are swimming in. They will not be aware of it until they have glimpsed another state of consciousness. Then they must see how easily they drop back into their habitual patterns, back into the muck they are used to.

DEFINING ATTENTION

As human beings, we have a most important tool to help us in our journey toward self-knowledge and greater possibilities. However, for the most part, it has developed in a lopsided and haphazard manner. That tool is *attention*. What is attention, how is it useful, how did it develop and have we ever thought about it?

"Attention" may be defined as the state of mind wherein a person concentrates on some feature of his environment to the relative exclusion of the rest. If his attention is haphazard, yet the primary means he has of collecting facts about the world or self-knowledge, then the knowledge he receives will likewise be fragmentary and limited. Thus we have a very limited and rather eclectic array of self-knowledge that is stored in us as associative memories. These associative memories do not give us any kind of reliable self-knowledge. Nor do we have any method for learning to focus our attention more accurately.

Child rearing, education, and the environment to which a child is exposed as they mature influence the quality of their attention. As a therapist, I find that individuals imitate the type and quality of attention of those who were around them during their formative years. The first assaults on attention begin in childhood. Parents instruct the child, "Pay attention to what you're doing," "Be careful not to spill things on the table," "Watch carefully how you're walking," "Don't hurt yourself," "Don't run, you'll fall," etc. This type of so-called "education" and directing a child's attention continues in school, where children sit for six hours each day trying to focus on what the teacher is saying when their bodies and minds want to move, create, or daydream. Their teachers, outside stimuli, hunger, and other bodily sensations haphazardly pull their attention around and gradually develop in them a lasting pattern of on and off attention, where one moment their attention is focused on something, and the next moment their attention is pulled toward any accidental impression that catches it.

The environment (impressions of people, surroundings, circumstances, and situations) binds a child's attention and programs it quickly. By the time they reach kindergarten, most children have developed what I refer to as "focused" attention. If a child lacks the ability to focus his attention as well as others, he may be labeled as having attention deficit disorder (ADD). Focused attention is an important capacity to develop in order to lead an effective life. However, if we wish to acquire true self-knowledge, there is a subtler, yet deeper, attention we must cultivate.

It is important to recognize that we have at least two distinct types of thought in which our attention participates. The first type is simply associative thought. This is a relatively random process of thinking that is active whether we are awake or asleep and is perpetually animated by either external stimuli or our inner environment of memories, emotions and sensations—it is similar to the motor of a car that is left running which is going nowhere in particular. We have little control of our associative thought process. The other type of thought is directed thought where we direct attention and thought in solving a problem, directing our actions, etc. This type of thought makes use of focused attention. Ordinarily, our attention is pulled about haphazardly by associative thought. Associative thought often interferes with directed thinking and prevents us from using our attention to think clearly. Learning to apply attention through directed thinking is where the possibility of our evolution begins.

Jacques Lusseyran was blinded at the age of eight in a school accident. He says the following about attention in his masterpiece, *Against the Pollution of the I*:

> Because of my blindness, I had developed a new faculty. Strictly speaking, all men have it, but almost all forget to use it. That faculty is attention. In order to live without eyes it is necessary to be very attentive, to remain hour after hour in a state of wakefulness, of receptiveness and activity. Indeed, attention is not simply a virtue of intelligence or the result of education, and something one can do without. It is a state without which we shall never be able to perfect ourselves. In its truest sense it is the listening post of the universe.[1]

Lusseyran went on to lead a children's resistance movement as part of the French underground during World War II. He was able to develop his attention to such a level that he memorized the details of each of his six hundred child accomplices, even though he couldn't see them. He served as head of the children's resistance until it merged with the main French Resistance. Lusseyran's blindness had forced him to develop not only focused attention, but other possibilities of attention that remain dormant in most of us.

Just as we have different types of thinking, we have distinct types of attention. The first is unfocused associative attention, developed randomly by the process of reacting to our environment. The second type is directed or focused attention and requires some intentional effort on our part. The third type of attention is more subtle than the others and is utilized in the process of *participation* that will be explained in last part of this book.

Our ordinary process of attention is associative, subject to any incoming impression, developing in a kaleidoscopic environment that constantly distracts us. The environment pulls on our attention, using up psychological energy and causing neurological patterns to develop randomly. Within this randomly developed system we gradually learn to direct our attention or focus on something we choose. The ability to focus attention is developed by efforts demanded of us by caregivers, education and our culture. Thus, within our so-called "conscious state," there is eventually developed an interior pattern of language, feeling, and sensation that either automatically and haphazardly pulls our attention about or which we are able to direct and focus to a limited degree. It is a testament to our organism that attention functions as well as it does, considering the poor education it has received.

Our attention almost always functions without our knowing or understanding it—except, perhaps, when we are sick or tired and we may notice a problem with paying attention. At times I notice a decrease in my cognitive awareness due to external impressions: If it is too noisy during a test, or when someone in a movie theater is wearing perfume or crinkling a bag, I might find I cannot sit next to that person and also pay attention to the test or the movie.

We may also notice an increase in the ability to pay attention after we have ingested certain chemicals or organic substances. For example, with coffee or a cigarette we might concentrate better. With methamphetamines, concentration temporarily soars to heights that delight, but soon wanes as the drug's effects wear off. The difficulty with all these "highs" is that the increase in attention is automatic (that is, requires no effort on my part). My body and psyche have not yet developed to the point where they can produce such an experience without such artificial help. Thus, a mechanical increase in my attention without my own effort depletes me, leaving me feeling used up, believing I require more of the drug.

Focused attention is primarily developed and directed through our visual function. As such, attention becomes intimately tied to vision and the manner in which vision operates. Even though he was blind, Lusseyran realized that vision was about moving forward and manipulating objects.[2] Science has discovered that the visual faculty is actually an extension of our tactile function. Attention, then, becomes an extension of our hands through vision. It allows us to apprehend objects, people, and even scenes at a distance.

Because we do not usually make an intentional effort to direct our attention, and it becomes gradually more intimately connected with and primarily activated by vision, attention becomes more and more automatic and a new faculty replaces it: the faculty of "correlation." Correlation is a learned cognitive function that labels objects, scenes, and experiences, which are then stored and linked in memory. Correlation allows us to use language to communicate about the physical world, and we use it to make the world understandable to ourselves. Unfortunately, correlation develops the words and labels into shorthand symbols, and these symbols gradually replace real attention and simply activate previously stored associations and memories.

Correlation, with its randomly stored patterns of associations and symbols pulls our attention about haphazardly, hampering our ability to think in depth or sustain an enquiry. In school, we develop this ability to correlate words, ideas, and situations in order to become "thinkers." However, just developing this correlative ability does not teach us how to think deeply. Instead, we become shallow thinkers, easily manipulated by advertisers, teachers, our parents, the government, and others. The net effect is we do not think for ourselves. Therefore, we cannot act from our true selves. Gurdjieff says the following about the effect of so-called "education" on our ability to think:

> . . . And [education] played a part because, based, as we have already said, chiefly on compelling the young to "learn by rote" as many words as possible differentiated one from the other only by the impression received from their consonance and not by the real pith of the meaning put into them, this system of education has resulted in the gradual loss in people of the capacity to ponder and reflect upon what they are talking about and upon what is being said to them.[3]

By the time we are adults, our heads are filled with such an assortment of associations that one association calls up another purely automatically. We are walking around, and for some reason we hear a song running through our head, or a person's face reminds us of Bill, and we suddenly remember how angry we are with him. This thought then reminds us further of the fact that he could never make a good living, but was very handsome, and so on. Such is the nature of our attention and thought. They remain undisciplined and shallow. Our inability to direct our attention becomes a problem when we begin to wish to know ourselves in a deeper way because there is a definite relationship between attention and self-knowledge.

Some years ago, ADD became a recognized psychological disorder, and soon many children had been diagnosed with it. These children were unable to focus their attention even for short periods, with very serious effects on their ability to learn. At the other end of life, Alzheimer's disease affects millions throughout the world. While there is no scientific evidence that the type of attention we have developed may somehow predispose us to Alzheimer's, loss of short-term memory and the inability to pay attention are symptoms of the disease. Of course, other factors may be involved in such disorders as ADD and Alzheimer's—for example, genetics, nutrition, environmental conditions, drug usage in either the parents or the individuals, or other determinants.

Our capacity to focus our attention deliberately is constantly under attack. You can see this clearly by just watching television for an hour. Notice how advertisers manipulate your erratic attention. They rarely allow you to focus on one image for more than a second. This ploy seems both intentional and unconscious. The unconscious aspect may involve the advertiser's inability to focus his own attention for more than a few seconds. The intentional aspect involves, of course, hooking the viewer. The ads, more often than not, include some pretty woman or handsome man using something (that is, driving a car or being admired for their looks). A great deal of advertising plays upon the fantasy that if you use their product, you will end up having more sexual satisfaction, or at least, avoid or alleviate some form of suffering, such as a headache, wrinkles, arthritis, etc. All of this passive television viewing is an assault on our ability to pay attention and establishes psychological patterns that become habitual.

As a psychologist, I have become increasingly interested in neurological patterning. If we do something more than a few times, our tendency to repeat that action is increased. Given a sufficient number of repetitions, it quickly becomes automatic, habitual. The benefits of this automatism may be useful for many endeavors, but it becomes problematic when it involves negative or useless tendencies, such as the inability to focus our attention. The more our attention remains unfocused, the more this lack of focus becomes a standard pattern for us. If our neurological habit pattern becomes one where our attention is pulled by any chance association, wouldn't we expect this tendency to increase with age?

Alfred R. Orage, a student of Gurdjieff's, addressed the question of habits. A brilliant writer and thinker, Orage worked extensively with Gurdjieff on the translation of Gurdjieff's two major works, *Beelzebub's Tales to His Grandson* and *Meetings with Remarkable Men*. When speaking about thought processes, Orage said:

> Theoretically, of course, we can place ourselves in any of many circumstances tomorrow; we can theoretically place ourselves in circumstances which will require us to think. But it is a thousand to one that we shall "choose" tomorrow's circumstances, not by their value to use as opportunities for developing thought, but merely in accordance with our already formed habits.[4]

Of course, the major instrumentality in forming these habits is our attention.

John G. Bennett, one of Gurdjieff's leading pupils, once likened people's attention to the assembly line in a peculiar sort of factory. In his analogy, the factory was very unusual, in that anyone could just throw anything he wished onto the assembly line. Attention would then only become the assembly line itself, acting as the glue that linked together all the diverse elements thrown onto it. We might surmise this factory would be terribly inefficient—one could not even be sure what the final product would be. In many ways we are similar to Bennett's factory in that we also manufacture products—in our case, behaviors, thoughts, and emotions—and if attention is our assembly line, and we wish to produce self-knowledge, we need to know specifically what we want to place on the assembly line and how to place it there.

Without attention, we are unable to understand ourselves or anything at all. Here, it is important to point out that knowledge and understanding are two very different phenomena. For example, I can look at the tools on a workbench and know many things about them, their shape, their composition, and even their weight. However, that knowledge does not mean I understand how to use the tools or their purposes. We are all in this situation with regard to our attention. It is a tool we use automatically, but poorly, all the time. We rarely direct it, and we understand only poorly its characteristics and purpose.

DEVELOPING ATTENTION

If you wish to learn about yourself and the possibilities of your own evolution, you must learn to use your attention. At the end of this chapter, I list a few informal practices that may give you a taste of new possibilities for developing your attention.

After many years, I have come to believe that real education, in contrast to academic education, can be found in what I call the "University of the Self." What I learn and understand about myself becomes immediately mine. You might notice that I used the words "learn" and "understand." Learning about oneself through practice produces a different quality of knowing than reading some bit of information in a book. It is through learning how to study myself that I can begin to taste understanding.

Understanding itself can be of two different types. Simple understanding means you can relate ideas and concepts to aspects of your own experience. Everyone possesses this type of understanding. It is the result of living in society, and, to some extent, a result of one's education. Deeper understanding actually begins with self-study. It is not a degree granted by a school or given by another person. True understanding comes from the invisible, inner university that resides within each of us. For most of us, because of our haphazard attention, it has become a rather dilapidated building, scarcely used. It needs restoration and funding! Attention is the tool we can use to restore and fund it.

Simone Weil, the mystic and philosopher, noticed that the children she taught displayed a very distinct type of attention. Her writings have helped me realize that a major feature of modern education is that our attention is trained to be a contracting, narrowing effort, as if we were contracting a muscle. Weil says:

> In order really to pay attention, it is necessary to know how to set about it . . . most often attention is confused with a kind of muscular effort. If one says to one's pupils: "Now you must pay attention," one sees them contracting their brows, holding their breath, stiffening their muscles.[5]

Weil alludes to a different type of attention that is possible for us, a type she characterizes as the ability to focus, yet remain receptive, *allowing new information to enter.* In speaking of prayer, she says, "The key to a Christian conception of studies is the realization that prayer consists of attention." [6]

I personally have experienced this different type of attention; not a narrowing, but the opposite, a type of active relaxation without muscular tension. It is not easy to describe, but one can approach it through working with Gurdjieff's Movements, which I will discuss in detail later. The Movements are demanding, not merely physically, but mentally and emotionally. They require me to develop a new type of "opening" attention, all the while relaxing the muscles. In other words, I learn to be attentive, while being emotionally open to whatever comes. To open in this way requires a kind of vulnerability, as well as a relaxation of the musculature.

The Work really begins for me as I struggle to direct my attention. Attention, our greatest asset, is developed and sharpened by practicing the methods the Work entails. I believe it is the most advanced methodology available for developing harmonious attention. In practicing it, I gain self-knowledge and the possibility of understanding my purpose in life.

GROUNDWORK FOR SELF-STUDY

Before outlining some practices regarding attention, let me offer some principles that in my experience are essential for self-study.

- The aim of self-observation is to see the truth about myself. My commitment to truth must include a passionate wish for objectivity.
- Everything I see about myself must ultimately include compassion for myself, real interest in my life and purpose, and interest and compassion for others.

Without compassion toward myself, the new impressions I gain in coming to know myself may easily lead to negative consequences. One of the reasons for these negative consequences may be my wish to be "good." After hundreds of generations of Judeo-Christian and Muslim culture, we all (except perhaps psychopaths or the truly enlightened) want to be good. As quickly as possible, I want to do away with what I see as the "bad" parts of myself. Those who begin on a spiritual path are especially prone to this and it likewise holds true for those in the Gurdjieff Work. In my experience, the impulse to do away with the unpleasant things I find in myself is a critical mistake. It can lead people to become even more unbalanced than they were before they started to seek self-knowledge. To counter this tendency, I use the following phrase whenever I see or learn something about myself: "Oh, this is so interesting. I must find out more!"

Another problem that highlights the need to develop self-compassion is that some individuals have a natural proclivity toward negativity or self-hate. They use the information they have gained through self-observation as a justification to be more intolerant toward themselves and others. The negative attitude toward others and the self-hate they have developed appears to allow them to feel superior to others. All of this is useless in relation to Work unless one recognizes it, becomes interested in it, and moves ahead to find out more about such a tendency.

DRUGS: OH DAMN, DO I HAVE TO GIVE THEM UP?

I am putting in this little piece about drugs at the very beginning, since it is very important. This Work has no place for recreational drugs. Whether it is the occasional use of marijuana, cocaine, psychedelics, or over-consumption of alcohol, all such usage will gradually cause you to stagnate. While alcohol has probably the most limited psychoactive potential for harm, you have no doubt seen the deleterious effects of alcohol abuse at all levels of society. It has destroyed many people in the Gurdjieff Work as well.

In general, the more psychoactive the potential interactions of a drug are, the greater the amount of psychic energy you will waste, and the more potential damage the drug can do to your psyche. For those who have used drugs, do not give up hope. This work, if applied earnestly, can help you undo the damage.

Many people turn to drugs to escape their inner contradictions. Gurdjieff said that drugs might be used to give someone a taste of higher states, but drugs needed to be abandoned as soon as possible. Drugs and Work do not mix. In fact, drugs may use up any real potential you might have for Work, due to their psychological and endocrinological effects. Drugs vary in terms of their danger and their effects, but the most insidious are the hallucinogens. I consider marijuana to be a mild hallucinogen.

Hallucinogens produce an altered state in their users. As your body metabolizes or digests these chemical compounds, it must call up its reserves of finer substances stored in the body, whose proper purpose is to further inner development. When you metabolize these special substances, you experience an altered state due to the release of finer chemicals. I wish this altered state carried a warning label. It would read, "Warning! This altered state you are now in, with all its vivid new impressions, might have been truly yours if you had worked. Now, it may be too late because you may have wasted all your energy. Stop now! Learn how to use your energy. Start working on yourself!"

Imagine that at birth, each person is given a limited amount of these unique substances. These substances serve a special purpose. They are construction materials for creating two higher "bodies," called by Gurdjieff the "Kesdjan body," and the "Soul body." [7] These higher bodies are the result of a special type of effort and their formation is only a possibility for human beings, not other animals. Their formation is neither guaranteed nor required for our lives on this planet.

Psychotropic drugs release and waste these unique substances. This is not their only effect. Psychotropic drugs create a psychological and physiological addiction that may make any authentic effort or work on oneself impossible. Drugs can sound a death knell for a person interested in Work. One of their insidious characteristics is that they can give us a taste of the real world, and this taste is something we deeply crave, and we begin to believe that through the drug, we have found a way toward this deeper life.

Early experimenters such as Timothy Leary opened a Pandora's box. While freeing creative energy from its prison deep within us, the psychedelic revolution also had a devastating effect. It obliterated the potential for inner development for many sensitive individuals. People who might have had the possibility of real evolution had it snatched from them through misuse of drugs. This misuse continues on a world-wide basis, and countless lives are wasted.

From my personal experience, and through watching the effects of such drugs on clients in therapy over many years, I can say without hesitation, if you are interested in these ideas, give up all recreational drugs. Otherwise, you are simply fooling yourself. You are better off just continuing your life as it is, enjoying it as best you can and not starting on this journey. It may prove disappointing in the least, and more likely, extremely depressing for you. Drugs gave you a taste of what is possible, but only through real effort can you develop this taste into something of your own. Quit the drugs and begin the journey.

PRACTICES

The aim of these practices is not self-improvement, but to begin to learn how to focus your attention, so that you are the one who is directing your attention, rather than allowing something in the environment to attract it.

I want you to try to verify for yourself everything I suggest in this book. Verification will require the exercise of your attention. No one can verify anything for you. It will require energy. Only as your study of your own sleep and lack of attention convinces you of your predicament, will you find the fuel for your further journey.

Consider that, up to this point, your attention has been mostly passive, serving cultural mechanisms that have helped you to fit in. You may not realize this until you begin to study how your repertoire of accidental associations has pulled your attention around. You may discover you are addicted to communication devices, such as TV, radio, computers, cell phones, the Internet, and advertising. Without your knowing, your attention has been manipulated and trained by unconscious individuals who are devoid of conscience and uninterested in your well-being.

Attention is developed *experientially*. Through these practices, you will receive new impressions of yourself. Some might be disturbing. Remember, the aim at the beginning is to simply become familiar with the characteristics of your attention, not to do it better. Also, do not assume that, by reading about these practices or even by trying these exercises once or twice, you will know or understand everything about the exercise or yourself.

Practices for Engaging Attention

1. Each time you pass through a doorway during the day, stop for a second in the doorway, and inwardly count "1, 2, 3." Then walk through. See if you are attentive enough to stop in the doorway before going through.

2. When you are eating, pay attention to the first bite of your food, and see if you can taste it while you are chewing and swallowing it. Only the first bite.

3. As you walk, pick a point in the distance and keep your attention on it as you come closer. Notice whether your attention is pulled about. Change nothing, just notice.

4. Place your attention on the second hand of your watch. Try to keep your attention on it as it circles the clock face once. Notice what interrupts you.

5. Sit for five minutes and think about some subject that interests you. Notice what your attention does. Sit for five minutes and do nothing. Notice where your attention is pulled. Do not try to direct it; rather, just be aware of how it moves about.

6. At a meeting where you do not need to speak and while listening to others, place your attention on the palm of your left hand for one minute.

CHAPTER 2

SELF-OBSERVATION

> Self-study is the work or the way which leads to
> self-knowledge. But in order to study oneself one
> must first learn *how to study*, where to begin, what
> methods to use. A man must learn how to study
> himself, and he must study the methods of self-study.[1]
> —G. I. Gurdjieff

A guiding principle of the Work is its insistence that you do not believe anything without verifying it for yourself—not a teacher, not Gurdjieff, not a group leader, or anyone else. Instead, each individual's task is to verify the truths that this "way" may illuminate; and a cornerstone of Gurdjieff's way is to study oneself through the practice of self-observation. Gradually, self-observation will lead you to the ability to "remember yourself," an ability and practice that will be explained in the next chapter. These two practices, self-observation and self-remembering, will help you understand yourself objectively.

In this chapter, we will look at the principles of self-observation, how to begin this practice, and the qualities of this special type of observation. As you will see, self-observation can give us new information about ourselves. In addition, it begins to utilize our capacity to direct our attention.

How is self-observation done? While we need an intellectual understanding of self-observation, directly achieving objective self-knowledge requires more than intellect, and therefore, the answer to this question is multifaceted. For some people one method proves more useful than another, but an all-around knowledge of the different methods of Work is the best foundation. We will begin with the intellectual premises of self-observation and move on to more practical methods.

I also wish to point out here that self-observation can be overemphasized in the Gurdjieff Work and result in lopsided development if it is not seen as an element in a larger framework of self-understanding. Although I will spend quite a bit of time describing self-observation throughout this book, I want to make it clear that it is only one of many steps on the ladder of inner growth. It is a most important rung of this ladder in that it creates a foundation built of facts of oneself that serves to fuel the wish to be a fully developed person. The aim to become a fully developed person who recognizes their purpose in life and is capable of fulfilling their role in a greater cosmic framework must be kept in mind to keep one from fixating on one or another technique. Self-observation is a beginning point that gives critical information about the habitual state of consciousness we live in. It is not meant to be the endpoint or aim of Work.

An additional concept to keep in mind is that all exercises and practices are best learned and applied over discrete periods of time. This allows for the gradual harmonization of the changes induced by the exercise with our already accustomed tempo of being. It is best when working with any practice to make it time limited rather than attempting to do it at all times. For example, when working with self-observation, it is important to have a clear idea in mind when you are working with it and decide ahead for how long you will work. This can be much better than trying any time you just happen to remember and will help you to learn when you can work and when circumstances may be too complicated.

Before diving into self-observation, we need some preliminary groundwork in understanding the human being as a complex machine. I will develop this groundwork more fully later, but I must say something about it here.

STATES OF CONSCIOUSNESS

The very thing that most people assume they have by nature is consciousness of themselves—that is, the experience of being self-conscious. Gurdjieff calls this a delusion that prevents us from seeking true self-consciousness. Generally, we have access to only two subjective or dreamlike states of consciousness. These are our states of sleeping and waking consciousness. Gurdjieff also says that our "waking" state of consciousness is actually a waking-sleeping state. According to Gurdjieff's system, there are in addition to these states, two other states possible for us: self-consciousness/self-remembering and cosmic/objective consciousness. I list the states of consciousness in Gurdjieff's system here in descending order, from the highest to the lowest:

4. Cosmic/Objective Consciousness. In this state, human beings can see things as they are. This state is often referred to as "enlightenment."

3. Self-Consciousness/Self-Remembering. Awareness of one's being We cannot achieve this state just by wanting to or by thinking about it, or believing we have it. It takes work.

2. Waking-Sleeping State. Gurdjieff defined this as our usual "Waking State." This is the state where we move around and engage in activities as if we were conscious of ourselves and awake, but we are not. This state is characterized by random associative thinking and daydreaming.

1. Sleep. The passive state in which we spend a third of our lives. We may or may not dream while we are in this state.

Psychology and current science do not recognize the higher states of consciousness delineated as No. 4, Cosmic or Objective Consciousness and No. 3, Self-Consciousness; they may consider these states the purview of mystics. However, for the purpose of work on myself, the most important states to consider are No. 3, SelfConsciousness and No. 2, Waking-Sleeping State. We must first study the waking-sleeping state of consciousness we are usually caught up in.

As Gurdjieff said, people have trouble coming to understand they live in a waking-sleeping state of consciousness because they believe they are already conscious. A primary aim of self-observation is to verify for yourself whether you are truly awake or self-conscious.

The Waking-Sleeping State, No. 2, is where we spend most of our lives, and thus we center self-observation, a fundamental practice for Work, on this state. Self-observation is our passport, bringing us from the "waking state" to a genuine experience of State No. 3, Self-Consciousness. Self-Consciousness is characterized by an awareness of yourself being alive, while doing whatever you are doing.

Contrast this experience with your normal state, where you are engaged in activities and yet are unaware of *yourself* existing. We may consider self-consciousness as a great step beyond our habitual existence.

When I first began to practice self-observation, I misunderstood the idea of "self-consciousness." I vaguely thought actors might be self-conscious or that self-consciousness was that state I sometimes felt when I was nervous about speaking in front of others. What we usually call "self-consciousness" is more of a heightened state of nervousness—an odd, embarrassed feeling, arising from the fear of making a mistake and being judged by others. It is not genuine self-consciousness. Although actors may approximate the state of self-consciousness, it is qualitatively different from the state we can reach through self-observation. As I learned to work, I found I needed to understand the meaning of self-consciousness in a completely new way.

Effective self-observation leads to some embarrassing insights. In particular, it puts a dent in our presumption that we are free and making choices. I have found, after a great deal of self-study, that almost everything I do is automatic. Every thought, emotion, sensation, and action, regardless of how much I ascribe conscious will to it, is for the most part entirely automatic or habitual. This automaticity is often difficult to accept, especially for intellectual types who enjoy solving situations and puzzles, thinking about ideas, and believe they are directing their well-trained minds. I hate to burst their bubble, but all this usual so-called "thinking" is simply the brain's automatic correlative ability already mentioned.

The habitual nature of all our psychological processes—our thinking, emotions, and reactions to information we receive from the five senses—is one of the primary reasons we tend to continually repeat the same behavior patterns during our lifetimes. What we refer to as being "conscious" or "awake," as distinct from being asleep in bed, is actually only the automatic functioning of thought, emotion, and sensation; functioning that usually takes place wholly without our awareness.

AWARENESS

We have no problem recognizing a change in our consciousness from our sleep to our usual waking state. However, we usually do not realize another change is possible for us. That is, we can awaken from our automatic waking-sleeping state into a place of awareness. "Awareness," as used here, is not merely the workings of the intellectual, analytical, or associative parts of the mind. The word "awareness" implies being mindful or heedful, alert and poised to respond rather than just react. Awareness links us with the further possibility of true self-consciousness. Awareness has the special quality that we simultaneously experience being present and existing in whatever we are doing while we are doing it, over and above our habitual behavior. When in a state of awareness, there is a certainty of our existence while we are thinking, emoting, or receiving sensations. From time to time we may experience this state of awareness accidentally, but accidental states of awareness are not sufficient for self-study.

It is of the utmost importance that we learn to distinguish awareness from our automatic waking state. Distinguishing the difference is akin to developing a taste for fine food or wine; you must experience and notice the difference in taste, that one is finer than the other. If you do not develop this sensitivity, then any old food will do. We can come to awareness as the result of a certain type of inner effort, and that is the effort of self-observation. I dislike using the word "effort," but there is no better one in English. The word "effort" does not effectively communicate the idea of self-observation or the state of awareness it leads to, because it connotes an image of having to lift something heavy. The effort we are trying is light and clear—the effortless effort.

Both self-observation and the state of awareness may be distinguished by certain characteristics: (a) a lack of self-criticism; (b) the absence of the need to improve or direct; and (c) a lack of self-analysis. Criticism or analysis may be present for some time and need not concern us, but it is important to realize they are not truly characteristics of awareness. Awareness that comes from self-observation simply *is*! When we experience awareness, we feel truly alive and self-conscious— that is, conscious of ourselves in the moment. Try reading this sentence over a few times, while at the same time, noticing or experiencing that you are alive in this moment as you read it!

BECOMING FAMILIAR WITH OUR CENTERS

One of the great gifts Gurdjieff brought to help us understand human behavior is the idea that the human organism operates by means of the integration of different "centers." These centers can be considered different kinds of "brains" or intelligences. Gurdjieff refers to humans as "three-brained beings" or "three-centered beings." Dogs, cats, and similar higher mammals are two-centered beings, having only a moving center and an emotional center. Humans have three distinct centers or brains. They are the moving center, emotional center, and the intellectual center. The third center, the intellectual center, is added to the other two. Besides the three main centers—so all-important for understanding our mind-body experience—our voluntary moving center is linked to two others: the instinctive center that regulates involuntary physiological actions in the body, and the sex center. Further, Gurdjieff tells us that the emotional and intellectual centers each have higher counterparts that we will look at more closely later on. For the moment, however, we will concentrate on the three basic centers: the moving, the emotional, and the intellectual. According to Gurdjieff, these three centers act like three different entities in us and barely communicate with one another.

The first part of self-observation, which may be overlooked by many people who become interested in these ideas, is to familiarize yourself with your different centers. This is not complex and is the beginning of a lifelong learning process that offers a great deal of knowledge. In order to begin, it is sufficient to notice which center is the source of the experience. For example, I see a car on the highway, and I notice it is a Japanese car, and I begin to think that I would like to buy a car like this. I think about all the different models. This associative thought process occurs as a part of my intellectual center.

Now I notice that there is one car I particularly like. It is a Prius, a hybrid, and I like it because it is very cute. This liking is an experience of my emotional center's activity. This center assigns a like or dislike, although sometimes it is neutral.

Another example of this center's activity: I have an argument with a woman at work, someone who always seems to disagree with me. If I want to do one thing, she says we must do something else. I don't like her. Every time I see her, I experience my dislike; this is an activity of my emotional center.

These examples may seem simple, but I assure you that many people do not know the difference between the activity of their associative intellectual center and the experience of their emotional center. Men seem to have more difficulty with this than women. I often will have a client say to me that they feel something is wrong about a situation or an idea that someone else has. They have all sorts of intellectual ideas about the situation, but they constantly speak about their experience by saying, "I feel he is wrong about this and that," or "I feel she is incorrect." In actuality, it is their intellectual associative center that has all sorts of reasons why they "think" she is wrong but they say, "I feel." When I point this out to them, that they are giving me different thoughts, they often realize that they have not been clear on what is a thought and what is a feeling.

The moving center's activity is easier to categorize. All you need to do is simply slow down some of your movements—walking, for example. Walk a few hundred feet slightly slower than you ordinarily would, and you can experience your moving center coordinating your steps and the marvelous controlled falling from one foot to the other.

It is also important to be able to differentiate the functions of the instinctive center from all the other centers and especially the moving center. We experience the activity of the instinctive center through our five senses of vision, hearing, smell, taste, and touch. There are other experiences of the instinctive center, including our experience of hot and cold, experiencing sickness or health, soreness of muscles, the kinesthetic inner experience of our muscles, automatic reflexes, heartbeat, and pulse, to name just a few. How can you differentiate between the voluntary moving center and the instinctive center? We are born with all the functions of the instinctive center fully operational and there is no learning involved. However, all voluntary body movements, our postures, and tone of voice are learned abilities.

In summary, becoming familiar with all the various functions of your centers and learning to classify them is a beginning step in self-observation. There may be areas where you are unsure and these can be sources for further study. This beginning classification of the experiences of your centers leads naturally to the next step in self-observation. However, my experience is that there is always more to learn in the area of classification, and it is a subject with unlimited potential for discovering new information.

BEGINNING SELF-OBSERVATION

When I first met with these ideas, I began to observe my own postures, movements, and other manifestations of my body. I also began to observe the postures of other people. It seemed to me that each of us had a very distinct number of postures. These postures not only indicated distinct physical manifestations, they also displayed emotional attitudes and even ways of thinking. I was intrigued by the idea that the repertoire of postures I observed in people was limited and was perhaps set and finalized by the late teenage years.

Very few new postures or movements are possible for people unless they undertake some specialized type of practice. I have found that the automatic postures of the muscular-skeletal system are fixed in us by our early twenties and will resist change throughout our lives. If you have ever tried dance or yoga, you might remember how awkward you may have felt at first. We feel awkward when we learn a new movement or posture because the effort takes us out of our habitual patterns. Actors or dancers can modify their postures and assume new ones. However, for the majority of people, the possibility of new postures becomes more limited as they age unless they do special work. Yoga, tai chi, and the martial arts are examples of practices that can provide an expansion of physical postures and a limited change in consciousness. What we need, however, are practices that can develop and integrate all the centers simultaneously.

In our organism, three major centers automatically weave together our movements, thinking, and emotions into a complex tapestry. Each center contains a negative and a positive part; that is, a part of each center says either "I like" or "I dislike" to almost every manifestation it makes or to any stimulus it receives.[2]

A tapestry or weaving is in many ways analogous to a system—a complete whole made up of discrete elements that work together. One of the inherent aspects of any system is that its basic elements tend to resist change and maintain their relative relationships, thus maintaining the integrity of the system.[3] Biological systems, whether they are a plant, a cat, or a person, also tend to resist change. If there is a change in one part of a living system, it will always affect the other parts in some lawful manner. For example, one positive outcome of our infatuation with sports and fitness over the last thirty years is that exercise makes us feel better, happier, and improves our thinking. In other words, physical exercise has a corresponding effect on the emotional and thinking centers.

When you study and become familiar with your postures, how they change and when, you may find that each posture correlates with an emotional state or a thought pattern. Just knowing about your postures alone can give you a great deal of information about yourself. One exciting aspect of studying the body is that it can provide an incredibly easy means of helping you to enter into a state of awareness. The study of the human body is a primary area for you to begin your self-study, as it provides a definite focus for objective self-observation.

In general, people are overdeveloped in one center, and the other two major centers remain relatively underdeveloped. You can verify this lopsidedness for yourself by simply noticing what parts of you respond more frequently to certain stimuli. Do you most often say, "I like," or say "I feel," or "I think," or "I'll do it"? You can notice the responses of others around you. Certain people tend to approach their life intellectually, looking at every aspect of what confronts them by thinking about it. Others will always have an emotional response, expressing strong feelings about everything before they think. Still others, physical or practical types, will not be able to think very long about something before they need to jump into action.

You may notice a certain stiffness of postures in people who have office jobs and do not get a chance to move about much during their day. Or, notice your own muscular tensions when you need to do some movement out of your ordinary repertoire, getting into a small car or bending to pick up some paper under a chair.

Begin to notice your physical postures at different times during the day, and pay attention to the way you move from one posture to another. Beginning to notice such things in myself is a first step in self-study.

It begins with the body, but later, we can notice our emotional states and thoughts as well. Beginning to notice in this way is the beginning of training your attention—that is, training your attention to observe you. The important difference between this type of observation of oneself and ordinary observation is that it is not automatic, but rather it is intentional and interested, and yet neither critical nor analytical of what it observes. It is "witnessing." Objective self-observation is witnessing without criticism or interpretation

PRACTICE IN SELF-OBSERVATION OR SELF-EXPERIENCING

As I stated before, self-observation is free from any self-criticism. The observing faculty within you is simply aware of your existence. This faculty is not concerned with making you better or changing whatever you observe. Its objectivity, or neutrality, is fundamental to the practice of self-observation. Developing a proper grounding in objective self-observation takes some time and will support deeper study of emotions and cognitive patterns.

Throughout this book I have been, and will be, referring to "self-observation" because it is one of the main practices in the Gurdjieff Work and the words "self-observation" are now part of the Work lexicon. We need to be clear that the term "self-observation" is often confused by people because the word "observation" is often associated with our ability to see visually and observe from the outside, as in looking at a painting or situation. I say that I observe someone crossing the street, or I observed that Jane had on a beautiful dress. As used by me in this book, the term "self-observation" has the following meaning: the attentive recordation of my experience while it occurs and in which I know I exist. It is not merely a visual activity and does not include analysis or interpretation.

For example, the experience of myself walking is bigger than visually watching myself walk. The recordation of an emotional experience of being upset is not fundamentally visual, although it may include aspects that someone else can see. The recordation of the experiences of my senses, such as taste, hearing, touch, etc., is also not visual (other than vision itself). I can be hot, cold, sweaty, experience my pulse, which are not visual experiences. Although these experiences may have visual manifestations that can be seen, these are not the experiences I have. Thus, to repeat, whenever I refer to self-observation, I mean the attentive recordation of my experience while it occurs and I know I exist. It is not merely a visual activity and does not include analysis or interpretation.

Beginning Self-Observation

1. Begin by paying gentle attention to the manifestations of your body—its movements, postures, gestures, tone of voice, and facial expressions.

2. Paying attention to only one or another body manifestation when you remember is all you need do in the beginning.

3. You do not need to change anything that you notice. There is no need to make it better or different.

4. If you find yourself describing intellectually what you notice, that is fine. Your aim is not really to describe, but it happens. It is interesting to notice your habit of analyzing and still gain new impressions of yourself.

5. There is no need to try to stop or alter any manifestation of your body.

6. If you are in a Work group, discuss what you noticed with others. (A Work group is an association of individuals who are attempting to work using Gurdjieff's ideas for their own self-development. It offers a forum for discussing ongoing observations and self-study.)

GENTLENESS

This simple way of beginning self-observation uses our ability to direct our attention. I have made a point of saying that this is a gentle attention. The word "gentle" is important. We all need to practice coaching our attention in this new direction of self-observation and bringing it back when it strays. Gentle attention is also a sly way to help you avoid the pitfall of muscular tension attaching to this directed attention.

We need to observe ourselves more, and we need greater under-standing of how it can work for us. As we persist in this practice, a great deal will be revealed. For example, self-observation leads to uncovering parts of our emotional life, as well as to latent abilities that we know little about. Self-observation also may also lead you into difficult places. That is why the simultaneous development of self-compassion becomes so important.

Self-observation seems simple, yet this is deceptive. Unbeknownst to us, we are disharmonized and it is difficult for us to be simple. The psychological disharmonization we suffer from is the result of multi-generational dysfunction. In other words, our current habitual inatten-tiveness is hundreds of generations old, allowing us the simple state of awareness only as an accidental experience. It takes time to learn to obtain objective knowledge through self-observation, and you need to be clear, patient, and gentle with yourself.

It is not necessary to go on a weeklong retreat to experience aware-ness and waking up, but the ability to maintain awareness in the midst of life is rare for people and must be developed. I may experi-ence moments of objective awareness accidentally, but these sporadic moments remain insufficient for any real self-development. Be patient. Begin with the study of your body's manifestations.

IMPARTIALITY

I describe self-observation in many different ways and yet say the same thing. We need different images that give the same message. I will add more details to the message each time I say it.

One of the difficulties of Gurdjieff's terminology for self-observation derives from his use of the word "self." In many ways, it might have been more exact to say "Jim-observation" or "Sue-observation," or my pref-erence, "biographical-I-observation." The word "self" is not exact. The word "self" connotes unity and essentiality, a unified whole that is one. However, you will see that the self you observe is far from unified, and so your observation may be more akin to observing only a part of Sue or Bill at any one time. Yet I use the word "I" all the time to describe myself, how I feel, think, etc. In actuality, I do not have one "I," but am a multi-plicity of different "I's." [4] That is not really a problem, since the emphasis is to develop your ability to observe, to develop an "observing I" that becomes familiar with all your "I's." Developing your capacity for self-observation is more important than the content of what you observe. Content may vary, but impartiality and acceptance of the impressions you receive must always be emphasized, and compassion included.

The aim of self-observation is to develop your own real "I." When I say "real I," I mean the part of me that begins as an "I" that is able to observe my multiplicity impartially. This real "I" that comes through self-observation has very definite qualities. It is objective and capable of impartial thought. Since it is born from and nourished exclusively through impressions of myself, it knows me. Eventually, it understands all the intellectual, emotional, and physically oriented "I's" in my psyche. Real "I" is capable of having a will; that is, it can carry out an aim. As we are now, we have no unified will. One "I" decides to do something like clean up the house, and a host of other "I's" decide to do other things—read a book or go to the movies. Rather than belonging to one will, each "I" has a separate will, and these different "I's" that make up the multiplicity of my "self" are continually at odds with one another. This lack of will leaves me in a situation where I really cannot make a decision that anyone—even I—can rely on.

CORRECT SELF-OBSERVATION IS IMPARTIAL AND TAKES PLACE IN THE MOMENT

Self-observation is not to be governed by likes and dislikes or any emotional reaction to what you observe; what you observe (that is, the impressions you receive) are simply recorded without liking or disliking—this is the definition of impartiality.

Certain people may have an automatic tendency toward negativity and even find they hate themselves as they receive new impressions of themselves. They may become hypercritical of what they observe and strive to become "better." Others will receive impressions of themselves and feel superior or prideful. None of these reactions should be countered in any direct way. Such negativity or pride will prevail unless you continually foster interest and compassion towards yourself. You need to be both curious and gentle. Simply emphasize the collection of more data, not whether the data is good, bad, or needs analysis. Then your real "I" can grow. Otherwise, you will tend to fall into liking, disliking, and analyzing, rather than coming to a state of awareness.

I begin self-observation by acting as if there is an inner witness to my physical movements and postures. This witness simply observes or experiences my body in action. The observation is impartial—there is no liking or disliking—and synchronous. It takes place as my body manifests and not as an afterthought.

In this way a separate, objective faculty is gradually created within me. This faculty is distinct from the actions of my body, distinct from my habitual sense of self, and distinct from my likes and dislikes. This new faculty is at first simply aware of my physical existence. It is a presence that grows in me.

Specific Areas for Self-Observation

1. General bodily movements: Experience your overt movements of the arms, hands, legs, feet, head, face, and torso. Be attentive and interested. Observe by experiencing your movements at times during the day without judging them. Do not try this exercise for prolonged periods. Quality of your effort is more important than quantity.

2. Posture: Notice when you are standing or sitting, and that you stand or sit in a particular way.

3. Gesture: When you are speaking to others, notice your gestures, the demonstrative movements you make with your hands, arms, and head.

4. Tone of voice: Notice when your tone of voice changes. When you are upset, notice whether your voice sounds shrill or sounds different from times when you are calm; and notice how your voice sounds at many different times. The telephone is particularly good for this study, since the other person's physical presence does not distract you. It is not important to understand or interpret your tone of voice, just be interested in the sounds you make.

5. Facial expression: This is a difficult area to study in oneself. Don't be discouraged by the difficulty, but notice your facial expression

from time to time. Sometimes you may notice a grimace or a smile on your face. It can be helpful to hold the expression for a few moments.

6. Sensation: When I begin to feel angry or upset, I can notice very quickly how my respiration may speed up or become shallow, or how I feel a change in some body processes, such as heartburn, heart palpitations, nervous sensations in the pit of my stomach, or sensations of anxiety in my upper chest. I can notice, in an impartial way, whether I feel cold, hot, itchy, wet, dry, and in what parts of my body I feel these sensations.

AUTHENTICITY

How is the type of self-observation we are describing different from any other type of observation? First, it is not an intellectual observation— that is, one that is almost always analytical or descriptive and comes to me in words. Second, it is not emotional, liking or disliking what is observed. Nor are the impressions to be analyzed after you receive them since correct observation takes place while you are doing or experiencing whatever is taking place. Observing is not one part of the intellect attempting to describe the motions of the body. All of these reactions or results will occur at times, but are not important though they can be noticed and accepted.

What makes this self-observation different? C. Daly King, a student of Orage and a psychologist who was instrumental in the development of the lie detector, says this, "Self observation presumes a real and valid distinction between the observer and the observed, between the being himself and his observed organism." [5] The result of this separation is awareness. Self-observation is a capacity we can develop that is neither thinking, nor emotion or movement, but a clear and precise recordation of our existence.

In summary, the beginning practice of self-observation is as follows: an inner part that is not your intellect, is interested in your body and its manifestations and observes and records them. No matter what this observing faculty notices, this inner part simply witnesses and remains positively interested. If you are correctly practicing self-observation, it can gradually lead to full, objective knowledge of yourself. Begin with the body, since it is the easiest part of oneself to observe objectively. Gradually, your capacity of awareness will become able to objectively observe your emotional states and your associative mind.

I also need to develop compassion towards myself while I learn more about myself. I need compassion to support me even if my personality does not like what I uncover. My objective faculty then becomes a special container that can hold the difficult aspects of myself that I might not otherwise be able to bear. Gradually, as my real "I" grows and is able to bear my unpleasant manifestations, new integration or transformation can take place.

It is important to keep in mind the qualities of impartial self-observation that lead to self-consciousness and awareness. However, they are not absolute by any means. You do not need to obsessively measure your observations to see whether they are objective and compassionate, just keep these qualities in mind. In a later chapter, I will point out some ways of working with self-observation where changing your manifestation might be useful. For now, you should simply try to work according to what you have understood and be patient and compassionate with yourself. Remember, self-observation is the work we engage in to come into the state of self-consciousness where we can experience what I have been calling "awareness."

CHAPTER 3

GURDJIEFFIAN CONCEPTS

In this chapter, we will look at some of the special terms and concepts that Gurdjieff emphasized in his practices and cosmology. These special terms are required to explain our current state of consciousness, and they can help us to think about the different states of consciousness in which we live. We will look at certain primordial cosmic laws. They are part of a complete cosmology that we will examine more closely in a later chapter.

IDENTIFICATION

"Identification" is a very special term in Gurdjieff's Work. Surprisingly, Gurdjieff himself mentioned it only rarely. People in the Work constantly talk about "not being identified." We speak as if we actually understand the concept. However, I am not sure we have thought about it sufficiently. What did Gurdjieff mean when he said people are always in a state of identification? I personally have used the word "identification" countless times and considered I understood Gurdjieff's idea. However, I realized I needed to understand it experientially, not simply intellectually. This realization led me to look for hints from Gurdjieff as to what he might be trying to tell us. I found an important clue in the following passage:

> It is necessary to see and to study identifying to its very roots in oneself. The difficulty of struggling with identifying is still further increased by the fact that when people observe it in themselves they consider it a very good trait and call it "enthusiasm," "zeal," "passion," "spontaneity," "inspiration," and names of that kind, and they consider that only in a state of identifying can a man really produce good work, no matter in what sphere.[1]

These words made me begin to think about my personality and my egoism. All those traits that define me and which I take pride in, those I consider to be me—could they possibly be just a glorified state of identification? Could the personality I treasure so much be just a statue erected in my honor, for my own continual glorification? If so, when, if ever, can I find examples of states where I am not identified? A frightening thought. Perhaps it is true I am never in a state other than identification. Just thinking, "I am not identified" in a particular situation, can it be that even this is a state of identification? What is the way out? I cannot solve this conundrum intellectually, like some Zen koan.

During this discussion of identification, it may seem to you that I am making identification "bad," which is what one might deduce from Gurdjieff's comment. However, I wish to open up the discussion a little by suggesting that the human tendency to be identified can provide a vast sea of opportunities for inner growth if I am able to utilize this identification and harvest new impressions of my behavior.

I want you to keep in mind the following definition of identification, which is very simple, and which I will use as the basis for further understanding. Identification refers to my attachment—that is, an inability to separate my authentic-I (to be discussed in depth later on) from that to which any of my "I's" are attached, be it an idea, person, belief, image, feeling, sensation, situation, material object, group, or anything else.

In trying to find a way out of my state of identification, my experience in psychology is a wonderful resource. Here again, I find a paradox in working with identification. The Work leads me to believe that I should not be identified and even asks me to struggle to "not be identified." This advice sounds simple, and it is, if I look only on the surface— if I do not ponder *how* I can be "not identified." My mind thinks it understands the instruction. In reality, however, it has little correspondence, if any, with the state of non-identification; or, as I prefer to call it, "disidentification." How do I know? The truth is, in order to disidentify, I need to be fully identified and, at the same time, notice and observe my identification. In short, I am willing to be in a state of identification, wake up, see that state and not tinker with it. Instead, my observing "I" witnesses me, identified. In this way, I may begin to taste what is called "separation." I need to be identified, experience it fully, and also be present to observe it.

In order to glimpse my identification, I need look no further than the hundreds of small worries and concerns that always distract me. For example, my inner considering of how others see me or whether they appreciate me or not. Other areas for self-observation are at my job, my activities and my concerns about them. How important is my identity as a teacher, carpenter, doctor, student, parent, or homemaker? What about my possessions? Every time I get in my car or put on a particular jacket, do they activate the same sequence of thoughts and feelings over and over? Am I worried about my health or the fact I am getting old and do not look the way I used to? Do all these worries signify I am identified? Yes, all these automatic likes and dislikes about myself and others, what I have or don't have, worries, prejudices, are symptoms of the disease of identification.

There is no substitute for the experiential evidence of my identification. It is part of the mechanism that maintains my sleeping state. Each of us is caught in our own particular web of identification, a combination of our haphazardly acquired reactions to the environment that became habitual. The key difference among people is not so much a difference in their level of consciousness or being, but rather in the content of their identification, their almost infinite attachments. The pattern of identification keeps a person locked in a finite repertoire of experiences by limiting what he has experienced, and his potential for new experience. In fact, it might be clear to you by now that identification is a type of prison that confines each of us to a limited life.

You may not believe it, but I have found it takes courage to be fully identified, fully engaged with my personality, and still willing to observe myself. It means I allow my personality to continue as it is. I don't try to change it. For example, I may find myself in a conversation with a friend, making some point about politics—a perfect situation for getting a taste of my identification. Most of what I know about politics I have learned from reading articles written by others. If I am honest with myself, I have actually very little firsthand experience; but strangely, I have a great many opinions, and I am sure these opinions are correct. In fact, when drawn into a political discussion, I love to voice my opinion and prove some point. I am attached to my opinion. I want the other person to notice how intelligent I am. I even make hand gestures as I speak adamantly about the topic. All my manifestations are a perfect subject for self-observation.

Again, impartial self-observation can bring me the experience of awareness that exists simultaneously with my state of identification. Gurdjieff says, "'Identification' is so common a quality that for purposes of observation, it is difficult to separate it from everything else. Man is always in a state of identification, only the object of identification changes." [2]

Self-observation, if I practice it correctly, begins with the body and can incorporate sensing (which we will discuss in the next chapter). If I establish a sufficient foundation in impartial self-observation of my body, I will begin to notice other elements of my personality, such as my emotions and thoughts.

"Disidentification" signifies inner separateness from the object of my identification. Disidentification is a gradual process that can occur through self-observation. It is the experience of separation from my continual attachment to every thought, emotion, movement, and sensation I have; it gives me a taste of my "real I" observing and separate from "it." In the beginning, the "it" is the manifestation of my body, a movement, gesture, or posture, etc. Later, as I add a new practice, *sensing*, self-observation naturally expands to my emotional states and later to my thinking process.

I can always begin with the body and consider for now that all my manifestations are connected to the body. The paradox we have here is that I can observe myself and can separate a part of myself from my body by actually getting more in touch with it. Gradually, I will find that I cannot separate from my body by using only my intellectual center, and that is where sensing will come to my aid. I also cannot use artificial means (drugs, holotropic breathing, a shocking reminder from a guru, etc.) and produce any useful, lasting results. Separation takes place gradually, through practicing proper self-observation and through sensing.

Later, we will return to look in more detail at the roots and pitfalls of identification.

SELF-REMEMBERING

> JUNE 5, 1950. When one begins to see that one can only
> begin to remember oneself for seconds at a time, it seems
> negligible. But what one must understand is that it is diffi-
> cult exactly because it is the beginning of a new state for
> us, the key to a new world. If it were easy and if results
> came more quickly it could not have the importance
> which it has.[3]—Rodney Collin

Observing "I" is a faculty that records my existence just as it is. It is a
unique experience in that it actually has two parallel functions. In this
experience of observation, one part of the "I" observes my behavior, and
another part realizes that I simply exist while this observation is taking
place. This parallel double function of the process of observation is to
allow me to experience the state of consciousness called self-consciousness or self-remembering. Self-remembering continually wakes me up
to the fact that what is observed is not as important as the fact that I
exist, a fact that is easily lost in the intellectual center's tendency to
describe or the emotional center's tendency to like or dislike. Gurdjieff
used the term "self-remembering" to indicate I need to recall and bring
myself back to recognize the true source of the observation that exists
alongside my observing "I." In this way I also exist and my experience of
existing is an integral part of each of my observations. One of the most
interesting passages in P. D. Ouspensky's *In Search of the Miraculous*
quotes Gurdjieff on the topic of self-remembering:

> "Not one of you has noticed the most important thing that
> I have pointed out to you," he said. "That is to say, not one
> of you has noticed that *you do not remember yourselves.*"
> (He gave particular emphasis to these words.) "You do not
> feel *yourselves*; you are not conscious of yourselves. With
> you, 'it observes' just as 'it speaks,' 'it thinks,' 'it laughs.'
> You do not feel: *I* observe, *I* notice, *I* see. Everything still
> 'is noticed,' 'is seen.' ... In order really to observe oneself
> one must first of all *remember oneself.*" (He again empha-
> sized these words.) "Try to remember yourselves when you

observe yourselves and later on tell me the results. Only those results will have any value that are accompanied by self-remembering. Otherwise you yourselves do not exist in your observations. In which case what are all your observations worth?" [4]

Self-remembering is one of Gurdjieff's key concepts. At first, the phrasing must appear strange. Why do we have to remember ourselves and what is it we need to remember about ourselves? Self-remembering points out that we forget that we even exist. We lose ourselves in whatever we are doing—even in self-observation itself. Because we can become so involved in trying to observe, we lose touch with who is observing. By the word "who," I do not mean my ordinary associative mind or my personality, but my potential real "I," a new and relatively free and independent reality within me. It is important to realize that this real "I" comes into existence only through my wish and efforts. One way the real "I" can arise in me is to act as if the real "I" already exists and is functioning. I act as if it is already there, separate and able to observe me impartially and compassionately. Simply acting "as if" is a means of bringing it into existence.

In order to discuss the meaning of self-remembering, we need a more exact definition of "awareness." Let us define awareness simply as being mindful (actively paying attention) that something exists because you notice it or realize it is happening. We are going to speak about self-remembering and the role of awareness in a few different ways because these concepts, although simple, may be difficult to understand.

Self-remembering is integral to the complete act of self-observation and represents its center of gravity. In self-observation, consciousness is split into an observing "I" and the object of self-observation, which we take in the beginning as the body. If you slightly emphasize the awareness of your existence as your observing "I" functions, as distinct from any impressions received of the body, your awareness will always include you existing in whatever you observe, and thus you will remember yourself. In other words, you observe or sense your body; at the same time, you are aware of yourself existing. Self-remembering should continue as you observe whatever manifestation of your body is taking place. This double awareness, your "I" observing "it" (your behavior, in this case your body) and the awareness of yourself existing as you are observing your existence, constitutes the act of self-remembering.

Summarizing, self-remembering occurs if I realize that I exist while I am engaged in self-observation. To facilitate self-remembering, my awareness of myself existing must be somewhat greater—that is, given a bit more emphasis—than what is being observed. Otherwise, the impressions I receive of my body's movements or other behavior will always overshadow the awareness of my existence. Try, over a period of time, to get a taste for this double awareness, the awareness of your "I" observing coupled with the awareness of your existence. Self-remembering is the simultaneous awareness of oneself being both the observer and the observed.

HIGHER WORLDS AND SELF-REMEMBERING

An equally important aspect of self-remembering relates to my personal valuation of the Work. What does this work signify to me? Does it simply represent the possibility of my individual evolution? Do I feel a responsibility to others who work, to the world, to the Work itself? What I can derive from the Work is determined by how much I value it, the energy I am willing to invest in my aim, and my understanding of the reasons the Work exists.

This aspect of self-remembering signifies the realization that a higher structure of being exists in potential within us, greater than the ordinary self. That higher structure is somehow "remembered" in us, even though we usually have no awareness of it. However, this "memory" is crucial to finding what is essential inside us and making a connection with it. This essential part of us is the link with our true self, the part of us that remains when false personality falls away, the part we will be able to depend on, irrespective of time or place. In many ways, it is our personal connection to the higher, to what is God for us.

Rodney Collin was a student of Ouspensky's. He was deeply affected by Gurdjieff's ideas and his esoteric writings have touched many. Collin clarifies the essential threefold nature of self-remembering and expresses it most beautifully when he says:

As we have seen, no phenomenon is produced by two forces; every phenomenon and every real result requires three forces. The practice of self-remembering or division of attention is connected with the attempt to produce a certain phenomenon, the birth of consciousness in oneself. And when this begins to happen, attention recognizes with relief and joy not two but three factors—one's own organism, the subject of the experiment; the situation to which this organism is exposed in the moment; and something permanent which stands on a higher level than both and which alone can resolve the relation between the two. What is this third factor which must be remembered? Each person must find it for himself, and his own form of it—his school, his teacher, his purpose, the principles he has learned, the sun, some higher power in the universe, God.[5]

To answer Collin's question, we must understand the fact that the Work opens up the possibility of touching a higher consciousness within and beyond us. It is no good simply wanting to be better and making random efforts. If we are to make real changes, we have to understand what this "higher level" is that we are striving for. A part of being able to make real efforts requires that we become familiar with two fundamental laws of the universe which Gurdjieff laid out very carefully for us and to which we are always subject. The quotation above introduces the "Law of Three," the idea that nothing can happen with only positive and negative forces.[6] To produce a result, we need a third force to reconcile the two opposing forces.

Octaves, Or The Law Of Sevenfoldness

The Law of Three is one of two major principles embodied in Gurdjieff's system. The other is the Law of Sevenfoldness, otherwise known as the law of "octaves." This law refers to the fact that, "every process, no matter upon what scale it takes place, is completely determined in its gradual development by the law of the structure of the seven-tone scale." [7] Thus, like the musical scale, a process may start at the "Do" of one octave and ascend to the higher "Do" of the next, through seven stages. These stages are not continuous or always the same, however. There are intervals at defined places in the octave where the energy runs down and needs a boost of energy from another octave. You can see where the intervals are by looking at the C major scale on the piano. They occur where there is no key or black note half tone in between the white notes—that is, between "E" and "F" and "B" and the "C" of the next octave. Taking "C" as "Do," we see that the intervals occur between "Mi" and "Fa" and "Si" and "Do."

Ouspensky discusses three important characteristics of octaves that we need to understand and which occur in all processes. Simplified, they are as follows: (1) there will always be a deviation in energy from the beginning of an octave to the end, often so much so that it may become its own opposite (the outcome of the process may be just the opposite of what is intended or expected); (2) processes do not stand still or stay at the same level (note) in the octave, but are always ascending or descending; (3) while descending or ascending, there are periodic retardations or accelerations in the vibrations of the octave. These retardations occur at the intervals mentioned above.[8]

Why is it so important to ponder these principles? The three basic characteristics of the octave can yield deeper understanding of many of our experiences in life that repeat themselves over and over. They explain how I can begin an activity heading toward a specific aim and sometimes produce a result that is the complete opposite of what I intended.

For example, I have been waiting all week to go out with my wife. We are planning a pleasant evening, with dinner and a movie. It has been a stressful week and I am really looking to unwind. However, on the way to the restaurant, a driver cuts me off. I get extremely angry at his driving, complain and curse about it. My wife says I should just relax and not get so upset. I feel she is acting superior and snap back that she does not understand how stupid the other guy is. I hurt her feelings with my tone of voice. Suddenly she does not appear to be having a good time with me. The fact that she does not seem to be having a good time stresses me out. My original octave—wanting a nice, relaxing evening—has turned into its opposite, a stressful interaction. This is a simple example, and you can easily find your own.

Every aim you have will tend to produce its opposite unless you begin to take into account how the octave may deviate and take a corresponding action to correct the deviation. If you look at your daily life, you may begin to notice that its octaves are constantly deviating. I find in my own life that I often start with a clear aim and end up confused because something unexpected happens in the process. Another example: I want to help a friend by sharing some small thing I notice about him. I am hoping it will make his life better and that he will thank me for giving him some advice to set him in the right direction. Lo and behold, I am amazed, angry, and saddened when he does not take my advice with great thankfulness, but is put off by my butting in. Trying to help others is an activity that often backfires.

Situations, energy, our consciousness, and everything we encounter at any moment is either ascending or descending, becoming finer or coarser, or higher or lower. For example, during the day, my energy level is in a constant state of flux. A few hours into the day, I am tired for an unknown reason. Then, a few hours later, I am feeling great, my energy level has gone up, but again, I have no idea why. This is also true of our blood pressure, pulse, heartbeat, breathing, thinking, emotional state, and even our sense of aliveness. We remain unconscious of the reasons for these fluctuations. The idea of octaves is a way of beginning to understand why things change as they do.

I have learned that almost any activity I begin has a tendency to run down without my noticing it. I might start to clean a room, write a paper, or attend a yoga class. Gradually, all these activities run down. I often leave the activity planning to return to it, but, often, I don't. It is in the very nature of the octave itself. Unless I keep my attention on my aim to complete what I have started, many of my intentions go unrealized. Each of us can familiarize ourselves with these broken or incomplete octaves in our lives. I might want to clean up my desk. I begin, then for some reason, I am unable to complete the task. I think it's because I must attend to a telephone call or another problem, but the real reason lies elsewhere. The octave of this intention has reached a stage, an interval (a slowing down or "retardation") in the octave, which requires more or different energy. If I am unaware of this slowing down, I will forget that, to complete my aim, I must pass through the interval and this requires something new. If I don't obtain it, the octave will stop moving upwards towards my goal and mechanically descend, ending back at its starting point. Octaves never stand still; they are always ascending or descending.

Gurdjieff also called the Law of Sevenfoldness "The Law of Discontinuity of Vibration," because of the need for another energy to enter at the critical points in the octave, but what happens in this octavic process is invisible to us as we are. He said:

> The principle of the *discontinuity of vibration* means the definite and necessary characteristic of all vibrations in nature, whether ascending or descending, to develop *not uniformly* but with periodical accelerations and retardations. This principle can be formulated still more precisely if we say that the force of the original impulse in vibrations does not act uniformly but, as it were, becomes alternately stronger and weaker.[9]

We have all had the experience of working on a project and reaching a point where we need new energy to continue. Particularly when I am working with a group of people, I notice how projects often need a renewed impetus. I am a very good initiator of a project, but I need others to come in and bring new energy to sustain it. I also notice that as a group nears the completion of a project, it often requires an even greater burst of energy. There is good reason for the common saying that the bulk of work on any project takes place in the last five percent of the time available. Often, our inability to muster the energy to bridge this final gap results in many incomplete projects.

Gurdjieff said that all of life follows from the characteristics of the octave and specifically from the retardation of vibrations. The Law of Octaves explains many phenomena in our lives that are otherwise incomprehensible. He formulated three characteristics of the octave:

> First is the principle of the deviation of forces.

Second is the fact that nothing in the world stays in the same place, or remains what it was, everything moves, everything is going somewhere, is changing, and inevitably either develops or goes down, weakens or degenerates, that is to say, it moves along either an ascending or a descending line of octaves.

And third, that in the actual development itself of both ascending and descending octaves, fluctuations, rises and falls are constantly taking place.[10]

STUDYING THE LAWS IN LIFE

According to Gurdjieff, the key to understanding the world, oneself, or anything else is through studying and comprehending the Law of Three and the Law of Sevenfoldness, the two great primordial laws. He refers to these laws as "primordial," because all actions and manifestations in our world are based on them. These laws stand at a higher level than our world. Bennett says, "When Gurdjieff says that the Law of Three is a primordial cosmic law, he means that it does not come out of the way the world works, but that it is a law that enables the world to be what it is."[11]

One of our great misunderstandings in an attempt to grasp the Law of Sevenfoldness and Law of Three is that we do not look for their manifestations in the right places. We spend an inordinate amount of time reading books others have written about these Laws. They were combined in a symbol that Gurdjieff brought to us that is called the "enneagram." Authors have picked up bits and pieces of psychology and even written whole books about "enneagram types." In my opinion, most of what we learn from reading—with few exceptions—will remain strictly an intellectual exercise for us unless we do our own research to find these laws in our experience.

I can only understand these two great laws through finding them first of all within my own life. Thus, my objective understanding of them is a function of how well I understand myself. Once we understand the operation of the Laws within our lives, we may then also see how they work in the world at large. These two objective laws manifest even within my subjectivity, and this subjectivity is a perfect starting point for my study. The Laws are at work in my anger, my useless movements, my daydreams, my inability to maintain an aim, my internal considering, and all the rest of my mechanical behavior. In fact, it is just in my subjective experience that I can find myriad examples of their manifestations. We cannot understand the Laws merely theoretically, and no one can teach them to us; rather, we must earn the privilege.

UNDERSTANDING THE LAW OF THREE

Every manifestation is the result of three separate forces, the affirming, the denying, and the reconciling. Gurdjieff calls them "Holy Affirming, Holy Denying, and Holy Reconciling." After seeing them in ourselves, we may understand why he regards them as sacred. For example, when you try to accomplish anything in your life, you can look at your effort as an affirming, active, or positive force. If you take notice of what actually happens, you can find your efforts are always met by resistance: a negative, passive, receptive, or denying force. The denying force includes extraneous environmental factors and intrapersonal factors that deflect initial activity away from its intended aim. However, if you take this resistance into account and treat it as feedback, you can make a correction. Feedback and correction lie in the arena of the reconciling force, the third, or neutralizing force. We can see that the reconciling process is required in steering a car, where we receive feedback from our surroundings and make continuous small corrections with small movements of the steering wheel. On an emotional level I can experience the reconciling force when I simultaneously recognize and bear both the positive and negative aspects of my own behavior. The reconciling force requires this effort of recognition and remains invisible without this intentional effort.

Any project I undertake is an arena where I can study the workings of the Law of Three in my life.

Practical Study of the Law of Three

In order to become familiar with the action of the Law of Three, pay attention to the frustration that often comes when you strive to accomplish an aim. Try the following exercise:

1. Pick some aim for the day. It might be as simple as doing something you have been putting off.

2. Notice what happens when you seek to fulfill this aim. Perhaps little things pull you away, you get tired, or interested in something else, or you do not have the time to do it, etc.

3. If you can persist in your aim, pay particular attention to your frustrations while accomplishing or not being able to accomplish it. Of course, you will need to pick some aim that is somewhat difficult for you and not simply something you enjoy doing, in order that frustration can raise its head. Then you may get a chance to see the Law of Three at work.

4. Your effort to accomplish your aim is the active force. The resistance or passive force will be everything, inner and outer, that gets in your way. The reconciling force is more difficult to see. You have to discover this force inside you and see how it works in your own experience, how it tastes. If you are able to stay with your aim, simply try to notice what makes it possible to stick with it.

Often, these primordial laws remain a mystery to people in the Work because they have not worked with them experientially; that is, they have not looked for them in the subjective experience of their lives. Our individual, subjective lives are important in the scheme of things, and each of us has the opportunity to understand these laws in the midst of our lives.

If I really engage my subjectivity, amplify aspects of it, and participate in it, then I can gain a wealth of personal knowledge. I may even see the workings of the two great laws. The knowledge I gain is truly mine, independent of any book I might read.

I can find the manifestation of the Law of Three in the very process of self-observation. I wish to observe myself and try to do it. Then, there is the resistance of my waking-sleeping state—that is, my tendency toward automatism, toward my usual habit patterns. Then there is some result. Where could the reconciling force come in during self-observation?

I have found I need to maintain a certain stance toward my own work, keeping my mind clearly on the Law of Three with its idea of the synergy of three independent forces. Without such clarity, my work will become negative or even stop. My stance is composed of three elements: (1) observation (affirming); (2) acceptance of what I observe or experience (receptive); and (3) compassion toward myself (reconciling). Without self-compassion that acts for me as the reconciling force, my self-observation can easily end in negative inner commentary, making further self-observation—much less, transformation—impossible. What I then would achieve in lieu of self-observation would be a mixture of bits and pieces of self-knowledge, with the simultaneous arising of an "automat," a critical, shaming entity that might stymie any further development.

HIGHER BEING-BODIES

The idea of the possible development of what Gurdjieff called "higher being-bodies" has existed for thousands of years. Theosophy and other doctrines have dubbed these bodies variously as "astral," "causal," "etheric," "soul," "mental," and so on.

Religions speak of the "soul" or the "spirit," but if you query their adherents closely, they admit they cannot really define these words. One of Hinduism's main tenets is that we live many lives; it seems to advise its followers not to pay too much attention to this life. The underlying assumption is that something in us will continue into the next life. We look at the plethora of theories, ideas, and descriptions of other bodies, the idea of some mystical, unknown part of us continuing, and the mind boggles. No wonder most of us dismiss the idea of having additional bodies. We consider our visible physical bodies as our natural possession and see them as similar to the bodies of other lower life forms such as dogs, cats, etc. In contrast, people speak of their "soul" as something invisible that will live after their death.

Gurdjieff stated that as we are, we have no soul. A higher body might arise in me that survives the death of the physical body, but this higher body can only come about as the result of a definite work. In his early teaching, Gurdjieff said we had the possibility of having four "bodies": (1) the physical body; (2) the natural or "astral" body that he calls the

"Kesdjan" body; (3) the spiritual, "mental," or "soul-body"; and (4) the "divine body." He says:

> The reason why it is possible for four bodies to exist is that the human organism, that is, the physical body, has such a complex organization that, under certain conditions, a new independent organism can grow in it ... The consciousness manifested in this new body is capable of governing it, and it has full power and full control over the physical body. In this second body, under certain conditions, a third body can grow . . .

> The first is the physical body, in Christian terminology the "carnal" body; the second, in Christian terminology, is the "natural" body; the third is the "spiritual" body; and the fourth, in the terminology of esoteric Christianity, is the "divine" body. In theosophical terminology the first is the "physical," the second is the "astral," the third is the "mental," and fourth the "causal." [12]

According to Gurdjieff, there is no guarantee I will develop higher being-bodies. They only arise through my sustained efforts. Gurdjieff's presentation of the possibility of immortality is tied to the development of my own individuality and real "I." He contradicts any assertion that we are already endowed with immortal souls that will continue to exist when the physical body is destroyed.

In *Beelzebub's Tales to His Grandson*, in the chapter entitled "The Holy Planet 'Purgatory,'" Gurdjieff tells us about the possibility of the development of the two higher being-bodies we mentioned earlier, the *Kesdjan* and *Soul* bodies.[13] Just as human beings are capable of reproducing another biological being through sexual intercourse, Gurdjieff says they may actually produce another being inside themselves, composed of finer material than their planetary bodies. Gurdjieff discusses in detail the development of higher being-bodies that can survive death.[14] However, he is one of the few teachers who speaks frankly not only about a life after death but also about the work we must do during this lifetime to allow for this possibility. He debunks the possibility of personal salvation unless there is a special preparation and work throughout this life. He emphasizes that the possibility of individual permanence beyond the death of my physical body depends on the creation during this lifetime of my higher-being body Kesdjan. The proper formation of the body Kesdjan can only be a result of real work on oneself.

We can also say that this body is dependent on the development of the emotional center. My emotions in their present state are, for the most part, disorganized. Generally, people have little real under-standing of the complexity of their emotional life. We are acutely aware of our emotions only at strong moments, when we feel either very nega-tive or very elated. Otherwise, our awareness of our emotional state is vague at best. Additionally, our emotions are often limited to either liking or disliking—in this way emotional development remains in its infancy. It is important to ask if is there is something within us that can go beyond like and dislike, that may have the stamina to withstand whatever is experienced emotionally and might truly mature into a real emotional body?

Some years ago, I was in the attic of my house on a hot day. It was a very uncomfortable and constricted space. I was remodeling, trying to install some wooden blocks on the rafters to support a skylight. I was lying semi-prone, sideways across the rafters while, at the same time, hammering nails to fasten the blocks between the rafters. It was an extremely awkward and painful position, my body was protesting and my emotional center felt very unhappy. In short, I was becoming very negative. Then a different part of me—a part I believe is closer to my essence—entered, and I found the force to complete my work. If I could express the emotional state in words, it would sound like this: "Well, this is extremely uncomfortable and painful, but it does not make any difference, you (meaning my body) are going to finish this job you have begun. It is not a matter of liking or disliking it, just continue and be aware of all your sensations and experiences."

This part of me was more genuine than my personality. It seemed to have a separate existence, at once confident and unifying. Compared with my ordinary state of consciousness, this part of me had a "will." It also had an emotional force that energized my body to continue despite its resistance. The entire experience was freeing and ecstatic. In some way, it seemed to me the most natural state in the world. Perhaps it was a state some deeper part of me has always known.

I believe there is a possibility of developing such a second body. If it can be a reality, it will be born from efforts to develop an inner emotional life independent of whatever is going on either inside or outside me. Gurdjieff's word for this first higher body, "Kesdjan," literally means "vessel for the spirit." The word "spirit" in turn, relates to the breath and the finer substances in the air—our second being-food—which can only be assimilated through inner work. (In Chapter 5 we will explain Gurdjieff's idea of three "being-foods" of which air is one.) If I maintain over many years the inner aim of becoming a full human being, regardless of what life throws at me, a new emotional presence can be born in me that is independent of the physical body. I believe the emotional force I felt in the attic relates to the creation of this second body. Efforts to continue working regardless of resistance can magnetize and assimilate the finer materials that are capable of coalescing into a new body. Gurdjieff says:

> We have no astral body, only astral "matter." From astral body, mental body formed, from mental, higher body still. Astral body formed when all desires ONE. We are like a heap of metallic powder, no one grain ever in the same place. But through "heat" can become ONE mass, each having its own place—Then mass as a mass can be used, it can be magnetized with "something." [15]

The development of the second higher or "Soul body" seems to be connected with the growth and maturation of what Gurdjieff called "objective conscience." That, of course, implies I have the will to actualize the responsibilities that having such a conscience would require. We sometimes have glimpses of objective conscience when we are faced with a momentous decision in our lives, aware we are standing at a crossroads. It may be that during the development of the Kesdjan body, we are also creating the energy we would need for developing the Soul body. I also suspect the production of these higher bodies may not proceed in a completely linear manner. The development of the two higher bodies is directly connected to what Gurdjieff referred to as "conscious labor and intentional suffering."

CONSCIOUS LABOR

Gurdjieff said human beings have the possibility of self-perfecting by practicing conscious labor and intentional suffering. The beginning of conscious labor and intentional suffering is the growth of self-knowledge and self-understanding; this growth is dependent upon self-observation and effort.

There are at least two requirements for conscious labor. First, a part of you is present while you are engaging in the action; it is therefore not entirely automatic. Second, you are clear about the aim of your action; you are doing this for a definite reason, and you are wishing to be present to yourself existing in this action and remember yourself. Again, this is an ability most people falsely believe they already possess. Self-observation is a requisite of conscious labor. Only through self-observation can you verify that actualizing conscious labor is rare, while making it possible for you to experience moments of it.

For example, I recently visited a friend who lives in a small cabin. The confines of the cabin required me to strip the bed in the morning and put away all the bedding. Before I stripped the bed, I had done a "sitting" where I was internally quiet and had little disturbance.[16] My friend continued to sleep at the other end of the room. I thought, "This is a wonderful opportunity for me to be present, consciously fold the bedding and put it away." I wanted to practice self-observation, observe and experience or "sense" my body.[17] Sounds like a simple task in such a quiet environment—but what actually happened? As I began to fold the first sheet, a part of me noticed I was not folding it completely evenly. Another part, said, "That doesn't matter, continue!" The same thing happened with the next sheet. Observing my body was lost while I was folding the first bed sheet. It never returned. While I was folding and putting away the bedding, I had completely lost track of my intention. Perhaps I should say I was no longer experiencing myself in present time. My mind had jumped ahead into the future, into what was going to happen after I had stored the bedding. Then I noticed another part of me was hungry. I was looking forward to eating some cereal and maybe even a banana. Then, I felt the wish to go swimming. After all, this was my vacation, etc.

You see, even my simple intention to be present while folding and putting away bedding was not so simple. My tendency to fall asleep at that moment, to think of the future, of eating and swimming, competed with my aim to be present in the moment, to observe myself. Conscious labor requires me to live and be conscious of myself in the present moment while carrying out an action or aim. I might think I am always conscious but it is clear I am not. It is actually a capacity that I can only gradually acquire. I believe, as children, we actually had more of this capacity to live in the present moment while a part of us was separate and present to our experience. I remember having this kind of experience when I was young, but my capacity for this type of presence gradually atrophied as I got older. I became more identified with the future and producing a finished task or product. Society's emphasis on future accomplishments gradually replaced my ability to do something in the moment and be present while doing it. Many of my childhood memories contain vividness, the result of the ability to be engaged and yet have a part of me that is simultaneously conscious of my existence.

In order to labor consciously, a part of me needs to be capable of remaining conscious while engaged in an activity. I have found this is a rare occurrence, but you will need to verify this experience for yourself. The most important point is that you yourself, through your own sincere efforts, must become convinced that you rarely labor *consciously*. Instead, you proceed mechanically and habitually, subject to every distraction that appears and takes you away. Being convinced of this by your own experience will develop your wish to be able to do some simple actions consciously. If you can do simple things consciously, more will be possible for you in an attentive state. If, however, you are incapable of simple conscious activity, then the idea of conscious labor remains a fantasy. Only you can judge the truthfulness of your own level of presence and consciousness.

A warning: As you become more familiar with your lack of consciousness in the present moment, and perhaps the difficulty of remaining present, you may become negative about your ability and your potential. However, it is important to understand that each of us needs to experience this frustration, because it shows you the truth of our predicament. This truth will gradually guide you in the right direction—toward self-consciousness in the moment.

It is very interesting for me to listen to psychotherapists in groups speak about "witnessing" or being able to have a witness to their actions. It all sounds so very easy, as if by saying it, it will then happen. I am afraid it is more difficult than simply saying you want to have a witness. It is similar to riding a horse. When the horse strays off the path, you must first notice it has strayed and then use the reins to redirect it. You must use the reins gently because being angry at the horse and jerking on the reins will only make the horse balk. Likewise, I first need to notice my attention has wandered before I can reinitiate witnessing. It takes gentle practice, practice, practice—and also, not to forget, compassion for our habitual condition. Conscious labor requires an attitude of openness. This is an attitude shift in that it is not the outcome of a task that is most important, but the development of your ability to remain in contact with yourself while working.

If I truly pursue the aim of being conscious—present—observing myself, my experience has shown me there will be some degree of suffering that accompanies my effort. This suffering will come from the new impressions—mental, physical, and emotional—I gain of myself. Inside me, this results in "tempering" (that is, an inner toughening without a loss of sensitivity). I become able to endure more experience, pain, or pleasure without falling asleep, distracting, or defending myself from the experience. As I have worked to engage in conscious labor, I have encountered depression, anxiety, grief, and joy. Compassion for myself has allowed me to benefit from the gifts these difficult emotions offer me.

Inherent in the concept of conscious labor—and its complement "intentional suffering" which we will come to shortly—is the idea of service. Service means supporting another, a community, a group, or the Work itself. It brings us to Gurdjieff's concept of "reciprocal maintenance." [18] Whether we wish it or not, we are always involved in the process of reciprocal maintenance, which feeds and maintains everything in the universe. That is, we are either eating, transforming the energy of lower forms of life so that we can exist, or being eaten, being utilized by nature in some way that we have little or no under-standing of. Nature and time continue to consume us whether or not we are conscious of them. Through service, I might extract something for myself as I serve what is higher. In this way, I become a conscious particle in the reciprocal feeding of everything existing, rather than an unconscious atom that is simply consumed.

INTENTIONAL SUFFERING

If we attempt to labor consciously, to observe ourselves, to lead a more conscious life, suffering will undoubtedly follow as we experience our state of waking-sleeping consciousness and realize we have lived in this way for our entire lives. We suffer intentionally when we make the effort to study ourselves. However, voluntary self-observation, if prac-ticed correctly, will also increase our psychological flexibility and give us truthful impressions of ourselves. If we become more flexible psycho-logically, it is a good indicator that our work is moving in the right direc-tion. If people or groups you meet "in the Work" seem rigid, take note.

Becoming more flexible allows me to be present in the moment and make new memories. Self-observation is the beginning of conscious labor. Suffering is a natural consequence of conscious labor: As you become more aware of your own mechanicality, your prison of habitual reactions, you see your subjectivity, negativity, limitations, rigidity, and other aspects of your emotional makeup. If you gradually learn to tolerate and experience your discomfort, you have begun the journey to flexibility and compassion for yourself and others. There is also incred-ible joy as I begin to learn in this way about myself.

Through my efforts, I begin to transform my energy, as the alche-mists sought to transform base metals into gold. However, beware of the possibility of going down the wrong road. As I mentioned, down one of the wrong roads you will find you are becoming more rigid, more judgmental. If you want to move toward objectivity, you might wish to consider the following idea: true objectivity must include subjectivity. I need to learn to accept myself and have compassion for all the subjec-tive states that overtake me that I am caught in.

Your body's manifestations are the first objects of your observation. Gradually, as you focus on the body, you can also become more objective toward your subjective emotional states. Collin says this about the situation: "When true self-remembering comes, one does not want to alter oneself, or others; one somehow rises above their weaknesses and one's own. There can be no blame anywhere. One swallows what is, and becomes free." [19] We are not planning to shut away our subjective experience. I have found I need to be careful of any group leaders or teachers with ambitions to power, who teach their followers to be negative about their own subjective nature rather than helping them *take an interest* in their subjectivity.

Self-study, if practiced correctly, gradually teaches you to suffer intentionally—that is, with intelligent purpose. My usual suffering is the suffering of my personality, a suffering that occurs mechanically when something does not work out the way "it" wishes. Then my attitude becomes negative and I suffer. In fact, we suffer much more than necessary, inadvertently, while attempting to avoid suffering.

At this point, I would expect you to ask, why would anyone intentionally want to suffer? Certain Buddhists might argue suffering is in fact not necessary, is illusory, and the aim should be to free oneself from suffering. I believe that Buddha did not mean we should not suffer. He was speaking of the unconscious misery we make for ourselves in reaction to life's circumstances. However, many people misunderstand the Buddhist message. They engage in mental gymnastics to free themselves from suffering. Obviously, mental gymnastics are just that, exercises to free oneself from what is an integral part of the human experience—suffering. All life forms experience suffering; the difference is how we experience it, the attitude with which we meet it. Mechanical suffering can eat up our lives. The only alternative, or should I say, the "only game in town," is to learn to use suffering intentionally for our inner growth.

Making use of suffering for my inner growth requires me to notice my experiences, be interested in them, articulate them to myself and others, and ponder their meaning. Only by pondering and making meaning from my experience can I mine the treasure within it. "Pondering," in this sense, means thinking and feeling deeply about my experience, trying to find its inherent meaning. Then my life—even my unconscious life—becomes a living laboratory where new learning and new memories become possible. Then I may experience both suffering and joy. However, this suffering is of a very special kind. Through it, I cultivate a real "I." This "I" can maintain an inner aim throughout the difficulties of my life. I will be able to depend on this objective "I" as it matures and gains strength.

Please note that when I refer to "pondering" and making meaning from your experience, I am not advising that you engage in continual analysis. Pondering and meaning-making means that I direct my thought to my experiences. Self-observation is really a registration and a witnessing of myself. Analysis, on the other hand, is an attempt to understand by fitting my observations into a certain framework. Work is different from analysis, since there is no framework to have to fit my experience into. However, Work does require that I ponder my experience and derive as much meaning from it as is possible.

In summary, conscious labor and intentional suffering start with studying and understanding myself. These activities cannot exist without struggle. Self-study and efforts to understand the functioning of my machine will lead to suffering. Through learning to labor consciously and suffer intentionally, one can develop a real "I" and real will. This real "I" not only can serve my evolution, but the evolution of humanity and the greater cosmos as well.

In this chapter, we have looked at a few of the major ideas that Gurdjieff brought us. There are many other ideas, but the ones we have covered provide a brief overview of the vastness of his cosmology, from the individual to the cosmos, in which everything has a purpose and a place. In Chapter 5, we will look more closely at his entire system of ideas and concepts.

CHAPTER 4

SENSING

GETTING IN TOUCH WITH THE BODY

One difficulty we encounter when we wish to study ourselves is the predominance of our associative mind. This is the "mind" that was "educated" in the classroom. It is an excellent instrument with which to begin our self-study, but eventually, we will require something more. In order to prevent self-study from becoming just another intellectual, associative exercise, we need to learn a method of Work called "sensing." Sensing is also a means of training attention. It gives our mind an anchor, because it is rooted in the energies of the body. This is key to developing balance among our three centers. In this chapter, we will learn about sensing and how to begin that practice. Sensing is a special practice for self-study—a practice, which, if developed properly, can help us learn about and fully experience all aspects of ourselves.

In order to be balanced, I must be grounded. What does "grounded" mean? Many people vaguely understand it to mean being in touch with the earth. I give it a more definite meaning here: To be grounded means to be in touch with my body, to actually experience it. When I am in contact with my own body, I can then proceed to be in contact with my emotional state, my likes and dislikes, my thoughts, and finally, the immediate environment and the natural world. If I lose this contact with my body and am caught up in only my thoughts or my emotions, I am only partially alive.

Being cut off from our bodies has become normal for us. Despite the hyperactivity of our head brain, we may still feel bored or depressed. Suspecting something might be missing, we will usually search to change our emotional state by using our mind. Most people have come to the point where they are so out of touch with the moment-to-moment experience of their bodies that they have to resort to all sorts of artificial means in an attempt to reestablish the connection. Sports, gymnastics, meditation, massage, hiking, biking, dance, and many other activities are attempts to reestablish this missing connection to the body. We may also use drugs and alcohol to try to reestablish this connection. In the last fifty years, movements in psychology and education have attempted to redress our poor connection with our bodies. Wilhelm Reich, a psychologist and contemporary of Freud, spoke of the muscular blockages to healthy energy flow within the body and the need to remove these blockages.[1] Psychological practitioners during the past twenty years have become interested in healing the "mind-body split." Such interest is important, in that it focuses attention on this poorly understood and neglected biological container—our body—and the disconnection that is characteristic of the mind-body split. Sadly, although contemporary psychologists evince a great deal of interest in discovering the wisdom of the body, they have found very few methods for developing a correct relationship to the body, nor do they understand how to study and strengthen this relationship.

Some people develop a destructive relationship to their bodies that is even worse than simply being out of touch. Either they try to over-control the body, leading to activities such as extreme sports or violent martial arts, or they overindulge its desires, leading to drug or sex addiction, extreme dieting, or overeating.

In my experience, if I can be in touch with my body, then my awareness and aliveness are increased exponentially when contrasted with the way I feel in my ordinary state of waking-sleep. If my thoughts about the future or past entrap me, or I am caught in current or past feelings without a connection with my body, then I am alive in only one-third of myself. My difficulty is that the disconnection from my body has become habitual, and when I want to establish a connection with my body, that habitual pattern of disconnection intervenes. However, with my efforts at self-observation and learning sensing, which we will soon explore, I can move into a state of awareness and be in direct connection with my body. Moreover, through this work, I establish new neurological pathways that eventually replace my old patterns of disconnection.

I am often asked to sit in on meetings where I hear other therapists say, "Notice what is happening in your body right now," or "Can you feel that tension in a particular place in your body?" At other times, they may suggest to a client or another therapist, "Get into your body." Easier said than done! After many years of practice, I know those instructions are not so simple. Very few people know what "Get into your body" means. They do not have a real taste of what it is like or how to do it without drugs or alcohol. Along with the lack of research on human attention, there is a definite paucity of research into how to connect mind and body.

What the therapist overlooks when he advises his client to get into their body is that the other person's ability to focus his or her attention is very limited, and the pattern of disconnection from their body is well established. Even if he or she could focus on the body for a moment, the flow of ordinary associations is so habitual that it often immediately overpowers any new impressions. Vipassana meditation gets around this tendency of distracted attention by having the participant focus their attention only on the breath and the area around the nostrils at first, to help him stay oriented, and later to focus the attention upon each part of the body. This type of practice can be useful for the development of attention in a controlled environment.

Gurdjieff brought a method of working with the body to develop the attention that was light-years ahead of any other method—it is sensing. But, before exploring sensing in more detail, a bit more about methods and practices in general is needed.

PRACTICES: MEANS VERSUS ENDS

What do I mean when I say "practices"? For the purposes of what we are exploring here, a practice is a tool that helps an individual on the path toward transformation and individuation. The problem with practices—yoga, aikido, meditation, tai chi chuan, self-observation, or any others—is that we tend to make them ends in themselves. The human tendency is to become addicted to security and feeling better, and by doing our practice, we probably will feel better. However, spiritual practices are not simply about feeling better. We need to view practices as a means to assist us in attaining an aim rather than the aim itself. Practices contain neither the meaning nor the aim of Work. For human beings to find their place in the greater cosmos, they must first work to become balanced and whole, and practices facilitate this.

Real practice for inner evolution builds an inner container to hold specific energies for transformation. In Gurdjieff's Work, we are interested in harmonizing all three of our major centers. The harmonization of my centers transforms me, and one might even say, results in a new type of human being capable of containing a higher order of experience. The "container" we are preparing will be able to receive and utilize energies from *two higher centers*.

According to Gurdjieff, these two higher centers—the higher emotional center and higher intellectual center—are already fully developed and complete in each person.[2] Individuals may briefly access these centers during times of great pain, fear, or need. They may also access them artificially with drugs, breathing exercises, various distortions of yoga (such as kundalini yoga), or hypnosis. However, to connect with the material from higher centers through such artificial means is always dangerous and unpredictable. Rarely, and maybe never, can the individual integrate that experience into the whole of him- or herself.

In order for us to become harmonious and able to access information from the higher centers, we first need to work on balancing our three lower centers. These lower centers must be educated, developed and harmonized with each other, which is the underlying reason for practices. In the past, esoteric schools used practices as an experiential means of connecting an individual with their true role in humanity's purpose in relation to the greater cosmos. Schools in the East existed where individuals who had reached a higher degree of consciousness preserved practices for self-development and guided those who went there to study.[3] These schools helped the individual to recognize that there was more meaning to life than the meanings they found within the material world they experienced. Sources for such practices include the great religions in their original forms.

Human beings are meaning-making entities; we are always trying to make sense of our experience. However, meaning exists on more than one level. We have the ability to differentiate between what the Work calls "horizontal" and "vertical" meaning. Horizontal meaning is limited and is usually confined within a specific culture, while vertical meaning is unlimited in scope. Symbols, such as the Christian cross, exist to represent the intersection of horizontal and vertical planes of existence and meaning, to aid those searching for self-perfection. Practices exist on the horizontal plane, where we live our lives; but practices also provide a temporary passageway for us, from the horizontal to the vertical experience, and connect us with our possible place in the cosmos. They provide us with a means to experience and transform potential energies within us.

FIRST-PERSON EXPERIENCE

The human body utilizes various energies to function, but our scientific knowledge is scanty on the subject of human energy. Endocrinologists catalog the various chemical compounds and hormones produced by the endocrine glands and treat dysfunctions due to over- or underproduction of these hormones. Most of their work deals with observable phenomena, aided by technology. Scientists primarily focus on the visible, material world and the energies that power it. In the scientific view, this is the prime "reality." Scientists have more difficulty in dealing with the invisible energies.

An interesting and overlooked characteristic of human experience is that our thinking, emotional, and inner bodily processes are invisible to others. Psychological experiences simply do not avail themselves to being examined under a microscope; thus, they remain invisible to external observers. In short, scientists cannot study in depth our actual thinking, emoting, and kinesthetic experience from outside of a person. Ultimately, we must study these functions within ourselves in order to understand their operation. Only through our own observation can we, ourselves, discover how we know we are not feeling well—physically or emotionally. Various diseases cause physical and psychological symptoms. However, our actual, lived, individual experience of either, no matter how the body manifests, remains invisible. Moreover, science still cannot measure a person's level of sensitivity or insensitivity to his environment, to himself, or to others. Thus, sensing, as used in the Gurdjieff Work, refers to an experience that cannot currently be measured scientifically.

SENSING

Sensing is the direct, bodily experience of the living sensitive energy within our organism. Sensing is not intellectual or emotional. Sensing allows us to utilize energy that can be brought up in our bodies as a focus for attention to help us maintain a state of awareness. Sensing directly connects us with the energetic experience of our lives, of the fact that we exist in this moment.

Don't confuse sensing with sense-experience—that is, seeing, hearing, touch, temperature, smell, etc. which arise automatically. Sensing is a means of accessing the state of consciousness where we can experience awareness. It is a potential capacity that requires development. It is essential to develop sensing, as it helps one to remain in contact with their body. We do not automatically have the ability to sense ourselves at will and this capacity requires intentional development.

Preparatory Sensing Practice

Do not be discouraged in any way if you do not notice any change. For some people the progress will be slow, but when it emerges, they can experience being firmly grounded by it.

1. Sit quietly in a chair.

2. Relax for at least five to ten minutes to let ordinary life go.

3. Place your gentle, unforced attention on the palm of your right hand. Notice if something changes in the state or the experience of your hand. If you do notice a change, then gently move your attention to the palm of the left hand and see if a similar kind of change takes place there.

4. Continue with the same practice for three to five minutes, switching gentle attention back and forth between hands. You are searching for a change in the energy within the hand after your attention moves to it. It may feel like increased warmth, tingling, increased weight, or a kind of knowing that you have a palm or that your palm really is there.

Note: You may realize that, before your attention dwelt on it, the palm of your hand did not really exist in your consciousness at all! Alternatively, you may simply notice that when your attention is on one hand, the energy in it is different from that in the other hand.

You may notice—but do not be discouraged if you do not, since this in no way represents whether or not you can sense or develop sensing—first that you find a new energy in the hand you are focusing on. Second, the development of this new energy is somehow related to your attention. Don't try to figure this all out, don't intensify it, or work with it for too long. It won't help and is beside the point. This exercise is only about noticing a change in energy in the hands, for three to five minutes maximum. Do this practice three or four times a week for one or two weeks, and then let it go. Later in this book, we will come back to it in different forms. People develop sensing at their own speed, so do not be discouraged. There is no rush here, just the opposite—relaxing and learning to be patient and gentle with oneself.

BEING IN THE BODY

A question that has interested me for a number of years is how the body organizes itself so that we are able to move. It was not until I had practiced sensing for many years that I experienced that the body uses a very distinct type of energy, not outwardly measurable, to organize both its movements and its stationary postures. This energy is finite and it forms itself into diverse patterns. This organizing energy of the body is a form of "automatic energy." Bennett says, "All our automatic associations—all the automatic work of our senses—all automatic seeing, hearing—all our movements that have not intention or choice in them—all these depend upon automatic energy." [4]

Sensitive energy is energy of a higher level than automatic energy, and we can utilize it in our work and develop a relationship with it through sensing. Sensitive energy has the property of making a connection to the here and now and facilitates our experience of awareness. It is quite different from the automatic energy that carries us along as functioning machines. Sensitive energy as experienced through sensing helps us separate from our automatism.

Strictly speaking, sensing only comes into play when the body becomes immediately here and now for me. Most of the time, the body has its repertoire of postures and carries on quite well without any awareness on my part, the automatic energy controlling sensations and movements. My postures and movements are normally automatic, habitual manifestations of my body. Yet, through sensing I can utilize any habitual movement or posture to create a separation of my "I" from my body and experience a state of awareness.

The body continually uses automatic energy to organize both voluntary and involuntary movement. Sensing provides an immediate awareness of my physical life in the moment. It connects the intellectual and emotional centers to the physical center through the wish to focus attention on the body's sensitive energy. Without sensing, we might never really experience the finer energy in either movement or stillness. If we remain ignorant of sensitive energy, we miss using it for our personal development.

Sensing has many benefits. Through it, we create a unique connection among the three centers, and our real "I" begins to receive new types of impressions. We begin to create this connection by strengthening the link between the intellectual center and the body. As you become familiar with sensing and its gift of new impressions, you will desire more of these impressions. Impressions are a "food" we need, which we will discuss in a later chapter.

SENSING AND INCARNATION

The religious among us take for granted that we have incarnated. By "incarnated," I mean we have a spirit that is now embodied in a human form. I beg to differ with this generally accepted and perhaps irrational fantasy. We live in bodies, yet we may not have really incarnated. Let's look at the situation. Most of the time, we are out of touch with our bodies and will become aware of them when hungry, tired, ill or sexually aroused. Until I began to work with sensing, I did not realize I had not fully incarnated, that I was not conscious and experiencing my body most of the time. In many ways, I had inhabited a house that I had not explored. I believe sensing is a means to begin real incarnation.

Being in one's body and experiencing it is actually difficult for many people. As such, they have not fully incarnated. Sometimes the aging process forces people to incarnate more. As they get older, the automatic ability of the body to move decreases, and people are forced into contact with their bodies and experience their aches and rigidity. I believe it is exciting and vital to learn as early as possible to incarnate during this lifetime and fully inhabit my body.

Sensing can become a tool to explore the real existence of my body, a method of gaining self-knowledge. Through sensing, I can learn about my body, my emotions and thoughts, and even their effect on my body. When I am emotionally upset, sensing helps to ground me, to contain and understand the strong or difficult emotions I am experiencing, rather than simply being overwhelmed by them or attempting to distract myself.

SITTINGS

In order to correctly develop the ability to sense, and before you try other practices or methods given by any group or any that you have found on the Internet, you should master the practice outlined here. In my experience, if I do not have a correct experience of sensing, other practices may either prove too difficult, or I will not experience what they were meant to demonstrate.

You should begin with relaxation. I have listed below some general guidelines for "sittings," describing their purpose, and also a relaxation method. Following these guidelines, I lay out Bennett's "16-point" exercise, an indirect means to help in the development of sensing.

I mentioned earlier that it is very easy for practices to become a means of changing one's state. Also mentioned was that people have a tendency to repeat something that results in a pleasurable change. For example, if you focus on the breath while witnessing your inhalation and exhalation, you may definitely change your inner state. For the most part, practices bring the practitioner into a pleasant, unusual, relaxed, or heightened state. Unconsciously, you may return to this practice simply to achieve this change. However such techniques are not ends in themselves. If you take them as such, they are not necessarily beneficial and may not produce any inner evolution. Instead of waking me up, the practice becomes another factor keeping me asleep. This distortion can occur with any practice, including yoga, meditation, or sittings. Remember, a sitting is designed to open up new possibilities for inner experience, but do not construe it as an aim in itself.

There are different kinds of sittings in the Gurdjieff Work, and each type serves a particular purpose. A common misconception about sittings is that they are similar to meditation. There are some similarities, but sittings require more activity and can involve all of the centers. One purpose of sittings is to prepare and support you to harmonize the fine energies elaborated during your sleep before these are dissipated by the automatic reactions required of you by your everyday life. They are usually done in the early morning after arising. Sittings do not go on for hours at a time, nor need you practice them for weeks at a time at a retreat. They are quite different. They are meant to be part of your life, so there is no need to go on retreat. You practice them for a limited period each day, rarely more than thirty to forty-five minutes. Another purpose is to prepare you to receive impressions from different levels of consciousness within you, the connections to which are not yet permanently established.

It is best to practice sitting before beginning your daily responsibilities. It is important at the end of each sitting to remain quiet and passive for a short while, to allow you to assimilate what has taken place within you.

General Guidelines for Sittings

The actual transformation of our nature is not something we do, but we can prepare to receive something new:

1. The best time to sit is in the early morning before being caught up in your day. Take your shower or bath and do not eat or drink before the sitting.

2. You need a very quiet place where you will not be disturbed for at least thirty to forty-five minutes. Lock your door and take your phone off the hook. Open a window to let fresh air in.

3. Sit in a straight-backed chair (unless you are very comfortable sitting tailor-style with legs crossed under you on the floor or on

a sitting cushion). The advantage of a straight-backed chair for many people versus the tailor position is that it fully supports your body. This support frees your mind and emotions from having to work with any bodily resistance and from the need to maintain any unnecessary muscular tension a particular posture might require.

4. Keep your eyes shut or preferably just barely open. The palms of the hands rest on the thighs or knees.

5. Before starting the practice per se, it is good to sit for five or even ten minutes quietly without doing anything, and allow your mind, feelings and body to wind down from any habitual activity you have begun even before work or breakfast.

6. Do a full relaxation. The relaxation described here occurs because of a gentle movement of your attention. There is nothing for you to try to do muscularly. Relaxation occurs by learning to move your attention gently. If your mind wanders (that is, your attention is pulled away), simply bring your attention gently back again. Give yourself about ten minutes for the relaxation so there is no rush. You can do a relaxation in your own manner or follow the instructions listed here.

Suggested Relaxation

- Begin by placing your attention at the center of the top of your skull.

- Gently move your attention to your forehead, down the back of the head, down the sides of the head to the ears.

- Move the attention to the eyes, nose, cheeks, and lips.

- Move the attention to the tongue. Take your time here and notice how the tongue is always ready to start talking, and see if you can just let it lie on the floor of your mouth.

- Then, move to the chin, back of the head and neck, to the throat.

- Continue to the upper right shoulder, upper right arm, elbow, wrist, top of the hand, bottom of the hand, all the fingers of the hand, the entire hand, and entire right arm.

- Then, move to the upper left shoulder, upper left arm, elbow, wrist, top of the hand, bottom of the hand, all the fingers of the hand, the entire hand, and entire left arm.

- Continue to the upper chest and upper back, middle chest and middle back, stomach area, and lower back.

- Then, move to the upper right hip, right thigh, knee (front and back), lower leg, top of the foot, bottom of the foot, entire foot, and entire right leg.

- Move to the upper left hip, left thigh, knee (front and back), lower leg, top of the foot, bottom of the foot, entire foot, and entire left leg.

- Continue to the navel area, buttocks, and genitals.

- Then spread a gentle attention over the entire body.

Remember, you do not have to try to relax. Relaxation gradually takes place as you learn to direct your attention this way. You may notice as you move your attention that you are holding tension in various parts of your body. Noticing the tension is what is important. There is no need to try to reduce the tension in any area where you notice it.

Bennett's 16-point Exercise—Preparation for the Experience of Sensing

Following your relaxation:

1. Place a gentle attention on the entire right arm: from the shoulder to the tips of the fingers. If your attention wanders, gently bring it back. Place your attention on the limb for no more than six breaths.

2. Move the attention to the right leg: from hip to the toes as one unit.

3. Move the attention to the left leg: from hip to the toes as one unit.

4. Move the attention to the left arm: from the shoulder to the tips of the fingers.

The first series of movement of attention through the limbs is now complete.

Remember, you are simply working with a gentle attention, not forcing, not trying to increase any state, but simply placing attention for a limited time, then moving on to next limb. If your mind wanders, that is all right, gently redirect your attention.

5.– 8. The next series begins with the right leg, the left leg, left arm, and right arm.

9.–12. In the next series, begin with the left leg, then left arm, right arm, right leg.

13.–16. The last series begins with left arm, right arm, right leg, left leg.

The above exercise represents sixteen movements of the attention. Repeat the entire 16-point rotation one more time, sit quietly for a few minutes and then leave it.

The aim is not to do your practice quickly, nor is it to change your state (although your state may in fact change). Work at the practice without tampering with yourself, without trying to be special or produce a special effect. Simply do it.

You may notice the following taking place: as your attention moves, an energy arises in each new limb in turn. This is a special energy for you as an individual, and it may be useful to you in ways you cannot now comprehend or appreciate. In my experience, I feel I am embarking on a sacred journey.

Remember: at this time, do not try to sense; rather, sensing may occur because of the honest, gentle, relaxed, intentional direction of your attention. You work with gentle attention, and then allow yourself to experience sensing.

Because of the wanderings of our unconscious attention, a habit that was passed down to us over generations, combined with our own habitual, undirected attention, the intellectual center alone is simply not strong enough to resist the flow of neurological programming that maintains the waking-sleeping state However, with practice, you eventually will be able to sense a limb or other part of your body of which you previously had little awareness—except perhaps when you injured it or were sick. Sensing develops your attention, forming a new pattern within you and creating new branches on your neurological tree. Recent studies have shown the brain to have a quality of plasticity. According to this theory of "neuroplasticity," thinking, learning, and acting actually change both the brain's functional anatomy and its physical anatomy.[5] Sensing is directly connected with the development of new patterns in the brain, forging new connections between centers; thus, it has profound ramifications for individual development.

THE ROLE OF SENSING IN SELF-OBSERVATION

The human organism is organized so that the intellectual, emotional, and moving centers are interconnected and influence one another. A cognitive-behavioral psychologist understands these connections. He makes use of the link between the intellect, or the cognitive part, and the physical and emotional parts. He may encourage his clients to be more physically active in order to lessen their depression. He recommends his client do some simple, physical exercise each day. When the depressed person begins to run for an hour a day, she begins to feel better emotionally. She may now be able to sleep better, whereas before she just stayed awake in her bed thinking about her difficulties and failures. Simple running has changed her sleep pattern and her emotional state. If she continues exercising, she may actually begin to function in a more balanced manner.

On the other hand, the psychologist may direct his client to think differently. He points out her tendency to think in black-and-white terms only, or that she tends to "catastrophize" when confronted by difficulties. Through learning to think differently, the client's depression or anxiety is reduced.

These examples show the interaction between centers and may give you a clue to the importance of sensing. First, sensing requires that you be attentive in a new way, which I refer to as "gentle attention." This type of attention is neither forced nor tense, but an open attention. Gentle attention is different from our normal focused attention, which is often at-tension. Usually, focused attention is a contracting movement that focuses and narrows the field of consciousness. Gentle attention by contrast, is characterized by expanding my awareness. Thus, while we are developing our ability to sense, we simultaneously develop the ability to practice gentle, open attention. We direct attention intentionally, rather than having it directed by outer life and accidental shocks from the environment. Directing our attention helps to ground us by connecting the mind with the body. When we are grounded, we experience our living existence and receive new impressions. You may find that the body enjoys being sensed.

Second, through sensing, we encounter energies within the body of which we were previously unaware. Thus, we are more conscious of our bodies and more able to experience its intelligence. Usually, as I stated above, the body uses automatic energy for organizing itself and we remain unconscious of it. However, with sensing, we have the opportunity to consciously participate in the experience of this special sensitive energy that is called up by being attentive, but without modifying it or trying to control it. The word "participate" has a special meaning here, which we will explore in depth in Chapter 16. *Participation* is an advanced method of self-observation and self-study.

Third, the effect of sensing, or in the beginning, simply directing our attention to a particular part of the body, has a definite effect on the intellectual center. It curtails daydreams, fantasies, and other useless patterns of associative thinking, without the necessity of stopping my thoughts. Later, when I am more experienced with sensing, it gives me an instantaneous means of self-observation. It bypasses the associative mind and immediately gives me increased impressions of myself. In other words, the mind's ordinary associative function cannot truly partake of the present moment. It is busy encoding impressions that have already occurred, rather than being able to experience them newly. Sensing gets around this continuous referencing of the past by giving a person raw impressions of himself in the moment.

You may have noticed already that I harp on the need for us to gain new impressions of ourselves. Impressions are actual food, although we are not used to looking at them that way. Without any impressions, we would die.[6] When deprived of most of them, we can become mentally unbalanced. The food of impressions is the material we need to deepen our understanding of ourselves.

If sensing allows me to become familiar with a new type of energy I have not experienced clearly before, are there corresponding energy systems in the emotional and intellectual centers? That is, are we also unaware of specific energies in the other centers? What are they? How do we learn about them? Can we also experience them? These are interesting questions to ponder.

You do not have to *try* to sense yourself. Simply work with the practices in this chapter to learn to direct your attention in a gentle way. A major benefit of sensing is that in practicing it we are humbled. We try to sense, but then don't remember our intention, or we lose track of ourselves, and this proves we are not awake, thus giving us direct experience of our inability to maintain our attention and connection with our own body. Do not lose heart for, if practiced, sensing will develop gradually, in proportion to your ability to relax while directing your attention.

CHAPTER 5

THE SYSTEM

> OCTOBER 22, 1955. I think the deep instinct to check everything, verify everything, seems absolutely essential. In fact it is this friction between the instinct to believe and the instinct to question which forces us to that state of self-remembering where alone things can be truly assessed.[1]
> —Rodney Collin

THE BIGGER PICTURE

Gurdjieff embedded his psychological theory and practices in a framework that encompassed the whole cosmos. In this chapter, I will touch upon some of Gurdjieff's unique ideas that will be covered in greater detail as we continue. I ask you: simply be open to the ideas and framework presented. It is important to recognize that many very sophisticated ideas can easily be discounted if one only looks at the surface of what is being presented or depends on accepted views of reality perpetuated by a society that does not encourage critical thinking for oneself. Gurdjieff's story is complex and unusual, and one might easily reject it because of these characteristics. The story, and even words and language, require you to think deeply about what he is saying and force you to depart from everyday associative thinking. In this chapter, we will examine Gurdjieff's explanation for what went wrong in ancient times that has led us to our present state of disharmony and sleep.

Gurdjieff places our planet Earth and its evolution within a larger evolutionary structure, a structure that has order, meaning, and a definite place for the "three-brained beings" that we are. The cosmology as presented in Gurdjieff's *Beelzebub's Tales to His Grandson* and in Ouspensky's *In Search of the Miraculous* is unique to Gurdjieff's legacy and is not found in such a complete form in any other written or historical material. It provides an entirely new and complete framework in which to explore the meaning and purpose of life. Gurdjieff's system ultimately connects the potential of humankind with our objective purpose, our place in the development and maintenance of the cosmos.

Gurdjieff's teachings look at humanity from two perspectives: the cosmological and the psychological. *In Search of the Miraculous* clearly depicts the organizational plan of the cosmos, including the role of stars, planets, nature, animals, and humans. Gurdjieff explained this organization to his early Russian groups, and individuals immediately realized that here was a framework of the universe that made sense both scientifically and spiritually. Gurdjieff elaborated his system in his large, allegorical history of the world, *Beelzebub's Tales to His Grandson*. The part of Gurdjieff's system that has always intrigued me the most is how human beings fit into the cosmological plan of the earth and universe, and specifically, why we are needed for the development of our planetary system.

Gurdjieff teaches that the universe, its stars, and planets are living and evolving entities. It is an idea that appears both revolutionary and simple. Our sun, a physical entity responsible for all of nature's marvelous interactions, is not a lifeless mass, but rather a living source or manifestation of intelligence. Gurdjieff lays out this plan of the evolving universe in what he calls the "Ray of Creation." To give us an idea of how a person might find her actual place in the universe, Gurdjieff defines the "world" of human beings and where we are located in a "chain of worlds" in the following:

> The chain of worlds, the links of which are the Absolute, all worlds, all suns, our sun, the planets, the earth, and moon, forms the "ray of creation" in which we find ourselves. The ray of creation is for us the "world" in the widest sense of the term.[2]

Each part of the Ray of Creation is linked to every other part. In other words, the Ray of Creation is the succession of living worlds, coming from the Absolute and moving downward, level by level, all the way to the earth and then to the moon. Gurdjieff calls this downward movement "involutionary," as opposed to "evolutionary," which would be the movement upward, toward the Absolute. The particular ray in which we find ourselves in our solar system, moves from our sun to the earth and ends in our moon. Speaking of the evolutionary movement, Gurdjieff says:

> But the moon is growing and developing, and some time, it will, possibly, attain the same level as the earth. Then near it, a new moon will appear and the earth will become their sun. At one time the sun was like the earth and the earth like the moon. And earlier still the sun was like the moon.[3]

Of course, we realize Gurdjieff is speaking of a time frame far beyond the lifespan of any individual, yet we can picture what he is saying.

Besides involution and evolution, there is an action of mutual exchange among all the aspects of the Ray of Creation and all its worlds. In *Beelzebub's Tales to His Grandson* he refers to this as "reciprocal maintenance."[4] It is easy to see reciprocal maintenance as the essential core of what we now call "ecology." However, Gurdjieff took the idea far beyond the limited horizons of present-day ecological paradigms. He describes life on earth as an integral part of the development of our solar system. The earth is not merely an accidental by-product of planetary formation; it is required to make a contribution to the evolution of the moon, and by extension, to the continued development of our solar system and its planets. The key component that produces the complex energy needed in planetary formation and maintenance is organic life on earth—that is, the complete, interrelated exchange of energies provided by the interaction of all living organisms on the planet. Gurdjieff says:

> Organic life is the organ of perception of the earth and it is at the same time an organ of radiation. With the help of organic life, each portion of the earth's surface occupying a given area sends every moment certain kinds of rays in the direction of the sun, the planets, and the moon.[5]

From the point of view of the descending or involutionary productions of the Ray of Creation, the solar system is the field of creative manifestation of the sun. Bennett writes, "The sun is able to evoke in the worlds subordinate to itself a creative activity that makes possible the arising of sentient and conscious experience." [6]

Organic life on earth, of which we are a part, is a film of living material on the planet's surface. This film receives radiations from the sun and distant planets; but each level of this film receives the radiations differently, be it a grassy field, a cow, or a human being. In turn, each form of life gives off a unique pattern of radiation downward toward the moon and upward into the solar system and the cosmos at large. Human beings have a special ability to receive and radiate various vibrations depending on the level of development of their consciousness.

According to Gurdjieff, the film of organic life is an organ of perception of the cosmos. It was developed to help maintain the earth and to develop our portion of the Ray of Creation—that is, to transmit energy, or food, to the moon, which is also evolving. That is one of our purposes; we serve as fertilizer or food for the moon. In this part of the cosmic scheme, we serve an involutionary purpose—that is, transmitting energies from a higher level (greater level of consciousness) to a level lower than ours. However, organic life on earth may also serve an evolutionary purpose, and indeed, Gurdjieff states that it is necessary and proper for it to do so. Yet, human beings are the only part of the film of earth's organic life that is capable of this evolution, or returning energy to the higher level of consciousness from which it was originally received. Moreover, people can only serve this evolutionary process and evolve individually if they develop consciousness of their role and intentionally fulfill it. Then, they may not only serve the evolutionary purpose of the earth, but also may transform for themselves some of the earth's energetic materials, creating a life within themselves that is conscious of itself.

In other words, the Gurdjieff Work directly aims to transform human consciousness so that individuals can take their rightful place in the reciprocal maintenance of all that exists. That is, they would not only provide energy for the involutionary ray, but also for the evolutionary ray. If a person can provide energy for the evolutionary ray that supports reciprocal maintenance, then they in return may develop true individuality. Thus, this work directs people to focus their attention on themselves as the prime area of study, as the way to personal individuality and evolution. Self-study and the possibility of evolution it brings us are the means for us to find our proper place in the interdependent, supportive framework of the life of this solar system, transforming the energy from the Ray of Creation that has passed to us from our sun.

Of course, there is no way that Gurdjieff or anyone else at present could prove or disprove the concepts explained in the Ray of Creation. Rather, their proof or disproof can only come through our own work and research. To repeat what Collin says in the opening to this chapter, "I think the deep instinct to check everything, verify everything, seems absolutely essential. In fact it is this friction between the instinct to believe and the instinct to question which forces us to that state of self-remembering where alone things can be truly assessed."

Modern education attempts to instill knowledge by emphasizing the study of outer life. By contrast, Gurdjieff and his authentic predecessors chose to educate us by focusing on the development of the inner life, the evolution of consciousness. The primary means is self-observation, questioning oneself, looking for the deeper meanings in our actions and lives. Through correct self-study, by studying how we relate to others, we can develop self-consciousness. Through self-study, I begin to understand the self-corrective action I need in order to fulfill my individual purpose. I can also begin to grasp the objective purpose of humanity as a whole.

We can access Gurdjieff's complete system through our own work of personal transformation. The cosmology—such as the Ray of Creation—provides a map of the landscape of which we are a part. The key elements that determine our place in this landscape are our consciousness and our will. They determine what we can understand and what we can do. The raw materials from which my consciousness can grow are the impressions of myself gathered through my work. Consciousness grows from these objective impressions. My will grows from the continuous effort I must make to collect these impressions, and fulfill the purpose for which I was designed.

THREE FOODS: EDIBLE FOOD, AIR, IMPRESSIONS

One of Gurdjieff's unique concepts is that, as part of the system of reciprocal maintenance, we take in more than one kind of food. First, there is the ordinary food we metabolize for activity during the day. This food comes from digesting plant or animal matter. It maintains all the physiological systems of every animal on the planet. However, two other foods exist, which we do not ordinarily regard as food. The air we breathe is actually a food. Consumed through respiration, air provides for the body's metabolic activities. The third and most important food for our development is the food of impressions that nourishes our intelligence and awareness.

Let us look at each of these foods in detail.

Food. The quality of edible food and water has become a growing consideration for a large group of more educated people in the world. People are interested in living longer, healthier lives. I agree that to eat well is very important. Yet, edible food alone is not the most important nutrient we take in. In fact, I wonder what our lives would be like if we spent as much time thinking about our inner life as we do about our physical health and the food we put into our bodies. Jesus said, "Man does not live by bread alone."

Air. Within the last fifty years, people have been forced to notice air quality due to the pollution of the atmosphere. The importance of the nourishing quality of air has become particularly evident because of the poor air quality so characteristic of many large cities. A few people vaguely understand that air has an intimate connection with the energy exchanges in the body. If you can open up your consciousness enough to recognize that air is integral to all living entities, then you might begin to suspect there may be something more subtle inherent in air. All animate entities breathe. Air links us all together. I may breathe the same air someone in China breathed a week ago.

The nourishment of inner life is connected with air. The word "spirit" relates to "inspiration" as well as "respiration." Just as two people might read a paragraph and each take different information from it, so it is with air. For example, a child and an adult take away different elements from a story they hear. The child may hear the tale, but cannot yet discern its complexity. The adult may understand and absorb its deeper, symbolic nature. It is similar with air because as each person breathes, he or she may take in different elements of greater or lesser quantity or quality.

Air is not simply the chemical substance current science makes it out to be; it contains much more. Just as traces of vitamins are available in food, so air contains minute elements that our higher parts need for nourishment. According to Gurdjieff, the more present I am, the more nourishment I can take from the air. Thus, each person, depending on his level of consciousness, digests air differently, taking in a better or poorer quality of material. I may experience a similar process when I drink a glass of wine with my dinner. With wine, I may distinctly taste different aspects of the food, appreciate subtleties that I would otherwise remain unaware of. In this case, I am receiving more from my food, more taste impressions. The same is possible with air.

If you are open to the possibility of air as nutrition, then the question should arise, how might I extract more from the air? After we realize air is a food, a very important one, new possibilities will arise for us.

Impressions. Gurdjieff also designates impressions as food. In large measure, we don't think carefully about the quality of our impressions, or even realize we need impressions to stay alive. To measure how invaluable any material substance is for human beings, we may ask the question: "How long could a person live without it?" Without food, we can live for up to forty-five days if we have water. Without air, we can live for only four minutes. According to Gurdjieff, if we were deprived of all impressions for even a fraction of a second, we would immediately die.

We know very little about the food of impressions. Modern science does not consider that impressions are food. It is only a marginal area of scientific research. Notably, quite a number of experiments over the years have studied the effects of sensory deprivation on human subjects. Research shows that severely reducing the quantity of impressions reaching the subject results in major psychological changes, sometimes including hallucinations.[7]

However, in other ways, people do recognize the importance of impressions. Our need for entertainment, travel, learning, and exploration is integrally tied to our need for new impressions. Designers of buildings, clothing, art, cars, and almost every material object available are very aware of the impressions their products will make. Note that when we think about impressions, they need not be confined to sense impressions only, but also include inner impressions received from our thinking, moving, emotional, and sex centers.

Recent interest in personal health has led many people to become more concerned with the food they take in. People's advocacy of organic foods and vegetarian diets may even become like a religion for them. They try to spread the word and profess that in this way they are helping themselves and the planet. With respect to the air we breathe, those living in large cities have recently become concerned about its deteriorating quality, but only to the extent that it should not harm them physically. As far as impressions are concerned, many, perhaps on an instinctive level, seek out beneficial impressions that art, music, and natural beauty provide. However, most people have no interest or understanding of the richness and importance of the food of impressions that becomes possible *only with self-study*. Without Gurdjieff's Work, the importance of this highest food would have remained unknown in our current era.

Over the last sixty years, parents have become more interested in the quality of their children's education, possibly because of the paucity of the education they themselves received. They have sought out systems designed to foster not only their children's intellects, but their emotional and physical parts as well. Examples are the Waldorf and Montessori systems. Without identifying or understanding the concept of the "food of impressions," certain parents sense that the impressions their children receive, as well as how they receive them, are very important.

Very few of us had parents who were concerned with the quality of impressions we received at school. Whether we survived public education, private school, or home tutoring, the emphasis was mostly on stuffing us with facts we learned to repeat back in order to achieve high grades. The emphasis was not on providing impressions of better quality, nor was there any attempt to teach us to take in impressions intentionally. Most importantly, no one taught us how to use our faculty of attention, the instrument through which we gather impressions.

Through work on myself, it is possible for an actual growth in consciousness to occur. This takes place as I hone my ability to intentionally receive and digest impressions. Normally, each of us receives impressions in the habitual, haphazard manner that we accidentally learned by having to react to life situations. What can improve my ability to receive impressions, help me to remember them, to appreciate them, to digest them?

For example, as I have been typing this paragraph, I am sitting in a rocking chair in my kitchen. In front of me sits a tall chair. On the seat of that chair is a roll of contact paper my wife purchased to line some shelves at the clinic where we work. However, I did not really see the roll of paper. My body, especially my eyes and memory, were automatically taking in the impressions of this paper roll on the chair, and yet, my mind did not take in this information. Until I became present, I didn't notice the pattern of the paper, the reflections on the wood surface of the chair, the light hitting the painted leg of the chair, or the position of the roll of contact paper lying on the seat.

In order to receive new impressions, I needed to be present and actually look through my eyes. As I began to work in this way, I noticed how the paper was lying against the back of the chair, since the seat was tilted a little. I also noticed the details in the laminated wood of the seat itself. I noticed nicks in the wood, the screws holding the back on, the dust build-up at the bottoms of the chair's legs, etc. Finally, I began to see the structure of the chair. In short, I was actually receiving new impressions, impressions that had been right there in front of me that I had missed.

Receiving impressions of the chair required only a slight change in my consciousness, but it produced a dramatic change in my experience. I actually began to register what I saw through my eyes as I was seeing. This is the beginning of the digestion of impressions. Prior to that change, I might just as well have been dead and buried, because I simply was not aware of my experience. I was not able to have or make new memories. Instead, my machine was simply replaying old memories, memories of sitting in the kitchen near the table in the morning. This example highlights the difference between automatically receiving impressions versus intentionally receiving the food of impressions. The subject matter in my example, though inanimate objects, may help you see what more might be possible when you shine the same light on yourself.

The further digestion of impressions once they are gathered is an area of study we know very little about and includes what we have referred to as "pondering." To ponder is to think deeply about something before deciding or reaching a conclusion. Pondering is very different than simply accepting the first conclusion that comes to mind. Modern education incorrectly reinforces a "quick conclusion" process by rewarding the child for raising his hand with the "correct" answer. Thus the child never learns about critical thinking, pondering, or consciously taking in impressions.

We are starving for new impressions. We take classes, go on trips, read books, and go to more and more movies. We engage in all these activities because we need fresh impressions. The difficulty is that we become impression addicts and yet are unable to digest the impressions we do receive because we are just not present. We seek more and more impressions, without realizing that their quality is much more important than their quantity. Moreover, our ability to be present to digest whatever impressions we experience is even more essential than their variety. To a certain extent, people recognize their hunger and intuitively lean in one direction or the other. Some gravitate toward more refined impressions coming from literature, art, music, the theater, a good movie, or their own creative work. Others take drugs to enhance their impressions, or indulge in overeating or other addictions. Some people need the intensity of impressions derived through dangerous sports or living on the edge sexually—where the excitement strengthens the impact of impressions. However, taking in impressions in this way does not necessarily result in any real nourishment or growth. After a time, the impressions become repetitious and cannot provide real food for inner growth.

The reason repeated unconscious impressions fail to nourish is that, in all such cases, there is no intentional work taking in the impressions, and thus, there is little nourishment for one's inner life. Results are only commensurate with the intentionality and consciousness of the person who receives them. Being passive to the constant stream of incoming impressions results in a state where we only remember moments of extreme beauty or fear—those situations where we have come into a heightened state of awareness for a few moments accidentally. Ordinarily, we do not gather impressions intentionally, ponder them, or attempt to make some meaning from them. Reading periodicals and newspapers is sufficient for most people. It gives them ready-made answers and facts about the world's situation that they can then spew out in discussions with others, using only their associative mind. I notice this tendency in myself and it is very difficult to counter.

The automatic flow of associations within me is a major feature of my ordinary waking-sleep, and does not involve new impressions. This automatic, and often chaotic, flow typifies ordinary consciousness and is quite different from the impressions received when I am awake and aware of the impressions I receive. In the latter case, there is an inner separate part of me that recognizes the new impressions being received and that I am alive at that moment receiving them. This process is not an associative one, but rather an experiential one. Gurdjieff said the following about our ability to gather new impressions as we age from childhood toward adulthood:

> . . . the capacity to get new impressions weakens with age. Children receive new impressions, but older people cannot; therefore in later life all that can be experienced is the arousing and recombination of these old impressions from childhood. Really new impressions can be obtained only by violence, because the rolls in centers are already covered up. It is difficult to penetrate to them because our force is limited.[8]

Thus, our dilemma. New impressions bombard us all the time, but our ability to experience them in the moment atrophies as we age. We can resurrect this ability, but only through intentional efforts to do so. Self-observation, self-study, sensing, and directing our attention are a few examples of such efforts that the Work provides.

THE NEED FOR GRADUAL TRANSFORMATION

I wish to emphasize that the process of self-study and self-development is a gradual one. We cannot accomplish change rapidly in either an outer or an inner way, but only by taking incremental steps. Real thinking, or "mentation," as Gurdjieff refers to it, requires a gradual and balanced development of our human capacities. He says:

> In short, only by a gradual change of the tempo of one part of the whole is it possible to change the tempo of all this whole without injuring it. I find it necessary to repeat that the "active mentation" in a being and the useful results of such active mentation are in reality actualized exclusively only with the equal-degree functionings of all his three localizations of the results spiritualized in his presence, called "thinking center," "feeling center," and "moving center." [9]

The human organism is a homeostatic system. In other words, each person's logical makeup is configured around his or her experiences and will resist any change. By default, my individual psychology will reassert its dominant pattern. I can only change gradually, so that the organism does not fall out of balance. However, even small changes that occur because of my increased self-awareness can lead to profound transformation. Therefore, the message is, go slowly and be interested in the small changes you notice.

WHY WORK ON ONESELF?

What is this work and why do we need to engage in it? The Gurdjieff Work is a vehicle for human self-development and self-perfection. It is based on the primary principle that human beings, as differentiated from all other animals, can evolve independently. This evolution is something more than accidental, physical changes or mutations to which all biological species are subject. Gurdjieff's premise is that human beings are capable of much greater development that encompasses more than merely changing the organism's physical structure. However, human beings are required to be active in their own evolution. This statement may seem to contradict the possibility of evolution occurring due to either accidental genetic changes or environmental demands. In fact, Gurdjieff distinguishes man as a being with special evolutionary potential, different from all other species.

Gurdjieff was very clear that not all of humanity could evolve using his system. Many people may find the idea very undemocratic and upsetting; yet Gurdjieff was very direct and uncompromising about his message. Whereas he admitted there might be general evolution for humanity solely with the passage of time, it would take eons, with no guarantee that it would actually occur. On the other hand, a quicker, self-directed evolution is possible for a limited number of individuals over the course of one lifetime. However, in order for such personal evolution to occur—in order for me to become conscious and aware, in order for me to see the true nature of the world and my relationship to it, in order for me to have new, extraordinary impressions beyond my usual associations—I must make self-evolution a primary aim throughout my life.

I believe one of the most disastrous consequences of our modern scientific period is the belief that evolution of human beings takes place automatically over time. At first glance, it does not seem so unreasonable and is even comforting to believe that nature, which includes humanity, is, just due to time itself, evolving. However, it has had a paralyzing effect on people who accidentally realize the terror of their situation—that is, the shortness of their life span and the inevitability of their own death. If a person even has the slightest belief that he or she is evolving simply by living, then why would one choose to work on oneself? There would be no reason to make any special effort, since evolution is occurring automatically.

There are even groups of people such as the transhumanists, who believe humanity will evolve because of new sciences and technologies, which will enhance all our mental and physical capacities.[10] They see technology as the means of ameliorating the undesirable aspects of the human condition: ignorance, suffering, disease, aging, and death. There is little doubt that technology allows for increased communication. Likewise, modern medicine has lengthened life expectancy in industrialized countries. However, the beneficial results, due to the increasing development of technology, appear to be more than counterbalanced by their detrimental effects.

In many ways, technological advancement may be a distraction from the exacting inquiry and struggle we need for inner evolution.

Technological innovation tends to increase the shared fantasy that we are evolving. Every new invention is trumpeted in the newspapers and on the Internet as if it will make the world better. However, inner work and evolution do not depend on technology. We can't purchase understanding at the Apple Store. Evolution may be possible only for the limited number of individuals willing to make the required efforts. Gurdjieff's Work transmits the message that groups of individuals are needed to play a conscious part in humanity's evolution, and that by playing their parts, they will also serve the evolution of this planet as well as their own development. Perhaps, such groups can even prevent catastrophe by providing the energies humanity, as a species, is required to produce.

THE FOURTH WAY

Gurdjieff referred to his work as the "Fourth Way." According to him, various methods of self-development have been available to people at particular times in human history. These specific practices, referred to as ways, consist chiefly of three types: the way of the fakir, the way of the monk, and the way of the yogi. These ways correspond to an intensive work with the body, the emotions, or the mind, respectively. The fakir masters his physical body by ascetic practices sometimes amounting to torture, and thus develops his physical will. He may experience higher energies and higher states of consciousness, but his intellectual and emotional capacities remain undeveloped. The second way, that of the monk or religion, is dependent on faith, or the development of the emotional center. Here also, the religious person may experience higher energies and increased consciousness, which he might call meeting with God. However, the religious follower often remains undeveloped physically and intellectually, since his way mainly emphasizes strict obedience and devotion and does not encourage investigation. Finally, there is the way of the yogi, which stresses development of the mind. The yogi may end up knowing everything, but he is deficient in the development both of his emotions and his physical will.

In Gurdjieff's system of the Fourth Way we work on our body, emotions, and mind simultaneously. Moreover, traditionally, studying any of the first three ways required special conditions, perhaps complete retreat from ordinary life. By contrast, the Fourth Way operates in life and makes use of ordinary life conditions. According to Gurdjieff, the Fourth Way only comes into being during certain historical periods, perhaps when a particular type of work is especially needed and when political and social conditions allow for Fourth Way groups to exist.

The concept of individual self-perfection through development of the psyche has many correspondences in religion, for example, in such ideas as "salvation" and "sainthood." Religions purport to offer a cure for the maladies of negativity and suffering that grip humanity. At the same time, there is a widespread feeling among many in the West that religions have failed. Gurdjieff was concerned not only with why they failed, but also why humanity suffers from its fundamental illness—whether described as sin or ignorance—in the first place.

According to Gurdjieff, our current situation is not the fault of Adam and Eve. It is ultimately not entirely the fault of humanity at large, but was due to an unforeseen cosmic event, the genesis of the moon. In the cosmology Gurdjieff recounts, a massive cosmic body collided with the earth and broke off large fragments, one of which coalesced into our moon. So far, Gurdjieff's explanation agrees with current scientific theory. However, what follows in Gurdjieff's account may seem extraordinary and unbelievable. In his book, *In Search of the Miraculous*, Ouspensky recounts what Gurdjieff said about humanity's predicament. It came about because we are, literally, "food" for the moon, along with the rest of organic life on earth. The concept of "food" here is more sophisticated than simple physical food (see the earlier discussion about foods, page 90). The food in this case comprises the radiations that all organic life produces, and perhaps especially, those of the consciousness and behavior of humanity. In *Beelzebub's Tales to His Grandson*, Gurdjieff's Beelzebub states that our dilemma arises from the implantation into us of an organ, Kundabuffer, following the collision that causes the moon's genesis. This organ prevented humankind from seeing the reality of our situation, that we are "food for the moon." [11]

In describing the genesis of the moon in the narrative of *Beelzebub's Tales to His Grandson*, Beelzebub introduces beings he calls angels, a kind of cosmic bureaucracy concerned with overall maintenance of larger cosmic systems, but not with the fate of individual creatures. The angels and archangels calculate that the fragments broken off the earth might leave their position and produce instabilities or "irreparable calamities" in the solar system as a whole. To offset a possible catastrophe, they decided that organic life and three-brained beings would be required to produce specific radiations for the emergent moon. As Gurdjieff explains, these three-brained beings in the natural order of things ought to have acquired what Gurdjieff calls "objective reason," or an accurate perception of reality. Consequently, they would develop "higher being-bodies," or souls. However, the "cosmic authorities" were still anxious. They feared the three-brained beings on earth might prematurely become aware of their objective situation—that their main purpose was only to produce a special substance or radiation for the moon, and understanding this, they would react with such horror as to choose to destroy themselves en masse.[12]

To guard against the possibility of humanity's mass suicide, the cosmic administrators implanted an "organ" called "Kundabuffer" at the base of each person's spinal column, reducing human beings to nothing more than "thinking animals." More importantly, as Gurdjieff put it, the organ produced "the-reflecting-of-reality-in-one's-attention-upside-down."[13] Thus, what is trivial seems important and what is important goes unheeded. Humanity's situation is all the more poignant because, while the higher individuals removed Kundabuffer later on, its effects continue forward to this day. *Beelzebub's Tales to His Grandson* is full of examples of the "maleficent consequences of the properties of the organ Kundabuffer." What are some of these consequences? Overwhelming egoism, heedlessness, waste, war, and delusion. Ironically, the very organ that was supposed to prevent us from destroying ourselves has resulted in a situation where we are in a perpetual state of war, almost continually destroying each other's existence.

What we need to take from Gurdjieff's historical allegory is that life, human life, is intertwined with the development of cosmic systems, particularly our solar system. Our existence and evolution is not some epiphenomenon or accidental by-product of blind mechanical forces. Gurdjieff always insisted that, willy-nilly, humanity must serve the purposes of Great Nature—because we are composed of matter and energy like everything else. However, he hoped that if we served Great

Nature consciously, we might retain something for ourselves, for our own individuality. Although Gurdjieff does not define "Great Nature," we can infer that Great Nature imbues the very genes of an individual planet's nature, that directs the interaction of biological life on a planet, with the possibility of evolution.

We may take the story of Kundabuffer literally. Alternatively, we may take it as a metaphor for our intrinsic dilemma: We are a part of the organic world; we are just the same as anything else, and our birth and death have no more meaning than that of a tree. Faced with our insignificance, we develop fantasies and cling to dreams to escape from reality. Gurdjieff gives us hope that we can awaken from our state of ignorance to what is really occurring, including the mechanical processes in which we must participate. We participate in these processes in one of two ways: unconsciously, where we retain nothing real for ourselves; or intentionally, where we become useful as part of the larger cosmos, and where we can potentially achieve our own self-consciousness and permanence.

As I discussed earlier, Gurdjieff pointed out that the erroneous belief that we are already conscious is the biggest barrier to our becoming so in reality; hence, the idea that our typical so-called "consciousness" is just a dream. There have been many versions of the profound idea that we live a dream life, and there is a need to awaken. In Christianity, the notion of original sin is very close to Gurdjieff's portrayal of Kundabuffer. We find in Christian thought the concept that salvation is only possible if one becomes conscious that one is a sinner. Here, it is important to understand that the original definition of the word "sin" actually meant "to miss the mark," not being bad.[14] However, as far as washing away our sins or weaning us away from the maleficent properties of Kundabuffer, it seems clear that traditional religious practices of prayer, worship, asceticism, and charity have proved mostly ineffective. Additionally, the three ways discussed earlier do not provide a balanced development. The way of the fakir, the monk, and the yogi are not sufficient to provide balanced development in the short span of one lifetime, because it would be then necessary to spend two more lifetimes developing the other two centers. Then, an individual would need a fourth lifetime to practice coordinating the three centers. Gurdjieff cut this work short with the Fourth Way. It can take only one lifetime, but a lifetime of extremely intensive work.

THE MALEFICENT CONSEQUENCES OF THE ORGAN KUNDABUFFER

Gurdjieff says the organ Kundabuffer caused people to see reality upside down. On my first reading of this idea some forty years ago, I certainly understood the words and I thought I understood what he was getting at. I realize now how superficially I took his words. Even now, Gurdjieff's assertion requires me to ponder on the question of how do I see reality upside down? Let us look at a few of Gurdjieff's ideas of the upside-down nature of human consciousness: our inability to notice our inner world and our preoccupation with the material world, inner considering, our shared suffering from the "disease of tomorrow," and the fragmentation of our once-unified psyche into many "I's." In the Appendix, you will find a simplified summary of the various topics covered that can be used as a guide to areas of personal study so you can verify and understand the dysregulation of the human psyche due to Kundabuffer. This summary is useful whether one regards Kundabuffer as an actual physical organ or the symbolic representation of the major psychological trauma that occurred to the human psyche.

At its simplest level, I see life upside down because I tend to make the physical world either the most important reality or the only reality. I place primary importance on my outer activities, such as acquiring things, a job, food, sex, and money. This visible, material world is where most of us spend the majority of our time and attention. There can be little energy left for people to develop either their creative abilities or their inner life. Further, my ability to ponder and look into the deeper meaning of my life is limited by my need to continually engage in commerce and make money.

Another way I see reality upside down: I find myself overreacting to many aspects of my life that, upon closer inspection, appear relatively trivial. For example, I have constant worries about different things I either need to do, have not done, or will be blamed for if they are not done, or feel a responsibility and pressure to do, etc. The list is endless, but the common thread running through them is an instantaneous emotional reaction to each situation that uses up my energy. I can sum up the entire scenario, repeated ad infinitum, with the phrase, "Making mountains out of molehills."

There is a fascination and fantasy about material things that has always gripped me. I love machines, especially the intricacies of how they work. I can be doing something really important and all of a sudden a mental association will pull me into a fantasy about making something. I often have little control or ability to direct my thoughts for extended periods. All of this time and energy is spent on material objects that are at first new and then will become old and need to be recycled. My attention is easily caught by the material world, and in the process, I become lost.

After attending many group meetings and practicing as a psychologist, I have verified that such tendencies are far from unique to me. An even deeper level of upside-downness is my inability at times to recognize the experiences that are truly important to me. I need to be forced to return to the more essential aspects of my life when some tragic event occurs.

The year before last, our friend's husband took his life. He had just turned sixty, was a successful doctor, but he had suffered from depression for a number of years. I recalled attending a wedding with him a number of months before his suicide. Prior to the wedding, I went with him and his son to a small deli to get some lunch.

I remember sitting with them on a bench and thinking, "He is such a loner; he never says anything, never asks about me and is so quiet." I knew of his depression and had tried in the past to strike up conversations with him. I remember now how I stayed wrapped up in my reactions to his solitude. It was only after he committed suicide that I realized I had missed an opportunity while sitting with him. I could have spoken to him about life, could have asked him about what he saw as the purpose of his life.

I would not have needed to get into any of his psychological issues, which would have been inappropriate anyway, since his fifteen-year-old son sat between us; but why didn't I speak to him about things I had found important in my own life? In retrospect, I realized I couldn't get past my own reaction and negativity to his silence. This is an example of "inner considering." I took his silence personally, and was caught in my inner considering.

INNER CONSIDERING

Inner considering can be defined as always considering myself first regardless of what may be needed by another person or a situation. I live in a self-centered world. Even at times, when I believe I have taken the other person into consideration, it is often just a show, because it is so important to me how I appear to others, or rather how I *imagine* I look to others.

It is almost impossible nowadays to have a meaningful discussion with anyone about what is truly important to us. We have no problem discussing politics, a soccer game, or what movies we have seen, but meaningful conversation is becoming an extinct creature. What is lacking in such discussions is what is really going on for me in my life, the deeper experiences I have, and the recurring questions that arise in me. I am generalizing here, but I am trying to paint a picture of a tendency in human interaction that is now a general predisposition. I notice I often do not want to speak about important topics because I surmise it might make the other person feel uneasy or cause him to think me strange. This is just more internal considering. Pop psychology has correctly noted that there is a tendency today "to make it about me." This pathology seems endemic to all of us at this period in our history.

The tendency to focus on and become lost in the relative day-to-day material requirements of life have left us with little inclination to ponder the meaning of our lives or life in general. We leave this area of human interest to so-called "great thinkers," contemporary philosophers, educators, and writers, most of whom seem to be rehashing in personalized forms what others have already said. We do not allow for the possibility that we ourselves need to consider life's important questions and find meaningful answers to them. Our inability to engage these important life questions relates directly to our educational system and the glorification of becoming a so-called "expert" in some small area of knowledge. In my experience, common sense and the ability to think widely about important questions have become the victims of modern education. We do not trust ourselves to think deeply. We unconsciously resist the uneasiness that comes from pondering a question and not knowing the answer. The uneasiness we experience is the result of expecting ourselves to know the answer beforehand without pondering it; the latter is another example of a widely held, but erroneous belief about our consciousness and ability.

Recently, I was on a trip with a friend I have known for a number of years. Each time we travel together, he is at one moment negative about the political climate and the next enthusiastic about the idea of getting people out into the wilderness to experience nature when they are young. After many such discussions, he asked me what way do I see to make the world better? I noticed that my first reaction to this question was one of considering whether I really wanted to discuss this topic with him at all. On this occasion, I decided to proceed and brought the conversation immediately to the psychological arena. More specifically, I spoke of the hypnotic, sleeping state of our civilization and the repercussions of having humanity "asleep at the wheel." I gave examples of how I personally suffered from this trancelike state of consciousness.

Surprisingly, I found him agreeing with me about almost everything. Gradually, I brought the conversation to the topic of our inability to direct our attention. I said that in my experience, so many problems in our lives seemed in some way to hinge on human attention, or should I say human inattention. Here, he also agreed. As we continued our discussion, I realized how important it was for me to speak to him about these topics, rather than just allow our discussions to ramble along in a friendly, neutral manner. I felt alive when we were discussing these important issues. At times, I was more present, noticed him more, and saw him for who he was. In short, I was awake at moments and aware of myself.

I usually kept quiet about these important subjects. I think this was because the discussion might not provide answers, but just questions. Somehow, that kind of conversation feels difficult for me, unfinished. I believe I should be able to convince someone of the importance of what I am saying. All of these habits remain unconscious in me unless I make an effort to work, in this case to bring up the uncomfortable questions that need asking. This is an example of an important effect of Kundabuffer—it keeps me from bringing these important aspects of life into the foreground of my consciousness. Also, in only considering myself, I cut myself off from others.

THE DISEASE OF TOMORROW

Another consequence of Kundabuffer is what Gurdjieff refers to as the "disease of tomorrow." [15] The human habit to put off a task has become a disease of our time, both personally and on a societal level. In this world, you need look no further than our inability to move away from our dependence on fossil fuels and develop alternate forms of energy. Politicians epitomize this habit to put off what needs attention today until the morrow. Clearly, if one procrastinates continually, time will pass, there will be little or no change, and generally, things will run down. On an individual level, the disease has equally devastating results.

I see many people in therapy who have put their lives on hold due to the disease of tomorrow. This habit has grown in them to such a degree that they complain about their situation vociferously, but are unable or unwilling to make even a small change. The habit of tomorrow can eventually bring about a state of confusion where they become depressed and unable to accomplish anything in their lives.

DISCONNECTIONS DUE TO KUNDABUFFER

Gurdjieff was one of the first psychologists to describe the human psyche as a multiplicity. Although we attribute "I" to every thought that pops into our head, Gurdjieff said we do not have just one "I." Rather, we are made up of many "I's" that are unaware of each other and are often in conflict. The psyche's multiplicity is both characteristic of our abnormal state arising from Kundabuffer, as well as the cause of the maintenance of this state. Various "I's" within the psyche are hidden from each other. From my own experience and from working with many people in the Work, I have found that every person who is interested in the Work has many "I's" that remain totally uninterested in the ideas of self-development. Such "I's" have neither the ability nor the energy to engage in Work. However, I must recognize these "I's" in myself, get to know them. If I remain ignorant of these different aspects of my psychological makeup, I will be ignorant of how these "I's" lead me astray and keep me asleep.

Another effect of Kundabuffer that is characteristic of the upside-down perception of reality is our inability to sense the interrelatedness of everything that exists. We see only discrete parts, but remain unable to grasp the whole. It is characteristic of postmodern society to generate specialists in the workplace, and this is symptomatic of the consequences and ghosts of Kundabuffer still within us. In many ways, the ecology movement implores us to understand the interrelatedness our myopia has obscured. You are probably familiar with the ancient East Indian tale that illustrates our problem. Several blind people stand around an elephant trying to describe it. One person grasps the tail and declares, "This is the elephant. It is tough with a brushlike end." Another grasps an ear and says, "No, this is the elephant. It is warm and floppy." A third grasps the tusk and says, "This is the elephant. It is hard and sharp," etc.

We can experience our instinctive wish to understand the interconnectedness of all things. Go out at night, away from the city lights, where the air is clear, and observe the heavens. If you allow yourself to quiet down (that is, just sit and let your thoughts spin down), you may notice when you look up at the sky that an instinctive part of you tries to "feel" the relatedness of everything. Our emotional center longs for this experience of interconnectedness. Gurdjieff says this is our birthright, and at times like these, we sense it. For me, this longing for relatedness is a sign that some part of me was once connected with the larger world from which I am now estranged.

A primary result of Kundabuffer is our inability to sense and even be interested in our purpose. In *Beelzebub's Tales to His Grandson*, Kundabuffer was expressly designed to prevent human beings from understanding their purpose. This lack of curiosity, the disinterest in wanting to understand and find one's purpose in life that is rampant today, is a symptom of Kundabuffer. People find a purpose in a vocation, raising a family, entrepreneurship, politics, yoga, kayaking, etc. All these activities can be enjoyable and substitute for a real purpose for living. Then, the ultimate question, "What is my purpose?" is simply put on hold indefinitely. In my experience, most people are not interested. They may have been interested during their teens when these questions naturally arise; but now, they have buried their curiosity and are just trying to survive. Or, they are happily wrapped up in their fantasies and are willing to follow and enjoy our culture's diverse assortment of distractions.

A MAJOR PSYCHO-HISTORICAL TRAUMA?

According to *Beelzebub's Tales to His Grandson*, when the higher authorities no longer deemed Kundabuffer necessary, they removed it. However, the human behaviors it had engendered continued long after its removal, down to this day. In the language of psychology, the neurological patterns people developed during the period the organ was in place imprinted themselves as distinct dynamic patterns in their nervous systems. Therefore, they continued the same patterns even after the organ was removed. We see similar phenomena today, where habit patterns remain as responses long after the original stimuli have disappeared. For example, an amputee may feel a "phantom" itch in a limb he no longer has. We also see a similar situation with post-traumatic stress disorder (PTSD). In PTSD, a person may experience a recurring stress response triggered by environmental cues, such as the reflection of a certain light or a sound that resembles some outside stimulus that occurred during the traumatic event.

In *Beelzebub's Tales to His Grandson*, Gurdjieff describes the many strange effects of Kundabuffer and discusses at length the subsequent character defects that appeared in people. The most devastating abnormal result of Kundabuffer was war. People began to kill each other, what Gurdjieff refers to as "the need of periodically occupying themselves with the destruction of each other's existence." [16] According to Gurdjieff, this was the first time three-brained beings had ever killed one another on any planet in the universe.

Self-perfection and the evolution of humanity have always been noble aims, but they have not been realized. If we accept what Gurdjieff has told us, that an organ like Kundabuffer was implanted in our earliest ancestors to restrict their consciousness, it is imperative to ask what might be the psychological repercussions of having had such an organ? Might it be that Kundabuffer, which was designed to limit certain experiences in the human organism, also blocked or dysregulated other normal functions? Might we get a glimpse of the answers by exploring what we already know happens to human behavior when people are restricted from exercising their full potentialities for long periods?

A concept that kept coming to the forefront for me when looking at Kundabuffer's effects was trauma. I began to realize that the results of Kundabuffer's implantation were dramatic and may have profoundly traumatized the human species. It seemed important to look at some of the known, predictable results of psychological trauma to better understand the consequences on people of Kundabuffer. Psychologists are increasingly aware of the deleterious effects of trauma as the result of war, societal violence, and other unexpected, painful aspects of life on individuals, families, and communities. If we believe Gurdjieff's description of the history of Kundabuffer, it might represent a core trauma on a scale so large it would affect all subsequent generations, including our own.

In my practice, I continually meet with clients who have been traumatized by past restrictions, often the result of events they experienced within their own families. What are common responses to being restricted? Let us look at a simple situation where a child is restricted from activities because her parents were overprotective. She may react with aggression, rage, despair, or simply follow the dictates of her parents. The reaction of aggression or rage is most interesting here, and I would guess it might be the most common response, even if it is repressed and her parents and even the child remain unaware of it.

Aggression has become so characteristic of human behavior that you can almost say it has become an instinctive reaction to stress. Keep in mind that according to Gurdjieff, Kundabuffer reduced three-brained beings to the status of "thinking animals." Higher mammals tend to become aggressive or depressed when restricted—you can observe this behavior in a zoo. In the wild, animals achieve dominance when necessary by aggressive behavior. Is it not plausible that the human response to long periods of psychological restriction (perhaps for a number of generations) might be a predilection to aggressive behavior? We find such aggressive behavior in jails everywhere on the planet, where inmates attack their guards and one another. In jail, people know they are restricted. But, since the implantation of Kundabuffer was unknown to the earliest humans that received it, they would experience Kundabuffer's restriction only unconsciously. However, such restriction could cause profound changes in their behavior. Aggressive reactions to such restriction may be lurking beneath our normal waking state. Additionally, if "we" were unaware of Kundabuffer and its implantation, then it actually means that our consciousness had been in fact split into two distinct parts: a conscious part which we experience and an unconscious part we are unaware of.

Gurdjieff gives us reason to believe the unconscious part of the psyche did not exist prior to the introduction of Kundabuffer. Kundabuffer, therefore, caused the development of a "subconscious." "The real consciousness of people, with all its potentiality, now resides in their unconscious." [16] Kundabuffer formed a barrier within people that left them with only certain basic life functions, while their higher functions remained suppressed and unavailable to them.

Summarizing, the implantation of Kundabuffer was done without our knowledge or awareness and a split in consciousness was created. We were temporarily denied the part of us that would have allowed us to develop normally, to become fully functioning beings with objective knowledge. The effect of Kundabuffer was also to create an unconscious part (new neurological patterns) in the human psyche that contained our unique, potential capacities for objective knowledge and understanding. Even though the organ was subsequently removed, our unconscious part, along with our inability to access our higher centers, continued to be separate.

ANXIETY

Anxiety can be another common response to restriction. Anxiety is the fear that something bad will happen to you. It is a state of hypersensitivity, usually due in some part to a psychic, emotional, or physical trauma. Restriction can be experienced as trauma. Restriction from their full potential might greatly increase a tendency in human beings toward anxiety reactions.

A behavior often connected with anxiety is aggression. In *Why Zebras Don't Get Ulcers*, Robert Sapolsky points out that human behavior in the face of danger and stress is different from that of other mammals.[17] For example, if a zebra senses a lion in the bush, it is immediately on full alert—until the danger passes. That is, the lion chases down the zebra and kills it, or the lion moves off and the zebra goes back to grazing. The zebra does not remain in a state of high alert or in a state of anxiety.

People, on the other hand, show a marked tendency to remain in an anxious state for days, months, years, and even an entire lifetime following a threatening or traumatic experience. Strangely, an imagined potential threat, such as rape, a car accident, or the stock market's decline can also evoke within us a state of anxiety and we may often respond aggressively. Anxiety can be triggered when we learn about a friend's sudden illness or injury. Because of our power of imagination, anxiety can become a chronic reaction. We fear—even worry—that our behavior may be restricted, for example, if we lose money on the stock market. Whether we realize it or not, a great deal of our anxiety about money is really a concern that our options will be restricted or our security threatened.

I have noticed that the longer I am restricted from my natural behaviors, the more easily I can become anxious, aggressive, or depressed. You can see this for yourself if you are restricted from physical activity even for a short time due to illness. The tendency is to become either anxious or find a way to numb out, fantasize, or sleep. You will also find that numbing out, fantasizing, and sleeping are states that appear in children who are forced to sit still for long periods in school. In this way, schools may unconsciously foster an atmosphere that leads to behaviors characteristic of anxiety; confusion, an inability to remain attentive, or hyperactivity.

According to Gurdjieff, over many generations people have lost their natural ability to cognize reality correctly. In any case, the restrictions resulting from Kundabuffer might have resulted in a "generalized" state of anxiety. "Generalized" in this case means a background state of anxiety now embedded in the individual and even in the culture. One could say the culture itself is traumatized and fosters behaviors we see in PTSD. PTSD is characterized by repeated flashbacks of an incident that may elicit defensive behaviors in response to stimuli that is similar to the stimuli that caused the original trauma. When we are traumatized, we fall back on survival mechanisms that include the more instinctive, animal side of our nature—the "thinking animal" of the Kundabuffer period. We then react like a cornered animal.

The stressed human "thinking animal" does not behave like Sapolsky's zebra. The addition of the third brain—the thinking brain—provides a different response to life-threatening situations. The zebra's responses are limited to freezing in place or running away. A person's responses to a threat, perceived or imagined, might include aggression, defensive behavior, and/or planning for future attacks. In addition, the traumatic experiences might elicit responses of paranoia, aggression, and anxiety, which might continue long after the danger has subsided. Carrying the possibility of danger forward in the associative mind, people take precautions to protect themselves. They form armies, build forts, and even attack preemptively. When they sense fear or aggression from others, they usually react with fear and aggression just like an animal—they lack the ability to bring in the third brain, the intellectual center, to help them understand how to respond. Responding is different than simply reacting automatically. Reaction is an automatic action, whereby responding requires one to consider a situation before one acts.

Another traumatic effect of Kundabuffer, besides the major split in our consciousness, may have been the partition of the psyche into many "I's." Gurdjieff explains that this partitioning keeps the different parts of the psyche from overwhelming us with their contradictions.[18] At first glance, partitioning might seem to be a mechanism to decrease anxiety, since, being unconscious of one's inconsistencies, a person would not have to face them. However, my guess is that, in fact, it leads to increased anxiety. If a person cannot explain—even to himself—why he seems to have so many contradictory behaviors, how can he justify them to the world at large? In short, having many "I's" leads not to harmony, but to further anxiety. For example, I may have a very important task to do and even want to accomplish it, but another "I" comes in and I go to the movies instead. As pleasant as the movie may be, I find that I am anxious afterwards because I did not do what I knew I needed to.

I must look for the effects of Kundabuffer inside me. It is important to see how often I am anxious and what I am anxious about. Impressions of my anxiety will give me an opportunity to see some of my psychological problems that arise not only from my own life, but possibly are a result of habit patterns that have been passed down from remote generations, patterns of anxiety.

RELIGIONS FAIL TO CORRECT FOR KUNDABUFFER

The great religions—Judaism, Christianity, Islam, Buddhism, Hinduism, Taoism, and Lamaism—have been, until the modern era, the primary vehicles for self-perfection. Each employs different methods, but each in its own way stresses the need for conscious labor and intentional suffering. The problem is that each of them has failed its followers. Humanity has been unable to develop consciousness and objective reason and fulfill the purpose for which it was designed. Nor have these religions been able to correct for humanity's abnormal manifestations—especially war, a mass insanity bequeathed intact to each succeeding generation.

Humanity stands again at a place where the degradation and deformed justifications of Christianity, Judaism, and Islam appear to be leading the world once again toward a major war. I began to wonder why have these great religions not achieved a more benign result? Why do religions appear to have become a factor that increases rather than lessens our predilection for war?

It would be very easy to say that the failure of religion is simply because human beings are too weak-willed to follow religion's precepts. The matter is more complex than that. Hungry people will eat anything. Starvation of the spirit requires the proper spiritual food. It is one thing to tell or show people what they should do—for example, tell them they should perfect themselves through various forms of abstention or by doing good works. However, it is another to understand the impediments. Perhaps a lack of understanding of the human predicament has contributed to the abysmal outcome of the teachings of great religions. If people have truly suffered severe psychological restriction for generations because of Kundabuffer, it is no wonder they distort and misuse the very tools religion gives them for their development.

I am not in any way excusing or justifying why human beings in general have been unable to use religion for their benefit, but I am interested in the problem of what religion may be missing. How is it that religion fails on such a large scale? Is there a mismatch between religion and people's interior landscape? This is an important topic for those of us who are interested in Gurdjieff's Work.

Worse than the failure of religion to help people perfect their being is the fact that, many times, religions often have just the opposite effect. Frequently, religion degrades people's inborn qualities as a means of social control. For example, Catholicism prohibits its clergy from having sex and procreating. This strange prohibition began in the Middle Ages, and we see its results in such unconscionable aberrations as sexual abuse of children by the clergy. Religions have also been utilized to promote aggressive behavior, as clearly demonstrated by wars, crusades, jihads, and even ideological wars within the same religion.

THE MYTH OF THE SOUL

Religions have perpetuated other more insidious and yet less obvious messages that have retarded the development of people's potential. For example, almost without exception religion perpetuates the false message that people have a soul, that some part of them will continue beyond death, which has had the effect of suggesting that they need not make effort. This message of a future life after death has degraded people's intuitive sense that they actually need to work to achieve inner development. The life-after-death message of religion—that our lives will somehow continue following the death of our body—is a disaster for many who have within themselves the possibility of self-development. The rationales for this erroneous message are manifold. They serve to calm the anxiety of the religion's adherents, putting them into a state Gurdjieff called, "self-calming." A religion may instill self-calming from a very tender age. It tells children and young adults that by following certain precepts—for example, praying to Allah five times daily—they will be taken off to some paradise following the demise of their physical body.

Religion can lull into deep sleep even those whose longings might have drawn them to work. It instills the mistaken notion that something higher exists within them already, and somehow this something will survive the death of their physical body. Therefore, why should they work? Hinduism, for example, elaborated the idea of life after death to such exaggerated heights that people feel resigned to their fate and fail to make the efforts that they can in this life. The same belief in an afterlife also fuels Islam, keeping its followers in constant hope of a better life after death, rather than seeing and understanding the objective causes of their situation here on earth.

Buddhism suffers in a similar way in its admonition to "free oneself from suffering." Many of its less-sophisticated followers believe they may avoid suffering by thinking their way out of it. To escape from suffering is presented as a noble aim and a means to achieve salvation, but even devoted Buddhists frequently misunderstand it. Some believe that by meditating for hours they will somehow achieve a state of non-identification that will help them survive death. Or, they believe that if they can think their way out of suffering, they will somehow avoid it in actuality. The mind is the culprit here. Eckhart Tolle's *The Power of Now* is an example of the so-called "effortless way." If we simply think about things differently then all will be well, and you will be able to get free from your suffering.

In my opinion, the aim is not to free ourselves from just any kind of suffering. Much of the suffering that we endure is simply automatic suffering, the continual worrying about money, the possibility we will get sick, the worry that people will not like us, etc. What we can do is learn to use the suffering we are all subject to, regardless of what it may be, in a conscious and intentional manner. I need to understand my reactions to suffering, the different types of suffering and their derivation. All forms of life suffer. How might I use suffering for my growth?

For example, when I was interning in psychology, the clinic's policy was to have each intern answer the telephone a few hours each week. I did many other jobs for the clinic I believed were more important and refused to sit around waiting for the phone to ring. Each month, the interns took part in a group meeting where they shared experiences and problems that had arisen that month. Another intern had found out I was not answering the clinic phone, and she verbally attacked me and tried to shame me during the next group meeting. I tend to react very defensively to being shamed and usually defend myself by being aggressive. This, of course, did not go over very well in the group. The matter was exacerbated because the group leader was the direct supervisor of the intern who had verbally dressed me down. Apparently, the two of them had been discussing my transgression for some time. During the group session, the leader also saw fit to try to shame me.

The entire incident was very painful. It activated painful memories of being shamed in my past. I easily could have taken this incident as simply the fault of the intern and her supervisor. In some ways, the intern was actually acting out her own difficulty with others who didn't do their duty. She tended to be very rigid and believed people just should do what they were supposed to do. However, I wanted to make more meaning out of this situation for my own growth. I needed to ask myself how was I responsible for what had happened and for my aggressive response to her raising the issue in the group.

The need to understand and find meaning in the suffering I experienced in this incident is important. To this day, I still find important material from this experience by reexamining my behavior and responses. Even if I was not fully conscious of my experience at the moment, incidents like these, which cause me to suffer, offer me a treasure house of information about myself.

I want to be capable of carrying out an aim that may involve suffering, doing what needs to be done rather than simply doing what I want to do. When you work to develop your consciousness, your understanding, and your will, you will find you gradually acquire the psychological container you need. If you can bear to suffer consciously and intentionally, you will be able to develop and find your place in serving humanity's highest objective needs. In this process your entire attitude to and experience of suffering may be transformed.

SHAME-BASED RELIGIONS

There is an additional reason why religion may have failed so many people so miserably—and perhaps it is the most glaring defect of all: It has devolved into set of doctrines based on shame. Religions attempt to keep their followers in line by relying on the human affect of shame, a topic I will cover in depth in a later chapter. Shame is a very poor, if not impossible, basis for a religion that attempts to develop consciousness in its followers. Shame, when used to coerce certain behavior to conform to the precepts of any religion, cannot produce good results. In

fact when people are coerced, they follow out of fear rather than understanding. We need to see how shame has been misused to coerce.

According to Gurdjieff and modern psychology, organic shame is a
naturally occurring affect, hard-wired into the human species. Gurdjieff
implies that it works hand in-hand with objective conscience. However,
he points out that since objective conscience has been driven into our
unconscious, real shame has also gone underground. Thus, pseudo-
shame has replaced organic shame. I feel ashamed for forgetting a
certain social convention or speaking the truth because it embarrasses
someone else. However, I may not feel ashamed for treating another
person badly.

Religion relies on pseudo-shame. Religions are filled with codes of
conduct that may have been important at one time, but may no longer
be relevant. Nowadays, adherents feel continually shamed if they do
not comply with many rules that they do not really understand. Some of
these rules are about sex, how and when to pray, what one eats, how one
dresses, how to address each other, and other questionable dictates. All
these rules serve to keep people in line and make them automatically
feel shame if they break them. Religions that were originally designed
to develop consciousness and individuality in their adherents and to
correct for the unforeseen consequences of Kundabuffer, have deterio-
rated with time and no longer serve their original purpose.

SUGGESTIBILITY AND HYPNOTISM

Due to the current preoccupation with the media, many people end up
in a trance state that is close to the state into which I bring a therapy
client when I hypnotize them. In that trance state, I can make use of
hypnotic suggestion to help them overcome a habit or tendency. It is
very easy to see that a great deal of modern life goes on while people are
in a trance. People are absorbed with the media, iPhone, newspapers,
TV, magazines, etc., while eating, drinking, and spending time with one
another. This trance state where people may believe almost anything
that is suggested to them becomes an integral part of their sleep.

Gurdjieff says that people will believe anything that they are told if it
is repeated often enough, with enough flattery, or by someone they take
as an authority. We see the results of this weakness in human percep-

tion today, and it has frightening and profound ramifications for our society. An important result is that our perceptive apparatus is less and less able to differentiate the real from the unreal. Television, movies, the Internet, and advertising take advantage of our suggestibility to bring us into a trancelike state that is very similar to that of dreaming during sleep. In this trance state, people can be made to believe what others wish simply through suggestion. Politicians and advertisers perpetuate these trance states by telling people things that make them feel good. Gurdjieff explained that this habitual trait is a result of the implantation of Kundabuffer in us. In *Beelzebub's Tales to His Grandson* he says:

> So, my boy, in view of this the Most High Commission then decided among other things provisionally to implant into the common presences of the three-brained beings there a special organ with a property such that, first, they should perceive reality topsy-turvy, and secondly, that every repeated impression from outside should crystallize in them data for evoking in them sensations of "pleasure" and "enjoyment." [19]

Repeated impressions, either from outside us or inside us, may be gradually experienced as pleasurable. Strangely, there is no requirement that the impressions be good or beneficial in order for us to experience them as pleasurable. Even pain can be pleasurable if it is repeated often enough. In fact, it can serve as a distraction. Teenagers cutting themselves or repeatedly abusing harmful substances are examples of activities that produce negative consequences and negative impressions, yet they continue to repeat them. Some people enjoy inflicting pain on others, and in certain cases, the ones on whom they inflict the pain also enjoy it. Pain and pleasure here are so interwoven they become difficult to tease apart. Such abnormalities appear to be increasing in modern culture.

BEING-PARTKDOLG-DUTY

Because of the cumulative abnormalities Kundabuffer caused in us, we have been unable to develop our capacities of consciousness and objective reason, all of which are part of our birthright. Gurdjieff calls the development of these objective faculties "being self-perfection." He calls his primary method for being self-perfection, "being-Partkdolg-duty," or the ability to practice conscious labors and intentional suffering. He says that three-brained beings on all planets in the universe utilize "being-Partkdolg-duty" as their primary means of self-perfection.[20] The words imply accepting the obligation to do what is right.

It is important to understand the terms "conscious labor" and "intentional suffering" and requires that I repeat some of the things said before. The practice of self-observation is the beginning of conscious labor. I gradually learn to be present while I am doing something, know that I am there, and know my aim. This is not an easy practice and requires persistence. "Intentional suffering" is a term that may bring to mind self-flagellation, fasting, or other self-deprivations. Nothing is further from the truth. Intentional suffering encompasses a much larger field of action. It refers to the ability to create and follow a life goal of developing an inner life. In the process, there will be resistance, such as periods of time where I encounter obstacles and either work through them or not. As I learn about myself, about my mechanicalness and my lack of consciousness, I experience suffering and the difficulty of my situation. If I learn to persist, my attitude and how I apply myself to my life can gradually shift and a new force grows inside me; this is the force of my own will.

I gradually learn to take an aim and stick with it even if it brings me suffering. The first common aim I share with everyone in the Work is the aim to know myself truthfully. Taking this aim as mentioned will provide suffering. It is suffering that I have found painfully real, enlightening, and joyful. Above all, it gives me a taste for what is true and real about me, about my life, and this taste of real life is unforgettable.

THE ITOKLANOZ AND FOOLASNITAMNIAN PRINCIPLES

To see what a predicament Kundabuffer has left us in, we need to look at a more advanced concept Gurdjieff introduces in *Beelzebub's Tales to His Grandson*. He explains how our faculty of attention was modified. This serious modification of attention caused a subsequent change in our being-existence. By using the term "being-existence," Gurdjieff is drawing attention to the quality and duration of our existence. Gurdjieff says:

> You must first be told that there exist in the Universe generally two "kinds" or two "principles" of the duration of being-existence.
>
> The first kind or first "principle" of being-existence which is called "Foolasnitamnian" is proper to the existence of all three-brained beings arising on any planet of our Great Universe, and the fundamental aim and sense of the existence of these beings is that there must proceed through them the transmutation of cosmic substances necessary for what is called the "common-cosmic Trogo-auto-egocratic-process."
>
> And it is according to the second principle of being-existence that all one-brained and two-brained beings in general exist wherever they may arise. . . .
>
> And the sense and aim of the existence of these beings, also, consist in this, that there are transmuted through them the cosmic substances required not for purposes of a common-cosmic character, but only for that solar system or even only for that planet alone, in which and upon which these one-brained and two-brained beings arise.[20]

I remember being intrigued when I first came across the concepts of the "Itoklanoz" and the "Foolasnitamnian" principles. I noticed Gurdjieff referred to them as "systems." It seemed to me he was justified in inventing such outlandish neologisms. He was describing something no one else had understood in quite the same way. According to Gurdjieff, nature originally designed three-centered beings (humans) to be governed by the Foolasnitamnian Principle, which involves the whole of us. However, due to the unbecoming manner in which human beings behaved, nature had to modify the human organism to follow the principle of Itoklanoz, so that our attention was activated and received the impressions of just one center at a time. On the other hand, when the Foolasnitamnian Principle originally functioned in us, the simultaneous and equal reception of associations from each center allowed us to direct our attention in an organized and purposeful manner according to our will. When our attention switched to functioning according to Itoklanoz only, we lost control of being able to direct our attention intentionally. I have noticed such a lack of control over attention in myself repeatedly.

Experiments in Experiencing the Principle of Itoklanoz

Try this experiment to explore the Itoklanoz principle.

1. Walk down the street and try to notice, without attempting to modify, the movement of your attention. One moment you are thinking of something; the next, your vision alights on a car, person, or sound, and then your attention is drawn there. Next, your attention moves to the temperature outside, then a worry passes through you. Do not take my word for this wandering, but verify it for yourself.

2. Next, try to walk down that same street and keep your attention on some subject you wish to think about. What happens? I'll bet your observation is almost identical to what you found in the first experiment.

3. Next, try walking again, but simply count a number sequence such as 2, 4, 6, 8, 10 . . . up to 150, and back. What happens then? Or try counting, 1, 4, 2, 5, 3, 6, 4, 7 . . . up to 150, and back.

We need to conduct experiments like these. Only then can you be categorically convinced you have little or no control over either your attention or the associations that are triggered by the environment or the inner flow of your thoughts and feelings.

Itoklanoz is a system whereby any chance stimuli, outer or inner, can elicit associations from one center or brain that continue until others from another center replace them. You see your energy, your life, and your being used up, your energy wasted on the flurry of activity in each center, stimulated by nothing more than chance impressions. Nature spends your energy this way without your knowing it.

Is there a way out of this situation? Gurdjieff says there is. He says we need to resist, or learn how "not-to-give-oneself-up-to-those-of-one's-associations-resulting-from-the-functioning-of-only-one-or-another-of-one's-brains." [21] I must admit, I never liked his formulation, or perhaps the translation bothered me. But Gurdjieff is telling us about such an important method that I pondered on it for some time. I believe it to be one of the cleverest means for the simultaneous development of both self-knowledge and real will.

My experience has shown me that people have a great difficulty "not" doing something—that is, to "not give yourself up to the associations of just one brain" might seem very difficult. I would express the effort we must make in language that is more positive.

Instead of trying to "not give yourself up to the associations of just one brain," try the following: maintain simultaneous awareness of the associations coming from each of your three brains. This kind of awareness may not be possible all at once, but we can try to get a taste of the experience that shows us how to proceed.

Experiment in Resisting Itoklanoz

- Sit alone quietly.

- While sensing just your right hand, simultaneously notice your emotional state. Note, I have not said, "try" to notice. There is a reason. Yoda in *Star Wars* was correct when he said, "Don't try, just do!" [22]

Practice this exercise on a regular basis for a week for perhaps just ten minutes each time. Your aim is to simultaneously have an inner part of you aware of both your body, by sensing, and your emotional state, by noticing. Through this simple practice, you can develop the ability to be aware of two centers simultaneously. You will actually get a taste of yourself that is closer to the way nature intended you to be. I have found we can expand on this experiment gradually, noticing thoughts at the same time, but we need care to develop the ability in quiet circumstances. Practice this experiment gently, never trying to force your attention or awareness. Instead, direct your attention deliberately, yet gently.

Gurdjieff said that because of the "unbecomingness" of our ordinary existence, nature had to change us so we would automatically give off the correct type of vibrations necessary for the general cosmic good. Nature needs human beings' intentional vibrations. However, we are not capable of fulfilling that role for nature because, first, we live by taking the ephemeral for the real; second, we have no ability to intentionally direct our attention. The chaotic movement of our associations is typical of our unconscious life. Just noticing the flow of these associations changes something in my consciousness. What has changed? Now, there is awareness. Awareness, separate from the chaotic vagaries of my attention, increases through the simple act of noticing.

Self-observation, noticing, self-remembering. They all regulate the chaos of my flickering, unorganized attention. Awareness in itself contains an organizing quality. Itoklanoz is random, chaotic. We can live our entire life in Itoklanoz, unless we develop a regulating function. Living under the influence of Itoklanoz is similar to a dream state where waves and currents of anxiety, pleasure, and sensation repeat themselves for no apparent reason. By contrast, in following the Foolasnitamnian Principle, I am able to direct my attention, to focus. The energies of the three centers can be coordinated, and each can supply simultaneous impressions to sustain my attention.

In this chapter, we have looked at an overview of some of the more complex ideas and concepts of Gurdjieff's system. Self-observation, conscious labor, and intentional suffering represent the primary foundation of this Work. They represent both the means to free ourselves from the consequences of Kundabuffer and provide us new possibilities of evolving as conscious beings. Gurdjieff's terminology may sound peculiar to us, but if we are honest with ourselves, we will recognize all too clearly the manifestations of egoism, selfishness, unwarranted anger, fear, and rage, which enslave us all. Read *Beelzebub's Tales to His Grandson*. Reread this chapter. If you find you have an automatic negative reaction to Gurdjieff's writing style or even have trouble accepting his cosmological model of the universe, don't let that dissuade you from recognizing the importance of his message: If you can allow the truth of your situation to sink in, then you will wish to work.

PART II

SELF-STUDY

CHAPTER 6

THE INNER LIFE

In the previous chapter, I alluded to the difficulties that religions encounter and how they have failed to achieve their aims in many ways. The reasons for this are that they do not understand basic psychological habits that have become firmly established in people and that these habits resist changes imposed either from the outside or by people themselves. To understand our predicament fully, we must understand more than these religions did about how we are constructed, the capacities we might develop, and the psychological patterns that have engrained themselves in us. Then we can develop a map of our inner landscape. This map must include where we are, where we are going, and at least some of the obstacles that confront us. In this chapter, we will explore some of the overlooked psychological structures that make change so difficult for us. One of the obstacles is that our personality, and especially, what Gurdjieff called "false personality," covers our true being, our essence.

ESSENCE, PERSONALITY, AND FALSE PERSONALITY

Gurdjieff made a distinction between a person's "essence" and "personality." [1] This difference was relatively unknown to twentieth century psychology, although current psychology has begun to approach it with its interest in "soul" development. Modern psychology roughly defines personality as the characteristic patterns of thoughts, feelings, and behaviors that make a person unique. Gurdjieff viewed personality as an appliance, a mechanism we develop in reaction to our culture that allows us to interact with others in that culture. Personality is therefore shaped by a specific time period in a specific culture. The persona or mask that each child develops is a means of adjusting to the relatively foreign environment that they enter at birth. Essence, however, is our true nature and remains the same regardless of the culture or time into which we are born. This is the part of us that can become the individuality of the true man or woman if it is nurtured and able to mature. However, since this part is unrecognized by society, and by parents and teachers, it remains undeveloped.

The normal personality becomes our instrument of learning. It orients us within the culture, learns its language, and acquires the skills we need to survive. Most of the attributes of personality, however, including moral beliefs, are learned in a haphazard and unorganized manner. In short, I develop a personality that is a mixture of my tendencies and tastes and an imitation of the way others behave.

The fact that essence and personality are distinct entities within us offers hope that something new can develop. If we were simply our personality, then our development would be limited to the variations a personality could assume in a particular culture. Essence, on the other hand, represents the core of our being and has the potential to develop. However, current culture is not at all suited to the development of essence. Quite the opposite. Modern civilization focuses almost exclusively on the development of personality, what we present to the world, at the expense of essence.

Gurdjieff draws a further distinction regarding personality that modern psychology fails to make. Everyone must develop a personality. We need it in order to survive and fit into society. However, an additional part is often pasted on to it, a part we really do not need for our survival. This part comes into being along with our personalities, and its existence is usually due to our insecurity and imitating others' behavior. In Gurdjieff's lexicon, this part is "false personality."

The concept of false personality does not really exist at all in current psychology. All a person's psychological attributes are generally thrown together under the rubric "personality." Gurdjieff's distinction is much subtler. As a psychologist, I view "false personality" as a system of defense mechanisms stemming from insecurity and imitation. Although the most successful individuals in our society may be rich, famous, or even brilliant, their success is often a means of compensating for some deep insecurity. Because of the poor quality of our education and caretaking when we were children, as well as the general lack of direction from those around us, people often feel a need to enhance themselves to compensate for the sense of inadequacy and insecurity they feel. This artificial enhancement is similar to an actor's role, the difference being that the actor realizes she is playing a role, whereas most of us are unaware of it.

We acquire false personality by imitating our parents, teachers, peers, and leaders. Its characteristics include the tendencies to exaggerate, lie, mislead, attempt to appear different than we are, cover up our perceived defects, hide our mistakes, hide our physical defects, be more concerned with how we appear to others than what we experience and feel inwardly, and so on. False personality makes it almost impossible to distinguish the real person from the added enhancements. Society virtually requires that all of us develop certain aspects of a false personality. The need to lie, for example, is endemic in social and political life.

Modern society is a fertile ground for fostering false personality. Examples in American and European culture abound. The dot-com image of instant success that the so-called "brightest" individuals in these societies enjoy, breeds a false image of human worth. Bill Gates and others like him are held up as icons to be emulated. These images create false self-concepts for the young to imitate—the successful person is one who makes millions of dollars with as little effort as possible—and accomplishes it while still young. Individuals in my son's generation (he is twenty-eight) often choose their vocation according to how quickly they may achieve wealth. The Paris Hiltons, Britney Spears, and rock idols become images that young people emulate, and these nonentities become the rage without any evaluation by the current generation of their actual worth.

Americans, at every level, from academics to gang members, live off images that have become almost totally artificial. Whether it is publish or perish at the academic level or becoming a big movie producer or Hollywood actor, there is less and less of what is authentic in people. More and more, the emphasis is on image. Children and adults are even taught how to project an image of themselves. It is a mixture of the usual personality and the false images a person feels she needs in order for her peers to accept and respect her.

Politics today has become entirely projection of image over substance. When someone with substance enters politics, it is very threatening to those who are in power. Either the person of substance is seduced by the power of the position or those who feel threatened peck them to death.

Harry Benjamin, a German endocrinologist and student of Gurdjieff's ideas, provides a wonderfully simple image that captures Gurdjieff's nuanced descriptions of essence, personality, and false personality:

> For instance, let us consider an egg. There is the yolk, the white and shell. If we regard false personality as the outer hard shell, and personality as the white, then we can see that for the yolk (essence) to develop into a bird it has to feed on the white (personality) and ultimately the bird has to break through (destroy) the shell before it can emerge fully into the light of day as a living creature.[2]

Benjamin's image very well captures my own experience. The false "I's" that are an integral part of my personality brought me the rewards that society valued, but also created many painful situations for me. I was lucky to have supportive friends in the Work that could endure my more artificial aspects as I worked through them. There are still many remnants of these "I's," but now I see them and have some compassion toward these false parts of my nature. I understand how they came into being. I can also see similar "I's" in others. This realization of my own false personality made me more compassionate toward others. Moreover, I have found other parts of myself I can truly depend on that represent more essential aspects of who I am.

If I become serious in my wish for inner development, false personality gives me an incredible amount of useful material. The defensive aspects of false personality cannot withstand the development of my inner life. False personality resists our efforts, but if we actually develop our inner life, this false part loses its grip or, as Benjamin says, the egg begins to crack. How then do we begin to pay attention to our inner life? What is it? How is it different from the outer life of the senses, and what is the relationship between the outer and inner aspects of human life?

INNER LIFE

Usually, we are unaware that we even have an inner life. There is a reason for this lack of awareness. My entire life is based on what comes in through my senses and what I am told. Society focuses us on the material aspect of life. As children we also had an inner world, a world that existed parallel with our outer lives. However, because of the need to rely on sense perception to manipulate the outer world, most adults leave behind the inner life of childhood with its capacities of imagination and creativity. There are, of course, exceptions among artists, writers, and others who focus their lives on bringing forth aspects of their inner world. However, even the inner life of the artist or writer comes primarily from his sense impressions within his particular culture and time. Few people make their inner development the primary focus of their lives, but that is what we are interested in here.

A basic principle of the Work is that other levels of consciousness are possible for us; other worlds exist. Not everything lies on the same level as the material world. Our inner life exists on a different level from our ordinary waking state. Keep in mind we cannot develop an inner life accidentally, because it is certainly not necessary for our personal survival. It is luxury in one sense, and in another represents an evolutionary responsibility. Nature is not particularly interested in its development.

Some four years ago, I was working on a remodeling project for the psychotherapy clinic where I practice. I had been a contractor for a number of years before becoming a psychologist. Because the clinic could not afford any of the contract bids it received, I acted as the contractor. This was an interesting time for me because I took this construction project as an inner task. I wished to handle the contracting differently from the way I had previously worked in this field. Contracting is definitely a stressful occupation due to the complexity involved. It had always been a challenge for me to work on myself while being involved in contracting and not totally lose my own sense of presence—that is, not become totally identified with a project. My aim in the clinic project was to try to accomplish the remodeling project with a more spacious, present inner attitude. To make a long story short, my plan worked well for a few months, until I had to give the clinic a completion date that would allow it to plan its move-in. I did not realize that when I decided on this end date, it would change my inner relationship to the project and to time itself.

The aim of my inner work, to complete the project in an unidentified calm state went out the window. I found myself waking up at 5:30 a.m., filled with anxiety because I might not have enough time to complete the job before the move-in date. The time pressure was killing my inner life. As the deadline loomed closer, my aim suffered. The more decisions I needed to make to finish the project on time, the more difficulty I experienced in remaining present.

At this point, you may be asking, "Well, what is this thing, inner life, anyway?" To answer that question, we first need to find out what it is not. Outer life is the world of schedules, money, responsibility, appearances, and the images of ourselves we project onto the world. Most people remain blind to the fact that while they are living such an outer life, they have a simultaneous inner experience as well. In fact, each person actually lives two lives, but we generally fixate on the outer. There are two worlds we can experience, but by default, we live in only one, the material world.

Five distinct streams of experience are constantly feeding the inner lives that we usually remain unaware of. These streams are composed of impressions flowing from the intellectual, emotional, moving, instinctive, and sex centers. The most important stream for this discussion comes from our emotional center. This stream is not the emotional state that we allow others to see, but rather what is really happening within us that we keep hidden from others (though we may reveal it to a therapist or close friend).

In general, people are not terribly interested in their inner life. A large number of clients who enter psychotherapy just want to have their dysfunction "fixed," and may not be interested in making any real emotional change. The idea there can be emotional growth beyond the teenage and early adult years is only a recent development. Of course, emotions do change over a lifetime because of accidental shocks from the environment and the unfolding of life itself. However, that type of emotional development bears no relationship to a focused development of my emotional center. My ordinary emotional experience usually becomes merely a repetition of what already has occurred. If a person gets angry easily or is usually depressed, these emotional patterns will repeat unless something changes. Emotional development, if not intentionally directed, remains dependent on accidental shocks from life. As such, it is haphazard, chaotic, and lacks structure. One of the best means to develop emotionally comes from the friction of collaboratively working with other people toward a common aim: in the case of Work, the aim of finding out the truth about myself.

The emotional development that I am talking about here leads to the development of the *mature human being*. This is a stage beyond attaining what is considered adulthood.

As an emotionally mature person my emotional center begins to understand others, is able to feel their emotional life, how they are caught, how it feels to accept them, care for them, and likewise accept and care for myself. My emotions expand and are not only centered on me and striving to get what I want. My emotional life expands because I emotionally experience my connection and responsibility to others and gradually to life itself. All this leads to emotionally experiencing the interconnectedness of all life and finding my place within this structure.

Ordinary, unconscious emotional life takes place the way a passenger rides in a train. The passenger (that is, the emotions) notices some interesting scenery as the train passes through the city and country. Some areas seem more pleasant than others. Certain areas are to be avoided altogether. From this noticing, the emotional part begins quite haphazardly to experience either liking or disliking, feeling good or bad, or pain or pleasure, depending on the landscape it is passing through. Likes and dislikes then become the passenger's emotional life, a narrowly defined life that could contain much more.

In a relatively short period of one's life—usually by adolescence—these haphazardly acquired emotional patterns are set. Then as we age, past stimuli and situations accidentally trigger the same emotions or feelings in the present when similar situations arise. Because inner life has halted at like and dislike and cannot proceed further, inner life has become the slave of outer life. These emotional patterns represent the usual extent of the inner life of most of us. We do not have an independent emotional life, but rather this inner part of us is programmed with reactive patterns from our past. An independent emotional life that is not activated and entirely dependent on outer circumstances that activate patterns of like and dislike within me, can only be the result of real work, and it is very difficult to come by. Growth of the emotional center requires bringing in another force, the third or reconciling force, a force that is capable of helping us pass beyond like and dislike.

Other experiences beyond like and dislike that can affect us emotionally fall roughly into four categories: love experiences, sexual experiences, peak experiences, and work experiences.[3] Our experience of love is perhaps the most profound and complex emotional experience we have, and even a small amount of it leaves us hungering for more. Sexual experience is a very important category, since the sex center is extremely active in everyone from about age twelve onward. In fact, the sex center pushes people around emotionally and can determine how they feel about others.

Sex can often take the place of an inner life, because sex energy intrudes upon emotional experiences and becomes mixed up with all our other emotions, especially love. Sex energy is a very high energy and that is one of the reasons it "magnetizes" us. When sexual attraction becomes intertwined with love and the physical appearance of a partner, a person may feel he or she can only love someone who matches a particular physical image.

People take notice of peak experiences. These experiences take us out of our ordinary emotional repertoire and are extremely intense compared with our usually vague likes or dislikes. However, because peak experiences stand out so much from the ordinary, they can easily assume an addictive role. If they are pleasurable and we wish to repeat them, we can become peak-experience addicts. People travel to exotic places, do dangerous activities, or go on retreats with famous people in order to have experiences that make them feel more alive emotionally.

In general, people eventually gravitate toward those experiences they like and try to avoid those they find distasteful or painful. This is a natural instinct, part of our survival mechanism. If something feels bad, the common reaction is that it is probably not good for us. We like to "feel good." We feel good when it is Friday, or when kayaking, driving, shopping, at the movies, the theater, watching sports on TV, playing sports, going to church, getting together with friends for drinks and dinner, just eating, etc. All of these activities affect and activate our emotional life. After a time, these types of emotional experience become similar to a computerized game. Feeling good is only activated by likes or dislikes. But can a person experience an emotional life that is more meaningful and freer than just being a reaction to like and dislike?

HUNGER FOR MEANING

I desperately desired to have meaningful experiences; however, I did not recognize my longing and emotional starvation for many years, nor did I see that my emotional state was completely dependent on like and dislike. Instead, I noticed I was bored or out of sorts. Certain of my pleasant emotional states became attached to outer experiences, such as making money, canoeing, shopping, etc. My emotional life was spent on a limited inner range of responses to outer life and the perpetuation of those responses. I found I was a creature of habit, repeating predictable patterns. Those patterns could be simple, such as waking and sleeping, or complex, such as worrying, feeling guilty, or striving for success. It really didn't matter what those patterns were. The most important realization for me is that I found they gave me the false impression of having some control over my life.

My first teacher in the Work was Willem A. Nyland, who had worked with Gurdjieff for almost twenty-five years. He used to say that for life (that is, biological life), it does not matter what our experience is, pleasant or unpleasant, whether we mechanically suffer or not. Biological life is satisfied to manifest in any manner. Life itself does not discriminate about the form it takes or insist that experience be pleasant. This is a very important principle. It gives us a clue as to why we may find ourselves repeating ad infinitum our negative behavior patterns, even those that are full of pain—life itself does not care what experience is manifested in the different forms it creates.

Most of us end up settling for a limited but secure repertoire of emotional patterns. Eventually, emotional energy runs down and we get depressed, take up a new goal (painting, yoga, spirituality) or just repeat the same pattern that has fed us in the past. Rarely, do these outer activities really feed inner life, although they can satisfy us for a time. For example, I have watched my own interest in photography wax and wane since I was thirteen years old. It is symbolic of the ebb and flow of excitement and search I experience, followed by a letdown or depression, and then renewed searching. It took some time to see that this ebb and flow of outer interest was a mechanical, unconscious means of attempting to nurture my inner life. In and of itself, it is not bad, but provides a very limited growth of inner life— this pattern kept my inner life ticking without real change.

I have also found that many people hunger to share their inner lives with others, but generally, there are few venues for sharing their realizations. Even if we have many friends, we still may feel lonely and isolated. The closest many people may come to sharing their inner life is with a partner, perhaps a close friend, or now more frequently, with a therapist. What has become customary is to share the more superficial aspects of our lives with others—problems with our job, the weather, sports, or discussing movies we've seen.

Obviously, our inner life is more than the life we see with our eyes. Vision fixes our attention on the surface. Although the eyes facilitate the body's movement and its ability to manipulate objects and engage in situations, all this activity gradually brings us into a trance of activity and reactivity. We do not develop the ability to think deeply about our experiences or what we are doing. Nor do experiences penetrate deeply into us, but instead we settle for a trance of activity. With our visual capacities and abilities to manipulate objects, we may come to see other people as objects also. The focus of our lives becomes the outer world of manipulating material objects. The focus of true thinking, what Gurdjieff refers to as "active mentation," requires more from us than seeing and manipulating objects.

A major characteristic of inner life is the search to realize meaning. Making meaning goes beneath the surface of objects and experience. It connects me with an experience greater than the automatic play of life I see around me. Inner development therefore represents vertical development (going deeper) and comes from self-knowledge and making meaning of the experience I have at every moment. Self-knowledge can lead to self-understanding and is not simply concerned with horizontal life, the life of limited mental associations and superficial interactions with others. Vertical meaning comes when we look at our experience and allow it to affect us in the moment rather than just thinking about it. In this way, we can take the simplest thing that happens to us and find new meaning within it. Intentionally making meaning of our experience and pondering experience brings us more impressions and gradually we experience more in each moment.

If I want an inner life, I have found I need to be willing to spend some time sitting quietly. Sitting quietly helps me pull out of the flow of ordinary life and experience my emotional state. I want to notice, without trying to change, what is going on within me—notice my emotions, thoughts, sensations—the actual experience of my existence that I miss most of the time as I am usually thinking about the future. When I sit quietly, I also become familiar with the patterns of emotions and thoughts that are constantly unconsciously repeating within me.

It is important to become familiar with our behavior patterns. Three distinct patterns are always flowing within us: a cognitive or thinking pattern, an emotional state or feeling pattern, and a pattern that provides us a vague sense of our body's condition. Being quiet can allow us to notice them. Cognitive patterns include what we value, what we think about, our confusion, automatic associations, etc. Our emotional state contains elements of how we relate to others, how we judge them and how we judge ourselves, how much enjoyment or depression we are experiencing in the moment, etc. These discoveries help us sort out what is valuable and show us what we may wish to let go of; although it may take us some time to actually let go of or change a pattern. The first step is to become familiar with the patterns. I have found that as I developed the ability to be in touch with my inner life, to notice it and be interested in it, a deeper part of me was activated and I experienced a new type of security, one more valuable than material security.

We are social creatures and wish to communicate our discoveries to others. When I discover new aspects of my inner life, I find it is both personal and relational. I think of Thoreau, who found it necessary to go off alone to develop his concepts and ideas, but he also wished to communicate them. Gurdjieff was also able to communicate his discoveries about the inner world to others. He went in search of esoteric knowledge, he searched alone and with others, and then he returned to share what he had found. My own experience has shown me that I need to remain in relation with others in order to keep my inner life energized and developing. It is here that group work is so valuable and which we will discuss at the end of the chapter.

WHAT IS HIGHER IN US

A major pitfall of modern life is its tendency to produce a hunger for so-called "specialness," the need to be a celebrity. Society tends to encourage everyone from birth onward to be unique and special. It often becomes a disease that engenders and supports false personality. Being special takes many forms, how we dress, being the best student, becoming a powerful politician, the richest man in Silicon Valley, the most respected physicist, or the leader of a Work group. Those in the Gurdjieff Work are not immune from this wish to be special and can easily miss seeing this feature of themselves in their self-study.

However, enjoying the specific thing that makes me special is not as detrimental as my need to be special. This artificial need fuels false personality. It can mix with normal personality so much that the two become indistinguishable. You may have met individuals like this, often salesmen types that are always selling something, usually selling themselves in one way or another. They are unable to turn off their selling. Sociologists might argue that without people's need to be unique, society's drive toward progress would be hampered. They are probably correct, if we simply define progress as the creation of ever-new material objects or better technology. However, my inner life may develop in an opposite direction from my need to be special, my wish to be seen and recognized for my achievements. No one may be able to see my inner development. If I don't seem special to others, my false personality asks, why bother?

According to Gurdjieff, we each have a higher emotional and higher intellectual center in addition to our three lower centers, but at present these centers are not accessible to us. An important characteristic of these two higher centers is that they are already completely developed. Our inability to access them is due to a number of factors: the lower centers are poorly developed or underdeveloped; the centers are unbalanced or one center predominates. There is also a lack of good connections among the centers. Moreover, false personality is overdeveloped and disharmonizes our inner states. False personality is extremely concerned with how I appear in external life and is instrumental in the development of false values that become part of me. Finally, I am usually unable to direct my three major centers to work together harmoniously. If I can actively mentate and develop my three major centers so they can work together, I might then be able to access my two higher centers and receive impressions from them. As mentioned earlier, Gurdjieff says:

> . . . "active mentation" in a being, and the useful results of such active mentation, are in reality actualized exclusively only with the equal-degree functionings of all his three localizations of the results spiritualized in his presence, called "thinking-center," "feeling-center," and "moving-motor-center." [4]

If I ponder his words, I can see the necessity for me to work on my centers individually and to make an effort to harmonize them. Gurdjieff's term, "active mentation," relates integrally to the development of inner life. If we become more harmonious—that is, if our centers are balanced in their operation—then we experience our lives more deeply and are able to receive more meaningful impressions from our experience. Those of us who are fortunate enough to recognize the importance of an inner life, then have an *obligation* to humanity. My level of education, my social status, how I came to this recognition of the importance of inner life, the path my life has taken up until now—none of this matters. I have only now, only the present moment to work; the responsibility right now to develop my inner being. This is what we are striving for—a higher level of being—but what is meant by the word "being"?

In the English language, no exact definition corresponds to Gurdjieff's connotation of the word "being." Let us think in terms of inner development. A person's being has little to do with his station in life or his possessions. It does not mean that a person with a highly developed being may not hold a position of power or be wealthy. How then does one define and measure being?

From the perspective of Work, I define an individual's level of being as the degree to which she comprehends the objective purpose of existence, her role in it and her willingness to fulfill her obligation in that role. A person who has great being understands her obligation and the work she is involved in. She understands how her individual existence relates to all existence. Additionally, being is a function of the development of the authentic self—that is, the extent to which essence has developed in a person.

On a personal level, I can look at my own life and evaluate how my activities either help or hinder the development of my being. This kind of inquiry inevitably leads me to larger questions, such as, what forestalled the development of human beings, keeping them from experiencing and developing their essential natures? Then we can reassess our culture's values. What in my culture is actually useful? Harmful? What enriches our being? What degrades it? An objective measure of a culture's authenticity would be the degree to which it facilitates the development of authentic being in each person.

EDUCATION

A major obstacle to the growth of real being has been education. It has left us crippled as human beings in many respects. When I began my search, I found a great deal of material that addressed my concerns in the writings of John G. Bennett, a student of Gurdjieff we have already cited a number of times.

A man of immense knowledge who traveled widely in the Middle East and throughout the world, Bennett followed Gurdjieff's example as a psychological researcher and became a prolific and important disseminator of Gurdjieff's system. In the early 1970s, Bennett introduced a nine-month training program at Sherborne House in England. Under his close direction, individuals in the program struggled to apply Gurdjieff's methods in a communal setting.[5] With the help of his editor, Anthony Blake, Bennett was able to make the most complex and important concepts and questions understandable, a daunting task and brilliant achievement.

Bennett's writings point out many of the failings of modern education. Among these is the concept of rote learning (that is, requiring children to memorize useless facts and numbers). His ideas for real education are quite different. The aim of education, in his view, is simply:

. . . to produce an independent human being, understanding his obligation toward himself and toward the
world in which he lives, feeling the necessity to fulfill that
obligation and capable of making the efforts and sacrifices
necessary to fulfill it.[6]

Obviously, modern education has failed in the task of encouraging
individual development. Instead, it tends to produce narcissistic traits
in its students, traits such as egoism, selfishness, vanity, and self-
importance. Education lacks a framework to help students to see their
purpose in the larger world. Educators still focus on rote memorization
and do not encourage the child to feel an obligation to the world, except
in the narrowest sense of finding a career in business or industry.

Although there is a proliferation of special schools in the United
States and Europe, such as the Waldorf and Montessori schools and
others, there is still lack of an understanding of the need for developing
the child's three centers. Teachers are in a state of waking-sleep themselves, and thus do little preparation to develop their pupils' inner lives
or speak to their inner needs. It is here, in their formative years, that a
child is most adaptable. During this early period, a child would be able
to learn to struggle toward an aim that is deeper than just achieving
good grades or learning to kick a soccer ball.

Incidentally, the current proliferation of sports education is
misguided because of its overemphasis on competition. There is no
question that competitive sports provide needed exercise for the physical body, but in many ways sports can be detrimental to children's
physical and emotional development—football is a good example of
this. Instead of teaching them coordination and collaborative team-
work, the focus is on winning above all, on crushing the other team.
Such competition produces either false feelings of superiority in those
who excel or anxiety in those who do not measure up.

Of course, even prior to formal schooling, the starvation and stifling
of children's being has begun. Many factors are responsible. The most
important one is that the parents' level of being remains undeveloped.
Thus, parents themselves are ignorant of how to teach their children
to be responsible beings. The education of a child's being begins with

the relationship formed with their parents or caregivers. Children may be unwanted by parents or considered burdensome. Sometimes, the parents themselves suffered abuse or neglect as children, and they perpetuate that behavior toward their own children. Some parents might try to hide that their child is not wanted, but such emotions cannot really be hidden from a child. Children sense how adults feel about them regardless of how they act outwardly. Thus, the emotional quality of the parents' bonds with the child determine whether the child's interest and joy in being alive are either encouraged or thwarted; and will, in turn, determine the child's attitude toward her life and the world.

Parents do not realize that the best education in the world cannot make up for the deficits in their own level of being, a level of being their children will imitate. They are not even aware that there are different levels of being. If the parents are vividly interested in the child, in life, encourage individual exploration, model for the child how to struggle and stay unidentified with trivia or negativity, then that child will have real tools to develop her own being. Simply put, parents are their children's best primary teachers. If they do not work on themselves throughout their lives, they deprive their child of the environment necessary for the growth of their child's being.

When modern educational methods are coupled with parents who are uninterested in their own self-development, what chance does the child have? Bennett says this about the child's environment:

> When children are born, they are subjected almost from birth to influences that will inevitably produce in them such characteristics as vanity, self-will, self-importance, distrust, deceitfulness, suggestibility, dependence on other people, and at the very root and center of their being, egoism.[7]

Authentic education must encourage children to be sensitive to their impressions and help them learn to contain and tolerate the myriad impressions they receive. Likewise, a parent's aim should not simply be to ensure that children are happy, but actually encourage them to allow their impressions to penetrate deeply, even the painful ones, rather than shrinking back from them. In other words, parents need to encourage their children to stick with their own impressions and create meaning from these perceptions, instead of accepting the words of a teacher or another person as a given.

Bennett points out that a child's upbringing is so incomplete and distorted, it actually forces certain parts of the child's nature into the unconscious. When referring to the development of the three brains, he says:

> In a normal human individual each of these three parts is capable of conscious experience but, largely due to harmful conditions of early childhood and subsequent abnormal education, children grow up so that their feeling and sensing brains disappear from consciousness. They are thus led to relate their own existence to one part only, the thinking brain, to the experience of which they attach the word "self" or "I." Nevertheless, the other two parts continue to act in them.[8]

Parents need to be especially attentive to their own attempts to distract or occupy their children so the children do not disturb them. If parents distract a child in this way, they are actually teaching the child to self-distract. Sadly, due to the overwhelming complexity of modern life, many parents unconsciously aid their children to distract themselves from unpleasant feelings such as anxiety, sadness, anger, or depression. Gradually the child loses her sensitivity for her own inner state or develops sensitivity without the means to contain, digest, and understand her emotions and experiences.

Gurdjieff speaks about education throughout *Beelzebub's Tales to His Grandson*. For example, in this most important passage, he describes a result of correct education and understanding:

> . . . after he had cognized with his Reason certain cosmic truths I had explained to him, he immediately acquired in his presence towards the beings around him, similar to him, almost that attitude which should be in all normal three-brained beings of the whole Universe, that is to say

he became as it is also said there, "compassionate" and "sensitive" towards the beings surrounding him.[9]

Gurdjieff is telling us that the acquisition of compassion for others is a lawful result of correct understanding of cosmic truths. He points out to us that this compassion and sensitive attitude is the attitude that all normal individuals throughout the universe have toward each other.

Gurdjieff spoke and wrote about developing compassion and sensitivity and demonstrated it in his own relationships, but it is still not emphasized sufficiently in the Work. In my experience, sensitivity and compassion are capacities that we can develop directly through Work and understanding ourselves. If a person has not developed compassion in relation to others, it is a good indication that he or she has not yet developed compassion for him- or herself. This is a result of a lack of adequate self-understanding. I need to have sufficient self-compassion before I can really experience compassion for others. And to develop compassion, I must understand objectively how we all are caught in our own prisons of habitual patterns of unconscious behavior. To experience compassion is a gift.

LOSING MY REAL SELF

The night before writing this chapter, I remembered a childhood experience. I was seven. My grandparents had saved enough money to send me to a camp in Massachusetts for two weeks. The other boys in my cabin were there for the entire summer and had been there for five weeks before I arrived; I was an outsider, but it didn't bother me at the time. I had only been at camp a few days when there was a big wrestling match in our cabin. Everyone, for some reason unknown to me, wanted me to wrestle a huge boy who was about a foot taller than I and about forty pounds heavier. I wasn't afraid of him, although perhaps I should have been, and I agreed to wrestle him. The aim was to get the loser to say "uncle" ("I give up!"). There was no doubt this boy was much stronger, but I was much quicker and I immediately got him into a headlock. No matter what he did, I wouldn't release him regardless of how much he thrashed about. I didn't squeeze his neck too hard because I didn't want to hurt him. I continued just to hold him. I realized that he was almost too tired to move, and I could if I wanted to, get him to say "uncle" just by putting some more pressure on his neck. Instead, I released my hold, got up off the dirty cabin floor and walked out toward one of the playing fields.

A part of me knew I had done the right thing, that it was the right way to be. It did not matter whether I won or lost or what the other boys thought of me. I simply did not care then what the others thought of me. My center of control was not outside me, but rather inside me. At age seven, I had touched a part of me that was mine, and that is the key interest in this story. What I didn't realize was that I would soon be separated from this essential part of myself by experiences that took place in my family, in school, and in a society that did not foster this independent part of me.

Having my center of control within me lasted another few years, but it was almost totally gone by the time I finished grade school. I remember how in the eighth grade, this center of myself was pushed out of the picture, downward into my unconscious, by another part of my psyche that was very concerned with what others thought of me. I can even remember the day when what others thought of me got the upper hand. How had this come about? What forces were at work? Many years later as a practicing psychologist, I found the answer to how this autonomous part of me was lost and began to find my way back to it.

Praise, blame, and shame play a huge part in our enculturation, particularly in our relations with caregivers and teachers. Praise and blame are almost always related to the outside world and the child's external, visible actions. There was little attention or importance given to my inner world, except if I was sad or acting out. My parent's focus on the external world and its importance established for me that the way I appear to others is more important than how I actually feel inside. This is the first great deceit. Parents and caregivers cannot help but focus on outer appearances because they themselves have lived under this slavery throughout their lives. Bennett says this about the situation:

> Children are made to think and to feel by influences that
> are brought to bear on them almost from birth that it is
> only their external manifestations seen by other people

that determine their value. Activity not seen by other people, either because it goes on in their inner experience or because it proceeds out sight of others, ceases to matter for self-satisfaction or shame.[10]

Bennett points out that children receive praise for the most ridiculous trivialities, such as learning to throw a ball through the air so it passes through a hoop or hit a ball over a net. Or, they are praised for how beautiful their clothes or hair look. Conversely, parents will suppress children's actions when they do not correspond to some arbitrary code of behavior.[11] What is unconsciously created in these children is vanity on the one hand and deceitfulness on the other. These traits, learned in childhood, determine the character of the adult man or woman. By that time, it is almost impossible to change, except through a special effort on one's part.

According to Bennett, when a child enters school he becomes the "slave of public opinion." [12] This slavery remains with him throughout his entire life, and very few escape it. Even so-called "nonconformists," whether they are artists, hippies, or wise men, are not immune. The artist or nonconformist outwardly may appear to have escaped from this slavery to public opinion, but it is usually only a façade. Inwardly, the rock musician, actor, or other so-called "nonconformist" is so desperate for others' appreciation that the "audience" becomes a survival necessity. We encounter such individuals all the time through the American media. They are desperately concerned, just as we are, with what others think of them.

In short, our caregivers, education, and experiences with peers program our behavior. We are taught to conform outwardly and hide our inner experience. We develop a policeman within us who is always measuring what others might think of us, and we adjust our outer behavior accordingly. Our inner life, which is usually active until we are seven or nine, gradually retreats and becomes stunted. Bennett says the following about this stunted development:

> He is unable to do anything without being influenced
> in one way or another by the thought of the effect of his
> actions on the opinion of other people who will be aware

of them . . . It is all the same whether this dependence upon the other people takes the form of subservience or revolt, whether he is concerned to please or to shock. It is the same because in either case, the possibility of inward independence and inward free judgment is stifled.[13]

ADDICTION TO SPORTS

The love of sports that is encouraged in children throughout their school years is a glaring example of the importance people place on performance in order to impress others. I remember how I reacted when I first read Gurdjieff's comments about sports. He spoke of how people die by thirds because of overusing one or another of their centers or brains. Gurdjieff says:

> Just as the spring of a watch has a winding of a definite duration, so these beings also can associate and experience only as much as the possibilities for experiencing put into them by Nature during the crystallization of those same Bobbin-kandelnosts in their brains.[14]

"Bobbin-kandelnost" is another one of Gurdjieff's peculiar terms, but the concept is simple once you think about it. Each one of our brains or centers—the thinking center, emotional center, and moving center—is analogous to a sewing machine bobbin that holds just so much thread. The "thread" represents the center's energy. Just as thread is unwound and used up while the bobbin is working in the sewing machine, so our energy (thread) is used up during our lives when we use that center. The thread gets used more or less efficiently, depending on our level of consciousness during our activities. When the thread is completely exhausted, the center dies. Gurdjieff exhorts us to learn to use our three centers simultaneously as a unit, in a coordinated and integrated manner, so that the thread in one center will not be exhausted before the others are unwound. Otherwise, one center dies prematurely, and we are left as only two-thirds of a functioning person. For example, we have seen how football players or boxers are severely injured or debilitated. In speaking about such debilitation, Gurdjieff says:

For instance, a one-third death on account of the Bobbin-kandelnost of the moving-center or "spinal-brain" often occurs there among those terrestrial beings who give themselves up to that occupation which the beings belonging to the contemporary community England now practice, thanks to the maleficent invention of the ancient Greeks, and which maleficent occupation they now call sport.[15]

On the positive side, sports represent one of the few areas where children combine their three centers in learning new movements and behaviors. In the early stages of learning a sport, the child may even struggle inwardly to learn these new movements. This struggle might serve as a useful tool for their character development—if the emphasis was on learning to handle the resistance that arises while learning any new activity. However, this aspect of sports is almost always lost; instead, competition and winning become the goals. Thus, sports are a mixed bag in terms of their benefit. They build the child's confidence and yet, at the same time, build self-centeredness and vanity. For children who are not good at sports, its competitive aspect frequently undermines their confidence.

A sport like tennis artificially resembles what Gurdjieff might call normal three-centered activity. It requires integrating the thinking, moving, and emotional centers within the whole activity. This integration of the centers gives the child a sense of accomplishment. But, accomplishment of what? Friends and parents cheer the child on for hitting a small ball over a net. Their self-worth and pride is bolstered by others telling them they played a good game. I picked tennis as an example, since I played from the time I was very young. I find tennis slightly less ludicrous than some of the contact sports such as football, rugby, or boxing, which require men to smash their opponents into a stupor in order to win the game and the adulation of friends, families, and, of course, the opposite sex.

Perhaps children realize somewhere in themselves that sports are stupid. Perhaps early on, they cannot really fathom why their parents smile and praise them so much for their sports acumen. My guess, however, is that this realization may be very short-lived and is quickly replaced by a kind of false superiority. No wonder. I have watched parents actually get into a fistfight at a Little League baseball game over a referee's call. I was both amazed and saddened. The father of one of the parents had to be ejected from the game by other parents. I realized that what these parents were actually modeling for their children was how to be unconscious, identified, aggressive, out of control, and overly concerned with what others thought about them.

Competitive sports are usually, but not always, about domination and power. Sports breed competition, and then only when some people feel they are competitive, can they feel alive. The superiority one feels if one wins the game builds vanity. This is due to its making you the center of attention and the praise you may receive from others. Also, winning is most enjoyable when the win is seen by others who then feel envious.

As a result of the worldwide adulation of competitive sports, society instills in children competitiveness and false superiority. Or, if for some reason, the child is not competitive, he may feel inferior or envious. The child's self-worth becomes attached to being successful at an activity that actually keeps him in a state of waking-sleep. In short, false personality receives nourishment and growth from competitive sports. The essence remains undernourished. Of course, one can feel a natural pride in sports activities. This pride comes from developing coordination; but as stated above, the idea of "personal best" is quickly lost and becomes secondary.

Worldwide, competitive sport has become such an addiction that it sometimes consumes the players' or spectators' entire lives. Periodically, some enraged fan kills a soccer player for making a play that caused his team to lose a game. Alternatively, fans release their hate on the player, and the player commits suicide after causing his team to lose. The unreality of sports and its emphasis on winning has become another drug to keep humanity asleep. Bennett sums up the glorification of the personality that education and sports engender: "Thus everything is done to enhance the importance of appearance and diminish the importance of reality. Therefore, what is the need to have an objectively satisfied attitude toward oneself inwardly?" [16]

We need to educate the body in more ways than sports. We need dance and movement education, especially during the early school years. With the exception of eurythmy classes in the Waldorf schools, most education is sorely lacking in any type of noncompetitive physical activity. Children's bodies are most flexible and they are most able to learn when they are young. That is the time for education in movement. Gurdjieff realized this, and we will explore the possibility of further movement education in Chapter 8 on the Gurdjieff Movements.

UNCRITICAL THINKING

I have found from experience that modern education fails in two other important respects. First, it fails to stimulate critical thinking. With respect to critical thinking, Bennett says, "Throughout all the different disciplines of school education runs one common thread: neglect of concrete meanings and reliance solely upon the ability to juggle with words." [17]

Second, our educational system fails to educate the emotions. Critical thinking and emotional education are interlinked, since in order to be able to think critically, one must have a certain degree of emotional development. We mistakenly believe that real thinking can take place only through suspension of the emotions. Whereas active mentation requires each center, including the emotional, to bring in needed material.

Reflection, or what Gurdjieff called "pondering," is the ability to mull over an idea or situation with attention, to be interested in it and look at it from many different angles—to find meaning in the words that describe something or some situation. Moreover, pondering requires me to bring in data from each of the three major centers, not just my head brain. It took me many years to realize I was never taught to think clearly or critically. Typical examples of my uncritical thinking were my reactions to the Iraq war. My thoughts and feelings about it changed depending on each new bit of information I received. As I received new information, it was funneled into the "I agree" or the "I disagree" columns in my memory banks, and then these thoughts (associations) automatically activated my emotional center, I felt either like or dislike depending on the associations. All of the latter liking and disliking was automatic, without any attempt on my part to evaluate what I was hearing, reading or seeing. Finally, the combination of thoughts and emotions were stored in my memory as unreflected (unexamined) data and were replayed whenever they were reactivated. In other words, I never really thought much about the material or my reactions. Rarely did I attempt on my own to make deeper meaning from the information I took in from newspapers, TV, and radio. I did not know how to think critically, which should include scrutinizing my own assumptions.

I was never taught the importance of making and realizing meaning. For example, the meaning of a sentence is quite different from the words that make it up. Meaning is greater than words. Words are symbols that condense human experience, merely a shorthand method of communicating. We learn words and their meanings automatically. What we then hear usually makes only a superficial impression, since we rarely attempt to think further about the meaning of the words. As such, the meanings we correlate with words are not really ours, and generally, people cannot think deeply about what they read or converse about. What we hear and see becomes part of our associative thinking automatically without our participation.

If we were able to think more deeply, life experience would nourish us more completely. Our lack of thinking deeply accounts for the shallowness of our experience. In fact, it has become common for people not to think deeply, especially about difficult questions. We are forever inventing new distractions to avoid the pain of analytical thought. Often, we habitually search for ways to numb out and/or amp-up the psyche, both a means of avoiding the effort required to think about experience. It requires effort to mine the psychological gold from experiences, and since no one ever taught us about the vast wealth our experience contains, this wealth of material remains unknown to us.

Some years ago, I became interested in the writings of Tom Brown Jr., who learned the Native American art of tracking animals.[18] He developed a school to teach Native American wisdom and ways. His method for teaching his students to hone their attention impressed me. At the beginning of his course, he assigned each student a 12-x-12-inch square of ground to study. Their task was to find out everything about that small square of land, to become completely aware of what was there.

As his students progressed, he would teach them the meaning of each thing they noticed on this piece of ground. He was training them to pay attention and create meaning from what they noticed. It is rare for people to stop and just look at something for a time, finding meaning in what they see, trying to really see without drifting into fantasy. To "see" in perhaps its deepest aspect here connotes understanding the essence of the experience through awareness.

Constantly, when I read Shakespeare as a child, I had to look up words. It was a wonderful experience, to look up a word and see how it fit into the action in the play. It required an effort on my part. It was different from the way I automatically learned language. In ordinary language learning, a word begins to take on meaning through the actions that accompany it. Gradually, it means something to me, but I rarely think about the word after that. For example, it was a number of years before I associated the name Oakland, a town just south of Berkeley, California, with an area that contained hundreds of oak trees. I had seen the name "Oakland" thousands of times, but had never really thought about it. You can find examples of this for yourself if you pay attention to the street names in the area where you live. You will find that you have seen the name of the street hundreds of times, but never thought about what the name meant.

The English language appears to me to be in rapid decline, in part due to the advent of computers. We generate more and more words and make less and less effort to understand their meaning. To test the truth of these statements, take any word in this paragraph and spend a few minutes thinking about its actual meaning. Have you ever done that? What images and experiences are associated with that word? Are there some other meanings for the word you choose that might never have occurred to you?

Part of our confusion in communicating with others is that an individual word means something different to each person. The meaning formed around the word is the result of correlating the word with a particular material object, situation, activity, or action. The intellectual center correlates automatically. Thus, we do not own the meanings of the words in our vocabularies, communication is inexact, people do not understand us, and vice versa.

The importance of language and communication is an area of knowledge where Gurdjieff broke new ground. He speaks about the development of language in *Beelzebub's Tales to His Grandson* and stresses the need for an exact language to communicate ideas from a higher level. With respect to the relationship of language to the higher centers within us, he says:

> It has already been said that the higher psychic centers work in man's higher states of consciousness: the "higher emotional" and the "higher mental." The aim of "myths" and "symbols" was to reach man's higher centers, to transmit to him ideas inaccessible to the intellect and to transmit them in such forms as would exclude the possibility of false interpretations. "Myths" were destined for the higher emotional center; "symbols" for the higher thinking center.[19]

In other words, education means educating something besides the thinking center alone. It means bringing in material that activates the other centers. In ancient societies, teachers used myth and allegory to touch the other centers and enhance the quality of the information pupils took in.

The relationship of the emotional center to critical thinking is an unresearched area. Real thinking, the ability to ponder deeply about a subject, is an active experience. It requires me to engage not only the thinking center, but also my emotional center, which supplies the appropriate energy and force. Otherwise, so-called "thinking" remains merely a passive process of word association.

Now, to go one step further. If the intellectual center is underdeveloped due to inadequate education, what then of the emotional center? What do we really understand about the development of our emotional center?

UNEDUCATED EMOTION

In retrospect, I realize I actually was given no training or direction in the development of my emotional life. No one around me, neither parents, teachers, nor friends were even interested in their own emotions. They never went beyond noticing they felt sad, angry, or depressed and wanted such unpleasant states to go away. Any emotional education I received was purely accidental. Luckily, I discovered music in junior high school and learned to play symphonic trumpet. I loved music; it was something that touched the emotional part of me and kept feeding it. And yet, this was purely activation of my emotions without any learning other than how to play a particular passage of music; other aspects of my emotional life would have to wait many years to be nurtured and educated.

What we notice of our emotional life is rather primitive. It is usually limited to feelings such as, "I'm feeling pretty good today," or "I'm a little down," or "I am furious with Jane, or the teacher, or my coworker, mother, friend, etc." If a negative emotional state persists for a long time, I may realize it and say, "I am depressed," or "I am feeling stressed." Is this the extent of our emotional life? No, not quite. Most people are also aware of feelings of pride and love for others, their friends, children, and family. So we do have a certain familiarity with emotions. We experience good feelings, bad feelings, liking and disliking, love and hate, and feelings associated with good sex or unsatisfying sex. Then I also recognize desires; I wish for what I need or want, such as money or health. Is this all there is? No, there is still a little more. I become afraid, anxious, inspired, or excitedly interested. Sometimes, I even feel courageous, ashamed, or embarrassed. I also have a whole group of complex feelings connected with sex. Is this it then? I am afraid so, except maybe for instinctive emotional states such as those activated by fear of death. Keep in mind here that all these emotional states are usually triggered by outside stimuli, and they occur automatically and are now habitual for each of us.

Most of what we experience emotionally is usually a mixture of the feelings mentioned above. There are actually quite a lot of them. But, think. Has anyone ever spoken to you in depth about these emotional states during your education? Rarely. Perhaps, they said, "Cheer up, it's not so bad," or "Don't be angry, you have no reason to feel that way," or "Stop crying, there is nothing to cry about," or "Don't worry about it, it is only one test." Not particularly meaningful responses—I know that no one ever made any attempt to help me explore and understand my emotional state.

Recently, there have been more attempts to teach emotional skills in some schools, but without the additional needed emphasis of teaching children how to make meaning from their emotional experience. Is it not ironic that perhaps our most meaningful experience as human beings—emotional experience—is not a more important topic of interest to educators? By default, emotional life becomes the focus of psychology and there the emphasis is primarily on dysfunction. The emotional life in a real educational program is studied very little and its importance is not realized.

When working with clients, I find that emotional self-regulation— teaching clients to strengthen and balance their emotional responses— is very important. Psychologists call it "teaching affect-regulation." All too often, we only notice emotions when they are at the extremes of experience. We express this in statements like, "I feel bad today" or "It's such wonderful weather." Learning to balance out our emotional state when it is extreme requires self-knowledge and practice. The majority of parents, teachers, and peers rarely model balanced emotional states for us. Quite the contrary. As I look back, teachers more often modeled how to overreact to stimuli they did not like, whether it was the personality of a particular child or some other small frustration. They could make a religion out of the smallest, most unimportant fact or the way to sit, write, or behave. At times, their behavior epitomized that of the overbearing and self-important egoist. Rarely did the teachers I had see their students fully. I found a few exceptions along the way, but the majority of my teachers were simply unconscious individuals doing a job.

What might the syllabus of emotional education contain? I envision enhancing children's relationships with their parents, peers, and authority figures by teaching both parents and children new ways to respond. We need to teach the children how they get their feelings hurt, how they hurt others, and how to repair the hurt feelings. It is really an education in relationships, teaching children about the common reactions to hurt that they may have, such as anger, sadness, and shame.

Then we need to teach them how to communicate in a meaningful way when they experience these emotions.

We also need to teach children how to remain in touch with difficult feelings like sadness, anger, grief, and loss, as opposed to dissociating from their difficult experiences. The latter is quite epidemic and is fueled by video games and other attempts to distract children from boredom or difficult feelings and make them feel better. Further exploration might include how to expand, rather than contract, their attention and interest, as they move toward adulthood and a vocation. Education of the emotions is not a mystery. All we need is to have sufficient knowledge about our own emotional states in order to design the tools the children could use. The curriculum would come from our own understanding gained through objective, compassionate self-study.

CULTIVATING INTEREST

How can we, as parents and educators, learn to avoid killing our children's fascination, interest, gratitude, and joy at just being? The answer lies within the question itself. Just as we underestimate and overlook the importance of the capacity of attention, we have also failed to develop children's affect of interest. Psychology considers interest a neutral affect, neither positive nor negative. Interest is intimately related to awareness and the development of the emotional life, but it may be destroyed in children very easily. Grade school teachers attempt to keep their students interested so that they won't lose control of their classes, but there are other reasons to foster interest.

Interest is actually an excited state of curiosity in which one wishes to learn. It is so necessary for learning and understanding any new subject, but in modern education, interest dies on the vine. Rote learning gradually erodes interest; its focus is solely on memorization instead of understanding. The child's focus is directed toward an end product, getting a good grade. With their attention left wandering, children do develop new interests; but they are interests in how they look, how they compare to others, how authority figures will perceive and treat them if they receive a good grade. In these ways, interest becomes adulterated when it is linked to our performance and how others think of us. To reawaken interest in our children and ourselves, we must re-interest ourselves in interest. It is not too late for us to take on the responsibility of reeducating ourselves and make up for the poor education we received. The hope for children is that enough of us become reinterested in everything so that we can model this interest for children, model aliveness. In order to accomplish the latter, I find that I must be more alive.

BALANCING THE CENTERS

By the time we reach adulthood, many people feel unbalanced and unharmonious. Gurdjieff states that the great challenge is learning to redevelop the three major centers so that they are in harmony with each other. Harmonization, getting the centers to work together in a balanced way, is also the best way to develop each center itself. I often remember Bennett's recommendation that we each need to activate or exercise each center each day. Over the years, this simple statement has taken on more meaning for me. It helps me to reharmonize whenever I find one center to be over- or underactive.

Throughout my life, I have been fortunate to be able to do physical work and learn many practical skills that universities do not provide. As time passes, I am somewhat less physically active, and I have had to develop a plan to keep my moving center in shape. Keeping in shape involves more than just physical exercise. It is better if some practical skill accompanies it, be it woodworking, sculpture, crafts, building, gardening, etc.

I have also realized that emotional development cannot proceed in a vacuum. I need engagement with others. I notice my clients' tendencies to become more isolated and sedentary as they age. Watching TV and being comfortable is addictive. Where they once might have thought nothing about getting into their car and driving to the beach or attending a weekend seminar, they begin to feel such excursions are just too much trouble. When they are more active physically, emotionally, or intellectually, they actually seem to have a greater life force flowing through them. Not surprisingly, one of the most useful interventions for combating depression is physical activity. This can be of even more value if it is activity directed toward an aim such as gardening, building, or dance, rather than simply going to the gym.

Bringing intentionality into the study of the three centers never becomes automatic. I have a responsibility to keep my three brains in good health, to learn how to exercise them each day. Eating organic yogurt and avoiding processed food is excellent for my body, but insufficient support for intellectual or emotional health. Of the three foods that I consume—ordinary food, air, and impressions—ordinary food is the least important for inner development.

The health and harmony of the centers is directly related to my ability to take in impressions. Real exercise of any center must also include gaining new impressions of myself. I can exercise my emotional center painting, dancing, or playing the piano, but if there is no part of me present when doing these activities, then something is missing and it remains unconscious activity. Also, it is important to learn how each center can influence the other centers. For example, if I hurt my back, the pain can severely affect my ability to engage fully in many tasks, even thinking. The pain I experience may also affect my receptivity to new impressions from relationships or other impressions coming from my emotional center. On the other hand, I notice when I am relaxed and spending time with others, I am better able to take in impressions of a higher quality that I might miss at other times.

You can see easily how one center affects another after an argument with a spouse, friend, or business associate. The emotions generated by arguments affect how we act throughout that day and even longer— we may then have an auto accident, have a stomachache, or forget our wallet. Getting very angry with someone is similar to throwing a large boulder into a lake. The waves go outward in all directions, create currents, bounce off the shore, and disrupt the entire surface. We should not take this to mean that we should never get angry. In fact, it is useful to get angry at times so we can study anger impartially and begin to understand it.

REAL UNDERSTANDING

There is a major difference between knowledge and understanding. Knowledge is information we process in the intellectual center. Understanding is actually the result of the relationship among the three centers. For example, I may have watched someone sewing a shirt, but

I have never done it. After watching, I now have knowledge of how to make a shirt, but something is lacking. When I actually make a shirt, I increase my understanding of the skill. My body and mind learn how to make a shirt, but still something may be missing—the emotional element. I wish to make a good shirt or wish to learn more about sewing and this brings my emotions into play. Then, I feel totally alive and experience the enjoyment of creating something.

However, I still need something else in order to be fully human. That is, the ability to "remember myself" while making the shirt. When I am in a state of self-remembering, I have many impressions that it is "I"—physically, mentally, and emotionally—who am engaged in the shirt-making. Self-remembering adds a whole new level to my experience and understanding.

What, you may ask, is different when I remember myself? During self-remembering and self-observation, I make an intentional connection between my centers, and I receive new impressions of myself, impressions that are a result of my centers being coordinated in the activity while a part of me registers this coordinated activity. These impressions nourish who I really am, that I exist, and I experience being more awake. All three centers come together as one in the moment; they line up, supporting each other. Something in me realizes I exist while fully engaged in the activity of making a shirt. We need self-remembering so that these impressions become a permanent part of our memory. Collin said:

> We were taught—and I understand it better every day—
> that understanding is not the product of one function
> in man, but the resultant of several functions working
> in harmony. For example, if one appreciates something
> with the mind, one "knows" it; if one appreciates it with
> the emotions, one "feels" it; if one appreciates it with the
> external physical organs, one "senses" it. But if one simul-
> taneously appreciates it with the mind, emotions and
> physical senses, then one really understands it. This is
> very rare as we are. It can be developed. But in order to do
> so, something like "self-remembering" is necessary—that

is, one has to remember all one's functions and their relations to the thing in question.[20]

Keep in mind the following: You can never fail in any effort you make
if you are clear about your aim. You are after impressions of yourself
simply existing in the moment. We will speak more later about the
importance of impressions as the highest and most important of the
three foods we consume.

REAL AND PSEUDO-CONSCIENCE

What is the difference between objective conscience and what normally
plays the role of conscience within us? You might argue there is no such
faculty as objective conscience, but the purpose of this discussion is not
to argue for one side or the other. I hope to simply stir up your thinking
about conscience.

In working with clients, I find that what they call their "conscience"
often plagues them. Their conscience is comprised of beliefs, guilt,
illusions, and sometimes, strange associations that have haphazardly
become deeply rooted and strangely connected. New associations and
experiences arrive and activate their conscience, full of previous associations. The previously stored data mixes with the incoming data and
this conglomeration subsequently goes into memory. For the most part,
their conscience ends up either plaguing them with guilt or justifying
their actions. They feel guilty about what they have done in the past
or justify what they are intending to do now. Sometimes they remain
stuck in indecision, not knowing what to do, because their conscience
is confusing them, guilt and shame are counterbalanced by desire and
justification. I refer to this conscience, the one we all have, as "cultural
conscience."

Cultural conscience draws its guidelines from society, our family
history, genetics, religion, personal history, and the rules and beliefs we
have distilled from past experience. Through immersion in our environment, these elements mix and haphazardly deposit themselves into our
inner structure. Of course, this mixture is different for everyone. Gradually, personality and cultural conscience molds behavior so that we fit
in. This type of conscience acts as a limiting function and determines

what we are permitted or not permitted to do. In many ways, cultural conscience is similar to Freud's superego, which functions to keep our behavior within certain bounds.[21] Is there another conscience, one not subject to my particular country, environment, and the idiosyncrasies of chance? If so, what is its nature?

While cultural conscience serves the purpose of limiting and guiding behavior, it is different for every person and in every culture. It changes throughout our lives; it is subjective. We might think that such subjectivity is a good thing, since it might allow for individuality. On the other hand, its subjective nature causes people to relate to each other haphazardly, depending on the configuration of their conscience. This results in misunderstandings, arguments, or even wars, depending on the degree of difference. Cultural conscience has proved an ineffective, inaccurate apparatus for developing collaborative relationships.

It is important to ask whether we could develop a different type of conscience, a more accurate and useful capacity. Is there something inside of us that could be developed into a real conscience? Was there once an objective conscience that was the same for everyone and still allowed for essential individuality? Gurdjieff says that, fortunately for humankind, this type of conscience did exist, and it still exists in each person. However, what he called "objective conscience" was driven so deeply into our subconscious that it has survived relatively untouched, though in an embryonic state. He says:

> They "educate" their children never to be able and never to dare to do as the "conscience" present in them instinctively directs . . . Thanks to all this, the conscience which might be in the consciousness of the beings of that planet is from their earliest infancy, gradually "driven-back-within," so that by the time they are grown up the said conscience is already found only in what they call their subconscious-ness.[22]

The resurrection of objective conscience comes through gradual work on oneself. Objective conscience is a birthright, but activating it requires some emotional suffering. I caution you, most people are not interested in developing their real conscience. We do not need it to survive on the earth at our current level of development. In fact, it requires a great deal of suffering in order to develop a real conscience. Gurdjieff says this about why it so difficult for us to experience our objective conscience:

> *Conscience* is a state in which a man *feels all at once* every-thing that he in general feels, or can feel. And as everyone has within him thousands of contradictory feelings which vary from a deeply hidden realization of his own nothing-ness and fears of all kinds to the most stupid kind of self-conceit, self-confidence, self-satisfaction, and self-praise, to feel all this *together* would not only be painful but liter-ally unbearable . . . But fortunately for man, that is, for his peace and for his sleep, this state of conscience is very rare.[23]

In order to develop our essence, we will need the help of our buried, real conscience to come to life. This conscience is not the conscience of guilt, but actually a faculty that can support and guide us. My experi-ence with guilt is that it is a very poor aide in supporting me and helping direct my actions. When my real conscience is active, I have a real guide for my behavior, one that I can trust. This conscience is valuable. Gurd-jieff says this about it, "This conscience is not suffering; on the contrary it is joy of a totally new character which we are unable to understand." [24]

GROUP WORK

Group work contains aspects of giving and receiving. Some of us are good at giving and others at receiving. We need both aspects in our search for meaning—activity and receptivity. Those who speak too much need to learn to listen deeply, to quiet down inside so they can receive. Those who never share their inner life need the safety of a real group in order to allow them to share the meaning they find in their work. A Work group accelerates individual growth; each person learns from the others. The group provides a field where we can study our reac-tions, interactions, automatic judgments, projections, and needs; all this is immediately available to the alert searcher who can separate even slightly from his own automatic reactions. Additionally, even in a small group, understanding from a higher level may enter, possibly because individuals may connect to their higher centers in the group.

I am writing this section after meeting with a small Work group. A general aim of a Work group is to support each member in their quest for objective self-knowledge and development of essence, of their potential. It is difficult for me to put into words how much I value meeting with individuals who share a common aim centered on the development of inner life. Here, I can get feedback about my own work, support others in the unique practice of self-observation, and support another's self-discovery. I have found that people become mirrors for one another in a group working with Gurdjieff's ideas. I get a chance to see myself in a different way from anywhere else. Additionally, I can learn from someone else, since each member will bring experiences that are somewhat different from my own.

In the Gurdjieff Work, I meet many people I would not meet ordinarily. Perhaps I should say that our personalities would not have brought us together. In life, we surround ourselves with those who flatter or at least do not antagonize us. If they do, we end the relationship, often blaming them for the bad situation. On the other hand, some people continue unrewarding relationships, but maintain an inner account book containing what they believe other people owe them for their efforts. Most of my behavior with others is unconscious. The study of my ordinary relationships in life and my list of inner accounts can be a source of important information for me. I can then bring this material to Work meetings and find meanings with the group's help that I would have been unable to find on my own.

Group work is difficult at times. Parts of me do not want to collaborate, do not want others to see me, and do not want to share. Efforts at collaboration can bring up issues of competition and power. Sometime ago, I had invited some good friends from the East Coast to come and be a part of our group in California. It became very problematic for the group. The new couple acted in a very superior manner. They were extremely judgmental and looked at others as if they were damaged goods. In retrospect, I realized their attitude was a projection of their own insecurity. It arose from their fear that they themselves were the damaged ones. At times like these, individuals get a chance either to see themselves and their reactions or leave and blame the group and others as a justification for their reactions.

Gurdjieff groups seem quite prone to this type of projection. The leaders and/or members of these groups often have little under-standing of group dynamics. In fact, leaders of such groups may often believe that any knowledge of psychology is worthless. Because of this tendency of group members and leaders to ignore the phenomena of group dynamics, such as projection, splitting, and kill-the-leader tactics, these unconscious activities can fracture the group, spoiling the opportunity for real work.

Below, I list a few terms from psychology that all group members should become familiar with, both within themselves and in the group. It would help to develop a watchful understanding and compassionate stance toward these manifestations.

Splitting: The tendency of an individual or group of individuals to think about themselves and others, and their behaviors, only in black-and-white—no shades of grey allowed. This type of thinking leads to group polarization, if not realized and addressed. Splitting is an uncon-scious failure to integrate the good and bad aspects of another person into a unified whole. Individuals in close relationships or groups only see each other in very limited ways, not as complex individuals. They often engage in unconscious faultfinding in others and will seek to muster forces to resist them or release their aggression toward other members. Splitting can tear a group apart and is an important dynamic for leaders and group members to be aware of.

Projection: Individual defects and fears about oneself, often related to past experiences and situations, are automatically and unconsciously projected onto others and color the way we view others and our interac-tions with them.

*Kill-the-leade*r: Although not a technical psychological term, it represents the tendency in a group for members to unconsciously project their own stresses and inadequacies onto a group leader due to their beliefs about the personal failings of the leader.

Despite the difficulties I have listed, groups are indispensable. They provide the friction, direction, support, mirroring, and opportunity for insight that arises from working toward a common aim. In some ways, Work groups are similar to a marriage. A person has traits that attract you, and after a time those same traits begin to repel you. Of course, group work depends on the group having a clear direction. This can be provided by one or more individuals who have worked on themselves and who understand correctly the Work concepts. I have found that only those who have achieved some objective understanding and compassion for themselves and others can correctly support members to objectively know themselves. They are able to coach others in the practice of Gurdjieff's methods. However, it remains for the members to do their own work and make use of the tools and practices for themselves.

CHAPTER 7

KNOWING MYSELF HERE AND NOW

In a previous chapter, I spoke of the three different foods that we consume. Impressions are the finest and highest food we can assimilate. Normally, the process of taking in impressions is totally unconscious and automatic. When we begin to work and to study ourselves through self-observation, we begin to be able to consume impressions intentionally. In this chapter, we will look at some areas where we can gather new impressions of ourselves and verify for ourselves observations that Gurdjieff made regarding human behavior. I will also present some different methods I have found useful for perceiving new impressions and exploring psychological material.

OPENING TO NEW IMPRESSIONS

What do I mean when I use the word "impression"? For our purposes here, it is an effect, feeling, sensation, or image at least noticed or retained in a state of consciousness as a consequence of experience. In order to gather new impressions of myself, I may need to study in a way that at first seems counterintuitive. Many new activities seem counterintuitive at first. For example, when I was growing up in New York City, the idea of downhill skiing had always fascinated me. When I moved to California at age eighteen, I brought all my belongings, including a pair of someone's downhill skis, in my Volkswagen; but I never did any downhill skiing because I could not afford it. By the time I turned fifty, all my friends had given up cross-country skiing with me, saying it was too much work. It was then I learned to downhill ski. I loved the majesty of steep mountains and wanted to learn something physically demanding that required skillful use of my body.

Downhill skiing is counterintuitive. The natural tendency when standing on skis on a snowy, steep hill is to lean uphill into the "safety" of the hill, but such leaning back uphill has unintended consequences. On a steep hill, if you lean uphill, the weight is reduced on the cutting edge of the downhill ski—this downhill ski's edge is the one that allows you to make a turn and control your speed—if this downhill ski loses the weight that the ski's edge needs to cut into the snow, you actually increase your speed, lose control, and risk falling. Keeping your body perpendicular to the slope is what is needed, and it instinctively feels and cognitively appears counterintuitive, but that is exactly what is required. Being perpendicular to the slope of the hill seems as if you are leaning forward, leaning downhill. However, being perpendicular puts weight on the downhill ski, enabling you to make a controlled turn. You use the turning motion to reduce your speed or allow yourself to ski at whatever speed you wish without falling. In downhill skiing, my intuitive, emotional, and cognitive habits prove incorrect. Simply put, when you are new at a skill, your body, mind, and feelings may lead you in the wrong direction. You may need to learn something counterintuitive to natural tendencies.

Another example comes from child psychology. When a child is acting out, a parent's automatic reaction is to try to put a lid on the child's behavior. The parent says, "Stop acting like that," or "Stop running around crazily," or "Don't be angry, you have no reason to be angry," or "If you don't stop that, there will be consequences, _____ [fill in the blank]." Rarely does the parent say something more understanding, such as, "I get it, you're angry. I don't know what it's about, but let's just scream about it. Go ahead, yell, get it out." Or, "I can see you have got a lot of energy. Let's take our bikes and I'll ride with you as fast as we can. Come on, let's race." Then the child could burn off some of his excess energy. This type of parental intervention seems counterintuitive, because it is outside the parent's repertoire. The automatic attitude displayed by most parents is to stop any of the child's behavior they find unpleasant because it is disturbing to the parent's waking-sleep. The parent will say things that are negating and limiting, attempting to alter the child's behavior by labeling the action "bad." Remember my skiing example when I lean back to stop myself from falling down the hill, fearful and thinking the steepness will cause me to fall. This tendency to stop myself from experiencing something unpleasant may not produce the result I want and may produce an exact opposite result than that which I hoped for.

Later, in Chapter 15, we will look more closely at the relationship of a parent's attitudes to the paradoxical results they have on children. Now how does this all relate to seeing things in a new way, gathering new impressions and work on self-development? Self-knowledge is there all the time and is not that difficult to find. Below is a simple exercise to demonstrate that it is possible to gather new impressions of oneself at any time in any place without having to go to Tibet to find new experiences.

A Simple Practice in Gathering New Impressions

1. Accept as an experiment the following hypotheses:

- You tend to filter—see the new through the old—many, if not all, the new impressions you receive.

- You do not know very much about how your filtering mechanism works (similar to the way you use an automatic transmission in a car and don't really know much about it).

- You really wish to gather new impressions in your life, specifically new impressions of yourself.

2. Sit quietly in an armchair. Place your elbow on the arm of the chair, and then move your hand under your chin and rest your chin on your hand.

- Do it just the way you ordinarily do, without any change at all.

- Now, repeat the arm-hand-to-chin resting movement five times, just the way you habitually would.

3. Without trying to change this gesture in any way, allow yourself to become familiar with your automatic gestures. You are simply getting familiar with them, noticing then, not changing them in any way. You may find it is very difficult not to change, or you may want to adjust something you have become aware of.

4. Now, let your body expand its repertoire by allowing your body to continue to move in another automatic movement.

- Notice the next thing your body will do with the hand under the chin. Perhaps it will scratch somewhere.

- It makes no difference what your body does, just notice it; and then repeat it a number of times.

5. The aim here is to intentionally allow your body to be automatic. The difference between the exercise and your habitual patterns is that you are intentionally allowing the gestures to be automatic while being present to the habitual movements.

This exercise may seem silly to you at first, but you may receive some new impressions from it. Remember, this is about learning through actual experience. You are gathering new impressions by acting counterintuitively.

I normally do not intentionally allow my body to move automatically. Now, by intentionally allowing my body to move automatically and even encouraging it, I am establishing a new relationship with my moving center. Actually, I am creating a new relationship with the automatic, habitual manifestations of my body. Later, this ability can allow me to connect in a new way to more complex behaviors and situations. These directions are a first step toward a method of participation. In Chapter 16 entitled "Participation" we will look more deeply into the rich possibilities of working in this way.

DENIAL

One of the most difficult things I have had to accept about myself is the degree of denial in which I live. Denial seems to be a survival tool for living in the modern culture. I drive to work in my car, and I notice Hispanic farm workers riding bicycles to work on the narrow roads near where I live. I wonder if they have a roof over their heads at night. I realize a part of me does not want to notice them too much.

Their situation reminds me of a time when I was three years old, walking with my grandmother in New York City. I was walking carefully, balancing on the curb at the edge of the sidewalk heading back to our apartment building. My grandmother was holding my hand as I walked on the curb. I noticed a Puerto Rican woman walking right next to the buildings going in the same direction we were. She was holding the hand of a child about my age. Inside, I realized even then that I would probably have opportunities in my life the other boy would never have. I felt sad and even some responsibility. Today, whenever I travel in third-world countries or see people living in depressed economic conditions, it pains me. I see poverty even in Santa Rosa, where I work. However, the continual exposure to impressions of poverty and inequality has gradually trained me not to see the issues before me.

As a civilization, our denial of the incongruities, inequities, and injustices apparent in our lives is epidemic. This myopia to the obvious becomes deeply ingrained. Perhaps the only real chance I have to transmute my state of denial is through inner work. The Work goes directly against my state of denial. The more I see myself, the more difficult it is to hide from the truth. The study of my personal denial has been for me a means to understand the multiple nature of the human psyche as the seeing dissolves the psychological buffers (barriers) separating my various "I's." [1] Buffers are psychological appliances that act like walls separating distinct "I's" from each other. We will look more closely at buffers a little later.

A Simple Exercise for Observation of Personal Denial

Make a list of the incongruities you can notice about yourself. They need not be complex. Some examples:

1. Notice how you spend money and whether or not you wish to save it.

2. Notice aims that you have now or have had in the past and how you spend your time instead.

3. Notice promises and commitments you make to yourself or others and how or if you fulfill them.

4. Notice the time commitments you make, and then see how you use your time.

5. Notice your prejudices, your likes and dislikes about others' behaviors, even with close acquaintances and how you behave with them. Is your behavior indicative of your inner feelings toward them?

6. Notice how or when you lie or exaggerate.

Do not use the information you develop from your list to criticize yourself or to make you better. Rather, it is a starting point to view and experience your habitual denial. There is no need to try to change. Change results from receiving impressions from repeated efforts at self-awareness. Self-awareness allows a new force to enter. We need now to observe, notice, and become familiar with what is going on with us. Then, at certain moments, we may glimpse a new possibility and find increased freedom of action.

Self-Calming

The idea of denial is now widely accepted in psychotherapy, as well as in popular culture. Gurdjieff frequently used the term "self-calming" to describe how we tend to suppress anything that might disturb our sleep.[2] The main characteristic of self-calming is its automaticity and the ease with which it takes us away from anxiety. Modern culture is addicted to self-calming. The depth of this addiction is so great that we usually are unable to see it in ourselves. However, we can easily see denial in others when their behavior is contradictory or does not conform to society's norms. For example, we are quick to say that someone who is addicted to illegal drugs, alcohol or gambling and is clearly destroying their life, is doubtless in denial. Surprisingly, society turns a blind eye to addictions like power, greed, and consumerism. They are considered normal and even held up as desirable.

Self-calming may take the form of daydreams; for example, repeated fantasizing about a new car, dress, person, shoes, camera, degree, money, power, an occasion where I will stand out, or perhaps the most fantasized of all, sex. The different modes of self-calming are too numerous to list here, but prove to be a rewarding area for self-study if I wish to know myself.

We learned self-calming in childhood, when we were overwhelmed by feelings of helplessness in situations we, as children, could not control. Its myriad varieties were created within us to defend our fragile psyches against being overwhelmed. Self-calming habits compensate for overwhelm and take on a life of their own. I may take a drink after work or smoke a cigarette as a means of self-calming. These activities produce a reduction in anxiety and easily become habitual and self-reinforcing. Each of us needs a certain degree of self-calming to help us adjust to the stresses of modern life. However, I may find the central focus of my day or week is propelled by the need to self-calm—the "Thank God its Friday" party, for example. Self-calming might entail compulsive listening to the radio the entire day with earphones, compulsive searching on the Internet, texting, or compulsively fantasizing as an attempt to block out a terrible moment of my past. You can often spot self-calming behavior by its characteristic of compulsiveness. I find I engage in the behavior regardless of the things I really need to do.

Study yourself and you will become familiar with your self-calming repertoire. There is no need to change anything at this stage. If you change one thing, it will almost always have an unpredictable effect on your other behavior. Simply become familiar with your patterns. Change will occur gradually as a result of your observations.

There is no need to judge the self-calming behaviors you find, although this will undoubtedly take place; they are neither good nor bad. The purpose of becoming familiar with them is to help you to know yourself and have moments of waking up, finding moments of choice as to how you wish to spend your time. Perhaps this tendency toward self-calming needs a more exact name. "Self-distracting" behavior might be more accurate. Each of us has certain "I's" that long ago became experts at distracting us from the deeper wish for growth. These "I's" do not want you to notice them and would rather remain hidden. The more you know and understand them, the greater your possibility of finding new ways to compensate for feeling overwhelmed or anxious, ways that will actually nurture you.

INTERNAL AND EXTERNAL CONSIDERING

> Only he may enter here who puts himself in the position
> of the other results of my labors.[3]
> —G.I. Gurdjieff

In *Beelzebub's Tales to His Grandson*, Beelzebub tells his grandson, Hassein, that the phrase quoted above was inscribed over the portal to the Holy Planet Purgatory. To put oneself in the position of the other results of the labors of His Endlessness means I must put myself in the shoes of another. As Gurdjieff says, I must "consider externally."

All religions emphasize taking others into consideration. But it really takes self-study to see that my life is mostly egocentric. People think and act as if life exists and revolves around them exclusively to fulfill their desires. If I look carefully, I find I almost always consider myself first, even when it looks like I am considering another. Sometimes, though, I can recognize a real need of another person. The situation calls me. Then, regardless of my desires, I can respond appropriately. Sadly, this recognition is the exception. Seeing so much of this self-centered behavior in myself, I became curious to find out whether this self-centeredness was intrinsic to me, was a learned habit, was part of human nature, or perhaps a function of all three.

I found that most of my self-centered traits were copied from others while I was growing up. Gradually, they became part of my socialized nature, reinforced by my own natural tendencies toward self-centeredness. Finally, society furthered the development of an entitled, self-centered inner considering in me. Eventually, I became an ordinary egoist just like everyone else.

Internal considering or self-centeredness is the hallmark of egoism. I myself thought I had many altruistic traits and was sure I did consider externally—at least sometimes—but what about those other times? Then I thought, "I must resist my egoism, give more to others. People who go to church and do good deeds are different, they are not merely self-centered." That is what I thought. The entire subject forced me to think more deeply about internal considering, egoism, and external considering.

Gurdjieff's dictum that to be a real altruist one must first be an out-and-out egoist, did not make sense to me until I was willing to imagine myself as being completely selfish. Then, a light bulb went on inside me. Of course, I thought, "The ultimate selfishness for me is to become a real, fully developed human being. Wouldn't that be the height of real egoism?" After considering, I realized I believed the answer to my question was yes. What got in the way at first was my thinking about ego. The term often has a negative connotation. However, egoism is not negative when its focus is the nurturance and development of my true human capacities. You could interpret Gurdjieff's statement to mean, "In order to be able to give to others, one must first develop oneself fully." Let us look at some of the finer points of altruism.

Generally, I give lip service to the concept of considering others. Considering others is an important aspect of living a responsible life. However, the word "consider" can have two quite different and even opposite meanings. Gurdjieff distinguished "inner" or "internal considering" from "external considering." Internal considering is concerned with how I imagine I will appear to others, with getting my full share, and with feeding all the insatiable needs of my personality. I find it is always an automatic reaction to outer stimuli, where I am afraid I will not get my fair share. When I consider externally, however, I deal with the real world and the actual welfare of others, finding and responding to what is needed in a situation.

If I wish to consider externally, I must first study my self-centeredness. Without a good deal of self-knowledge, I can fall into being what I call "church" good. This type of outer conformity does not lead to greater freedom, but to another type of bondage. It is conforming to what I believe others think I ought to be doing. Learning to consider externally is a gradual process. It requires being present in order to see I stand in front of choices. I must first learn to experience my self-centeredness when I notice the needs of others. Only then, might I choose how I will respond.

When I am the center of the universe, I am preoccupied with what others think about me or what I want. A waitress does not respond to me as quickly as I feel she should. Immediately, my hackles are raised and I am ready to strike. When I speak to her, I may mask my feelings and sound only slightly annoyed. I believe I am in full control, but my annoyance with her is obvious to everyone. In another situation, I may feel someone has not realized who I am, not given me enough respect or not acted toward me the way I would have acted toward him. These people have not considered me enough! I want them to "externally consider" me, whereas constantly I am "inwardly considering" how other people view me. Of course, I am especially concerned about my friends and clients in business since my ability to earn a living depends on them. As long as people see me the way I want them to, I believe it really does not matter what I do or feel inwardly. When a person feels and thinks one way inside and behaves completely differently outwardly, we say he has a psychological split. Gurdjieff might say that one "I" is unaware of another. People are generally unaware of their interior splits.

When I feel someone has not considered me sufficiently, a certain something begins to take place in me emotionally. What is this something; more precisely, what does it taste like? Am I able to let go of the taste or does it linger? I believe it is the taste of hatred—I am angry, hate being treated that way, and hate the other person. Alternatively, I am hurt, and my anger masks my hurt feelings and vulnerability. This is a wonderful arena in which to study hatred or hurt. Perhaps you may object to the use of the word "hatred," or maybe you believe I should simply call it annoyance. Maybe you are right, but feel it, taste it. Then decide for yourself if there is not a slight tinge of hatred there.

On the other hand, how does it feel to consider externally, to consider another? Can you put yourself in another person's place? To learn how to put myself in another's place is a way to free myself from the slavery of inner considering. As long as internal considering always occupies me, there is little room to recognize the needs of another person or a situation. Only by studying inner considering can I get a realistic picture of my relationships. If each of us remains caught in the world of inner considering, it is actually impossible to have a real relationship.

Inner considering is an integral aspect of personality, and you must be gentle and clever to see it. The taste of inner considering is bitter, and it even may feel physically toxic, if you are able to notice it. I get tastes of it all the time, but remain unaware of them. Just as I may eat dinner automatically, not really tasting my food, I miss the taste of inner considering because it has become so habitual.

Seeing myself through my own efforts is very different from having a teacher, leader, friend, or therapist point out how I am. Another person's viewpoint can undoubtedly help me. However, very few people can imagine the wonderful transformation that is possible when they initiate their own work. Self-initiation allows you to carry your wish forward, and experience overcoming your resistance or inertia.

In my experience, external considering is an aspect of our capacity for compassion. My search led me to ask the question, how can I possibly have compassion for another unless I first develop it in relation to myself? I will return to this question throughout this book.

STRIVING AND WISH

What does it means to strive toward a goal? Striving relates to desire or wish. We want an academic degree so that we can be an accountant or a stockbroker, and we strive toward that goal. We get frustrated along the way and learn to push through to get a job or make money. Some of us are luckier than others, and our striving gets us to our goal. Others are not so lucky and fail. We rarely ask ourselves, what is unique about striving?

To strive means to expend emotional energy. We call this energy "wish." Without wish, it is virtually impossible to accomplish any aim. Wish is a word we are all familiar with. We wish all the time. We wish to go on vacation, get a new car, find a girlfriend or boyfriend, get more money, and on and on. We squander our wish, our special emotional energy, without ever understanding it. Most people have never thought deeply about the experience of wishing.

Often, when I raise the topic of wish with clients, they look at me and cannot quite understand. I say to them, "You cannot get up and open my office door unless you wish to." Sometimes I challenge them to leave my office without wishing to. They sit on the couch and look at the door. Then something clicks. They realize they are frozen on the couch. They cannot get up and go to the door unless something in them wishes to. Up to that moment, their wishing has been mechanical, automatic, unconscious. They never realized they were using their ability to wish all the time. Their wish was only connected with getting material objects, a relationship, money, a good grade in school, a job, or sex. Unfortunately, their brief glimpse into the power of wish is generally short-lived. Rarely does anyone mention it again.

In the Gurdjieff Work, the energy of my wish determines how much I can work. If you have no wish for work, rest assured, you will not move from your present predicament. Sometimes I can feel a deep wish as a yearning for more from my life, sometimes even as a sensation in my chest. Pay attention to this deep longing if you feel it. Notice how it fluctuates, is stronger or weaker at different times, how it periodically comes to the surface and then descends beneath your awareness.

To get in touch with wish often requires being quiet for some time. Sit quietly in a chair for fifteen minutes. Then ask yourself the question: "What do I wish for in my life?" Sit quietly and see what happens. If an answer comes in words, then repeat the question. Continue questioning a number of times, until you can differentiate between an automatic answer and the emotional force, the wish, the longing that is drawing forth the answer.

FRUSTRATION AND RESISTANCE

Counter to the wish to work is resistance, experienced as frustration, an automatic emotional reaction to effort. No one has ever taught us about resistance and our automatic response to it—that is, frustration, negativity, or anger. Gurdjieff says this resisting force is the second fundamental force in the universe, the "Holy Denying." [4] However, this force only becomes "holy" for us as individuals if we can appreciate its importance in our work.

Resistance, the denying force, is unknown to modern education. The only places we find anything remotely resembling it are in physics or Marxian dialectic. Not only do we not study our resistance, it annoys us, and we try in every way we can to get around it. Finally, we just get mad. Although traditional psychoanalytic theory has recognized resistance for almost one hundred years, current psychological research does not address the subject.

If we become sincerely interested in resistance, curious about our frustration, interested in the capacity hidden in our unconscious reactions to resistance, we might find a great treasure, a source of unlimited energy. But few are interested in finding the meaning within or behind resistance. Instead, we are interested in the iPhone, the latest movie, or just going to sleep. I say "we," because I am talking about myself also. I am not immune to anything I am writing about here. In fact, I am a continuous victim of my unconscious behavior; but at least I can see it at times. My semiconscious life, like everyone else's, is the unfortunate result of the lack of real education, particularly, the education of my emotions, but at least I realize my position. This realization motivates me and helps me to engage in my reeducation.

The hidden treasure that lies within the force of resistance is that it presents us with the possibility of developing real will. Without resistance, we cannot develop will. Real will recognizes the effect of resistance, takes it into account, and uses it as fuel. We had experiences of real will in the past, when as small children we desperately wanted to move from crawling to walking, wanted to speak, write, or overcome whatever frustrated us. Children demonstrate the will to struggle; they fail and yet they persist. As we know, mistakes and failures are an integral part of the learning process. When learning to walk, we got hurt when we fell, we were frustrated, but it also elated us to try again. We have forgotten how incredible it all felt. We were in touch with the miraculous, the impossible.

In accomplishing the transition from crawling to upright walking, we overcame resistance, almost drowned in it, but then used it, and finally walked with it. In fact, walking is a beautiful example of how we use resistance to fall from one foot to another. Of course, walking quickly becomes a habitual, unconscious activity and you can only notice its characteristics if you are in pain or if you pay attention to it. As an experiment, try and notice your walking. Slow it down, and you may find out what it is all about. Without resistance, without being able to push the floor away, we cannot go forward. Now, wouldn't it have been nice to know all these years that walking was actually a controlled fall? Verify it yourself.

Learning how to use resistance is the first step in learning how to intentionally struggle. It is the foundation for developing authentic will. Real will is not what we call "will power," which is merely the dominance of one center over another or the momentary dominance of one small wish, or "I," over others. I must be conscious of resistance in order to engage in real struggle. If I only struggle unconsciously (that is, struggle to get what I want from a situation) without awareness of resistance, then I will never realize the role of resistance and the part it plays in my inner development. Resistance becomes a gift if I can learn to use it.

Chapter 8

THE MOVEMENTS

After so much intellectual explanation, it is good to speak about a practice that I have come to love in a special way, a practice that fully involves the body. Words are inadequate to describe the uniqueness of this Gurdjieffian practice. Ballet and certain ethnic dances may give a clue to what Gurdjieff's gift of music and body practices contain. In this chapter, I will try to give you a taste of what I believe is an example of an objectively complete system of education.

A Method Of Balance

Gurdjieff described himself as a "teacher of dancing." One of his greatest gifts to us was the group of dances and exercises he referred to as "Sacred Dances." We now call them the "Movements." The Movements provide education of the three centers in its most accessible form.

Movements are practiced in a group, with a teacher at the front of the room. The students stand in various arrangements, but usually in six files facing the teacher. Ideally, there are at least two rows. Generally, there is piano accompaniment. The pianist sits in such a way that he or she can see both the instructor and the class, so they can respond to the teacher's indications and see what the students are doing.

The class often begins with exercises that are either part of the instructor's repertoire or invented by her in the moment. They are tailored to the energy and ability levels of the class. There are multiple demands on the students. They must engage their attention and work on all three centers at once, while working on the exercises or the actual Movements. The demands on a student depend on her ability, experience, and the movements she has previously studied. The first demand is that the student learn the positions of the given movement and their sequence. This is her individual work. Second, she must work in time with the music as well as heed any instructions. Third, the student must collaborate with the other members of the class, line up with her file and row, and stay in touch with the class as a whole. The physical demands of mastering the Movements can create a container for the emotional and intellectual demands that become evident as the student struggles to learn the particular set of gestures.

A movement may include a series of leg positions and leg movements. Simultaneously, there may be a complicated series of arm movements, head movements, bending, and even singing at times. In more advanced movements, students displace from their usual positions. The displacements and combinations of students' positions in files and rows add another layer of complexity. In many ways, learning Movements mimics learning a language, except the entire body is expressing the language. We must engage the entire body, our emotions, and mind in order to learn the language of the movement. It is difficult to describe the beauty, intricacy, and yet brilliant simplicity of the Movements, harder still to describe the experience of doing them. Learning the Movements is similar to learning to play an extremely difficult piano piece, but in this case, the instrument is myself.

No matter how well I execute the movement gymnastically, that is not the aim. More important is learning about myself while in movement, for I can never exhaust what the Movements can teach me. They permit me to gather seeds of understanding myself that I can only come to when I struggle. The Movements exist on an objective level and are similar to a library that I have access to for moments at a time. An individual begins just where he is, and the practice of working at the Movements reveals insights commensurate with his or her work.

The Movements are unique and vastly different from any other way or form. They are unlike Tai Chi or other martial art that contains a very limited set of gestures. Proponents of martial arts would argue that their particular form contains great meaning. However, martial arts are meant as an individual practice (although performed in a group setting). In contrast, Gurdjieff intended Movements to be both an individual and group practice. Their collaborative structure requires an awareness of others that immediately sets them apart. Gurdjieff spoke of three lines of work: work on myself, work with others, and work for the Work. While practicing Movements, I become aware not only of working on myself, but of working with others as well, an extremely important aspect of Gurdjieff's Work.

Other differences from martial arts become apparent. The Movements seem structured, artificial in some ways, yet very organic in others. We perform them neither to make us feel at ease in the face of attack nor to master the gestures so that they become automatic and we can relax. They bear no resemblance to "authentic movement," as it is strangely called, where there is no demand to move in a precise manner. They demand your attention, and demand you learn how to move in a new way.

THREE-CENTERED ACTIVITY

Movements are the most sophisticated and complete system I have encountered for developing a correct relationship with the body as well as simultaneous coordination and development of our three main centers. Almost every moment of our so-called "waking" consciousness is associated with automatic, unconscious movements. Our inability to inhabit the body leads to various dysfunctions ranging from susceptibility to disease to proneness to accidents. We hold our bodies rigid when there is no need to, wasting an incredible amount of energy. Similarly, we cannot relax when we wish to. All of this unnecessary muscular tension wastes energy, disrupts our sleep, and affects sexual experience. We lack grace in our movements, and only trained dancers or athletes seem to move in a way that is appropriate to our species. Most of us inhabit our bodies the way we stay in a motel. We treat the body as if we were just passing through, and we never get to live in our own home.

Movements are in many ways like a hologram of the Fourth Way; that is, they are a means of teaching our three major centers to work together—the intellectual, emotional, and moving. Working with Movements, for me, is a primary arena for three-centered study of myself. I believe Gurdjieff designed them to allow us to approach higher knowledge and connect with our higher centers.

The Movements demand both outer and inner work. The outer work is concerned with learning the form and directing your body to move with the music and the others in the class. However, the deeper emphasis in movements is on inner work. The Movements engage me in learning how to struggle, learning about my own psychology, and understanding the beauty and force of working with others.

Movements help me to see the prison of my self-image. I see my reaction to frustration; how difficult it is to maintain my attention in a nonhabitual way—even for a few seconds—and how to move in concert with others in an intricate pattern. Persistence through participation in the Movements will gradually give a taste of three-centered work, how it feels to be a complete human being. It is a taste not easily forgotten.

Three-centered work is different than most of the activities that I engage in. I can be shopping in the grocery store or even doing therapy, and my mind can wander, my emotions can be activated by any thought or sensation. In short, I can do many things in life with one center while the other centers are either not engaged or drift off in fantasy or go in a completely different direction. This is easily verifiable if you drive a car. You drive automatically while your mind and emotions are haphazardly engaged in associations that have nothing to do with driving.

The three-centered work the Movements demand is different, but is not foreign to our nature. Yet, ordinarily, most of our activities require us to engage only one center at a time. However, in Movements, a single movement may contain a separate task for each of the three centers. Each center must work on its own task, and then I have the effort of blending them together. Through this struggle, I can experience a previously unknown part of myself, a part that has always been there, only in embryonic form. Although initial efforts at learning the piano or other musical instrument, learning to swim, play tennis, or other complex behaviors may require different degrees of three-centered learning, none of them remotely approximates the learning possibilities inherent in Movements.

EMOTIONAL AWAKENING

Nature completes the development of the moving center by the time an individual is approximately eighteen years old. We then live out our lives with hardly any more development in this center, other than perhaps learning a new sport or a dance step. Nevertheless, since real understanding of myself requires a balanced development of all three major centers, I can develop the moving center further by directing and developing my body's abilities in conjunction with my emotional and intellectual centers. Movements at first may feel artificial and unnatural, but the unaccustomed positions bring me out of my habitual way of moving and shocks the other two centers awake. These shocks then generate new impressions for me and require me to engage in three-centered activity.

Practicing Movements can teach us how to raise our own energy level. In addition, the emotional development that becomes possible through Movements goes far beyond the struggle with frustration or vanity. Moreover, the emotions the Movements and its unique music evoke are of a special type, at times allowing one to experience the higher emotional center. Gurdjieff speaks about the possibility of "objective" music; that is, music that has the same effect on any person irrespective of their culture.[1] The Movements music contains such an objective quality. Working with Movements provides a unique opportunity to experience a timeless and objective world.

For most people, our emotions are an enigma. We are aware of how we feel when we succeed or fail in achieving some small accomplishment. However, the subtleties of the emotional center elude us, and most of the time, we aren't interested in anything subtle. We can only guess what being in touch with more subtle emotions would be like. Working in Movements may give us a glimpse of these subtle aspects of our true nature.

Although the Movements are part of group work, they are also uniquely tailored to awaken my emotional life. I find them to be one of the few activities that place me simultaneously in front of my own limitations and in front of opportunities for development. Here is the paradox: We all would like to have a teacher of our own who is uniquely suited to us. The place we fail to look for this teacher is inside us. The Movements provide the conditions for activating our own teacher and a place where we can listen to this teacher.

Working in Movements encourages us to develop a new attitude toward learning, to bear the friction, frustration, and energy that working with difficult movements generates. In order to execute the desired movement correctly, something may need to break apart within me and reunite in a new way. This deconstruction and reconstruction is similar to the healing process in psychotherapy. Disintegration is required before new integration can occur. Each time I practice the Movements, I can discover something new, some important aspect of myself that I could not find any other way. Ordinarily, one might need a lifetime of activity to develop what the Movements can develop within just a few years. Work with the Movements can reawaken the original "sovereign learner" that was present in us as children.[2]

I feel an indescribable harmony and beauty when working with the Movements. The music and the positions convey an experience that transcends my ordinary life. At times, when I have struggled to master a series of positions, the music combined with my effort bring me to a place in myself that feels timeless. For many people, this sense of transcendence may be the overriding reason they work with the Movements—they touch a different world locked within them.

I find it sad that many, who appreciate Gurdjieff's Work intellectually and emotionally, may remain relatively uninterested in developing their moving center as well. They may never achieve the full understanding they seek without initiation into the Movements. Without Movements, the Work may give us only knowledge, ideas or concepts, without the full possibility of understanding. The practice of Movements brings Work ideas into our experience in a form accessible to anyone who is sincere. Movements offer me a place where I can directly experience knowledge, ideas, and concepts in a manner that provides understanding that can never be achieved with our ordinary mind. The two fundamental laws of the universe (the Law of Three and the Law of Sevenfoldness) to which we are subject can never be understood with the intellect alone. They must in fact be experienced and this requires a special work and transformation of my being. Work with the Movements provides a container where this transformation may be undertaken.

For me, work with Movements has been a place of deep, inexhaustible learning. I have experienced a harmony, joy of moving, and an understanding that represents the most complete life experience I have ever had. I encourage anyone who is sincerely interested in personal development to begin working with Movements with all deliberate speed. Movements can become a source of inspiration and transformation for all those who sincerely wish to work. But you will need to search for a group that understands the Work and appreciates the inner process involved in working with the Movements rather than simply mastering their performance.

PART III

THE ELUSIVE "I"

CHAPTER 9

WAKING UP TO NEW POSSIBILITIES

> All this is inherent in saying that there is the action
> that is beyond control of any power at all, that Gurdjieff
> calls the "Merciless Heropass." As the system grows in
> complexity, a certain moment arrives when it is no longer
> possible to control it because anything that is done to
> control it introduces more disorder than it can rectify.[1]
> —J. G. Bennett

We will need to develop greater sensitivity towards ourselves as we begin to understand more clearly our place in the greater world. We especially must understand how to transform our emotional life. In this chapter, we will look at various aspects of the human psyche and the problems inherent in personal self-study. As a background to keep in mind as we explore some of the subtleties of Work, I introduce Gurdjieff's "Strivings." These strivings provide a larger framework so that we can understand our place and purpose in the enlarging world. I go on to introduce a range of psychological topics that I have found of particular value in my personal work.

FUNDAMENTAL STRIVINGS

I believe that two of the fundamental questions about life that should arise for a truly responsible person are the questions of the purpose of life and the role of humanity. For me, these questions came to the fore when I was in my early twenties studying at the University of California, Berkeley. They have resurfaced continually throughout my life and have taken on greater importance for me as I have matured.

When someone first meets this Work and is sincere, he may sense an objective source from which it emanates. A person's first contact often leads him toward the cosmology and philosophy of Gurdjieff. Questions may arise as to why this possibility of Work exists and why it attracts him. It is not for everyone.

Many of the practices I have already mentioned do not exist in a vacuum. They were designed to accomplish a number of aims. That the personal, psychological work relates to a larger objective framework is for me its most important aspect. This raises the question of the purpose of Work and the purpose of life that I surmise has no doubt arisen for each of us at one time or another. Our work suffers when we ignore the foundation that gives it purpose and meaning. The Work is a system that demonstrates the interconnectedness of everything that exists and assigns a purpose to each separate interconnected piece. In this way, it solves the ancient question of separateness and oneness. A person, planet, flower, action, or anything else we can conceive of can be placed within this system. The aim we share is for each of us to understand as much as we can of our individual purpose within this larger integrated whole. In order to summarize the place of human beings in this larger world, Gurdjieff elaborated the "Obligolnian Strivings."

Below are the Obligolnian Strivings. They are Gurdjieff's shorthand version of the objectives to keep in mind for our personal work. Gurdjieff links them to the development of the divine function of genuine conscience.[2] These strivings reveal larger responsibilities inherent in an individual's real purpose. I have listed them below in their entirety because of the great importance I place on them.

> The first striving: to have in their ordinary being-existence everything satisfying and really necessary for their planetary body.

> The second striving: to have a constant and unflagging instinctive need for self-perfection in the sense of being.

> The third striving: the conscious striving to know ever more and more concerning the laws of World-creation and World-maintenance.

> The fourth striving: the striving from the beginning of their existence to pay for their arising and their individuality as quickly as possible, in order afterwards to be free to

lighten as much as possible the Sorrow of our COMMON FATHER.

The fifth striving: the striving always to assist the most rapid perfecting of other beings, both those similar to oneself and those of other forms, up to the degree of the sacred "Martfotai," that is up to the degree of self-individuality.[3]

HOW TO WORK

This book is more about the how of working on oneself rather than a mere intellectual discussion. That being said, certain fundamental concepts are important to keep in mind. Three main concepts underpin the work of the transformation of consciousness:

1. Not identifying. Positively restated as the practice of disidentifying, to witness one's existence, to separate an inner part of oneself.

2. Self-remembering: to remember the existence of oneself and one's aim.

3. Not to internally consider. Positively restated as to externally consider.

Each of these factors is both an aim and a practice, but I will simply use the word "practice." Two of these practices—not identifying and not internally considering—seem to have a negative connotation, because I am attempting not to do something. As such, they have a contracting feeling. The other is positive: self-remembering. However, if I frame not identifying and not internally considering positively, something changes in me psychologically. For example, if I externally consider, rather than not internally considering, I experience something quite different. In addition, I find "disidentified" to be a much clearer term than "non-identification" or to "not to be identified." To "disidentify" connotes a positive action. It conveys a different image; I find even my bodily experience of this word is different. The idea that I might disidentify places me in a positive frame of mind rather than trying "not to identify." I will speak more about "disidentification" below.

Here again we are talking about the "how" and not the "what." The "what" is the aim. For the "how," I need certain things in hand. I need to investigate my habit to always consider internally, rather than externally, not an easy task. In addition, I may need to experiment with "amplification." Amplification occurs when I *intentionally increase* the manifestation of a reaction or thought somewhat more than I would normally manifest it.

For example, in order to study internal considering, I might actually accentuate it in a given situation. You must try it for yourself. In my experience, if I am willing to amplify a trait I see in myself, then I am taking a step toward increasing my consciousness of it, and how it affects me and others. In this way, I can experience its effects both emotionally and physically more distinctly. I'll explain this with an example of what Gurdjieff calls "negative emotion."

Some years ago, I had a profound emotional experience that persisted for a number of months. I was studying for a licensing examination in psychology. While I was preparing, I became very anxious. I decided early on that it might be impossible to expect my anxiety simply to evaporate. I realized that, even if I could manage to reduce my anxiety in practice exams, I probably still would be terribly anxious during the actual exam. Therefore, I made a commitment to experience my anxiety deeply, to take my practice tests fully expecting and inviting the anxiety to be there. This tactic helped greatly, and I passed the exam while experiencing only a bit more anxiety than during my practice.

However, the real gift was my realization that anxiety is a definite type of identification. My anxiety has specific, somatic indications that are fairly recognizable to me. Perspiring, tightness in my chest, and a little bit of shakiness made me feel as if I were ill. At first, this may seem like a simple deduction, but it had profound repercussions for my work. I began to notice the times I felt similarly ill during the week. It felt almost as if I was catching a cold. By increasing my sensitivity to these physiological sensations, I realized I felt a little bit sick whenever I was anxious, worried, or according to my realization, identified.

Gurdjieff said we need "alarm clocks" to shock us awake from the usual trance state we consider "being awake." I need alarm clocks as reminders to work, to observe, to remember myself. Pretty soon, I get used to one kind of alarm clock and need to invent a new one. An alarm clock may be as simple as a note left on my dashboard reminding me to work or wearing my watch on the opposite wrist.

I noticed I could use the sensation of feeling sick as an alarm clock. It helped me remember myself (remember that I exist now as I am doing something) and pay attention to my state of identification; usually, some worry or another. My anxiety or sick feeling became a key, telling me I was identified. When you are sick, what do you usually do? You want to stop feeling sick, and you take a variety of medications to that end. It might seem silly if I said that one should attempt to sink deeply into feeling sick. However, I found that was precisely what was useful in relation to my anxiety: to experience the actual sensations my body produced.

I gradually found that I needed to look more closely at the relationship of somatic experience to my negative, identified states. Negative emotions (unpleasant emotions) include anxiety, worry, anger, fear, jealousy, greed, the need for power and control, paranoia, guilt, blame, self-pity, and hatred, to name just few. Confusion and feelings of overwhelm also seem connected with identification and negative emotions. I became very interested in the physical or physiological sensations each of these identified states produce in my body and began to pay particular attention to them.

AMPLIFICATION

Let me make a distinction here. There is a difference between identification with a negative emotion, repression of a negative emotion, projection of a negative emotion, and finally, the useful expression of a negative emotion. We are so used to repressing our negative emotions that we don't see them. They don't go away when we repress them. Instead, we hold them as tensions in our body, and they may go unnoticed for years, until such constant stress makes us ill.

For example, one of my clients holds tension in her neck and shoulders when she is stressed. I suspect her tension in these areas arises from an unconscious attempt to defend herself or keep from experiencing a painful emotion. Perhaps it is sadness, fear, or shame. It does not help to tell her, "Relax your neck muscles," or "Don't tighten your neck and shoulder muscles." This would be like saying to myself, "Don't internally consider," or "Don't identify." In fact, I have discovered people are usually unaware of their habits of holding their muscles in a particular pattern of tension. They may not even experience any tension at all in the areas where they hold it. They suffer from what psychologists call "muscular amnesia." They tensed these muscles at some time in the past, and through repeating the tensing in similar situations, their muscles do not remember; that is, they have no somatic consciousness of being tense. The muscles in this case need to be shown how to "remember."

Therefore, in the above case, the "what" my client needs is more relaxed neck muscles. You might think the "how," will be to simply tell her to relax her neck and shoulder muscles. But this method does not work. Instead, I said to her, "I notice your neck and shoulder muscles are tight by the way you are holding yourself. I want you to tighten the muscles in your shoulders and neck right now. I want you to tense them. Okay, now hold that tension. Can you feel it?" After a short time, she said, "Yes, I can feel it." Now I told her, "All right, now loosen the muscles, very slowly, just a little bit at a time."

It seems so simple. Yet, for the first time in perhaps forty years, the amplification of her habitual muscular tension has helped her to come in touch with her own body in a way that hitherto was impossible. In her entire adult life, she was unaware of her muscular tension; but now, the amnesic tension in her neck muscles relaxes, and she becomes conscious of how she was holding her stress. I had her repeat the tensing and slow relaxing until she became truly familiar with the tension in her shoulders. Next, I helped her to use these new impressions of herself to make connections with the emotions that caused her tension. Very often, a simple investigation of some somatic tension can lead into a deep exploration of a person's life and provide new understanding.

I am proposing that the same sequence of amplification I use in therapy can be useful for us in our self-study. What we need is to engage in the particular identification, be it complaining, anxiety, worry, etc., and become familiar with it, not to try "not to identify." Instead, be identified, but also be present with your identification.

If you notice the sensations in your body when you become upset or tense, and then sense your body and continue to experience the unpleasant sensations, you are engaging your identification and will receive new impressions of yourself. This "how"—noticing your ordinary bodily sensations and then sensing when you are upset—can provide new impressions. By contrast, the attempt to "not be identified" usually occurs within the thinking center alone and usually produces very few new impressions. Instead, I think about work and fantasize that I am not identified. Thus, when you find you are identified, sensing indirectly changes your identification, subtly loosening its bonds. This is what I call a "backdoor approach" to small experiences of freedom.

The entire work of amplification is a practical means to explore the difference between knowing something about Work ideas and actually practicing them. By working with identification and internal considering, I can transform my life. Knowing about something is good for discussions at a party. Practice is the only thing that actually changes me.

Clients often experience new emotions when they begin to pay attention to their sensations and emotions as I have described. I usually do not bring up the technique of sensing since this requires practice. Instead, I have them concentrate only on the sensations in their body associated with some emotion. For example, rather than trying to figure it out or tell me about their sadness, I might first have them keep their attention on the sensations accompanying their sadness, wherever it occurs in their body. Sadness can come from having cut themselves off from their grief. Often, they realize that, for many years, they have been defending against certain emotional experiences by tensing certain muscles, in effect attempting not to experience their somatic sensations. Or maybe they realize they have missed the enjoyment they had as a child when they were more fully in their body. Through the simple somatic work of paying attention to their sensations that come up around strong emotions, their emotional world opens up. Not surprisingly, amplification and release of tension from repressed emotions brings additional positive changes in their mental and physical states as well.

Note that this work is done slowly and in small increments. The musculature has become configured in a definite way and has learned to contain many complex emotional patterns. Just a small release in certain muscles can have profound ramifications. Through gradual work, the body and psyche have a chance to integrate the new material. This is another reason that gentleness, patience, and compassion are so necessary when I study myself.

In a slightly different way, each of us is stuck like my client who held tension in her neck and shoulders. For example, I was waiting in a checkout line in a Whole Foods Market. The cashier was having a wonderful time talking to a customer about vitamins. The store was crowded and I was about four people back in line. I noticed tension in my stomach and upper chest area. I wanted to get going. I also noticed I had some rather unpleasant internal talking going on, phrases such as, "Come on already, don't you see how long the line is?" or "How dumb and inconsiderate can you both be?" and "Will she ever just get her money out of her purse?" etc. Then I realized I wanted to study my state, see myself truthfully, understand my identification and the lack of separation between automatic inner behavior and the situation I was so caught up in. What to do?

Inwardly, I amplified my inner voice and silently said to myself, "What a jackass this cashier is, how unconscious, doesn't she see the number of people? And the person who she just checked through, she is an idiot also, no consideration for others at all! What idiots they both are! How long will this moronic discussion about vitamins go on? She'll have scurvy before she can even take her vitamin C. Someone should call the manager. I should say something now like, 'Hey! There are other people waiting!'" Then, a small miracle took place. Amplifying my self-centered, identified state through this inner dialogue (which, by the way, caused even greater tension in my body), a part of me separated inside in a manner I could not understand at the moment. This part was simply aware of all my experience. Something inside me received direct impressions of me internally considering, not considering the other, not able to externally consider.

I must emphasize that I did not try to separate, nor did I try to "not be identified." Rather, a part of me was simply aware of my inner and outer identification, and I activated that observing part by engaging in and amplifying my identified inner dialogue. The separation comes of itself. The separate part is relaxed, as if the amplification has freed it up. I have found a new "how" that works to take me toward my "what"—learning about my state of identification. Moreover, a part of me, for some unknown reason has become disidentified. The key is that I creatively allowed myself to express my feelings inwardly in order to amplify them, and this brought about the state of disidentification. This use of the thinking center to modify our experience is an example of creativity and experimentation, which I will discuss in depth later.

To repeat: The method of reaching this state of disidentification is not complicated. Simply amplify your inner state, put something more into it, up the ante. No one need know what you are doing. Paradoxically, you will remember this type of effort better than merely thinking about non-identification.

A person may say to himself a hundred times a day that he should not identify, but when a difficult situation confronts him—someone blames him or something unexpected occurs—he drops back into identification, whether it is worry, annoyance, feeling pressured, etc. All the self-talk about not identifying is useless and remains just talk. When it really comes down to it, he cannot "not identify." He cannot remember himself or understand his experience of always being identified, even though it is a continuing pattern. However, he may find the very thing that is useful for studying his identification to be in a completely unexpected direction—to be found in being present while intentionally amplifying his identification.

To summarize, in relation to the Work aim of not being identified, it may not be useful to try to accomplish this with only my thinking center. I may, in fact, need to amplify my identification—the inner talking, annoyance, and/or muscular tensions that accompany it—in order to catch a glimpse of it.

A word of warning about amplification: when used for Work in this way, it is an inner practice. Your amplification only takes place inwardly. By that I mean, you must not amplify a physical manifestation of anger outwardly toward another person by beating them up! This would not only be injurious to the other person, but also self-injurious. Amplification is a method to be applied judiciously; I do it by simply amplifying my own inner dialogue. Then it often gives me the surprising results of experiencing being disidentified.

THE STUDY OF NEGATIVE EMOTIONS

The study of negative emotions and the possibility of their transformation is perhaps the greatest challenge of our species. I believe that unless we begin truly to understand negative emotions—especially shame, anger, fear, hate, and depression—our chances of survival as a species will continue to diminish. All of these painful emotions are dysregulated in us. All except hate are hardwired in us and can be found in people in every culture, but they do not function as they were originally meant to. That is the reason I am devoting an entire section of this book to the study of negative emotions. The Gurdjieff Work brings tools to this study that no other discipline offers. Many people have long realized the need to transform hatred, but the tools they brought to the job were insufficient. They may bring their knowledge to a situation, but lack self-knowledge and knowledge of the automatic, psychological structures of human beings. Academic research has not seriously discovered any means to study or understand how to work with hostility among individuals or nations. Diplomacy is only as successful as the individuals engaged in the mediation are wise, mature, experienced, committed, and, most importantly, conscious so that they can be awake to meet the waking-sleeping behaviors of participants. Rarely have any of these negotiators actually worked at transforming—or as I call it, "metabolizing"—their own hatred into something positive. Nor have these individuals worked on themselves. Therefore, they can have only partial success working with others on the world stage.

Modern psychology focuses on the individual. Most of the time, this individual is interested only in getting through his suffering as quickly as possible so he can feel happier. The psychological community is just beginning to recognize the deeper relationship of psychology to the larger world, but psychologists lack the framework with which to view this larger world. Gurdjieff's approach offers such a framework, as well as the tools for studying negativity and unconscious suffering. However, in order to begin the inquiry, we need to be able to fully engage our own, personal negativity. Engaging negativity does not simply mean to get around it, through it, or banish it to the netherworld. Engaging entails entering into the cave of negativity to meet the dragons, the guardians, and the gatekeepers who guard the entrances and keep us from seeing its underlying causes. Gatekeepers and gatekeeping are subjects well worth studying, and we will begin to explore them below.

As I stated earlier, to understand negative emotions fully, we need to investigate the difference between: (a) identification; (b) repression; (c) projection onto others; and finally, (d) the appropriate expression of negative emotions. Let us focus on anger to flesh out some of these differences.

Generally, we manifest anger automatically in two ways that often intermingle with one another. In the first instance, you get angry with someone for an act of omission. This is a difficult type of anger with which to begin your self-study because you direct your anger at another person; you are always identified and feel justified in your anger. It appears he has wronged you, or you think what he has done will cause you some harm in the future. Inwardly, you are saying this person did not consider you sufficiently; you inwardly justify your feeling and often express it outwardly. I call this "reactive anger," and it usually gets expressed. Because you don't notice the anger coming until you are in the midst of the interaction with the other person, it is very hard to study. Moreover, the other person will usually have a reaction to your expressed anger. Thus, the situation can escalate in a way that will likely cause you to forget any aim of self-observation; you are identified, that is, completely attached to your anger.

In the second instance, you do not express your anger. Instead, you repress it, bottle it up and place it in an invisible psychological bag, the resentment bag, which you carry over your shoulder. This bag can carry only so much weight before you need to empty it. Some people are actually able to carry a steamer trunk on their shoulder—avoid them! Generally, you are not aware of the bag's weight until it is about to crush you, then you may outwardly explode, projecting your anger onto someone else (that is, projected anger). Whether repressed or projected, the anger usually masks your more subtle feelings, such as hurt, sadness, fear, or shame, that are at the root of the anger and which you are unable to experience. Because of our tendencies to either repression or projection of anger without the ability to understand it, people have not developed the communication skills to effectively communicate anger in a useful manner—useful for both themselves and others.

We can experientially study the effects of our anger. One way is to pay attention to the actual physical sensations that accompany the emotion. For example, anger is usually accompanied by contracting and tensing the muscles of the chest, abdomen, arms, or face. We may also find tension in other muscle groups, in the neck and shoulders or genital area. We may experience a residue of other more subtle emotions that accompany anger. We may actually also feel sad, guilty, or depressed, even if we feel justified in our anger. Often, the physical sensations surrounding anger may make us feel ill. We can start our study of anger with the study of the physical sensations and other emotions that follow an angry outburst. Now let us look more closely at repressed and projected anger.

When you repress your anger, you are still identified with it. It hasn't gone away. Followers of Gurdjieff's ideas quite often miss this fact that they are still identified even if they are not expressing their anger. All that has happened is you have managed to keep a lid on it. However, if you can be in touch with your anger and sensitive to the other emotions that accompany it, such as shame, hurt, sadness, fear, or anxiety that sit just below the surface of anger, then you may understand its real cause. Sensing will help you observe and distinguish what is actually taking place in you or held inside. Sense your body when you are in the grip of anger. There is no need to attempt to change your state. Rather, stay in touch with your body, using sensing to experience how uncomfortable and painful your experience of anger feels, or just stay with your physical sensations. You may find tensing of the muscles, weakness in the limbs, or a vague feeling of not being well, such as an upset stomach or cold symptoms.

There are powerful links between shame, anger, and hate. The nature of shame makes it very difficult to study because no one wants to experience it, and we very easily default to anger rather than experience shame. The study of anger includes the study of the accompanying affects that we shy away from experiencing. Shame is one of the most common affects that underlies anger. It is dysregulated and no longer resembles its original biological function. I will look at the dysregulation of shame in greater detail in the next chapter.

Projected anger is often more subtle than it first appears. For example, in my experience, part of me is constantly criticizing myself, monitoring my progress, critiquing my life. At times, I get exceedingly angry with myself for the way I do something, especially if I do something stupid that may be seen by others (shame is at work here). I put up with my constant self-critiquing because I have no other choice nor any control over this critical part of me. However, just let someone else monitor or critique my behavior and immediately a button is pushed inside me, and I project my anger onto them.

This projection takes place because I have developed hypersensitivity toward anything remotely similar to my own critiquing. Although I cannot escape my inner critic, I will not tolerate criticism from someone else. When I feel criticized by another person, it may be that I have endowed that person with a projection of my inner critic. Then, I accuse him and shout at him or resent him, feeling fully justified in my anger because he has treated me so badly.

The way to handle negative emotions is to recognize them and be present to them as they manifest—not through an attempt "not to identify," or through repression or projection, but by containing or "cooking" in the energy of the emotion I am experiencing. When you are cooking in Gurdjieff's soup, as someone once said, you have a chance to taste yourself!

GATEKEEPING

Gatekeeping is a psychological concept originally from Kurt Lewin's work on communication and media work and which is adapted here to help us understand an important aspect of our inner world.[4] As the name implies, a gatekeeper is a psychological mechanism that opens a metaphorical gate to certain experiences and keeps others out. It is a process through which information and ideas are processed. I was very excited when I first learned about gatekeeping. I realized I had found a crucial piece to the puzzle of self-development, as well as a link to understanding self-hate. Understanding gatekeeping has been immensely valuable for my self-study, and I believe it can be extremely helpful to others interested in Gurdjieff's ideas.

Gatekeeping has a close connection with Gurdjieff's concept of many "I's," which we look at in depth in the next chapter. The gatekeeper's restrictive nature, allowing in only certain experiences and keeping others out, limits my ability to see myself fully. If you begin to study gatekeeping in yourself, you will find your gatekeeper is constantly evaluating you and others—it is rarely quiet. You can often notice its running narrative when you interact with others. The gatekeeping dynamic often determines our emotional states and feeds negative emotions. I often find that some small mistake I might have made in the morning affects my emotional state the entire day. This is my gatekeeper in action. The gatekeeper finds it very hard to accept that I make mistakes. It views and judges me in a very restrictive way according to criteria developed in early childhood, judges others continually, and enjoys gossiping about them. It never stops judging and is very concerned with how others do not sufficiently consider me.

Let us look first at an example of gatekeeping in action. Recently, a client complained to me how angry and hurt she was by her adult daughter's behavior toward her. She had always had a difficult time with her daughter and had been estranged from her for a number of years. Recently, her daughter had moved back into the area and their relationship had begun to improve. She was expecting her daughter to call her and wanted to get together with her for Mother's Day. However, my client never received a call. It didn't occur to her that she actually could call her daughter. A week later, her daughter called and wanted to meet. My client was so angry and hurt that she could not keep herself from telling her daughter what a terrible daughter she was, how a normal, dutiful daughter would have acted, and how her daughter should be ashamed of the fact that she hadn't even called her on Mother's Day.

This type of shaming, blaming, and criticism is typical of the gatekeeping dynamic. If you want to find the gatekeeping dynamic in yourself and others, just remember one simple word—blame. Blaming is our culture's mechanism for the release of stress and anger. Almost everyone is addicted to either blaming themselves or others. We could call our age, the age of the "blaming/shaming paradigm." If we are to move into

a new paradigm, we need to understand how this blame/shame paradigm works. Let us look more closely at the above example.

At first glance, the scenario appears to be a mother being critical of
her daughter's behavior. However, that analysis barely skims the surface.
The behavior is a symptom of the abnormal way we live out our negativity. The gatekeeper is like an editor of a newspaper who decides which
stories to run and which stories must be killed. The term "gatekeeping
dynamics" personifies this process. The word "dynamics" is shorthand
for a series of moves similar to chess, where one party tries to beat the
other, to checkmate him. Here, the dynamic involves the mother feeling
hurt and making her daughter feel bad enough about her actions that
the daughter will feel the way the mother herself does—that is, hurt
and sad. The mother in this case is judging the daughter's actions. As a
psychologist, I hypothesize the mother judges her own behavior similarly. In her statements to her daughter, she unconsciously, or worse
still, intentionally, attempts to make her daughter feel hurt, guilty,
and even angry with herself for her lack of foresight in not calling her
mother. Where did the mother learn such a strategy and what might its
real purpose be?

The mother is engaged in the gatekeeping dynamic with her
daughter. She wants her daughter to feel her pain. How interesting! Pain
for pain. Very Old Testament. Doesn't it make sense? It is the motor
driving the gatekeeping dynamic. The mother erroneously believes that
by causing her daughter pain, her own pain will be relieved. Thus, at
the core, the gatekeeping dynamic is always an attempt to relieve an
intolerable feeling, whether it is sadness, hurt, overwhelm, confusion,
or inability to control oneself or a situation, etc.

The gatekeeping dynamic originates in childhood. It is created as a
defense mechanism to help the child handle being emotionally overwhelmed. The gatekeeper forms in the psyche and restricts our experience in order to mitigate or reduce the pressure of these overwhelming
experiences. Originally, gatekeeping may be extremely necessary for
the child, because it provides a defense to an overwhelming experience.
When a child receives harsh treatment from an overly strict parent,
suffers emotional or physical abuse, or experiences a situation in which
she is shamed or told she has failed, the gatekeeper is born and leaps

into the breach. The child handles the overwhelming experience by then allowing in only certain stimuli and excluding others. The child quickly registers that certain of her actions will result in painful consequences. The gatekeeper takes over in an attempt to reduce the possibility such experiences will occur by closely monitoring the child's behavior. Alternatively, in a situation where the child has been told she has failed, she may "choose" to view herself as a failure. The child narrows down her intuitive understanding of herself and the situation, even though, at a deeper level, she may realize she simply made a mistake.

Perhaps it was a math exam and the teacher never carefully explained the material to you, or for a host of reasons, you could not understand the subject. In this situation, your gatekeeper allows in the information "You have failed the test," and excludes the teacher's poor instruction that left you confused. Through hundreds of such interactions, a psychic structure—your gatekeeper—forms inside you. It will always limit your view of yourself or others by restricting the possible perspectives—seeing only what is good or bad, right or wrong, ugly or beautiful, dumb or smart, success or failure, etc. The gatekeeper becomes the limiter of your actual experience of life. It also loves to limit the experiences others should have as well. It is a constant inner critic who compares your behavior to the narrow, unconscious standards it previously established to protect you. However, the gatekeeper encompasses more than just an inner critic. It is more difficult and slippery as a subject of self-study.

The long-term result of the gatekeeping dynamic is that your gatekeeper restricts your life experience and limits your ability to experience life fully. The gatekeeper automatically decides what it will allow you to do and what it won't. It bases its decisions expressly on helping you avoid the emotional experience of being overwhelmed.

Gatekeepers develop within every culture to limit the experience of its members. The gatekeeper keeps us seeing life upside-down, distorts and minimizes information, makes mountains out of molehills. That is, it keeps you addicted to behaviors that prevent you from seeing your life. It views you in a limited manner and disregards your other attributes; thus marginalizing and restricting your life experience. It can be very important for self-study to recognize the gatekeeping dynamics that reside in you.

Practical Study of Gatekeeping

Studying your gatekeeping of others:

1. Notice how you always criticize others.

2. Notice, through sensing, where in your body you experience this constant criticism, notice tensions in various muscles.

3. Gradually notice the unique taste of the above experiences, so that you are more alert to your experience of gatekeeping.

4. Try to find some meaning from these experiences. For example, you might notice how your criticism does not allow you a full picture of others, but pigeonholes them instead.

5. Notice how this part of you enjoys thinking and feeling negatively about others.

Studying gatekeeping in oneself:

1. Try to notice when you feel embarrassed or ashamed.

2. Notice the gatekeeper's inner dialogue. Perhaps you said something silly, did something wrong, made a mistake in a meeting, or someone embarrassed you. Then the gatekeeper follows this up by shaming you more.

3. Try to sense your body when you are feeling shame, notice the somatic experience, tolerate it without attempting to change it. In this way, you will become familiar with it.

4. Get a taste of this inner gatekeeping, how it feels inside your skin.

5. Notice how the gatekeeping dynamic tends to hang on and perpetuate itself. You may be thinking about your embarrassment days or months later, and it will evoke the same thoughts, feelings, and sensations.

Working with negative emotions is not easy. The Work literature does not discuss how negative emotions are born, activated, and nourished. Learning about your gatekeeper gives you experiential data about the birth of these negative emotions. The gatekeeping dynamic begins to shed light on how we carry around our negativity internally. It is an important subject if you wish to begin to free yourself from negative emotions and identification.

Gurdjieff did not find it necessary to delve into how our negativity and identification begins. He viewed negativity and identification as mere mechanics—operations of the human automaton. However, I have found it very important to study how these negative states are born and perpetuated inside me. The aim is not to analyze the concept of gatekeeping. It is, rather, to enrich your impressions and understanding of your gatekeeping mechanism.

The study of gatekeeping is an indirect means of loosening the bonds of negativity. I have not found another method that works so well. Studying the gatekeeping dynamic shows me how negative emotions develop their deathlike grip and can lead to a more useful way of meeting my negative states. Understanding gatekeeping is like shining a beacon into the darkness where my negative emotions arise.

BUFFERS

"Buffer" is a Work term for a psychological barrier that develops between distinct "I's." A buffer serves to isolate one individual "I" from another. Buffers are similar to the bumpers between railroad cars. The cars represent different "I's." The bumpers keep the cars separate from one another and dissipate the shock of one car bumping up against the other. You can imagine the damage that might occur if these buffers were not there to keep the cars from running into each other. In people, buffers prevent an individual from experiencing the dissimilarity or complete opposite aspects of his many "I's."

In the Work, we encounter intense energies as we pursue self-observation and other aspects of Gurdjieff's teaching. These energies may intensify our emotional issues. For example, if someone suffers from anxiety or has a tendency toward alcoholism, these proclivities may become intensified. The Work places additional strain on our psychological structures. Gurdjieff in his groups intentionally created difficult situations. He believed that by producing friction among people working together toward a common aim, it would help people to see the truth of themselves. However, because the Work tends to dissolve psychological structures such as buffers, we must proceed gradually. At certain junctures, people require support.[5] The buffers developed over many years; thus, even though we may imagine a new way we wish to be, buffers can delay or derail our progress. Transformation requires the gradual dissolving of buffers, and it is accomplished, in part, through objective self-observation. There can be no transformation without increased self-understanding and without developing compassion for myself and others.

METANOIA

Metanoia is a Greek word, which, according to Maurice Nicoll, a British psychiatrist and a major exponent of Gurdjieff's ideas, certain Christian writings have mistranslated as meaning "repentance."[7] He says this word has developed a negative connotation, but that the correct translation of it is to think in a new way.

Our work is based on the possibility that we can receive new impressions of ourselves through self-observation, and that we can assimilate these impressions. I need to experience metanoia, to open to the possibility of thinking in a new way. New impressions of myself are the catalyst to convince me that I have work to do. I must realize I have contracted a deadly disease—sleep—and only I can find the cure for it.

As I mentioned in an earlier chapter, impressions are the highest food we take in. However, we habitually filter this new food. Because we live in a waking-sleeping state, it is almost impossible for us to be present at the reception of new impressions, unless we make a certain effort. Some people are unable to receive any new impressions at all. Instead, they only receive impressions from previously stored memories activated by incoming stimuli. Each of us has developed an unconscious habit pattern of repeating old impressions stored in our centers. We each have our own variants of the pattern, but it is unconscious in all of us. This pattern cuts us off from receiving new impressions.

You can observe the idiosyncratic manner in which people filter impressions by noticing how different people describe the same situation. The Japanese film *Rashomon* brilliantly illustrates this phenomenon.[8] In the movie, each person who observes a rape and murder describes it in a wholly different way. You may have noticed that very few people can agree on the simplest thing they witness. Each person sees different aspects of the same situation based on habitual proclivities and the focus of their attention. Thus, new impressions are almost always mixed with automatic memories and projections from the past. Therefore, nothing is ever new, unless a new part of us is present, the observing "I." Additionally, we do not ordinarily notice what is taking place directly in front of us in the moment. If we knew how, we could receive many new impressions.

I perceived a striking example of the power of automatic memory some years ago. I went to a Christmas party at a good friend's home. My friend was greeting everyone at the front door as any good host might. He would make some small talk for a moment or two and then stand aside to allow people to enter. When he first opened the door to me, I knew something was different but struggled to figure out what it was. Then it hit me. He normally had a full beard, but he had shaved off one side of his beard and mustache. Suffice it to say, most of the people who came to the party did not notice that half his beard and mustache were missing. Their automatic memory had retrieved the way he should have looked and simply filled in the missing parts.

Another example also involves a beard. This time, it was mine. I had a beard for twenty-five years, and eighteen years ago, I decided to shave it off. A few weeks later, I had lunch with a friend who had studied Work ideas for many years. Yet, he never commented nor noticed that my beard was gone and still hasn't. Perhaps, he thought it would be rude to do so, but my intuition tells me that was not the case. In contrast to him was my son's reaction. He was about ten at the time and reacted quite differently to the absence of my beard. When I came home, I didn't have my key and had to knock at the front door. My son opened the door and stood transfixed, afraid and not ready to let me in. He did not recognize the person who stood in front of him. He was present in the moment and immediately noticed what was different about me.

The reception of new impressions is also made more difficult due to our limited ability to focus our attention. A major cause of our inability to focus our attention is due to habits formed in us in reaction to the pace of modern life. We are in a rush, the pressure of time has become a disease for many of us, and it is so chronic we don't realize how it affects our psychological and physical health. It starves us of new impressions and habituates us to the wandering of our attention. Time pressure and my habitual inability to be present in the moment results in my attention continually wandering, taken by any stray association from inside or outside me. There is scant time to notice details or even what is directly in front of me. In other words, there is no time for me to be aware of myself existing. As we age, the internal structures we accidentally developed because of the wandering of our attention become more rigid unless we undertake a specific type of work to expand our capacities and train our attention in a new way.

This inability to intentionally receive new impressions leaves people starved for them. At the present time, the proliferation of movies, the Internet, television, email, and sound bites seem to be unconscious attempts to feed a voracious populace with an artificial food of new impressions; but the massive quantity of these substitute impressions are poor nourishment. Computers must be faster, television and movies need to be in 3D. Even sound has to be intensified so people can feel alive and nourished. The younger generation now needs earbuds hooked to an iPod to receive constant new impressions and feel part of current culture.

What is the cumulative effect of all this noise on our attention? How can we find a new way to develop our attention so we do not starve for lack of real impressions? How can we wake up to our heedlessness and undergo the metanoia that will enable us to learn of our own reality? We need to turn ourselves around—but who are "we"? Each of us is a multitude. There is a critical need to understand the multitude that we are, the many "I's" that inhabit our being. Without this understanding, our real self is left wandering in an inner landscape without a map or compass.

Chapter 10

MANY "I's"

MULTIPLICITY

In this chapter, I will examine Gurdjieff's concept of psychological multiplicity and present information on the subsequent psychological dysregulation of our emotional lives. You can find the concept of multiplicity in Gurdjieff's Work as far back as 1917. It is also mentioned in the works of Sigmund Freud, Fritz Perls, and other seminal thinkers in psychology, but not investigated sufficiently by psychological theorists. Gurdjieff was much clearer about the psychological causes and ramifications of the psyche's multiplicity. He says this:

> Man has no individuality. He has not a single, big I. Man is divided into a multiplicity of small I's. And each small I is able to call itself by the name of the Whole, to act in the name of the Whole, to agree or disagree, to give promises, to make decisions, with which another I or the Whole will have to deal.[1]

The concept of multiplicity has been fundamental to my understanding of the psyche. I have found it so important in psychotherapy practice that I often take the time to explain it in detail to my clients. I find the explanation helps them understand their own multiplicity. Gradually, some even begin to see distinct "I's" within themselves. This facilitates their ability to accept their contradictions and develop greater self-compassion. For those of us involved in Work, we can go further than a client and begin to grasp the discontinuity of the self due to multiplicity and the resulting fragmented nature of human behavior and existence. The concept of our multiplicity begins to explain a person's inability to carry out a task or behave in a consistent and dependable manner. The self has no permanent continuous single "I" directing it; therefore, I experience a world filled with the results of my contradictory behavior. I have one "I" at the steering wheel one moment and another "I" the next with spaces of dreamlike sleep in between. This is the normal state of consciousness for almost everyone.

THE FIRST THREE "I'S"— MULTIPLICITY BEGINS

According to Gurdjieff, we are actually seven-centered beings. These seven centers include the five lower centers: instinctive, moving, emotional, thinking, and sex centers; and two higher centers: higher emotional and higher intellectual. Generally, two of the three major lower centers (the intellectual center, emotional center, or the moving center) remain relatively undeveloped during our lifetime. One of these centers is usually more developed and predominates. Our many different "I's" gradually develop as the organism and the lower three centers develop. It is important to keep in mind that the development of many discreet "I's" is not normal and is actually a dysregulated development due to the influences and habit patterns induced by Kundabuffer.

The first distinct "I's" develop in response to the activity of the three major centers: the moving, the emotional, and the thinking centers. Each of these centers or "brains," as Gurdjieff called them, develops its own patterns of behavior. These behaviors include likes and dislikes, habits, desires, fears, organizational ability, and a host of other behaviors. Moreover, each of these centers contains both a positive and negative part. Thus, each person from birth actually begins with three distinct "I's" that in most cases develop vastly different desires and end up having little in common with each other. Even from the very beginning, we are a multiplicity.

Gurdjieff's formulation of the three centers or brains is stunning in its simplicity. It elegantly describes how each person on the planet has developed one brain or center that predominates. Thus, we can observe three types of people around us. Gurdjieff labels them, "Man Number One," "Man Number Two," and "Man Number Three" ("Man" includes women). In Man No. 1, the moving center predominates; in Man No. 2, the emotional center predominates; and in Man No. 3, it is the intellectual center. No one of these types is better than the other; however, one culture may stress the overdevelopment of one center over another. In Western society, it is the head-brain, or intellectual center that is now over-emphasized. We see all three types every day. For example, we see the accountant or professor, who in general leads his life dominated by his head brain; the artist or musician, whose emotional center predominates; and the athlete or carpenter, who is ruled by their moving center. This is not a strict rule. There are many exceptions. An individual may work in a vocation that does not correspond in any way to his or her predominant center.

From birth, these three distinct kinds of "I's" blend and interweave with the individual's responses to his or her inner and outer environment to form other "I's." These new "I's" are similar to small sub-personalities with very specific ideas, beliefs, and habits.

DIFFERENT TYPES OF "I's"

As Gurdjieff says, we do not have just one "I," but many. A primary aim of my personal work would be to develop one real "I" that understands all the others and eventually has the ability to direct them. For this reason, there needs to be a more exact language to discuss our situation. Assuming I am open to the concept of my multiplicity, then what I call my "self" can be understood to be a multiple entity. In the discussion that follows, I will refer to the "I" we commonly refer to as "myself," as "biographical-I."

Biographical-I is built from the experiences of my life. Many parts of my biographical-I, (different "I's" within biographical-I) are actually imitations of others' ideas, emotions, movements, and attitudes. Other parts are more original. They have developed from my reactions to situations I have encountered during life. I experience these parts as a unity, because they inhabit the same body and use the same name throughout my life. Thus, I experience a continuity of sorts that gives me a false impression of wholeness. Gradually, the experiences of these two kinds of "I's"—the imitations of others' behavior, plus my own behavior— form memory patterns. These patterns interweave to become my repertoire of reactions to life. I then repeat these behaviors throughout my life in reactions to a belief, situation, person, idea, mood, or attitude. The behaviors of the different "I's" and their patterns cumulatively form the structure of biographical-I. Although, biographical-I can be very complex, its repeating pattern of reactions limits its experience and development.

Biographical-I repeats patterns, sees things in the same way, and reacts to situations in a preset manner. It is difficult for it to react any other way. Some "I's" may be interested in Work ideas, but others are not. You may find that one of the "I's" of biographical-I aims to clean house, but another wishes to read a book all day. One of your "I's" makes a commitment to your wife to spend the evening with her, and another "I" goes to a movie with a friend. Yet, you say "I" to all these conflicting aims. Therefore, your biographical-I may set many aims, but you can accomplish only some of them; others never will come to pass. Gurdjieff would call this behavior "law-conformable"; it cannot be any other way.

Try to open to the concept of multiplicity now. Then, through your own self-observation, verify that your own biographical-I is a multiplicity. As you get to know yourself better, you may find there are distinct groups of behaviors you exhibit at different times that will seem incongruous to you. Biographical-I is filled with such incongruities—its very existence is actually a tapestry of many "I's."

The ultimate aim is to nurture the parts of me that eventually become my authentic "I." The authentic-I is conceived and nurtured only by receiving new impressions of me, which come from intentionally engaging in self-observation. The impressions I receive from intentionally observing myself become food for a different level of consciousness within me, that of awareness. They arise only because of intentional work to know and understand myself.

Ordinarily, impressions enter me automatically without any work on my part, similar to going to the movies, where I am passively fed impressions from the screen that cause me to react. No real effort on my part is made. In life, shocks can occur that might awaken me from time to time, because unexpected and painful situations arise. This shock may show me how I really am—self-centered, foolish, and insensitive. The difficulty is that these shocks occur too infrequently to provide any continuity in my inner work. It is continuity of practice that builds confidence and understanding. Additionally, the natural human reaction to shocks is to try to reduce them and to keep things calm and predictable. Intentional work, on the other hand, allows me to create my own shocks. At least, it helps me to put myself into conditions with others that increase my chance to receive these important awakenings.

Gradually with time and work, an authentic-I grows through my efforts. Authentic-I is nourished by certain foods. As I mentioned, accidental shocks can feed it, but between shocks, authentic-I starves. I have to learn to feed it real food on a regular basis—that is, the food of impressions taken in while I am observing myself through my own efforts. That is the only food that contains enough energy to feed a higher level in myself where transformation is possible. I believe there is no substitute for this kind of effort. Yoga, meditation, faith, or instruction from a teacher cannot replace self-observation and self-remembering.

While you are working to create an authentic-I, you will encounter resistance, which comes from many areas, but mainly from your own tendency toward psychological rigidity. Rigidity is due to the human habit to repeat previous reactions. Psychological rigidity is universal, but part of our rigidity arises because we actually have difficulty forming new memories.

For most people, memory is simply a passive storehouse for experiences. Each moment, these stored memories replay themselves automatically. This automatic replay causes us to miss new impressions of ourselves in the present moment. And more importantly, we do not clearly remember moments that are only a replay of old memories. In order to make new memories and not just replay old ones, a different quality of consciousness is required. It is in the state of consciousness, signified by the word "awareness," that new memories are created, and these are the memories that are truly important and will actually be remembered by us.

Thus, without awareness of ourselves existing in the moment, we actually miss completely new impressions. We often measure our happiness and satisfaction in the present moment against past memories, and this constant comparison of present to past experience in memory, dilutes our experience of the moment and prevents us from receiving fresh impressions. This entire mechanism of automatic memory-reaction patterns, Gurdjieff refers to as the "formatory apparatus." [2] It is the dominant part of consciousness that allows us to react to day-to-day experience. Formatory apparatus handles new situations just the way it did previous situations, and we need make little effort, for it is automatic and acts with forms (patterns) from our past experience. It is like a bureaucrat or filing clerk.

Our intellectual faculties are too heavily influenced by the past. Memories that replay themselves continually become stale. This staleness leads us to feel out of sorts and impedes our ability to experience and appreciate the newness of each moment.

During our lives, certain types of memories become associated with difficult emotional experiences, perhaps something painful that happened where we experienced suffering. We then attempt to avoid replaying such unpleasant memories, and repress them. We wish to avoid suffering at any cost. This automatic unconscious need to avoid suffering can become a motivating force for addictions of every type. Avoidance of pain and suffering creates further limitations and rigidities in our behavior. If not countered, this rigidity changes the inherently flexible nature we had in childhood into that of a more limited machine—an automaton that always predictably repeats the same limited set of reactions. We give lip service to this when we say, "Oh Bill, he can't help being that way," and it is true, because a machine cannot behave in a creative or new way, but only as it has been constructed or programmed.

In speaking of the difference between a human being and a machine, Lusseyran says that a person has an "I," and that is what differentiates us from a machine.[3] As unconscious, rigid automata, we have no actual "I." To create a real "I" requires work. In speaking about the conditions under which this "I" can grow, Lusseyran says, "It nourishes itself exclusively on its own activity." [4] I have verified Lusseyran's statement in my own work. Only through sincere efforts can authentic-I come into being in me. I believe that having an authentic-I is my birthright. Yet, few of us actually claim this birthright, largely because we only vaguely sense the possibility of its existence. Few are willing to embark on the journey of creating an authentic-I and nurturing it to maturity, because it is not held up as an aim by society. Authentic-I would, by its very existence, change the actual composition of biographical-I. Having an authentic-I could mean that all the aspects of my previously disharmonized self could be integrated.

It is important now to look at one aspect of biographical-I, which is the dysregulation of the natural affect of shame. What Gurdjieff refers to as "instinctive shame" is clearly described in *Beelzebub's Tales to His Grandson*. This affect is extremely important because of its relationship to conscience. Reconnection with objective conscience is one of the cornerstones of Gurdjieff's Work.

OBJECTIVE AND SUBJECTIVE SHAME

In *Beelzebub's Tales to His Grandson*, Gurdjieff describes instinctive shame and the degeneration it has undergone. When discussing some of the deleterious effects of Roman civilization, Gurdjieff says:

> And the Romans were the cause why as a result of successive changes, the factors are never crystallized in the presences of the contemporary three-brained beings there, which in other three-brained beings engender the impulse called "instinctive shame"; that is to say, the being impulse that maintains what are called "morals" and "objective morality." [5]

According to Gurdjieff, instinctive shame has gradually disappeared and been replaced by a pseudo-shame that governs our manifestations. He says the following about pseudo-shame:

> Here it is very interesting to notice that although, as I have already told you, thanks to the inheritance from the ancient Romans, "organic-self-shame"—proper to the three-brained beings—has gradually and entirely disappeared from the presences of your favorites, nevertheless there has arisen in them in its place something rather like it. In the presence of your contemporary favorites there is as much as you like of this pseudo being-impulse which they also call "shame," but the data for engendering it, just as of all others, are quite singular.
>
> This being-impulse arises in their presences only when they do something which under their abnormally estab-

lished conditions of ordinary being-existence is not acceptable to be done before others.[6]

Psychologists define shame as a "natural affect," one of the nine biological affects. An "affect" is a psychological term for an observable expression of emotion. However, each affect also has a distinct inner physiological experience. The other eight affects are anger, disgust, dismell, fear, joy, sadness, interest/excitement, and startle.[7] For the remainder of this section, I will primarily refer to pseudo-shame, the type of shame modern people generally experience. Otherwise, I will use the term "instinctive" or what Gurdjieff refers to as "organic shame" when referring to the pure affect of shame that is hardwired in us.[8]

Shame is perhaps one of the most important areas of self-study we can engage in, and yet it is one of the most difficult to study. This pseudo-shame is now mixed with so much of our behavior—intellectual, emotional, and even somatic—that it has become an integral part of our being. As such, we are usually unaware of its influence upon us. Without realizing it, shame has developed a deathlike grip on us. Our culture has wielded it as a behavioral weapon, somewhat like a cattle prod, since we were children to force us to fit in. Use of shame coercively in this way can wound and brutalize a child's essential nature.

Our caregivers were our first teachers of cultural or pseudo-shame. Others who influenced us when we were young—that is, our families, teachers, friends, enemies, etc.—reinforced it in us. We learn pseudo-shame by imitating gestures, facial expressions, postures, tones of voice, and most importantly, emotional reactions. In short, we master all the various behaviors of those around us. In psychological parlance, a child introjects (that is, replicates within herself) the various negative affects of her caregivers. She unknowingly becomes similar to them in the way in which they behave emotionally. Even if a child hates the way her mother or father acts, and swears she will never act that way, she nonetheless picks up certain parental traits she may remain unaware of and yet will still manifest during her adult life.

Having introjected emotional shaming techniques of a caregiver, teacher, or friend, the child then proceeds to police herself by inner talking and inner emotions—that is, by gatekeeping and utilizing self-shaming. The gatekeeper can even cause physiological pain when she does something she believes she should feel ashamed of. Thus, pain accompanies shame, and sets in motion certain endocrinological changes. This triggering of the endocrine system by emotional shame occurs instantaneously. The scientific study of emotions and endocrinology has given us a basic knowledge of the relationship of the adrenal glands to fear and anxiety; however, I do not know of any study of the endocrinological effects of shame.

By the time we are in our late teens, pseudo-shame has developed into a mechanism that inhibits our behavior and causes us internal pain. One need only witness teenagers' addiction issues. They use drugs not solely because they wish for ecstatic experience or to fit in with a group. Drug addiction often comes about to deal with the pseudo-shame teenagers feel. They are not so handsome, beautiful, or smart as some of their friends. They have disappointed their parents. They unsuccessfully attempt to repress certain self-images in their minds or the contradictory emotions they experience due to their multiple "I's" activating the pain of pseudo-shame. Finally, lack of support from a society that constantly uses shame to belittle them fuels their need to rebel in order to release their rage and hatred. Or they become addicted to drugs in order to soothe or numb the emotional disharmony they experience. Their rage is often a means of getting back at those who have made them feel ashamed. Similar rage in adults can be seen as rebellions in many countries such as India and China, and even the United States, where whole sections of society are relegated to live in down-trodden conditions while the upper echelon look down upon them and judge they should be ashamed of their inability to get a job or better themselves.

Pseudo-shame is also used to repress and limit children's emotional expression. Children, who are taught to repress their emotions by being shamed when they do express them, may be emotionally crippled as adults. Parents tell children not to be angry, not to show sadness, not to be afraid. They say, "You have no reason to be angry," "You shouldn't be afraid," etc. In these cases, pseudo-shame combines with the repression of emotion.

Clients I see in therapy are often tortured by the pseudo-shame they carry around. Pseudo-shame can be activated by thinking about their past actions, their life, their body image, their age, the negative emotions they experience with partners, children, and others, or just about anything else. Their shame combines with the pain they feel about past failures and decisions, or the fear and anxiety they anticipate in a failure lurking just ahead. It is especially painful and difficult to sort out what is actually happening when pseudo-shame, mixed with repressed emotion, is activated in close relationships like marriage.

Shame comes up in so many ways, I am continually surprised people don't realize its effects on them. One reason is that it comes in small bursts accompanying flashes of thought or emotion and is quickly covered over by defense mechanisms like denial or by buffers. Simple examples of pseudo-shame abound. For example, most people experience it if they are on the toilet and someone inadvertently opens the bathroom door. Or, I may say or do something incredibly stupid in front of my peers. Can you just imagine going into a restaurant on a date, eating an excellent meal, and when the bill arrives, realize you have left your wallet at home? You can easily find countless examples from your own experience.

Instinctive or organic shame is different from pseudo-shame. Instinctive shame is a natural function, arising from its inherent connection to objective conscience. It should act as an alert system for our behavior, to help us change behavior that we experience as counter to our essential nature. It should prompt us to ponder the repercussions of our actions. "Let your conscience be your guide," said Jiminy Cricket in the Italian children's book *Pinnochio*.[9] However, our culture has hijacked the essential roles of conscience and instinctive shame. A child is taught to be ashamed mainly when her behavior violates social taboos. The artificial taboos that activate pseudo-shame gradually mix with the real affect, instinctive shame, and its physiological cues. Inevitably, pseudo-shame replaces organic shame.

Shame has become a means to control behavior. We constantly employ it in our close relationships with our children, family members, significant others, and even in making a living. We need to sniff out our bodily experience of shame and study it. In relation to others, it masquerades as blaming someone else or making them feel smaller by cutting them down or humiliating them.

Study of Shame

Yourself and Others:

1. In discussions and arguments, notice how individuals try to make others feel stupid and/or ashamed about their behavior or what they are saying.

2. At work, when your supervisor speaks to you about something you did incorrectly —or when you speak to a subordinate—notice the attempt your supervisor or you automatically make to have the other person feel shame for his error or stupidity. You can find the evidence in the tone of voice, the emotional message behind the words, or feel the tension that comes about during these types of conversation. Do not try to change your behavior at this time. That is not the point. Just gather impressions.

3. When you have made a mistake at work or in another situation, notice how you defend your position, decision, or action to yourself or others. See if you can notice and feel the shame you are experiencing. We do not like to make mistakes.

4. When you discipline your children or redirect their behavior, notice how you may subtly shame them as a means to get them to follow your directions.

Cultural Examples:

1. If you follow politics, notice how almost every remark made by political figures in speaking about their opponent is an attempt to shame them.

2. In church or any place of worship, notice how shame may be evoked during the sermon.

You must verify for yourself that we live in an atmosphere of shame and are rarely aware of it. Most people do not notice it, nor do they have any interest in it. We have become so used to shame that we overlook how detrimental and unhealthy it is. Our shame has almost nothing to do with Gurdjieff's "instinctive shame." We have gradually internalized pseudo-shame and now use it against ourselves and others. It is also a major component of the gatekeeping dynamic, the inner critic who is always watching us. If I want to free myself from my negative states and my constant identification, I have found I need to become familiar with pseudo-shame and experience how it affects my behavior and emotional life. Then, I will have material and understanding that can lead to self-compassion and some freedom from my artificial shame.

FEAR AND POWER

I recently read an article in a psychology-networking magazine about a conference that took place in Los Angeles with some well-known speakers in the field. A major theme of the conference was how psycho-therapy might be more helpful in a world that is out of control. I asked myself why none of them addressed the problem of our addiction to power. A few therapists mentioned the topic, but as a group, they largely ignored it. I am very curious about the subject of power, because I believe it directly relates to fear and anxiety.

When I was contemplating a dissertation topic, I became curious about the underlying causes of fear and anxiety. I've always tended to have a reductionist approach when trying to understand a complex situation; that is, I wish to understand the complex nature of things by reducing them to their simplest interactions. However, when I studied fear in myself, I found I could not reduce fear to anything simpler in me than experiencing an absence of feeling safe. When I do not feel safe, or worry something will happen to make me unsafe, I react with fear. Thus, fear in me is the reaction to a lack of safety. And what is fear really besides the psychological affect? Fear also had many physi-ological symptoms, various sensations in my body went along with the fear. There was a muscular attempt to constrict my muscles so I might not feel some anticipated pain. This turned out to be an important clue.

I began to test my hypothesis about safety on more complex negative behaviors, ranging from violence to various addictions. I questioned clients, studied their behavior, and tried to search out their underlying anxiety. In each case, I found that violent, negative, or even addictive behavior was as an attempt in many clients to avoid experiencing the physiological sensations of fear, that were, themselves, a reaction to feeling unsafe—clients constricted their muscles, went to the movies, shopped, etc. Thus, behaviors as simple as overeating, overworking, gambling, and compulsive consumerism may all relate to the need to feel safe—even though the feeling of safety might be spurious or short-lived. In fact, such behaviors merely distract one from the experience of feeling unsafe and do little to help one really feel safe. I have found that there is also a subtle connection between safety and power. When I feel safe, I also tend to feel more confident, and is not confidence very similar to real power?

The connection between a lack of safety, fear, and power made me more curious about the insatiable need for power that people have. I wondered if fear, itself being just a reaction to a lack of safety, could induce this terrifying addiction to power that so many people suffer from. Is the unquenchable need for power activated in people as a reaction to counteract their fear that is a symptom itself of a lack of safety? Many people engage in various activities in order to feel powerful, to feel as if they are in control and appear confident to others.

It may be that the heroin addict, right-wing fundamentalist, dictator, terrorist, alcoholic, gambler, and wife-beater only seem to have different, distorted motivations. Perhaps the root of it all is really based in their need to be safe. This need may cause a terrorist, who desperately wants to belong to a group so that he can feel safe (perhaps in heaven), to do something as extreme as blow himself up in a café. It may cause another to start a war; a third to take a loan on the family home so he can gamble; or another to shoot up drugs until the tension, anxiety, and pain of living are obliterated. The situation, behavior, thought, or feeling that activates the need for safety is different for each person, but the aim always seems to be to reduce the experience of anxiety, fear, or the lack of safety.

Fear and need for safety are fertile areas for self-study. Fear and anxiety can serve as alarm clocks. They tell us we are identified, asleep, and that perhaps a molehill has become a mountain. Until we come to know fear in ourselves, we cannot even imagine the extent to which it runs our lives. Fear causes the release of certain hormones in our bodies. To be afraid continually can be devastating to our physical and mental health. Until I came to realize the degree of fear I had and worked with this affect, I did not understand what it feels like to have moments where fear did not direct my actions.

What are we afraid of? People can be afraid of anything: another person, a situation, the past, present, or future. One valuable area of personal study that I found is the connection between fear and shame and my own fear of experiencing pseudo-shame. I found that I do not like the physiological sensations that accompany this shame and am fearful of them. The connection between anxiety/fear and shame would require another book in itself, but I mention it here to spur you on to become interested in these more subtle emotional connections for your own self-study. Modern psychology is just not studying these areas and they are almost impossible to objectively study as a researcher by observing others from the outside. The mechanics of our emotional life can only be experientially studied.

The increased frontal-lobe capacity of our intellectual brain compared with those of other animals gives us the ability to imagine our future. Thus, we can make ourselves afraid of anything and everything. I believe the dysregulated experience of fear is an effect of Kundabuffer. That we have developed so many fears about the future, about situations that may never occur, about our health, and so on, seems indicative of a phantasmal perception of the world. Truly, we are "seeing the world upside-down."

Studying Fear

Try the following steps:

First, make a list of all the things, situations, and people that make you feel afraid. What may seem like an intellectual exercise actually has practical value. The task of bringing confused, fearful thoughts and situations clearly into focus will change your relationship to those thoughts and situations. Then you can engage the fears that operate at the preconscious level. Often, we may notice something just below the surface of our usual state, but our attention is so quickly distracted that we usually do not pay it any mind.

It is difficult to become aware of preconscious material unless it comes fully into your consciousness. For example, something is bothering you physically, but the unpleasant sensation is just beneath the surface of your awareness; and yet, some part of you notices. It is like a skin irritation or the beginning of a muscle ache, or a cold is starting. Only when the ache reaches a certain level do you notice it. However, were you to look back carefully, you would realize you had experienced several moments where this ache had poked into your consciousness.

Second, pick one of the fears from your list that has a strong influence on your behavior, one you really want to work with. Let us say the fear you choose is about money. You may feel you never have enough money; you live with this fear constantly. Regardless of their financial circumstances and how rich they may be, many people live in fear of not having enough money. The fears surrounding money seem universal. For example, I find that couples that come to see me for help and have been together many years, have never discussed money. They are afraid to discuss their finances, due to the fears such a discussion would engender.

It is very important to get a taste of how topsy-turvy fear makes our lives. We fantasize about fearsome events and the reaction pulls our attention away from the present moment. Gradually, we lose our ability to live in the present—the future seems so much more dire and immediate. Most of the fears we continually experience are clues that we are identified and feel unsafe.

Fear & Money

Here is a practice to help you become familiar with your fears surrounding money. You may need to do preparatory work before you actually can be present to experience your fear.

1. Sit quietly for ten minutes with your eyes closed.

2. Intentionally think of an issue about money that is bothering you— that is, where some fear has attached itself.

3. Imagine the worst thing that could happen in this scary situation. For example, my checks will bounce; I won't be able to pay back my friend; others will think I am a failure, etc.

4. Make this imagining as real as possible; flesh out the images to make them realistic. In other words, names, dates, places.

5. For five minutes, while maintaining the image you have created, pay attention to the sensations that arise or occur in your throat, upper chest and stomach area.

6. Try for five more minutes to maintain the fearful image while slightly emphasizing your bodily sensations.

This practice will facilitate your learning about yourself. It is not to become another avenue for self-criticism, but simply a practice to stimulate your interest in understanding your own fear. It will help you to gain self-compassion through engaging your attention on the fear. Don't overdo it! Ten minutes, no longer, is enough.

If you familiarize yourself with the sensations that accompany your experience of fear, you will see that the intellectual center alone is inadequate for self-observation when it comes to strong emotions like fear and shame. You must study your fear and other strong emotions not only with your mind, but experientially and somatically. Until you can tolerate fear or shame in this way, it will be very difficult to study fear in actual life situations; but practicing in this way will help you prepare by becoming familiar with the bodily sensations that accompany such emotions.

The exercise shown above is one example of how to use the body to help with self-observation. Such a practice is also useful for studying other strong negative emotions, such as shame, anger, jealousy, anxiety, and greed. I have used these exercises myself to learn about my strong emotions, such as anxiety. Gradually, a desensitization to my anxiety occurs, along with the exhilarating observation that some other part of me exists separate from my anxiety and even my need to be safe.

CONTAINMENT AND FLEXIBILITY

What is the psyche? It seems to be a rather vague term. It is not our personality, if one defines personality as the characteristic patterns of thoughts, emotions, and behaviors that make a person unique. The psyche is larger than our personality, and it contains so many aspects that are not seen by others. The personality is really a small part of me that I present to the world. There is a much larger psychological experience than just my personality occurring within me. Sometimes we see "psyche" defined as the human spirit or soul. Elsewhere, it is the human mind, as the center of thought or behavior. For our purposes here, let us consider the psyche to be a container having many lenses through which experience is filtered and held.

It is very easy to conceive of the body as a container of experience. It is a large object that accompanies us until our death. Our psyche, however, is a container of a completely different nature. Its dimensions are not limited by space or time, although it does have other limitations.

The boundaries of the psyche can be rigid or fluid, and we can experience this through our interactions with different people. The flexibility of the psyche is determined by our individual filters—that is, our predispositions, genetics, family environment, cultural heritage, society, and so forth. Flexibility in this sense refers to the different available filters within the psyche through which a person can view a situation. The more different filters I develop and the larger the spaces within these filters, the more flexibility I have. For example, the flexibility of a police officer's psyche will probably be less than that of a psychologist in responding to people's behavior. Through his education and experience, the psychologist has hopefully developed a greater tolerance (bigger spaces in the filter) for people's behavioral differences. Police officers, on the other hand, experience stress due to their daily risk of danger to life and limb; and they must strictly enforce the law. The people they encounter and their training gradually constrict the parameters of their psyche (smaller spaces in the filter) and their view of others. They can become suspicious and rigid, and tend to interpret events strictly in black and white terms. In this way, they develop a somewhat rigid worldview because of their job.

The psyche is further constrained by our beliefs, which become an integral part of the personality. For the most part, our beliefs have developed from a limited set of experiences—from imitating parents' and peers' opinions and feelings. Certain inborn traits may influence beliefs, but cultural patterns leave an indelible mark. Depending largely on the degree of flexibility of our parents and peers, our psyche develops greater or less permeability. For example, if I grow up in a fundamentalist, white, Christian household in the Southern United States, my tolerance for sexually explicit films, gay men or women, or people who question my religion's views may be very limited. We can determine the flexibility or rigidity of each person's psyche by its degree of permeability—that is, the ease with which it allows in new ideas and concepts.

By the time we are about twenty, the pattern of the personality, which is really just one aspect of the psyche, is pretty much set. But if we study and practice Gurdjieff's ideas and methods, it is possible to gain new impressions and self-knowledge and increase the flexibility of our psychic container. If we are open to what we experience, our psychological container can expand. This stretching allows in new impressions and feeds essence.

New impressions may cause me suffering, but if I value these impressions, the suffering can be illuminating. The suffering I personally endured when I received new impressions of myself led me to new discoveries, and I found out things about myself I never would have suspected. The greatest gift was I realized I needed to be self-compassionate, this was the critical component of flexibility and crucial for me in the development of my authentic-I. Without compassion for myself, I would have continued a process of further calcification of my psychic lens, developing more beliefs, more knowledge, and more negative opinions about myself and others. Eventually, without compassion, my psyche would have only allowed in a sliver of the available light.

FAILURE OF RELIGION TO CONTAIN OUR TRANSFORMATION

Religion, as mentioned earlier, often inculcates rigidity in its adherents. Originally, the aim of all religions was to develop and fulfill human potential, what Gurdjieff called "being self-perfection." The practical means for achieving this goal varied from one religion to another, but all aimed at liberation and development of the essential self. However, all the great religions now suffer from having developed a rigid power structure. The leaders, whose original purpose was to guide new members of the flock, became the power possessors and built up an authority structure. They became the ultimate arbiters of what was acceptable and what was not. They, and only they, were allowed to interpret the tenets of the religion. Followers were then labeled "good," if they adhered to the established structure and "bad," if they did not. Of course, you probably realize my comments about religion also apply to almost any group that forms to promote anything.

The primary drawback of most religions has become the requirement that its followers rigidly adhere to doctrines their leaders have codified and enforced. Such leaders may have little or no understanding of their religion's inner meaning, or equally important, no understanding of psychology whatever. Consequently, both the leaders and their flock obey only the limited doctrine they have promulgated: what is allowable and what is not. Gradually, their psyches become more calcified and inflexible than they were before they embraced the religion. The result is predictable. For example, Christianity, originally based on divine love, makes a 180-degree turn and creates the Inquisition.

Psychological rigidity is a danger for Gurdjieff's followers. Certain individuals rise to positions of power and then fool themselves into believing their positions indicate they have developed higher levels of being. They then either intentionally or unconsciously coerce others into compliance with their rules, whether the rules make sense or not. The leaders do not bear the whole blame for fostering a herd mentality, however. Followers in any group allow themselves to be led because they wish to feel accepted and safe. In part, they may conform because they eventually want to have power over others, just like their leaders. They try to associate themselves with those leaders and enjoy the celebrity they believe such an association will bring them. I have seen the dynamic many times. Groups can gradually become rigid over time and stifle creativity in their members.

Gurdjieff's ideas contain inherent power, and people rightly feel a high respect for them. However, the power possessors in certain Gurdjieff groups have developed a tendency to squeeze the life out of this Work. Because people walk around with rigid facial expressions, thinking they are non-identified and serious, it does not mean they are. If I put on a somber face, it in no way means I am actually conscious, non-identified, or working on myself. It just may mean I am asleep in a new way. This type of behavior goes completely in the opposite direction from evolution. It leads me away from returning to the source of my life and away from the creation of a permanent "I." All of us need to recognize our rigidity, understand it, and bring humor and compassion to our self-observation.

The main difficulty in countering the predisposition to rigidity is that group leaders are often unfamiliar with or uneducated about these tendencies in themselves and others. Leaders should make it a point to learn about psychological dynamics. They must realize that the purpose of Work is not to perpetuate their power or a dead, repetitive formulation of Work. Nor is it to find personal aggrandizement by developing a group that is big, organized, and powerful.

"I's" FROM IMAGES

What attracts us to another person? It is usually a combination of his or her personality and appearance or sometimes just his or her appearance. When someone is physically attracted to another person, they all too often project onto the other person attributes they are hoping to find. Our ability to project images is a powerful force. The architect, designer, writer, or artist is perhaps most familiar with the positive aspects of projection. He begins with a mental image and becomes adept at bringing that image into physical being. However, even artisans who create images as part of their vocation sometimes only poorly understand the process of projection.

Unconsciously, we create images all the time—we are image-making machines—but rarely are we conscious or knowledgeable of the projective process involved in how we are attracted to others. Our projections are haphazard and may end up being destructive. Our habit to project our ideal image onto an attractive subject is one of the reasons it is rare for us to choose a partner who is, as Gurdjieff says, of the right psychological type. We rarely meet the corresponding type of person we should be with, because we live in personality rather than in essence.[10] Personalities are driven by unconscious images randomly accumulated during life. Our personality accumulates such images everywhere, through discussions with friends, through examples of people we admire, or from bombardment by the media. The power of images is fully recognized in politics and business, and politicians and corporations wield this power for their own self-serving ends.

How can we begin to study the ways in which images drive us? The answer is not difficult: by studying the images and values that live within us. Images and values today have become almost synonymous. Our images become intimately tied to our values. We might even say images become the building blocks of values, not vice versa. Images not only contribute to the formation of values, but the values they form create other images of the same kind. Not surprisingly, our values and images motivate us. They provide the emotional energy that moves us toward the goals images have created for us!

These values and images become distinct "I's" within us. We become identified with them, attached to them. We may have tens or hundreds of distinct "I's" that accidentally formed from and around images. They may arise from accidental pairings with pleasant experiences or simply from personal attraction. Just as images can be sources of power and energy to motivate us, they can also create havoc if they remain unexamined. For example, teenagers may go to a rave and take a drug like Ecstasy. They become not only addicted to the drug, but also to the image of dancing wildly and fitting in with a group of "free," unfettered spirits. Then, the images they carry away from the rave may motivate further drug use that can result in severe psychological injury.

We gather information through our senses and higher functions, including our thinking and emotional centers. Our thinking associative function is far too slow to allow us to correct and adjust our behavior quickly, because a plethora of information is involved that we need to collate and codify. Thus, image creation is a shortcut. It condenses this morass of complex information coming from our three major centers and helps us decide how to proceed. Images are also the language of the emotions, and the emotional center is instrumental for us to adjust our behavior.

For example, if I have an image of being successful, it creates a certain bodily sensation and feeling. I feel confident and powerful. Conversely, if I have an image of myself failing, this image likewise activates my emotional center in a different way. I may then feel apprehension, depression, or hopelessness. One of the problems I face is that my emotional center creates images so quickly that I identify with them before my thinking center can recognize the identification. Gurdjieff used the phrase, "We attract forces according to our being." [11] Likewise, the images that inhabit us attract and determine the lives we live.

Whether we realize it or not, we all live through these inner images. The minimalist who eschews all worldly possessions lives that way because of his image that minimalism is the proper way for him to live. Likewise, the person who must possess the most expensive car or be with the best-looking partner is pushed around by images that have accidentally adhered themselves in his psyche.

Unconscious images also play a big role in determining our relationships, the friends we become close to or those we pass by. We even measure our ongoing relationships through images. We compare how the relationship really looks to the image we have of it. Our images also influence our expectations and opinions of people. Although we are usually unaware of it, images determine our emotional attitude to almost everyone and every situation.

To study your images, look at where you spend your time and money. If you find yourself shopping for clothes or browsing magazines that contain beautiful things, pay attention to these activities. This is not about classifying your behavior as good or bad, but rather becoming familiar with it, which you will find to be much more valuable. See if you can contact the images within you that are motivating your behavior. There is no need to change or feel guilty. Simply familiarize yourself with the images through which you are living.

To appreciate the power of images, imagine the following: a car accident in a suburban neighborhood. A six-year-old boy with a new bicycle is killed on his very first ride. One of the neighbors backing out of her driveway did not see the boy and drove over him. The image of this situation encompasses not only the catastrophe of the ending of the child's life, but also the pain of such a tragedy. In one image, you feel the effects on the parents, the neighbors and neighborhood, and on the driver. You feel the repercussions, recriminations, and self-blame of everyone involved, and the guilt and pain that may last a lifetime. The image contains all this emotional content. One image can compress and store millions of small pieces of information.

I find images act like glue, causing distinct "I's" to coalesce within me. They keep me in a state of constant identification. Becoming familiar with those images has helped develop my ability to reflect more clearly upon myself, what psychology calls "reflexivity." It is not about feeling good about myself or sorry for my actions. Reflexivity is a human capacity that truly sets us apart from the rest of the animal kingdom. It needs careful cultivation to yield any harvest.

VANITY

Now that I have—hopefully—got you interested in the importance of learning about and studying the images that motivate you, let's look at one of the results of these images that seems to afflict all of us and from which there appears to be no escape—vanity. I commonly use a dictionary of psychology to look up different psychological words. It was interesting that I could not find any reference to vanity in that book. I thought, now this is strange. There are various psychological disorders that have vanity as a symptom, such as the narcissistic and histrionic personality disorders. An ordinary dictionary defines vanity as excessive pride in or admiration of one's own appearance or achievements. Any objective study of oneself should include the study of one's vanity.

I have found my own vanity to be an inexhaustible area of self-study that relates to shame, fear, and false personality. Gurdjieff says vanity is a result of the organ Kundabuffer. I have found that almost everything I do, feel, or say, is related to vanity; a part of me craves to be admired either by my vanity "I" admiring itself, or by other people.

Vanity is an emotional state that can attach itself to everything I do and adds an unnecessary element, spoiling my life, similar to adding too much salt to food. This emotional element powers false personality. It also provides a dissociative force that disrupts my attention and causes me to fantasize, taking me out of the moment and preventing me from paying full attention to what I am doing. The only possibility of freedom from this curse is to bring it fully into the light of consciousness, to find it hiding in almost everything I do, and to tolerate the experience of it once one begins to see it clearly. Only through this exposure, can its bonds be somewhat loosened. Release from vanity does not come through attempting to stop it, but through continued observation of it.

THE PURPOSE OF TRANSFORMATION

Lynn Quirolo, a friend of mine and student of Bennett, said, "Transformation has always been an elective." She pointed out that there are few cultural supports for development of a spiritual ethos within our society.[12] In the world today, people wish for spiritual transformation and join so-called "spiritual" organizations and movements simply as a means of finding emotional security. No real transformation usually occurs, because no real work takes place.

Recently, I was speaking with someone whose close friend had returned to her homeland of Pakistan. Her friend was dismayed that many of her educated acquaintances there had joined one or another religious group in order to feel secure and assured they were not about to be slaughtered. Fundamentalism, of course, is not a new phenomenon, and the fundamentalism in Pakistan is but one example of it. It has been going on for hundreds of years, and it is built on fear. In the United States, the evangelical, fundamentalist movement sprang up 150 years ago, and has burgeoned because of our need for safety and anxiety reduction. Few if any of these spiritual movements lead to real transformation. Instead, they merely promulgate rules and dogma.

The current ecology movement requires greater understanding of humanity's role in planetary development. Many of those interested in ecology have a vague, inarticulate belief that Nature, our planet's system of balancing organic life, has a definite place for human beings and wants us to evolve. Suppose this belief about the nature of the earth were fundamentally untrue. Nature may not at present be interested in humanity's evolution in any way. Nature only needs to balance the required vibrations of all living organisms to fulfill its own function in the planetary harmony of this solar system. If the human race does not voluntarily produce the required vibrations, they will be extracted from us in one way or another. Nature had resorted to overpopulating the planet so that the quantity of vibrations would suffice. Vibrations produced from unconscious suffering because of famine, disease and war also serve Nature's purpose. Gurdjieff hinted that Great Nature, to which planetary Nature is subordinate, may have a definite purpose for the evolved portion of humanity to fulfill.

Chapter 11

PITFALLS ALONG THE WAY

Misguidance

In this chapter, I will look at some mistakes people are prone to when they try to "do the Gurdjieff Work." If people are working on their own and their only references are books, they may completely misunderstand what they read. If they join a group, they are dependent on the group leader's direction and guidance. Sadly, such guidance in certain cases may be misguidance.

All too often, individuals believe that because they are "in the Work," attending the Work activities somehow shields them from making their own efforts, or relieves them somehow from having to think for themselves. What does it mean, then, to be authentically engaged in Work? For me, it means looking carefully at what I am doing, being willing to experiment, to initiate my own efforts, and be creative in my Work endeavors. It does not mean to mechanically repeat what others have already done or said. I cannot merely follow instructions without examining my motivation or evaluating what I am doing.

When I first contemplated writing this book, my primary motivation was to transmit to others some of what I had learned in applying the ideas and methods of Work. My secondary motivation came from witnessing some of the lopsided psychological development that can take place when Gurdjieff's methods are incorrectly applied. As a psychologist, I am familiar with many modes of dysfunctional thinking, emotional expression, and behavior. I have realized that improperly applying Gurdjieff's teachings can produce results that may lead to dysfunction, rather than harmonious development. Some of these results are difficult to correct, and therefore, care is necessary. I will discuss some of the problems in this chapter.

Where and how have individuals gone wrong in their attempts to work? Primarily, I believe people stumble when they try to change themselves too soon after finding these ideas. They haven't yet developed the proper stance toward themselves and the impressions they gather through self-observation. They want to change what they consider "negative" traits too soon. This tendency seems to originate from a naïve wish to be good. They make shallow changes to their psychological landscape, rather than remaining with their observations and digging into them for deeper meaning. In other words, the aim for quite a long time simply should be to nourish observing "I," without changing anything. Most efforts to change are a reaction to what the intellectual center has seen, perhaps for the first time. These efforts to immediately change what you do not like are usually not only ineffective but may be harmful. They also prevent you from seeing reality—that is, the truth about yourself.

DANGERS IN GROUP WORK

Many individuals have difficulty handling the increased energy released through Work. When additional pressure is put on them in the cauldron of a Work group, their drinking or other addictive behavior may increase and some people gravitate toward multiple affairs that destroy their primary relationships. Others might become more anxious or egoistic. If a person has a proclivity toward leadership, he or she may take a position of power in the group. In many cases, group leaders have little psychological knowledge or understanding of themselves or others. When confronted by behavior that disrupts the group's cohesiveness, they tend to look the other way or, worse still, react inappropriately to the people involved. For example, differences may arise among group members or criticism may arise about a leader's decisions. In these cases, the leader may make a unilateral decision without consulting the group members or defend his decisions without taking into account the group members' concerns.

Some leaders fall into the trap of believing they know what is best for others and then find people gullible enough to follow their direction and recommendations. Psychologically dependent individuals tend to blindly follow a leader's advice to them about how they should lead their lives, although the leader of a group may have no knowledge of what these members really need.

In California, there are a number of large groups where individuals have fallen under the spell of completely authoritarian and incompetent leaders. They waste years in such groups only to eventually realize they have been following the dictates of a person whom Gurdjieff refers to as a "hasnamuss." [6] A hasnamuss is someone who intentionally leads people astray and manipulates them by taking advantage of their weaknesses. It is worthwhile to read in detail Gurdjieff's description of the hasnamuss.

In some groups, members are unintentionally infantilized. Members develop an inability to make decisions for fear the leader will disapprove, and this often curtails creative group energy. Creativity is then replaced by anxiety or by wanting to do the right thing. Moreover, wanting to please the leader is often just an unconscious attempt to gain more power or to gain the recognition one never received as a child. Many believe they can become more powerful through developing a close association with a group leader. Some people in spiritual groups crave to be close to the leader. Through such close relationship, they erroneously fantasize they are important and powerful. In reality, such close proximity may simply result in more egoism or strengthening of false personality. A person then believes he must be "something" or at least is "okay" if the leader speaks to him in confidence. People will adjust their behavior so even the leader is fooled into thinking they are special, and then the leader himself wants to have such people around. The sleep of ordinary life is then simply replaced by the sleep of being in a group and believing that I am special.

Humans are very cunning creatures and can be so cunning as to even deceive themselves. Gurdjieff was aware of such tendencies and made a point of stepping on people's psychological "corns" to keep them from falling into an even deeper sleep in the belief that they were special.

PERSONAL RESPONSIBILITY

Those of us in Work groups need to pay more attention to our psychological wounding, wounds received in childhood and later from relationships. If an individual has unfinished psychological work, especially developmental work—that is, areas of development that were missed while growing into adulthood—it is important to take personal responsibility and look into them. Psychotherapy of limited duration can be very useful in this regard. Otherwise, when individuals reach a certain point in Work, unattended wounds may hamper their possibility of further self-development. In my experience, it is never too late to look into developmental issues that may be hindering you, and I encourage you to explore self-discovery through psychotherapy. Those studying Gurdjieff's ideas can benefit from psychotherapy without having their work diluted. In fact, psychotherapy will enhance your understanding of yourself and others.

Below, I look at some of Gurdjieff's major psychological ideas, and point out what I see as incomplete interpretations, as well as the consequences of attempting premature change based on incomplete understanding. Some of these topics have been discussed before but now I want to go a little deeper, beginning with a reexamination of the idea of identification.

DIGGING AT THE ROOTS OF IDENTIFICATION

"Identification" is a term people in Work groups constantly use. They do not want to be "identified." What do they mean? Sometimes, they use the term "not identified" as an excuse to remain unengaged in their lives—or even not to feel what is happening to them. Many people in Western civilization suffer from lopsided overdevelopment of the thinking center, including people in the Work. The admonition to be "not identified" may add to their tendency to retreat into their intellect. They may even act in a distant, aloof manner that allows them to feel superior to others. However, this attitude of superiority has nothing to do with not being identified. On the contrary, it is just replacing one kind of identification with another. Identification, as I am using it, means you lose consciousness of yourself while you focus your attention on something else, something that you become attached to. Another synonym for identification that we may keep in mind is attachment. Identification and attachment are the same for our purposes here. In many ways, people have been trained to lose their awareness and be identified through their upbringing and education.

For example, imagine someone is a doctor, a carpenter, a banker, or a homemaker. Identification with what they are and the images attached to these roles gives many people their only sense of identity. However, this attachment becomes a type of slavery that can restrict their possibilities. When a person is so attached, we say in the Work that these people are identified with their roles in life. What would it mean not to identify with a life role? We have heard the admonition in the Work to "be in life, but not of it." Can people learn to be fully engaged in life and yet realize their professions, actions, and their accomplishments are not all there is to them? Can they keep a part of themselves present, free from the role they are fulfilling in life?

In the Work, it is said that identification is the cause of our unconscious suffering. How do we learn about the identification that causes such suffering? One thing is clear to me, we do not learn about identification by trying to not be identified. It is not effective to tell myself to "not identify." It is like telling myself not to worry, not to think about a pink elephant. As soon as I instruct myself not to do something, there is a tendency to do just that. Let us look more closely at how our state of identification might have come into being.

Our sense of identity begins at birth and so does identification. How are the two related? After we are born, memories are gradually glued onto our new identity as we gather experiences in life. These experiences are unique to our particular culture. These memories and our attachment to them identify us as Americans, British, French, or Japanese. They may also identify us as adolescent, or middle class, white, black, etc. Thus, we unconsciously develop a self, an identity that is constellated from our experience. It is a set of memories that gradually comes to consider itself as "I." Finally, we associate this stack of memory images with a name. We say, "I am Sue," or "I am Bill." In this way, we become Sue or Bill, and Sue or Bill, in turn, become a teacher, doctor, cashier, or carpenter.

This "I" has come into existence through identifying itself as part of what it has experienced, the things it wants and receives, what it can do, and how others relate to it. My "I," from its earliest moments, is identified by being equated with my experience. Just as Ivan Pavlov's dog salivates when a tone is paired with meat powder, we say "I" because we have paired our experience with ourselves. In other words, people are identified at every moment. They become attached to the images their experience has generated. However, when we are young, another part of us is still operating, at a preconscious level. This part simply registers our existence; it is not completely identified yet with who we are (what we are doing and how we appear before others), but simply notices that we exist. This noticing usually occurs at a level just below our usual waking state. However, this part eventually atrophies in most people and ceases to function. Work is actually a means to reactivate and develop the latent part that was present in us earlier. How, if we are always identified, do we free ourselves or even begin to observe the continuous state of identification into which this noticing part became immersed?

A first step might be to reformulate my aim. I believe we might better express the idea, "I don't want to be identified" as "I wish to become aware of my identification." Not only do I need to become aware of my constant identification, I must study it in depth and understand why it exists. Whether I like or dislike being identified makes no difference. My aim is to know the state of my identification and, in this way, loosen its hold on me. I do not try to eradicate it, which in any case is impossible.

Imagine I am unjustly imprisoned, and there is no way I can plead my case. My only way out is escape. Now, if I try to break out by smashing myself against the prison walls, obviously I will not get free. I can try many different methods, but all of them still might be to no avail. To the guards, it makes no difference whether I am guilty or innocent, weak or strong, smart or ignorant; I am simply another inmate. This is our situation. One of Gurdjieff's greatest gifts to us was to point out the direction we must go in to free ourselves: first, to notice and then clearly realize that we are in the prison formed from our constant identification with every thought, emotion, and sensation we experience; and, second, to notice how we feel about ourselves based on the way we appear to others and what they think of us. The way out is not by pleading to the courts or smashing ourselves against the walls. Nor can anyone else free us. In order to escape, we must investigate our bonds and understand our prison more precisely than even the guards themselves. Our one ray of hope is that the guards are usually as asleep as we are. If we wake up, they may be sleeping; then there is the possibility of escape.

I must point out that investigation does not mean destruction of the prison or rioting for better conditions. Investigation means to be curious about what is right in front of me. I must become a detective, while still in prison, and notice what confines me. Psychologically speaking, I must look at how often I get upset, how often I am negative, how often I am in a state of revolt against the conditions that are a part of my life, how often I just give up and just stare into space or at the TV set, how often I am in a trance and confused. In short, I must study my behavior completely, and in this way, come to understand my identification. Only then, as I come to know every aspect of my bondage, can I experience a glimpse of freedom, a disidentification.

I observe myself in order to verify that I am always identified—from one moment to the next—with a thought, emotion, or sensation. My attention is caught by one of the multiple "I's" within me and focused on what takes that "I" in the moment. One moment, it is a thought about what to buy for dinner, then a worry about how much money I have in the bank, then a sensation of being thirsty or tired and wanting a cup of coffee. An "I" attaches itself to a thought, emotion, or physical sensation at every moment. For all practical purposes, the "I" *becomes* the thought, emotion, or physical sensation. Likewise, groups of oft-repeated patterns of thoughts, emotions, or sensations ("I'm hungry") become specific "I's." Nothing else in the world matters or even exists for that particular "I."

If I can verify in the moment that I cannot "not identify," then I am studying my identification and, at the same time, experiencing a moment of freedom. That is, not all of me is completely at the mercy of my identification. Something new is actually disidentified. Again, what helps me personally is to "act as if," pretend that some small part of me is separate from my usually identified self. In this way, I can be compassionate, curious, and interested in what is taking place. I cannot be completely identified if I am observing myself, because I am willing to observe while I am identified.

Paradoxically, it might seem impossible to create something separate within me that witnesses me; yet, through acting as if this part exists, a small part separates. I taste the experience of this unidentified, separate part. In other words, I study myself and bring consciousness to my constant state of identification. This new part that sees me eventually becomes the seat of my real "I." It disidentifies from the larger, self-centered me who is much concerned with how I appear to others.

Here, a real danger enters. As soon as my observing "I" allows me even the slightest objective look at my actual behavior, my ego/personality and/or my gatekeeper cannot bear it. In reaction, I begin to try to change myself. I want to make myself better. Some other "I" begins to label certain behaviors as "good" and others as "bad." I try to effect such changes in my usual state of identification and thus, I can produce no real change. Real change and inner transformation are results of that small separate part, the beginning of real "I." I need to feed this "I" with real impressions of myself. Think of these impressions as films. We would normally not take a friend to a movie and constantly edit it by immediately commenting on each scene. Likewise, the growth of my real self depends on truthful impressions, not only those I call "good" ones. I am not a churchgoer hoping that God will see only my good acts. What God would see, if he were to see me—and what I need to see—are impressions of myself just as I am!

Seeing ourselves truthfully requires courage. You can just stay on the surface of your life and get along quite well; perhaps with less agitation if you do not know the truth about yourself. Nonetheless, if you have any inkling that you are not all you thought you were, you might wish to take steps to see yourself as you are.

Practices to Facilitate Separation and Study of Identification

The practices described below are just a few examples of how to stay with and study your identification. They may help you to develop a new, separate part within you that gradually becomes familiar with your continuous state of identification. The aim of learning about your state of identification is tri-fold. First, you gain impressions of yourself through development of an objective faculty that sees your continually identified state. Second, you increase your understanding of yourself. Third, you develop compassion for yourself in your present state of bondage. This tri-fold aim can fuel your wish to work as you begin to understand the nature of your prison.

1. Notice, when you are standing in a grocery store line or other tedious situation where you must wait for somebody else to serve you, how you respond. Do not try to change your behavior. Perhaps you are in a rush, you think the cashier is too slow, or you find the person in front of you is annoying, or you just dissociate, move into a trance state. Allow your emotions to continue just as they are and simply notice your emotional state.

2. When you are upset or feel anxious about a problem and you notice the anxiety, you may feel tension in your shoulders or stomach. Amplify the tension and allow the unpleasant emotion to manifest in your body. Simply be interested in the state of tension, without any attempt to stop or alter it. Stay with it. It is similar to surfing. You don't fight the wave, but learn to ride it.

3. In the early morning, if you realize you are worried about a problem, take the time before starting your day to sit quietly. Then, intentionally bring the worry to mind and experience its effect on your body and your thoughts. Remain with your anxiety, learning to tolerate it, experience it and feel its effects in your body. Try this for five minutes, and then let it go and sit quietly for at least two minutes. Finally, let the entire exercise go and move into your day.

Practicing these exercises will throw into relief my continuous state of identification. I need to see my state as I am—always identified—before I ever have a chance to free some small part. My identification will continue, but now at least something in me notices this continuous state.

SELF-OBSERVATION AND POSTURE

As I mentioned earlier, one area for observing my mechanicality is to observe habitual movements or postures. It is an area where I can make small changes, relatively free from undesirable psychological consequences. Note here that I am using the body as a reminding factor and an instrument to help in Work. I believe in starting gradually, not attempting to make big changes that may quickly disrupt the little psychological balance I have.

Keep certain ground rules in mind before beginning this study. First, I make a small change in posture—for example how I hold a pen or make a gesture—not for the purpose of assuming a new posture or doing anything unusual, but solely to become more familiar with my mechanicality. It gives my nascent real "I" something to observe.

A few things you may notice by making small changes. First, the seamlessness of the body's habitual movements, how one movement flows smoothly into another. Small changes in movements interrupt this flow and can provide hooks for my observations. Second, by changing small habitual movements or doing things slightly differently, my real "I" begins to get new impressions of me. The real "I" can only grow when I intentionally feed it impressions, received from direct, deliberate practice. In this way real "I" is nourished.

It is not necessary to change anything either inside or outside you merely for the sake of change alone, or in order to appear different so as to impress others. It is possible to make changes to the intellectual and emotional centers, but you need to understand any changes you make before you try them. Below, I address a major problem I have seen and experienced personally. It concerns the attempt to stop certain manifestations of ordinary emotions.

NONEXPRESSION OF NEGATIVE EMOTION

Rodney Collin said this about negative emotions:

> The miraculous in relation to negative emotions begins with the idea of second conscious shock—the transformation of negative emotions into positive ones. It begins for me with Ouspensky's saying that if we had no negative emotions, we would have no chance of development, so they would have to be invented. They are our own inexhaustible raw material for transmuting into that divine energy which otherwise is incommensurable with our logical efforts.[1]

In the previous chapter, I introduced the concept and study of negative emotions—that is, how we might use them for our growth. The nonexpression of negative emotions has become a cornerstone of the Gurdjieff Work. However, in my opinion, this aspect of Work is widely misunderstood and can lead to unintended negative outcomes. Ouspensky says of this topic:

> For instance, although he [Gurdjieff] undoubtedly gave the fundamental basis for the study of the role and the significance of negative emotions, as well as methods of struggling against them, referring to non-identification, non-considering, and not expressing negative emotions, he did not complete these theories or did not explain that negative emotions were entirely unnecessary and that no normal center for them existed.[2]

I would point out to the reader that it is Ouspensky, not Gurdjieff who states above that no real center for negative emotions exists. It does not appear that Gurdjieff himself made that statement.

We must first ask, what is meant by negative emotion; specifically, what might Gurdjieff have meant by the term? Keep the question in mind. There is no doubt the nonexpression of negative emotions can produce a psychological effect and even produce energy for Work. However, some people more than others seem better able to make use of such nonexpression. Others, with a different psychological makeup may experience some unpleasant results. Their emotional state may become unbalanced. Believing the nonexpression of negative emotions is good for everyone is like saying one size shoe fits all.

Gurdjieff does not mention the nonexpression of negative emotions in any of his writings. However, Ouspensky speaks of it on three separate occasions in *In Search of the Miraculous*. The most important of these sections occurs the first time he mentions it. Ouspensky reports Gurdjieff as saying:

> In the sphere of the emotions, it is very useful to try to struggle with the habit of giving immediate expression to all one's unpleasant emotions. Many people find it very difficult to refrain from expressing their feelings about bad weather. It is still more difficult for people not to express unpleasant emotions when they feel that something or someone is violating what they may conceive to be order or justice.[3]

Note that Ouspensky reports Gurdjieff as speaking of "immediate expression." Struggling to restrain the immediate expression of unpleasant emotions is a means of studying my reactive emotional habits. Gurdjieff uses the example of someone complaining about the weather. In this situation, a person might try for the next moment or two, instead of immediately complaining, to restrain himself, see what the experience is like, find out about where it is coming from, and notice its automatic nature; then express it and be present while doing so. In other words, holding back the immediate expression of an unpleasant emotion is a means for self-study and creating energy and interest in one's psychological structure; the aim is not to immediately change, but to study oneself. Gurdjieff is not instructing people to be good.

Ouspensky goes on to quote Gurdjieff as saying: "Besides being a very good method for self-observation, the struggle against expression of unpleasant emotions has at the same time another significance. It is only one of the few directions in which a man can change himself or his habits without creating other undesirable habits." [4] I believe this is where the problem really begins. The word "immediate" from the first quote has been left out. If a person struggles against the immediate expression of unpleasant emotions, it is not a big shift, and in fact can help in self-study. The unpleasant emotions Gurdjieff speaks of seem to be simple ones, such as constant complaining about one's body or the weather or the unnecessary fears or worries that are peculiar to each individual. These types of negative emotions are very different from strong emotions such as anger, hatred, or depression.

An unpleasant emotion may involve not liking the way someone sings, for example, or being annoyed that someone has not considered me, etc. However, a strong negative emotion such as anger goes far beyond my simple annoyance at not being considered. In fact, it may be perfectly justified for me to feel angry when I see injustice, such as the abuse of a child by an adult or the discovery of betrayal. Psychologically, we need to admit we do not really understand what the repercussions would be if we tried to stop the expression of an emotion such as anger, either outwardly or inwardly. If I struggle against the actual expression of a strong negative emotion and never express it outwardly, that is a very different situation from struggling with the immediate expression of an annoyance. It is also important to consider that if I do block the outward expression of a strong negative emotion, then what happens to it? Is this repression actually useful for my work? I am unsure that Gurdjieff made the statement exactly as Ouspensky quotes him the second time. It goes against all current psychological understanding and my own experience. Nowhere can one inflict more psychological injury on him- or herself than through the continued nonexpression of negative emotions. Attempting to not express major negative emotions can immediately alter our psychological ecosystem and provide some very unpleasant surprises. This is not to say that someone who is constantly angry and expressing it might not benefit from an anger management course or learn how, more usefully, to express his anger.

Because anger is a powerful emotion that Gurdjieff did not directly address, it may be useful to understand a little more about it. In order to look more deeply into anger, we need to understand two additional psychological terms.

Sublimation defines a situation where an individual diverts the energy of a sexual, biological, or emotional impulse from its immediate goal to one of a more acceptable social, moral, or aesthetic nature. For example, a man sublimates his sex drive by redirecting his energy and becomes a great athlete or mountain climber. Sublimation is a very natural process, usually not harmful. Most of us use it unconsciously.

Repression occurs when feelings or thoughts are pushed down into the unconscious so that we cannot access them in our normal waking consciousness. Repression may lead to neuroses and neurotic behaviors. It is generally disharmonizing, psychologically and physiologically.

The nonexpression of negative emotions appears to be a misinterpreted practice in the Work. It is an intentional attempt to produce energy and receive impressions of myself. In my opinion, it is an advanced practice. Many people in ordinary life already repress strong emotions almost all the time and it creates havoc in their lives. They are often taught to repress such emotions in childhood and it is already habitual. There is a great deal we can learn about ourselves from the study of negative emotions, without attempting to repress or stop them. Negative emotions can present us with a rich field of new material. It is not advisable to take on the practice of nonexpression of negative emotions too early; and perhaps not at all, if we can find a more appropriate method of using these difficult emotions for our work.

EXPRESSING FEELINGS

In modern society, we are told from earliest childhood not to be angry, not to be sad, not to be prideful, not, not, not, etc. Due to such admonitions from caregivers and teachers, many people enter adulthood with a great many repressed emotions. In these individuals, certain emotional states are expressed habitually while others are repressed, and they have little control over any of them. They have developed a behind-the-scenes gatekeeper who decides for them what is acceptable to express and what is taboo.

In many cultures, we teach women it is all right for them to be sad. However, they are not supposed to be depressed but must be cheerful. Women also are taught not to be angry or show their anger. These statements are of course generalizations, but I have found they hold true for many women. Men are also short-changed. They are taught not to feel sad or depressed. If they do have to express anything, let it be anger or aggression. These behavioral strictures have loosened somewhat. Men have become more accepting of emotion and are now allowed to show affection toward one another. Unfortunately, however, the behavior patterns that were previously modeled for men are now bleeding over into women's lives as women take on other roles; they are then required to appear tougher and emote less.

When speaking of the difficulty men have in expressing feelings, psychologist Robert Johnson says: "It is difficult to feel much pleasure or joy in life when one is burdened by a self-image that says: in order to be a man you must be tough and cool as steel." [5] Johnson points out that many men are simply unable to bear the suffering and alienation they experience when they repress their feelings. Thus, they take refuge in drugs, alcoholism, gambling, workaholism, and even sexual obsessions as a means to avoid their difficult feelings. All these refuges are emblematic of what Johnson refers to as "immature masculinity." We will look in more detail at the archetypal images that mold and form identity later in this chapter.

My experience has convinced me that before I stop the expression or other manifestation of a negative emotion, I must first understand that emotion. However, in order to understand the emotions, I need to really experience and study them. I must develop my ability to be aware of them at the moment they manifest mechanically in me; that is, my observing "I" must be active. I need to be curious about these negative, difficult emotions and compassionate toward them. Perhaps at times, I even need inwardly to amplify them in order to study them. If I attempt to cut them off too early, I may generate a lot of energy, but I will miss the more interesting aspects of myself that lie beneath these difficult emotions.

We all get angry. Some of us express that anger in a nonviolent manner but others cannot. Many people either repress their anger and then become angry with themselves, or project their anger onto others. We cannot understand anger by either repressing it or simply projecting it mechanically. A great many of my clients hold back feelings like anger and do not express them. In fact, the people who hold back emotional expression the most seem to be the most dysfunctional. Simply put, many individuals, who do not have an inkling of Work ideas, automatically repress their negative emotions. It has not helped them one iota. We must question if directing individuals to practice the method of nonexpression of negative emotion is either correct or helpful. I believe there is another approach that employs neither repression nor projection onto others.

I have found anger rarely exists as a pure emotion. There are usually hidden emotions that arise with the anger, including fear, anxiety, shame, sadness, grief, loneliness, or a feeling of overwhelm (an emotional state where too many emotions or thoughts flood into us). The tendency in modern culture is to repress anger for fear of reprisal. However, the anger usually comes out—inappropriately—later. We see the results of repressed anger all the time—in road rage, abuse of elders and children, and addictive behavior. If you repress your anger, you may be unable to see the subtle emotions that cause your anger. You will need to study anger in yourself to verify what I am saying here. Just how angry do you get when someone cuts you off on the road, does not serve you properly in a store, or is inconsiderate to you? What is this experience of anger really about? How does it taste, what is underneath it? Can you really observe it objectively? You may find the answers to these questions by repressing your anger outwardly, but I doubt it. It may be more productive first to practice being present with the anger, feel it deeply and only then, disidentify from its manifestation.

I believe the study of anger and rage is immensely important at this time. Many dysfunctional aspects of our culture are related to the inappropriate manifestation of anger, running the gamut from annoyance, abuse, addiction to drugs or rage at a government's addiction to war. What could be a more interesting field of inquiry for human beings? If we try to not express something that is constantly being expressed in our society, it may prevent us from acquiring a real understanding of our true nature. It may be that we are really not so nice underneath our personas. We need to bring our anger out of the shadows and study it.

ANECDOTES OF ANGER

A Personal Example

I come home at the end of the day. My wife is not home, but out with others. I am tired and still have a number of things to do. She comes home an hour later and is in a great mood. I get angry with her, but there is a part of me watching from inside. I speak to her about how angry I am that she was not home. As we talk about it more, it becomes clear the issue was not her being out with friends, but rather my deep fear of abandonment that has been there ever since I was a child. That material, that knowledge of myself, I could never have touched had there not been something within me—observing me—at the moment I was expressing my anger. On the other hand, if I had I just repressed my anger by keeping quiet, I might simply have ended up resenting her, believing I was the superior, more conscious one—since what one should do if one is "in the Work" is not express negative emotion.

Keeping quiet when I am angry and seething inside, instead of discussing my feelings, is such a typical way for couples to interact that it seems endemic to relationships. The repression or nonexpression of anger in such a situation ends up being a dead-end road. The anger is invariably expressed later in ways that may be more deleterious to the relationship. Repressing anger and not knowing how to express it can lead to more serious and dysfunctional behavior later on. However, learning to express anger in a nonviolent way, where I am freer to be curious and observe myself, can lead to self-discovery and to the development of compassion for myself and others. Of course, it takes practice and time to learn this kind of nonviolent expression.

Before continuing, let us clear up again any issues that might lead to misunderstanding. I am certainly NOT advocating screaming or engaging in violent acts. I am suggesting there is a better way to learn more about your negativity than by repressing your anger. Realize you are upset, and outwardly allow that upset to manifest, but inwardly emphasize self-observation. By working in this way, a number of other things may occur simultaneously. First, you would gain impressions of yourself as you felt your pride, shame, fear, and your blaming attitude. Second, you can feed the compassionate, objective, observing part of yourself with these impressions. Third, you would develop greater flexibility and tolerance for negative or unflattering impressions of yourself. Finally, you would gradually learn to discharge your anger in a nonviolent way, through sensing your body and through self-observation. You might even improve your ability to communicate difficult emotions.

Two Related Examples

After an already frustrating day, a woman from my bank calls to say one of my checks has bounced. I am upset and angry about the situation. I believe it is the bank's fault, but I don't say anything. I believe I am remembering myself, but of course, this is not the real meaning of self-remembering. I am stopping the outer manifestation of a negative emotion. I am in the Work; I repress my anger. I feel good about repressing it because it means I am superior to others, I think, and am proud to be in control of myself. Later, I go home and my wife tells me I need to pick up our son because she wants to go for some coffee with a friend. I scream at her, telling her how unfair she is, because I worked all day. I get into an argument with her. She doesn't say anything, but just leaves. I feel angry and terrible. What happened here? To find out, let us look at another similar experience where I actually learn something about my inner structure.

When the bank calls, I get upset. I realize that I am angry just as I am beginning to express my anger. Noticing this, I wish to experience my anger fully. I continue to express it, but now I remember myself (I am self-conscious) and there is an observing "I" present during the expression of my anger—it is interested in learning about my anger. Here is my inner experience and what I find out.

Yes, I am angry at the bank's mistake, but what is really happening inside me is that I am afraid and embarrassed that the check I wrote to a friend will bounce. I am concerned and angry about what he will think of me (I don't want to feel shame); in other words, I am engaged in inner considering. I hate myself for some reason I cannot even understand. I am blaming the poor woman at the bank who did not make the mistake, and I feel guilty about that too. I feel out of control, overwhelmed, and want to make it right, but don't know what to do. Now, the important part. I can only access all this information about myself if a part of me is detached, compassionate, and objectively observing as I manifest my annoyance and anger, if I am self-conscious.

What actually happened in this situation is that I outwardly became angry with the woman from the bank before I could catch myself. Feeling my anger, I realized it and then began to be present as I expressed the anger. When it was all done, I actually apologized to her for my behavior; but by that time, I had gained quite a lot of information about myself. As I went over the material, I realized my anger was really a result of the shame I felt and my own gatekeeper attacking me for not doing things correctly.

In these examples, it is important to look at the possibility of delayed negative outcomes due to repression of anger. In the example with my bank, when I repressed my anger with the bank about my check, that anger later spilled over onto my wife, who had no idea what was going on. She then, might feel hurt, repress her anger at me, but end up resenting me. Her anger might come out later or maybe she would just continue to resent me. I would probably forget the whole scenario by the next morning. My "forgetting" would be a mechanism of denial, of not wanting to deal with the way I acted. When her resentment and anger finally came out toward me, (it might be much later) it probably would not make sense to me.

The above examples from my life illustrate how displaced anger can lead to resentment that often develops in marriages and other close relationships. Such dysfunctional emotional patterns spill out into the larger society and prime people to be angry at the slightest provocation. In other words, these people are "easily offended, waiting to happen."

Another way we can observe repression of emotions is when we discourage our children from feeling angry or showing it, as our parents may have done with us. We give them messages early on that anger is not a good thing when we say, "You have no reason to be angry." However, they also sense that their mothers, fathers, teachers, and others live within a continual atmosphere of their own anger. The anger is blurted out in stores, at school, and by parents when they lose the little control they have. We live in a very angry society. As a society and a world, we have not learned to transmute anger, nor do we understand its psychological twin—hatred. In my opinion, we will never be able to understand these difficult emotional states unless we study them from within.

SELF-OBSERVATION AND NEGATIVITY

I hope you can see what a wealth of experience can come through observation of your anger, in contrast to the scarcity of material available when it is repressed. An interesting side note here involves sensing when we are having negative feelings. The energy of the moving center is much faster than that of the associative mind, and thus can keep better pace with our emotions. Therefore, using sensing to gather impressions of our emotional state can be a more informative tool for us than thinking. With respect to the speed of our various centers, Gurdjieff says (see the Glossary for an explanation of the term "hydrogen"):

> The thinking or intellectual center is the slowest of all the three centers we have examined up to now. It works with "hydrogen" 48 (according to the third scale of the "table of hydrogens"). The moving center works with "hydrogen" 24. "Hydrogen" 24 is many times quicker and more mobile than "hydrogen" 48. The intellectual center is never able to follow the work of the moving center. We are unable to follow either our own movements or other people's movements unless they are artificially slowed down.[6]

Some of my most important findings come when I am present with my negative emotions, really being with a negative feeling, without self-judgment. Even if I have expressed my negative emotion and made a mess of the situation by doing so, I still can salvage the experience if I begin to work, have a part of me present and somewhat separate from my negative state. I often find deep insights come from this kind of separation.

We generally acquire meaning from our experiences unconsciously and unintentionally. However, we can intentionally search for meaning by expressing our emotions and thoughts while at the same time attempting to be present. If I can be present, then something in me observes. This observing part of me can receive impressions from more than one center. The different "I's" Gurdjieff refers to bump up against each other without any buffers to separate them. I may feel a little bit overwhelmed, but that is fine. We need to be overwhelmed at times. If we stop a negative emotion too soon, it may lose its effect on us. We end up just thinking about our experience, without the participation of the other centers. If our emotions are curtailed prematurely, we may get the false impression we can control our feelings. We miss the cues about what is really activating our negativity. However, if we can find its source, then we have understanding instead of mere knowing. Miraculously, this understanding brings me choice and freedom of action.

As mentioned earlier, I am not, I repeat, not, advocating resorting to violence or verbal abuse. However, being "good" Christians has not worked. The Crusades and the Inquisition are vivid examples of attempts to coerce people into being good Christians. Fundamentalist movements throughout the world fall into the same pattern. In many ways, religious fundamentalism comes from the need of power possessors to repress the rage of people made to feel powerless.

As I have often pointed out, we have to be interested and curious about what is happening within us—whatever it is that comes up—just as we are, and not as we might want to be. Interest and curiosity are requirements for finding the treasure of objective knowledge upon which all of our development as true three-centered beings depends.

LOSS OF INTEREST AND CURIOSITY

Interest is one of the nine natural affects we are born with. The capacity for real interest is frequently destroyed or at least stunted by the end of grade school. In our quick march toward adulthood, we often lose the ability to be genuinely interested and curious about the world and ourselves. Wanting to be good or wanting to fit in and be like others easily kills interest. If we become curious about our negativity, admit our negativity, feel our anger, and be truly interested in it, then our interest brings new impressions. We can even be interested in our anger after we have made the so-called "mistake" of becoming angry. We remain curious. We examine whether we can bear experiencing our unpleasant manifestations. For all we know, experiencing our unpleasantness might even lead us to being able to bear others' unpleasant and often negative behavior, rather than just reacting to it automatically. We may become curious about the other emotions that sit beneath their anger. This work with the emotions is not easy. It is not for the faint of heart—not for those who only want to feel happy or be good.

In psychological parlance, interest is considered a positive affect. It is the critical component of attention. As children, we are interested and curious about everything. The faculty of human attention tracks the natural affect of interest. Gradually, we focus our interest in various directions and exclude others, and our attention follows this same pattern. Because of this natural process of exclusion, our field of interest also tends to narrow over time. In general, our interest is drawn toward the outer, material world and our inner world is excluded. Even in the material world, interests narrow as time goes by. However, we need to counter this narrowing, contracting force if we wish to develop ourselves. This is why each of us must seek out and rekindle interest and what is called the "sovereign learner" within each of us.

Elizabeth Schreiber wrote this about the sovereign learner: "The sovereign learner has an autonomous relationship to curiosity, play, and practice; the sovereign learner can claim discipline as a tool necessary to support the deepening of self-awareness and engagement with the world." [7] The sovereign learner is a capacity that is forced underground when we are young. In some ways, this part of us desperately needs to come out of its cave. In order to access this part, we need to recall how to notice the newness in almost everything, the incredible spectacle before us each moment. We also need to familiarize ourselves with what keeps us from noticing newness.

A Practice for Rediscovering Interest and Curiosity

Simply sit for one hour, without any agenda. Keep your eyes open. This is not meditation. It is a means to allow you to slow down your automatic behavior and help you notice the subtleties of your experience—what is going on within you. Your associations gradually spin down and you may have moments of "noticing." Noticing is very close to awareness, but it is momentary. Slowing down while sitting can produce a state that may release other inner energies. Some people may complain they are unable to sit and do nothing for an hour. This is just the pressure of habit. If you gently persist, resisting the compulsion to be sucked into your automatic agenda, you will undoubtedly learn something about the way you are wound up. You may possibly rediscover your interest.

This kind of practice can wean you from being interested mechanically, exclusively to whatever accidentally attracted your attention in the past. When people say, "I am interested in sport, but I am not interested in art," most often, they are talking about their enslaved or mechanical interest. If you practice the above exercise, you may reawaken your natural interest and curiosity.

Stopping Thoughts Is Not A Good Idea!

Another erroneous idea, prevalent in some Gurdjieff groups, is that I can and should attempt to stop my thoughts. I remember being at a meeting twenty-five years ago and hearing Robert de Ropp, a teacher in the Work, advise people to try stopping thoughts. Ouspensky also mentions this practice in his book, *The Fourth Way*. In my experience, this formulation of Work ideas is incorrect and impossible, and this kind of practice can result in serious psychological damage. It can completely unbalance the entire human machine.

The mechanism that balances the interrelated systems of the human body is magnificently sensitive. It continually adjusts for changes in breathing, emotional states, thinking, physiological and endocrinological changes, digestion, etc. Our associative, cognitive faculty begins in infancy and is an integral part of our mechanism. Any attempt to change the flow of associations by trying to stop thoughts directly runs the risk of doing more harm than good, regardless of any increased awareness that may result. Associations are a means of correlating new material with old and comparing aspects of different impressions. The speed of thought is variable and is neurologically balanced, maintained, and developed from fetus to adulthood. Trying to stop thoughts is equivalent to taking a wrench, without any knowledge of automobile engines, and jamming it into the pistons of a highly-tuned sports car while it is running at high speed. Parts may be bent and even ruined forever. Reduction in associative thoughts, such as that produced through meditation, occurs gradually and indirectly. It occurs because I have taken a certain posture, focused attention on my breathing, or repeated a mantra; these methods work indirectly to reduce associative thought.

Another danger in trying exercises like stopping thoughts is my immediate tendency to want to increase any pleasurable change in my state that results from the exercise. We believe, "If a little is good, let's do more." Just because we can, does not mean we should. Nowhere is this truer than when we notice a change in our state of consciousness. We notice a small change, we like it or feel it is unusual, and then we quickly move to increase it. This tendency can result in lopsided development. Buddhists say it creates new "samkharas," or fissures, in the psyche.

For example, let us look at meditation, which may bring about a change in my state of consciousness. In my opinion, some individuals become addicted to the meditative state and unconsciously use meditation as a means to avoid the trials and anxiety of ordinary life and even perhaps as a means to repress or deny their inner contradictions. That is not the way toward evolution, only another means of escape. The same can be said for retreats of every type. Practices of one type or another are often the centerpiece of these retreats. Individuals who conduct these retreats may claim the retreat will develop some psychic, physical, or emotional aspect of us. However, if we overdo any such activity, it can become another means of self-calming or disharmonize us. The retreat may open us up to possibilities within, but only with efforts to harmonize the centers and long practice can we actually attain what we glimpse during a retreat. In our attempt to increase a pleasurable psychic state, it is easy to go overboard and tax our capacities. Because of this, we need to go slowly in any practice and gradually build up our ability as if we were building up a muscular capacity.

Numerous individuals suffer the ill effects of wrongly conducted yoga practice, meditation, and also the Gurdjieff Work. One of my friends suffered a psychotic break while at a ten-day meditation retreat. Although she had practiced meditation, this was her first long retreat. She needed to be hospitalized and took quite a long time to recover. I give this example only as a warning that our mechanism is very delicate, and for some individuals, care needs to be taken. In summary, never try to stop your thoughts!

DANGERS OF BREATHING EXERCISES

As a rule, exercises to modify breathing are usually completely incorrect and dangerous, particularly in the beginning of your work. There are breath-modifying exercises associated with Gurdjieff's Work, Kundalini yoga, Vipassana, and Stanislav Grof's holotropic breathing. They produce changes in one's state. If they are practiced incorrectly, they may unbalance you. This happens because you connect a positive change in your state to modifying your breathing. Often there is some self-hypnosis involved here due to your wanting your emotional state to change. Then you may feel that if a little is good, more is better. This is how addiction begins. I have watched many individuals, friends and clients who become addicted to the change of state that came about from changing their breathing.

From experience in many sittings and practices taught by Gurdjieff's pupils, I have never come across any exercise that has been verified as given by Gurdjieff that advocates modifying breathing. In fact, just the opposite is true. Gurdjieff's advice was to allow the breathing to adjust itself and not attempt to modify it.[8] Some exercises brought by Bennett from the Naqshbandi Sufi line do suggest changes in breathing. While I highly respect Bennett's work, I would suggest you apply caution when you try such exercises. I consider them to be advanced methods. All too often, inexperienced individuals try them. They experience a change in state and then jump to the erroneous conclusion that the change is a good sign and that they are developing their being. That is not always the case.

In summary, the body is always dynamically balancing its intricate mechanism to meet the inner and outer changes in our environment. The instinctive center automatically adjusts the breathing. You would not want to take on this responsibility. In no way should you make a voluntary change in your breathing.

BEING SPECIAL VERSUS BEING ORDINARY

As we discussed earlier, I always like to think I am special. One of the more common mistakes in this Work is to believe that being associated with these ideas makes us special. Group work can accentuate this specialness. Remember that when we work in groups, the Work may exaggerate some or all of our idiosyncratic traits, both good and bad. If individuals have a big ego, it will get bigger, and if they have been looking for something that can make them feel superior, then they can certainly find something in the Work that can. Yet, this is not the purpose of Work.

We will each eventually have to face one difficult task—to learn to be ordinary. *Participation*, an advanced concept developed from Gurdjieff's Work, is based on allowing me to be what I am, while being a spectator from the inside. I need to find the subtle balance that allows me to witness my ordinariness. This I will speak about in more practical detail in the last part of the book.

My need to be special, to stand out, to think of myself as superior, and to wish to always augment myself somehow might eventually prove to be counterproductive for real development. We often wish to look better and hope others will mirror our magnificence back to us. Then we can feel as if we are finally something. What is so laughable is that we cannot stop doing it, nor would it be advisable. This aspect of my vanity is excellent for self-observation! I mention this showboating tendency because those who suffer from it have the most difficult time simply learning to be ordinary. This disease of vanity is a result of incorrect caregiving and education. Bennett said this about it:

Vanity is a special form of subservience to the opinion of others which prevents the growth of any true individuality, and yet vanity is fostered in children by every word of unmerited praise or flattery which they hear from the day they begin to become aware of the attitude of other people toward them.[9]

The study of how we wish to stand out and not be ordinary brings us to study our pride, greed, and the quest for personal power that derives from our basic insecurity. These desires are wonderful subjects for self-study. Again, there is no need to change anything, but rather work to become familiar with the different psychological forces within you.

Experiment in Observing My Specialness

This experiment works best when relating to others in the following circumstances:

1. In meetings, notice how you wish to say things that stand out.

2. In relation to your physical body, notice how you might dress to be noticed or how you attempt to cover up your physical defects.

3. In the way you move, study how you may be embarrassed and do not want others to see your mistakes; or conversely how much you may want others to notice how well you do something, often something incredibly simple.

4. In personal or work relations, the same as above—notice embarrassment over your errors and wanting to be seen when you do something well.

Of course, this is the short list. We need to lengthen it as we discover more about ourselves. The aim is not to find things we dislike about ourselves, but rather to notice the uncomfortable emotions that accompany our need to be special. This kind of study can put us in touch with our uneasiness and is another clue to escaping from our prison.

To be ordinary is to move against all of society's overt and covert messages that teach us we must excel, be special, and even be famous and powerful. Our psyches are full of these distorted images and archetypes. In the world of archetypes, we find gods and goddesses with various idealized attributes, such as the mythological figures Jupiter, Venus, and Mercury. We can become enslaved by our conformity to these vaguely experienced archetypes without even realizing it or knowing about these mythological beings. To be ordinary is actually freeing in and of itself. It is the simplest thing in the world and affords a place to be able to observe oneself and others. It is simple, but not an easy place to find in oneself.

CHAPTER 12

A TRANSFORMATIVE APPROACH TO NEGATIVITY

The Gurdjieff Work has highlighted the role of emotions, and negative emotions in particular, in the development and transformation of our lives. Ouspensky speaks about the "second conscious shock," an important moment in the transformation of impressions, which can only occur by working with our emotions. Gurdjieff left no instructions regarding how this work is to be done.[1] Other than telling us to try not to express negative emotions, the Work does not give us very much information about working with them. This lack of direction led me to seek out a means to understand and make use of my negative emotions. I found that unpleasant and painful emotions can be transformed for the development of real being. This is an area where modern psychological practice can offer some useful tools to the Work. In this chapter, I will explore the role of negative emotions and negative behaviors in our lives in more detail along with ways to work with them, and what we learn here will be applicable to all of our emotional states.

My personal work has shown me there is no way to harmonize our emotions, other than to become more conscious of them. Although our emotional state plays a part in almost all the activities of our lives, we neither know nor understand much about these emotions, other than we like some of them and wish to avoid others. Religions prescribe how we must act and the actions we must avoid. They inculcate fear in their teachings in the hope that people will change out of fear of going to hell and hope of going to heaven. Christianity and Judaism point to the Seven Deadly Sins: wrath, greed, sloth, pride, lust, envy, and gluttony. But these examples of our negativity and shortcomings do little good because they do not help us to change the way we are. Very few people ever study their emotions or understand how they work. Without this knowledge, nothing can change.

Perhaps we need to rethink the concept negative emotion and what it might mean in relation to Work. It may be that it needs a new definition. I would like to remove the onus of negative emotions and the wish to get rid of them; but, since Work has used the words "negative emotions," I will continue to do so at times. However, what I will mean by negative emotions are unpleasant and difficult emotions, those that are painful rather than pleasurable. I suggest that it is possible to learn to use these unpleasant emotions as a continuing source of immense energy for transformation. Negative emotions are an untapped goldmine. The ore that is to be mined is the deeper and truthful understanding of how my essence has become entrapped in patterns of thoughts, images, and emotional states. I cannot extract this gold by blocking over the entrance to the mine or throwing out the ore, but need to find a means to dissolve the material that is binding the gold. Dissolving is done by experiencing these emotions and behaviors and being present while they occur. Using my unpleasant emotions and my unbecoming behaviors in this way, rather than attempting to stop them, is quite contrary to the conventional idea of good and evil. By the way, Gurdjieff referred to the idea of "good and evil" as the most pernicious and harmful idea in human affairs.[2]

Unpleasant emotions use a great deal of energy. They can generate even more for my being, if I can transmute their energy instead of allowing it to block my access to my higher emotional center. Transmutation of negative emotions is radically different from seeking to avoid, suppress, not express, or project difficult feelings onto others. It is a hazardous business and requires compassion since we are very complex beings. As we shall see, we cannot simply make it happen just by wanting it to occur. Understanding the roots of a negative emotion is much more transformative than attempting to make it disappear.

CONTINUING THE STUDY OF NEGATIVE EMOTIONS

The study of negative emotions requires that you have already developed some degree of interior separation—a nascent authentic-I that is interested in your life. As you probably have understood already, I believe it is a mistake to try to change too quickly or to repress negative emotions.

Within our anger, fear, disgust, shame, pride, or jealousy, we can discern deeper meanings. A negative emotion does not exist in a vacuum. There is almost always a deeper emotional context hiding beneath it. For example, anger often masks stress and fear, or it can be a symptom of deeper distress. In many instances, anger may represent a coping or defense mechanism to help a person handle feelings of sadness, loss, or overwhelm.

When I face a difficult or confusing task, I may get angry in response to the stress I feel about being capable of completing it. In past relationships, others may have shamed me for not doing something well. Alternatively, I may have shamed myself, believing I should have done better, even if I had no previous experience with the task at hand. As I mentioned earlier, you may find through self-study that many negative states have a component of shame attached to them.

Sometimes we view basic fear as another negative emotion. However, fear is actually an instinctive function, an affect that is neither good nor bad. Biological fear is hard-wired in us as a survival mechanism. "Environmental impingement" is a term from psychology that refers to experiences and woundings you incur during your life because you were treated improperly or without respect. Due to environmental impingement, instinctive fear is paired with painful experiences and other emotions. In this way, the natural affect fear becomes the emotion fear, which is then mixed with extraneous impressions. If we try, we can remember certain emotions that were paired with fear when we experienced some difficult situation. For example, I tell a joke to my parents that I heard at school, and I thought it was funny. My father thinks it is inappropriate and smacks me across the mouth. This is painful and shaming. I may never be able to feel at ease just joking around again for fear that I will experience pain and shame—fear has now been paired with pain, shame, and joking around. People joking around can bring up a fear response in me. In this way, the instinctive fear that originally operated to protect me has been distorted.

The idea of pairing experiential content with a natural affect comes from classical conditioning theory and originated with the work of Ivan

Pavlov.[3] I mention classical conditioning because it sheds light on our associative processes. Pavlov's famous experiment with dogs, mentioned earlier, paired the ringing of a tone with feeding meat powder to dogs. The tone was presented just before the meat powder was given. The dogs salivated in response to the meat powder, their natural response; that is, all dogs salivate when presented with meat powder. Gradually, Pavlov used only the tone without the meat powder, and the dogs would begin to salivate all the same. The same thing happens with a natural affect such as fear. All people experience fear naturally, but fear pairs up with stimuli we associate with certain events, people, or actions and then becomes "learned" fear as distinct from instinctive fear.

Each of us has had many experiences that caused us to feel afraid. If the biological affect fear is paired with another stimulus, the pairing may cause me to feel fearful in situations other than where fear is really appropriate. Learned fear affects not only our emotional center; it affects our thoughts and our bodies as well. For example, the natural fear of falling off a cliff or driving too fast produces physical sensations and hormonal changes in my body's chemistry. However, because of pairing, I may experience the same sensations and hormonal changes when I have to meet new people at a party, make a mistake in a speech, or am unable to pay the bills.

When such learned fear is locked within me and has no outlet, it can easily become an ongoing state of anxiety. The stress from the anxiety then affects my body and thoughts in the same way instinctive fear would. People develop many intricate behaviors in their attempts to avoid learned fear and make their anxiety go away. Anxiety is often the result of unrecognized, repressed emotional fear that remains unintegrated. Often, unexamined beliefs are at the root of the anxiety. Anxiety breaks through when repressed learned fear associated with such beliefs can no longer be held in, either mentally or physically. Then a person experiences a panic attack or similar feeling of being overwhelmed.

Anxiety-reducing behaviors run the gamut from reading a novel to alcoholism to going to scary movies, from compulsive shopping to drug addiction, from an excessive need to succeed in our careers to gambling our livelihood away. Anxiety is there so often, but I do not notice it. I simply must be willing to remember myself and study my behavior. The more curious and knowledgeable I am about my negative emotions, including anxiety, the more emotional balance I may find.

People are often ashamed of their anxiety and try not to show it to others, but we need to understand it and learn how to properly contain and transform it. Only by studying our anxiety and not attempting to dull it through any form of self-medicating can we learn about it.

In therapy, medications may be useful when a person's anxiety has reached such a level that it affects his ability to function. There is no shame in taking medications to help reach a more grounded state so that some therapeutic work can occur. The important thing is not to forget the inner work. Drugs alone, without the work to understand myself, may end up being a psychological crutch. There are exceptions, where an individual's actual chemical makeup may require medications to allow him simply to function normally in the world.

In other words, negative emotions are a source of energy for our personal evolution, but that energy may be trapped in unconscious habit patterns. If we could use them for our work, these energies would become what Gurdjieff called the "Holy Denying" force. King has this to say about good and evil and the study of negative emotions:

> Correct Self-Observation of emotions, including nega-
> tive ones, is the non-identified observation of their
> organic symptoms in one's own body. In respect of nega-
> tive emotions it will be found that such Self-Observation
> in fact leads to the alteration of the symptoms and very
> shortly to the disappearance of the emotion itself.[4]

King was on the right track, but I find his formulation somewhat simplistic and possibly misleading. He gives the impression that the negative emotion will simply disappear quickly. In my experience, it is not disappearance but transmutation that occurs, and it takes time and continued self-study. It is too easy for people to interpret King's description as a quick means to get rid of unpleasant emotions. Merely observing the negative emotion can actually create a higher level of energy within me. If I can continue to observe my negativity over time, the negative emotion may be psychologically changed and integrated in my emotional center in a new and positive way. This is actually what the alchemists meant when they spoke of turning base metals into gold.

The transformation of our negative emotions takes place when we are awake, while we actually experience the emotion. It is the natural outcome of our capacity for separation. We work with our observing "I," not trying to change anything, while we actively participate in what is happening. Active participation without us seeking to change our behavior allows us to experience a state of self-consciousness and awareness. Awareness can provide the possibility of our experiencing reconciling force. Exposure of our negative emotions to the light of consciousness gives us a wealth of information about ourselves.

If we can truly express a negative emotion outwardly without violence and maintain an objective part that is present as well, that experience will transform us in a way no amount of thinking or feeling alone will do. In other words, my ability to learn to express emotions—negative or positive—without violence or inner repression, is integral to my transformation.

On the other hand, if at first we try to directly alter an emotion, be it positive or negative, it is usually because we have reached some judgment about it, a mixture of thinking and feeling. A simple example with a negative emotion: you believe you should not outwardly express your anger, so you try repressing it. You find you can repress it in certain circumstances, but not in others. You are frustrated by your inability to hold back your anger and feel as though you have failed in relation to your Work aim. Your frustration eventually becomes disgust with yourself for your inability to keep your anger in check. Eventually, this disgust feeds into your tendency to dislike and be disappointed in yourself. Gradually, you come to hate yourself and the fact that you cannot control your anger. Your gatekeeper has new material now and can busy himself.

This self-hate then will need to express itself. Perhaps you will need to self-medicate in some manner because your negative feelings about yourself have become too strong. You then start looking at pornography because you just need a break from your disappointment and self-hate. Your wife finds out about this addiction and now you are furious at her and ashamed she has caught you. Now you need to stop that also, so you begin drinking. Before you know it, you no longer get angry because you are so occupied with the other diversions you have developed to comfort yourself. And so it goes. This simple example is not fiction, but is taken from life.

In general, when we place an inner taboo on some emotional manifestation such as anger, it may end up backfiring on us emotionally. Rather than allowing us to forget our anger and experience more joy, it has the opposite effect. We have unconsciously set up a merit system within us that our future actions must meet. However, we cannot meet the requirements of our self-imposed merit system, since it lies hidden within our unconscious almost all the time. Therefore, we fail, and then we dislike ourselves even more. That feeling of failure causes us to move the manifestation of our anger from its outward expression and focus the anger on ourselves. Thus, self-hate will eventually increase. Any system of taboos that an individual cannot adhere to will result in self-hate or some other negative behavior. It is all the same if someone else created the taboos or we created them.

In summary, we need to study very carefully and seriously the idea of transformation of our negative emotions, a core idea of Gurdjieff's system. We need to study and observe our emotional states and not try to banish the negative ones too soon. The painful emotions need the light of observation more than they need our criticism. Nyland once told me something very simple and helpful: "In the light of the sun, the ice will melt." So it is with negative emotions. Allow your negative emotion to continue, even express it in words, and simply have the courage to participate with it. Allow your observing "I" to experience it in the moment. If you aim to early toward the nonexpression of negative emotion, you may be not only "throwing the baby out with the bathwater," you may be throwing out the bathtub itself.

NOTICING, IN THE STUDY OF EMOTIONS

The first thing we need to do to study our emotions is to simply notice them. When you notice anger, fear or worry, sadness, a compulsion to do something, immediately pay attention to your bodily sensations that accompany that emotion. There is no need to think about the emotion; we need to connect with our bodies when we notice emotions, either positive or negative ones. Otherwise, our self-study will remain only in the intellectual center and not give us actual impressions of the emotions. Thinking about emotional states produces almost no real result unless we also experience the emotion in our bodies.

Noticing an Emotional State

First, you notice that you are _____ (fill in the emotion). Then:

1. Sit down. Stop or reduce your outer activity, if possible.

2. Place your attention on the sensations occurring in the main core of your body, that area that extends like a tube about 4 to 7 inches wide, running from your throat to your navel.

3. Pay attention to the sensations in this area. Stay with the sensations. Your emotional state may continue.

4. When your mind wanders, gently draw it back to the sensations.

5. Do not try to change the sensations.

6. While remaining with the sensations, notice whether any other emotions are floating around in this core area, such as sadness, stress (felt as anxiety), hopelessness, overwhelm, fear, disappointment, etc. Just make a note of these emotions, but do not attempt to change them. Continue to bring your attention back to the somatic sensations. Perhaps an idea or an image will come up—just be interested in it without analyzing.

If you are able to practice studying your emotions once a week, you will gradually develop the ability to intentionally notice and experience your emotional state. This practice is a good model for studying all emotions, including the negative or painful ones. Remember, the beginning stage of all study in this area requires noticing. Noticing is different from merely thinking about something or thinking about myself, thinking about studying myself, or thinking about observation. Noticing is a faculty that is actually relatively undeveloped in most of us. In Bennett's gem of a book entitled *Noticing*, he says:

> Noticing is connected with the "I," with the real "I." But because we have nothing prepared that is able to give this

a place in us, it is just a moment. It is also fair to say that noticing is something that happens to our essence; but because we cannot remain conscious of ourselves in our essence until very considerable changes have happened, we notice, and then our personality takes over. After the moment of noticing, though very interesting things may happen, they no longer have that extraordinary quality. From that moment onwards, we think, we see, we argue with ourselves, we run away, we avoid things, all the different ways in which the personality can react to a situation.[5]

At first, noticing may seem to be a very ordinary human capacity. However, noticing can have very positive benefits for our development if we practice it. Linda Moore, a good friend, one of the editors of this book, and someone who has been involved in Work for many years, made this profound comment to me about noticing: "Unless we notice, we will never be in a position to choose our direction or act for ourselves. Noticing is a transition from one state of existence to another. We have largely neglected the significance of this transition—which is not a process in time—because we fail to understand its relevance to freedom. Noticing is the opening of possibility. How can we train ourselves to grasp this kind of opportunity?"[6]

TRANSITIONS AND INTERVALS

Ordinarily, people move from one activity to the next with no space in between. However, if we give ourselves time to pause, usually called "time to think," it affords us a chance to behave differently. Transition periods during the day are an opportunity to become familiar with psychological material and behavior we usually don't notice. In these intervals, we may gather new impressions. Otherwise, the seamless nature of our automatism makes it difficult to experience anything new. Associative memories tend to fill in the gaps in our experiences and there is little space for new impressions. However, during the transitions, we can find the intervals in the octave, where we can notice something new and different. Thus, these intervals can be good stopping places where I can pause and work.

Transition Periods During the Day

1. During your day, pick a few transition times; for example, when you arrive at work in your car. Before you get out of the car to start your workday, sit in the car for one to two minutes without doing anything. Then notice what comes up for you or simply what you notice. You may notice how long two minutes actually is. See if you can be still for two minutes, before you begin the next sequence of your day.

2. When you are asked to get something done at work, sit quietly for one to two minutes before you begin. Notice the pressure of time. Direct your attention gently to your breathing, then your neck muscles, then your throat, chest and stomach. Pay attention to the sensations in those areas. Do not try to change anything!

3. When you are speaking with someone, let them speak for a minute or two minutes, and instead of speaking, just remain quiet and listen—hold your own thoughts while you listen.

4. When you eat lunch or breakfast, sit for a few minutes before and after the meal without doing anything.

Again, the purpose of experimenting with transitions is not really to change anything at this time, but to become familiar with the pressure of my habitual life and also look around and notice. Actually, creating and paying attention to the transition periods is already a big change. A general rule is that we do not really need to change our behavior in the early and middle phases of Work. Transformation comes through the addition of observation and the resultant state of awareness as we see the truth of ourselves.

As an analogy, imagine you are driving on a highway. You habitually miss the exit to your destination because you tend to daydream, and you get annoyed each time you miss it. You finally figure out you cannot be sure of taking the correct exit unless you become familiar with the signposts along the highway. Observing oneself and sensing oneself is akin to becoming familiar with the highway your mind travels. Taking the correct exit will not be possible before you are very familiar with your own internal landscape, currently invisible to you.

Through Work, we make invisible patterns visible. It is similar to a hunter going after invisible prey. These exercises make the prey visible for a moment here and there, help you gain impressions of the prey (in this case, you are the prey), and remain compassionate about what becomes visible. Gradually, you can become compassionate and knowledgeable as you gain a more complete picture of yourself.

As you become more familiar with the seamless nature of your habitual patterns of movement, thought, and emotions, you will be able to notice more transition points. Recently, I have become very alert to the transition time just before getting out of my car. I sit for a minute or more. I sometimes catch myself at the instant before exiting. I look around and notice the external impressions. At other times, I simply stop while stepping out and maintain that posture for a few moments, experience my body leaning on the car door, as I get ready to step away and close the door. In some ways this is changing something, but my aim is not to change; it is to pay attention at this moment of transition. This is the beginning of experimentation, where a rather insignificant adjustment gives me new information about myself. Experimentation is an advanced area of Work, and one should approach it only gradually and carefully.

An essential part of our work is bringing into awareness what is obscure, including embracing aspects of our experience we previously deemed undesirable. Let us get a little experience with this by looking at depression. Later in this chapter, we will discuss other emotions.

DEPRESSION

Depression is an important topic of self-study. As you work, you will undoubtedly encounter your own depression. It is important for any seeker to know as much as possible about it. You need to study your depression and find some of the gifts that it has to offer.

Depression is often the result of unconscious material that has been repressed, marginalized, or denied. It will often recur because of the path your life is taking. Our values, that is, what we feel is important to us, determine how we spend our time in life. I can go through my entire life without examining my values, how I spend my time. Depression can be a signal that I need to reevaluate my life or, at least, stop and take notice that I am depressed. It can help me derive deeper meaning from my experiences or even change my values or the direction of my life.

Sometimes, there is psychological material you may have put off looking at. Depression can be a symptom that you need to bring this material forward, understand and then integrate it. For my essence to grow, I need to bring this depressing material out of the shadows and into the light of my awareness. The way I meet this new material will determine whether I can extract any insights from my depression.

If we suffer from depression unconsciously, we tend to self-medicate or look for ways to avoid becoming depressed. People sleep more, drink more, put off more, shop more, get angry more, etc. If on the other hand, if they can meet depression with curiosity, they can learn a great deal. Having compassion for yourself when you experience depression, rather than just feeling sorry for yourself will allow you to gather new impressions and derive more meaning from your experience.

I have noticed that depression feels very much to me like a bad cold, but much worse. As I sit here writing this paragraph, I am suffering from a cold. I do not get them often and like to brag that I have not had a bad cold in more than ten years. Well, this looks like a real cold and feels like one too. What are my tendencies? I want to get it over with so I can feel well and get on with my life. The cold is forcing me to curtail my usual activities and I am a little bit annoyed about that. I want to just stop writing and take a nap, but my throat and nose tell me I probably will not be able to nap anyway. I am wondering just how long this cold will last, will I be able to sleep tonight, will it get worse, will I be sick for a week, what about my clients? I wish my cold would be over now! My wish to end it is a very important clue about depression. We want to get it over with, be rid of it.

As a society, we attempt to banish depression to the netherworld. We do not like dark places. We only need to look at how shopping malls bring in natural light to dispel any depressive feelings in their shoppers. Western architecture, transportation, dress, and products are meant to camouflage and cast out depression. Medications, counseling, theater and comedic films are meant to reduce our suffering from the depression lurking just beneath the surface. People unconsciously schedule their days and vacations to mitigate depression and their fear of it. We are actually trying to free ourselves from the suffering inherent in depression. Depression is even construed by Work people as being a negative. If people are depressed, there is a reason to avoid them.

In reality, depression is very important for us. Thomas Moore, in *Care of the Soul*, sees depressive disturbances as a possible impetus for individuals to reevaluate their lives and to go deeper into themselves.[7] A few psychological theorists now de-pathologize (take it out of the "illness" or psychological disorder category) depression and are beginning to view depression as a necessary element in the human journey. It is time for those of us in the Work to become more interested in it. We need to talk more openly about our personal and collective experience of depression.

JEALOUSY

What do we know about jealousy? Have you thought about it, or its twin—competition? Both are strong motivators. Yet, since childhood, they remain almost invisible to us. We might experience unpleasant feelings when we believe someone appears to be better than we are at something, looks better than we do, or has something we want. They might look younger, thinner, better dressed, seem more alive, have more money, or seem smarter. These perceptions of the other person activate suffering in us. We call it "jealousy." Such experiences are very important for self-study because they can allow you to observe a group of inner masters who direct your negative emotional life and cause you to suffer mechanically.

Jealousy develops very early in our upbringing. Parents, relatives, teachers, friends and the media hold up to us the activities and achievements of others as being wonderful. Their admiration leads us to strive to be that way too, because we desire the same admiration and recognition. They tell us to get good grades. If we receive an "Excellent" on our Kindergarten report card, smiles and good feelings from teachers and parents come our way. If someone else gets a better grade, draws a better picture, is more popular, is better looking, is not afraid, is funnier, is more clever, then you want to be like them. You feel jealous if you are not getting the same recognition. Thus, jealousy begins as we begin school, or even earlier if our parents favor one sibling over another or make them compete against each other.

Teaching children to be jealous seems conscious or intentional; it is an integral part of the educational system. Jealousy is insidious and becomes second nature, one of the motivating forces that fuels our waking-sleeping state. Jealousy increases the unbecoming aspects of personality and inhibits the growth of essence. Other culprits that promote jealousy are advertising, merchandising, and consumerism, and the competitiveness they engender.

Modern advertising is designed to induce imitation, jealousy, and competition. We see a beautiful woman or man, having certain things or looking a certain way. These images are held up to us as ideals to which we should aspire. If we become like them, look like them and have what they have, then others will feel jealous of us and appreciate how wonderful we are. Almost every major business uses advertising to sell its product and engender jealousy. One of the most bizarre aspects to me of modern media's exploitation of jealousy is that it can make a hero out of the most venal or even despicable characters. As long as someone has made a fortune or even inherited one, he is, in the media's eyes, worthy of emulation.

COMPETITION AND CONCEPTS OF MASCULINITY

Competition is jealousy's twin. From our earliest days, we are thrown into competition with others. It is not sufficient just to be ourselves; instead, we must be better than others. Leaders in education, psychology, and politics may argue that competition is necessary for society to move forward. This idea is so prevalent that anyone who would disagree with it runs the risk of being considered crazy or naive. I began to doubt the benefits of competition quite a number of years ago. When I mention my doubt to others, they act as if I am a little strange. In recent years, there have been others questioning the role of competition.

Terrence Real, in writing about male depression, says that from the youngest years, the isolation a man feels is supported through the presence of competition at every level.[8] A young male client of his, upon meeting another bicyclist on the road, instead of wanting to find out about him, wants to "blow him away." [9] He says the reality is that when men enter into relationships with other men, it is often tinged with jockeying for power, which throws men into the paradox of having to one-up the other as a means of entering a relationship.

In *Beelzebub's Tales to His Grandson*, Gurdjieff alludes to the destructive nature of sports. However, I doubt he ever could have imagined what has happened today, to men in particular, with the growth of the sports industry. Sports now deify competition. Men have become addicted to sport and to drinking together while watching sports events. In first-world countries, sports bars are the rage. In second and third world societies, men can justify killing a soccer player if he misses a goal. The hypnotic effect of spectator sports plus alcohol has become a lethal potion that curtails men's inner development. Many images are now firmly embedded in our psyche from our universal preoccupation with sports. In his book *Knights Without Armor*, clinical psychologist Aaron Kipnis reports on his investigations of the archetypal masculine images that have imbued American society.[10]

One is that through athletic prowess, men will become successful and attractive to women. For example, high school football in the United States is a sport responsible for three hundred thousand to one and a quarter million injuries in young men each year, where the aim is to crush the other team; the football player has become the icon symbolizing American men's values. The attendees at such competitive sports include a surprising number of women who unconsciously reinforce men's distorted archetypal images.

Watching spectator sports is now a means to compensate for the boredom and emptiness of men's inner lives and allows one man to feel closer to another by being united in a shared interest—beating the other team. The word "beating" should be our clue. Kipnis traces such tendencies back to the Roman gladiators. He posits that contact sports allow the audience a vicarious release from their own frustrations and aggressive tendencies.

Another hidden message of contact sports is that men must prepare themselves to be injured and mutilated as part of their duty to protect women and children. Kipnis says, "Much of the conditioning adolescent boys receive is the perfect preparation for turning a playful life—the affirming boy into a complacent soldier, unquestioning cannon fodder, a killing machine—a real man." [11] Such conditioning, he says, sends men the message that only through performing heroically will they receive love and affection both from women and powerful older men. They must repress their pain, practice martyrdom, and further the myth that heroes don't need attention. Competitive sports foster false personality at the expense of essence, which is left unnourished, like a beggar on the street.

Again, verify all this for yourself. The simplest arenas of study are sports events, television broadcasts, and the hero worship given to successful sports figures. Famous sports figures become gods, empty idols who glorify useless pastimes, such as hitting a ball into a hole. In and of themselves, sports are fine as a distraction. When they become a way of life, emulated by thousands of young men and women, we should at least question the meaning of such fascination. They infect our young with a competitive virus that remains with them throughout their lives.

Competition appears whenever any group meets or anywhere you find yourself in close connection with others for a definite aim. To glimpse competition in yourself and others try the following exercise.

Study of One's Competitive Habits

When you are in a group where you usually talk:

1. Do not speak for half an hour.

2. Notice the emotions that build within you.

3. Sense your body and your posture.

4. Notice any tendency to find something objectionable in what another says, how you need to correct him or her or to make your point.

5. Notice the automatism to join in when you hear something that makes sense and others are agreeing with it. Notice wanting not to be left out and feeling you should maybe add something, so that you too will be noticed.

This practice will give you impressions of your competitiveness. It is not bad, not something to be stopped, but definitely something to notice.

FEAR AND FALSE PERSONALITY

The pressure of life and the fear it produces are such big topics that I feel compelled to add a bit more about them here.

I have found that fear is an underlying emotion in almost all people. It appears to be both universal and the foundation for false personality. Of all the emotions, fear seems ubiquitous. It has the chameleon-like ability to blend in and disappear into every human emotion or thought.

Years ago, a friend said to me, "Fear is the attempt or wish for something not to happen, or to avoid the experience of what is happening." Over the years, I have been able to verify this simple definition through my experience. The basis of fear is part of our intrinsic biological need for security. As I mentioned earlier, natural fear is a biological affect that alerts us to danger. For example, when we stray too close to the edge of a cliff, we feel fear. It also helps us recognize when we are in a situation beyond our abilities; thus, it serves as a basic survival mechanism.

By contrast, in the formation of false personality, fear serves a quite different function. There, the natural affect of fear is distorted. It becomes fear-anxiety. The development of our actual personality appears to be necessary to adjust to culture and allow for the diversification and development of the human species. Perhaps without an individual personality, we would all act the same. On the other hand, I do not really need false personality for my survival. It is an artificial appliance and, therefore, fear-anxiety easily roots itself there. One trait I have found in my own false personality is my habit of exaggerating as a means of bringing attention to myself.

False personality depends on embellishments that take many different forms. Obvious ones include how we dress to impress others, our preoccupation with how we look or what others think about us. Less obvious embellishments are hidden; for example, how we judge our own worth.

Embellishments of personality take many different forms. Almost all of these are false and therefore inherently vulnerable, and thus, the perfect receptacle for fear-anxiety. Yet, it is not fear of death or injury that our false personality suffers from, but an artificial fear of embarrassment or pseudo-shame, a fear of what others think about us. This kind of anxiety is the fuel for Gurdjieff's concept of internal considering. It also can serve as a clear example of an unpleasant or negative emotion. The effect of others' opinions can be devastating to false personality. We read that Gurdjieff made it a habit of stepping on people's "corns," or the embellishments of false personality.

Our personality and the ego formed at its center is on an impossible quest, the creation of a secure world for us. Life is inherently insecure and unstable, and dynamic because of its lack of complete predictability. Yet, we spend almost all of our energy trying to make life—this dynamic exchange of energies that is changeable, alive, creative, flexible, growing, and disintegrating—into something stable and static. Of course, physical security is a biological imperative. We need shelter for our children—a cave, a house, dependable caregivers, and the like. However, our drive for stability at all costs may actually deaden us. Our inability to accept life's ups and downs—perhaps its most basic characteristic—can turn life into something frightening. To stave off the certainty of decay and ultimate annihilation, people occupy themselves with artificial, dysfunctional interests. They are preoccupied with the accumulation of wealth; they plan for retirement and pay for insurance of every type. These are all attempts to stabilize the inherently unstable. Our fascination with machines, technology, and money is, in many ways, part of our addiction to making life secure, repeatable, and predictable at the material level—in essence, more machinelike. Benjamin put it this way: "The personality craves for security in a very insecure world; it—the product of perishable matter and doomed to eventual dissolution—demands continuity for itself and permanence, which it is quite unable to secure for itself. Therefore, the personality's basic reaction to life is fear." [12]

We are overly concerned with protecting ourselves, building ourselves up, having more money and physical comfort than is necessary. We overindulge. We become violent when our security is threatened. It is all because of our desire for security and the impossibility of ever attaining it in the physical world. However, very few of us look to our inner lives for security.

Fear also appears to be the core emotion that causes people to form nation-states. The more I have observed the politics of the United States and other major world powers, the more they appear to be run by fear, although greed also plays a primary role. The major world powers are simply the most proficient countries at this time at manifesting their automatic reaction to this unconscious need to achieve the impossible—to make life feel secure. Politicians intentionally manipulate our natural tendency to wish to protect ourselves and our families. They may even create a state of increased insecurity in order to justify war, violence, or dominance.

What are the common responses to fear-anxiety? Some people become depressed. Others feel subdued and anxious. Still others become aggressive and violent. The dominant response of humanity appears to be aggression that runs the gamut from arguments to war, or preparation for future violence. Countries develop weapons and raise armies. This default to violence has become a habit pattern. It is our current response to any perceived or imagined threat.

Another by-product of fear-anxiety is our tendency to lie, to hide the truth from others out of fear that it will make us vulnerable. Turning to physical violence to dispel fear-anxiety now parallels what has become the disease of lying to achieve emotional security. Violence and lying are predictable results of society's reactions to the fear and anxiety that underlie our psychological insecurity. If we could understand the twin dysfunctions of deceit and fear-anxiety, we might profoundly change the future.

Every individual person is a cell of the human membrane spread over this planet. If groups of us increase our self-understanding and compassion, this membrane becomes more flexible, and this process might allow new energies and possibilities, in conjunction with more conscious energies, to enter the mainstream of human life.

STUDY OF PERSONAL FEAR

I began to study my own fears some twenty-five years ago. I had no idea then that this would become an actual practice of Work for me and one that would yield a wealth of important material for understanding myself. It began one morning when I was awakened by my anxiety at

5:30 a.m. I lay in bed and became acutely aware that I was nervous, felt tension in my chest, and noticed various concerns and worries swirling in my mind about the day ahead. A part of me wanted to deny and avoid these worries and just wanted to get back to sleep, but this was not to be. I also was angry and frustrated since I was so tired. Finally, I got up and showered, but I noticed feelings of dread, small fears, thoughts, and anxieties swarming about. I felt overwhelmed and I wanted to escape from this feeling.

As I was just about to launch myself into another day, a most unusual image came to me. I saw myself sitting down quietly on the edge of the bed. Something was telling me, "If you are going to suffer all day with this anxiety and tension in your body, then instead of running into activity to try to get away from it, sit down on the edge of the bed. Call these fears up one at a time—invite them in and meet them."

Most of me didn't want to. Sitting there while calling up my fears about the day ahead seemed like a waste of time and couldn't possibly help. Another part of me felt desperate enough to try anything. So I sat on the edge of the bed for thirty minutes. During that time, I intentionally connected with the fearful sensations in my throat and chest areas. While maintaining that connection with my sensations, I thought about each problem and fear, one after the other, until I exhausted the list. I tried to experience my fear and anxiety as deeply as possible in my body; I allowed and even willed myself to experience my fears and sense my body.

Gradually, a subtle change occurred. It was not only that my fear lessened, but rather than feeling overwhelmed by each fear, a new part of me was able to tolerate it, and that changed my relationship to fear. I was learning to engage my fear. I had discovered a way to enlarge, strengthen, and increase the flexibility of my emotional center and allow a new type of integration to take place within me. Additionally, I had made explicit all my fears and worries. I felt that they were all on the table, so to speak. This way, they were much less scary than if I had stuffed them down and boxed them into one corner of myself.

I have continued my study of fear-anxiety and have taught others about this and similar methods. It may very well be that my interest in fear and anxiety is due to my psychological type. However, I have seen the same patterns in many others and hear about similar patterns in clients of other therapists. The suffering they describe often centers on fear.

The study of fear has major implications and holds the possibility of releasing us from our emotional slavery. Fear binds us into habitual, self-destructive patterns. It limits our possibilities in so many ways that volumes could be written. However, those of us in the Work can study the effects of fear and anxiety on us and use what we find for our development.

Important aspects of fear can be observed in how people handle stress. Everyone has a habitual way of handling or avoiding it. A person can sit and read a magazine; engage in hobbies, sports, or exercise; go to a movie; smoke a cigarette; have a drink; smoke a joint; go to a baseball game; or, can have an argument with someone they care about. More dysfunctional methods of handling stress may include having an affair, emotionally abusing your mate, becoming addicted to substances, compulsive shopping or gambling. For the most part, the way we handle stress goes unnoticed in our lives. Even people who have been engaged in Work activities for many years remain ignorant of the causes of their stress. They don't know what they do to relieve it, how it feels in their bodies or especially, how it affects their emotional lives.

In couple's therapy, I often find that the inability of one or both partners to handle personal stress is a key to difficulties in the relationship. If the couple is unaware of the part stress plays in their lives, they blame (gatekeep) each other. They persuade themselves that if the other only would change, the relationship would improve. It takes some time for individuals to understand that they project the burdens of the stress they each carry into their relationship and onto the other, and there is really no one to blame. Nor would everything in the relationship be fine if the other person changed. Difficult situations in a relationship are almost always symptomatic of a dynamic interaction dependent on both parties.

Some relief is attained in a couple's therapy when one member begins to take responsibility for his own stress and be accountable for it. Then both can begin to own their stresses and how they have acted them out in the relationship. This accountability results in greater trust between the couple. Then they can both see that the acting-out is not really the other partner's fault. It is the result of the "actor-outer's" inability to understand his inner stresses and the ensuing dynamic interaction. They then realize the importance of being aware of their level of stress and of learning how to meet it creatively. Each of us needs to learn how to soothe ourselves when we are stressed. All too often we expect our partner to soothe us, are unable to express this need, and this expectation causes a great many hardships in close relationships.

Psychological self-soothing is not what Gurdjieff called "self-calming." In response to the stresses of modern life, self-soothing can be a means to manage disharmony. Modern life is filled with so many situations that produce fear and anxiety that some degree of stress is inevitable. To live in a state of constant worry and anxiety is an incredible waste of energy, and thus it is necessary to learn to talk with oneself and calm down. Many people never learn this technique; instead, they use drugs or alcohol or engage in other unconscious behaviors to reduce their stress.

The greatest loss of personal energy I see in clients is from constant worry, perhaps the most useless negative emotion we experience. It often results in a chronic state of anxiety in which the intellectual center joins the emotional center in worrying about one thing after another until the body has no choice, but to drink, sleep, or find another way to relieve the tension. Chronic anxiety becomes a habitual pattern of behavior. This state can be very difficult to get a handle on without a definite approach.

In couple's therapy, integration and stress reduction for the couple often requires each member to take time away from the relationship. However, it is often quite difficult to convince certain couples that time apart is necessary, especially where both people feel compelled to keep hammering on each other as a means to work their problems through. However, after just a small break, a few days spent alone with one's thoughts and feelings away from ordinary life, a partner can return to the relationship emotionally softer, because he or she is back in touch with a deeper part of themselves.

Softening toward yourself is not about justifying your actions or subduing your conscience, but rather it is about how you speak to yourself. Most of us can be more compassionate and understanding with others than we can with ourselves. It is important to notice how we inwardly treat ourselves and what sort of attitude we have toward our inner self.

PATTERNS OF INDIVIDUAL STRESS

Over-drinking, over-eating, over-smoking, over-working, over-sexing, or under-sexing are examples of dysfunctional stress-reducing behaviors that lead to the need for automatic self-calming rather than intentional self-soothing. Gurdjieff alludes to the fact that self-calming has now become part of our nature. It is often difficult see it in ourselves. Self-calming does not work because it is mechanical and actually results in even more stress. The latter is due to the fact that what is causing our upset and imbalance is never really dealt with, but repressed or denied. We need to study this cycle of over-doing, of being out of balance. However, it is not easy to observe such unbalanced behavior even when our machine repeats it continually. This repetition of wasteful behavior is characteristic of our waking-sleeping state and difficult to change.

Generally, the parts of any system tend to keep the system in order by resisting change. In some ways, cohesiveness or the resistance to change defines a system. This holds true whether the system is an actual machine, a person, or a relationship. When you exhibit dysfunctional behavior resulting from stress, your organism resists your ability to observe this pattern or change it. Why would this be so? Because you need a special energy to carry out the observation, and your system does not believe there is any energy to spare. It has habituated itself to spending its energies in a limited number of ways and within a certain time period. In fact, people are so pressured by time and habit they are often unable to stop unless they are hurt or sick. Thus, time pressure works as part of the system to resist any attempts you make to observe yourself. Just being able to notice your stress is a small beginning that can lead to a big shift.

Although one part of us wants to learn about our stress-induced behaviors, other parts have a vested interest in perpetuating them. Our buffers keep us from seeing the contradictions. If the parts do make contact, it may feel exceedingly unpleasant—it feels like even more tension. Buffers, in certain ways, are defenses against suffering and inner tension; but as far as handling stress or reducing suffering, they often produce a paradoxical result. A buffer may block out stress in one area that then pops up somewhere else. However, whenever we study and gather new impressions of ourselves, we weaken the buffers. That may not be possible when we begin Work. Gradually, however, we may increase our ability to be aware of our inner contradictions, thereby weakening the buffers indirectly as we accumulate self-knowledge.

GENDER PREJUDICE

I hope most of us in the Work are aware we harbor prejudice toward people of different colors, genders, cultures, economic or educational levels, height, weight, and perhaps most importantly, psychological type.[13] However, our understanding of prejudice is usually quite vague and remains at the preconscious level (that is, the level of consciousness that lies just beneath our ordinary waking-sleeping state). If you are quiet and sit in a chair alone for fifteen minutes, you can notice a stream of words, images, songs, and sensations that is constantly flowing within you—this stream represents the surface of the preconscious level.

As a psychologist, I found it was important for me to become familiar with my own prejudices. One area of particular interest became gender. Gender prejudice has become a part of our psychological inheritance. In many of the developed countries, some new inroads are being made toward dissolving prejudices, especially gender prejudice, but in general, prejudice is the norm, clearly visible and bolstered by societal institutions. However, most people remain relatively unaware of the reasons for their prejudices.

Generally, men tend to hold prejudice toward any woman who threatens what they believe is their God-given right to hold the lion's share of power. Women, in turn, tend to be prejudiced toward men in reaction to men's behavior, which only serves to reinforce men's domineering and patriarchal nature.[14] Historically, women have suffered due to the abhorrent manner in which men have treated them in these patriarchal cultures. It might very well be that all civilizations that transitioned from horticultural hunting societies to agricultural societies needed men's superior strength to keep the farms going. Men thus controlled the means of production. They have since maintained their control by creating systems of government, religion, family, society, and laws that perpetuated their dominance. Women have generally had little power, even when heads of state have been women. It is only within the last one hundred years, with the advent of technology and birth control, that women have been able to change the outer form of their lives and wrest some control for themselves. And only during the last thirty years, has there been a change in the way men have viewed and treated women.

The fear, resentment, and prejudice women generally hold toward men lies along a spectrum ranging from caution to hatred; in all likelihood, this is due to the treatment they historically received during their lives. Women have been, and still are, beaten, enslaved, and treated as chattels. Such treatment in varying forms appears to be deeply rooted in every major culture. The mistreatment of women even extends to women themselves, who keep their positions in some cultures by mistreating lower-ranking women and mutilating female children. In some countries, women resist any release from the established patriarchal structure and persecute or ridicule those women who want to free themselves from such constraints.

I find in my psychotherapy practice that many men, unconsciously, are actually afraid of women. Their predisposition toward the degradation of women and the feminine seems to have its roots in their insecurity. This insecurity has resulted in men's need to act as if they are superior to women, even if there is not a genuine need. I also find that most men are wary of the potential hostility that women may have toward them. Women's greater connection to their emotional centers also gives them an advantage in understanding men's emotional states. This advantage can seem threatening to men.

Because women have greater access to their emotional centers, they are more capable of developing close relationships. Men, due to their more competitive nature and lack of experience with emotions, have greater difficulty developing such relationships. Men's innate prejudice toward women and fear of them also adds to their habit of objectifying women; that is, they treat women as objects and devalue their greater emotional development. A symptom of this is men's over-focusing on the physical beauty of women; this becomes an addiction for men in modern culture and generally leads to too many partnerships based mainly on physical attraction. Such partnerships are inherently unstable. The study of gender prejudice for both men and women is a requirement if a new type of relationship is to form between them.

PREJUDICE TOWARD OTHERS

Another aspect of prejudice is the automatic need to feel either superior or inferior to others. Few individuals get in touch with the underlying reasons for such prejudices or how they restrict their relationships. Superiority can be a defense against feelings of inferiority or insecurity. Alternately, an attitude of superiority can come from introjection (that is, the imitation of parental behavior and/or others' values and opinions). Such feelings of superiority or inferiority cause us to miss the actual experience of others—we simply cannot let them in or see them for who they are. We are either dismissing them as inferior and discounting them or elevating them as superior and making more of them than they deserve. In both cases, we are inhibited from making a real connection. The habit of feeling either superior or inferior to others can also create difficulty within a group and exacerbate people's inability to tolerate differences.

Human beings love to organize and create structure; however, structure by definition means exclusion of certain elements. The design of a building cannot contain all designs or all types of rooms. The building's design serves its function and is limited to the particular purpose for which it is built. The structure of a gymnasium is different from that of a medical clinic. Moreover, once a structure has been created, it will, by its very existence, resist change.

Likewise, once our psychological structures are in place, usually by seven to ten years of age, but for some not until the late teenage years, we tend to maintain and reinforce them automatically. Generally, we include those experiences and people we are familiar with and exclude others. The unfamiliar often seems dangerous. It produces fear or anxiety, the basic underlying dynamic of prejudice. We need to study these prejudices we hold toward peoples' race, their appearance, manner of speech, attitudes, etc. This is a very fruitful area of study because prejudice can be very subtle. It operates in almost all interactions among people; and yet for the most part, we remain unaware of it.

SCHADENFREUDE AND GOSSIP

Schadenfreude is a German word signifying pleasure derived from others' misfortunes. I was struck by this word when I came upon it because it was symbolic of so many negative feelings I had noticed in myself and others. The study of how interested each of us is in the difficulties others are experiencing is indeed a "dark" study—a study of part of our own shadow side.

Because my grandparents raised me, I was constantly around older women, friends of my grandmother, all homemakers, with no vocation outside their homes. When I would arrive home from school in the late afternoon, my grandmother would be sitting with a few friends. The major subject of their conversation was the other women they knew, their husbands, marriages, and how they all were doing. One woman named Harriet always had a strong effect on me. Harriet exuded a poisonous atmosphere, and I intuitively felt I could not trust her. When she was with my grandmother, I could feel a marked contrast between the two of them. My grandmother, although enjoying the gossip and schadenfreude, rarely had any real negativity or vehemence attached to her statements about their friends. However, Harriet's conversation seemed to be filled with hatred for everyone. The only time Harriet would praise someone was when he had made a lot of money.

As I got older, I began to experience an increasing aversion to Harriet. I disliked her and did not even want to talk to her. Many years later, I learned she was dying from cancer. A part of me did not want to see her, but another part felt I had to, that something was required of me. I visited her as she lay dying and immediately felt that the poisonous vibration had left her—as had my aversion for her. It was a healing moment for both of us and I found myself feeling compassion and caring for her.

Gossip, especially negative gossip, is endemic in society. Newspapers and television have raised schadenfreude to an art form. I have studied my own tendency to be fascinated by what is happening to others and take particular interest if there is some difficulty they are going through. I have found this to be a difficult area of self-study. It requires being disidentified and compassionate toward yourself as you see these habitual attractions. I sometimes wonder where my gossiping tendency came from. I thought I was free from it, given my distaste for it in childhood; but apparently, a certain part of my childhood environment stuck with me. I had introjected certain tendencies of those who were around me when I was young. The study of schadenfreude is an excellent topic for group work, a topic that brings out of the shadows an aspect of being human. By discussing this topic in a group, we can see it more clearly. It loosens up our tendency to hide what is not very becoming about us.

You can also make an outer study of schadenfreude by watching any television news program. When a fire breaks out somewhere in the United States, all news stations drop what they are reporting to focus on it. Television is now so degraded that there are programs that follow sexual deviants and murderers for hours of broadcasting time each day. Children and adults become immersed in schadenfreude through watching these programs. Some even aspire to become television reporters in the mistaken belief that these programs having something to do with "current events." Such addiction to schadenfreude is common everywhere and is now a full-blown disease that poisons the very essence of humanity.

Questions to Consider When Studying Schadenfreude

What is the draw of such gossip, what do we get from it, how does it feed us, and what part is it feeding? You can also observe similar traits in others, the news, politics, and the increasing tendency in our society to distract our attention from important issues by fixating on disasters or the trivialities of the abhorrent behavior of people. Finally, study any personal enjoyment you find within yourself at the misfortune of others whom you dislike or of whom you feel jealous. It is an excellent topic for getting unexpected impressions of yourself.

SLAVERY TO IMAGES AND BELIEFS

As we saw in an earlier chapter, images are a means of condensing beliefs, and we all harbor images that influence our lives. Although I will refer primarily to images throughout this section, bear in mind that images and beliefs become almost inseparable. Through images, I can get an understanding of my beliefs and vice versa. My images and beliefs affect and determine my emotional state and my behavior. For example, financial success is an image that affects almost everyone. Even those who live in absolute poverty and have little chance of ever being financially secure still hold on to the image of being rich. That image can even give them hope.

Looking beautiful or handsome to appear attractive to the opposite sex is a pervasive cultural image. Images surrounding physical appearance affect every aspect of modern culture. Modern society projects images of how we must dress, where we must live, the car we must drive, where we must be educated, and our vocation. Images are a yardstick against which we measure ourselves to find our place in society. We wish to impress other people. How we speak, think, write, and the projects we are involved in—a political election, our church—are all aspects of the images we live by.

There are a host of images connected to what we expect from ourselves, other people, and life. Some are well defined, others less so. They relate to desires for closeness, dependence, independence, and other emotional states such as happiness or fulfillment. We move from one image to another throughout our lives. Instead of connecting with our real being, they often distract and falsify our experience.

We can work with images directly in order to understand how images are connected with our power to wish, a very important aspect of Work. Images move us. When you get up in the morning and go to work, there are hundreds of unconscious images living within you while you are waking up, getting dressed, arriving at your job. Study your images. It is a large and fascinating topic. I predict that if you study this material seriously, it will yield a great harvest of information about yourself. I list below some areas of research in which to explore your images.

Areas for Studying Images

What are the images that control or are connected to:

-How you look?

-How you dress?

-Your home?

-Your job?

-Your art, jewelry, car, any material possession?

-How you want others to see you?

-Your children?

-Your values?

-Your future?

-Your death?

-Being happy?

Which beliefs and actions fit with your self-image; that is, do you think of yourself as a kind person, a churchgoer, do you work in a hospice, do you give to charities, do you recycle?

What are the images connected to how you:

-Control your life, and what images are there around this need?

-Want to be told what to do so you can feel secure?

-Need others?

-Are afraid of being controlled?

Which images hold and represent for you the ideas of:

-Success?

-Failure?

-Love?

-Kindness, hatred, sadness, courage, beauty, etc.?

You can also substitute the word "belief" for "image" in these lists, or simply add it.

As you can see, the list is long, but it will be different for each individual. You will find images lurking around things, people, and situations that are important to you. The point is not to dissect the images, but to become familiar with them. Just the act of noticing them can free you a bit. Remember, you built up these images and beliefs over a long time, and understanding them can help you understand your behavior.

Self-study creates a special type of suffering and a special reward. It is a part of what Gurdjieff means by "intentional suffering." It is not martyrdom. It means I wish to see and am willing to suffer what I do see in myself. The suffering occurs by itself and is the result of exposing our unknown parts to conscious exploration. Intentional suffering is not becoming more critical of ourselves or developing more rules about how we should act or be. It is really becoming a scientific researcher, interested in and curious about how I came to be the way I am, and what I am. I have found that in this exploration, I can receive understanding of myself that greatly outweighs any suffering I might experience.

PART IV

PSYCHOLOGICAL INVESTIGATIONS

CHAPTER 13

PSYCHOANALYTIC CONCEPTS

TRANSFERENCE AND COUNTERTRANSFERENCE

To investigate further the mutual relevance of Gurdjieffian and mainstream psychology, we need a basic understanding of some psychological concepts. Out of the entire realm of psychological material, let us look at a few that hold particular relevance for self-study. They are: *transference* and *countertransference*, and *projection* and *projective identification*. I want to dispel the notion that an understanding of such concepts should be exclusive to psychotherapists. In fact, transference is the major player in human interactions. I believe it should be a required topic of interest in every field of human interaction and everyone should try to understand it.

Freud coined the term "transference" in the early twentieth century. In the textbooks it is defined as, "the passing on, displacing or transferring of an emotion or affective attitude from one person to another person or object." [1] "Countertransference" is actually transference of a particular type. It refers to the phenomenon of the therapist who transfers his or her emotions onto a particular client. Here, I will use the term transference for both. I will discuss projection and projective identification later.

When transference occurs, a person may come to have a distorted perception of another individual, a group, or a relationship. The term is used now primarily by therapists to describe the client's reactions to the therapist during the period of therapy. [2] During therapy, a client might love, hate, or develop erotic feelings for his therapist simply as a repetition of unresolved interactions with important people from his or her past. Transference is important as an aspect of self-study for me personally. It takes on added importance within group interactions.

When friction occurs among people who are united by a common aim, such as they may be in a group, transference and its repercussions are unavoidable.

Gurdjieff was known for forcing his students into situations where they would be in close contact with others, inevitably creating friction. By creating such friction, people would drop the masks of their personas, and they were forced to see more clearly who they really were. Gurdjieff was actually utilizing transference. The Prieuré, where Gurdjieff centered his work in the 1920s, was a cauldron of transference. I am not sure if Gurdjieff was aware of Freud's terminology, but he was working with transference nonetheless.

We were not raised by perfect caregivers, nor taught by perfect teachers. When our parents did not understand us, when they tried to control us or ignored us, or when they met our needs in a self-serving or inadequate manner, we were often emotionally wounded. Teachers, friends, and other relationships also may have wounded us throughout our lives. In relation to our upbringing, Gurdjieff said this:

> Every man comes into the world like a clean sheet of paper; and then the people and circumstances around him begin vying with each other to dirty this sheet and cover it with writing. Education, the formation of morals, information we call knowledge—all feelings of duty, honor, conscience, and so on—enter here.... Gradually the sheet is dirtied, and the dirtier with so-called "knowledge" the sheet becomes, the cleverer the man is considered to be.[3]

The writing on our "clean sheet of paper" consists of many emotional experiences, as well as learning. If such experiences were abusive—that is, if they caused us pain or shame (in the negative sense we discussed earlier)—we do not forget them. Instead, we compensate for them somehow and learn to walk through the minefield of life without always showing our wounds, but we still experience them inwardly. However, because we are not conscious of past woundings, they become invisibly woven into our psyches, and we unconsciously compensate for them in our relationships. This compensation causes us to project aspects from previous relationships and the woundings we received onto new relationships and situations; thus, transference comes into being.

Say, for example, you failed to win the approval of your father, no matter how hard you worked; and in fact, your work was an object of his disapproval. You subsequently may have trouble when confronted by a male authority figure, such as a teacher, boss, or even a friend who might criticize your work. You may then experience lowered self-esteem, an inability to trust yourself. You may even suffer somatic symptoms, such as a headache or stomachache when you interact with others who remind you at an unconscious level of your disapproving father. You may find you react angrily to the slightest bit of criticism or get depressed should someone question your decisions. Your sensitivity to the woundings activated in you in these situations need not be gender specific. If a woman disapproves of you, you may react the same way you would with a man.

When you are on the job and your supervisor points out some details you missed in a report, outwardly you might appear very obliging and say you will of course take care of the mistakes; inwardly, however, you resent him because he does not appreciate you and can only find fault with what you do. At the same time, you hate yourself for your ineptitude. The resentment of your supervisor arises because you transferred onto him feelings associated with previous wounds you received from your father or someone else who was important to you. The transference will limit how you feel and act in this situation. Specifically, it will filter how you perceive your supervisor and what you will be able to communicate to him. In other words, you cannot see your boss as he is and cannot see the situation cleanly. Rather, you view him through a mixture of emotions cluttered with memories from experiences that have little to do with him or the present situation. The interaction may also be complicated further by your supervisor's transference onto you. There is something about you he never has liked, and he cannot quite put his finger on it. He also may be extremely stressed and afraid of how your mistakes might ultimately affect him. He may live in constant fear of not doing his job perfectly. And so it goes, round and round. The transference phenomenon is active all the time in relationships, tugging behind it a trainload of psyches bursting with undigested experience.

Transference is a hidden aspect of identification. When in a relationship with another person, it is always a transference relationship. You transfer onto others; likewise, they unconsciously transfer onto you. You act and react differently to different people, creating greater transference issues with some people than with others.

Lack of awareness of transference can be a source of unnecessary suffering in close relationships. However, if you can become aware of your transference, you have greater choice of action. Almost everyone is unconscious of transference, including therapists who are supposed to be very knowledgeable about the process.

Transference is very visible in certain situations. It is clearly present when a father and mother argue about childrearing. For example, the father may want his wife to be stricter with the children, just as his father was with him. We might say he learned to be strict from his father, but at a deeper level, the relationship with his children is activating transference within him in relation to his children. The original wound occurred due to his overly strict father. Now that he is in a position of authority, he plays out a part similar to the one his father played, like an actor on stage. Thus, our interactions with others may not be as simple as they seem. More often, they are cluttered with old patterns of transference having little or nothing to do with the present situation.

Studying transference in yourself and learning to see it in others is not easy, because whenever we are with others, we are in a state of transference all the time. Gurdjieff might have said we are identified at every moment. Transference is a major form of identification, so prevalent in relationships that it is difficult to see. I am caught in a web of transference without realizing it.

If your parents are still alive, it is a rather easy place to view transference in action. You will often hear people talking about how great their parents are and how well they get along with them, or just the opposite. Some will tell you how angry they feel toward their mother or father because of the way their parent acts and find themselves acting out old behavior patterns that disturbed them during childhood. You may find your behavior is often changed when you are with your parents. It provides a great field for study.

PROJECTION AND PROJECTIVE IDENTIFICATION

Projection involves attributing your own thoughts or emotions to another person; that is, you believe the other person has these thoughts or holds these emotions about you because you yourself have these thoughts and emotions. Specifically, you may deal with your emotional conflicts, your internal and external stressors, by falsely attributing your own unacceptable feelings, impulses, or thoughts to another person.[4] Examples: (1) a man, unable to accept that he has competitive or hostile feelings about an acquaintance, says, "He doesn't like me"; (2) a woman, denying to herself that she has sexual feelings about a male coworker, accuses him, without basis, of flirting and describes him as a "wolf."

Another important concept that operates at the very core of relationships is projective identification. It takes place in relationships all the time and often results in negative outcomes. Projective identification is more complex than simple projection. It occurs when I project onto another my own thought, belief, or emotion that I am afraid of or that is unacceptable to me in some other way.[5] In this case, however, I do not fully disavow my own impulses or fears and may even remain somewhat aware of them. I believe my actions and reactions to the other person are justifiable responses to the other person's behavior, because I am sure they are a certain way—the very way I fear, of course! Then, in what almost can feel like magic, I induce the very feelings or behavior in the other person I mistakenly believed, or was afraid, were there.

For example, I might be afraid my wife is going to be sarcastic and belittle me. She might tell me, "You know, there is a better way to wash the vegetables than what you are doing." I recognize that I also have certain impulses in myself; I am often critical of the way people do things and think I know better. I may even have some notion where these critical impulses came from, but I don't like them. Now, the destructive black magic of projective identification begins. I hear her comment about the vegetables and this makes me feel she is being sarcastic and belittling toward me. She is actually not belittling me, but simply starting a discussion about cleaning vegetables. I act offensively toward her trying to defend against what I believe is her belittling comment. Now, a dynamic begins that changes my wife's behavior—she begins to re-explain why she said it. I am now convinced that she is behaving in a way that is more characteristic of the very fear I have projected onto her—that she will belittle me. I get a little aggressive with her, tell her, "I know what I am doing," to defend against what I know is coming, and then, in exasperation, she says something that is actually belittling, "You know you don't make any sense, you are acting like a child!"

To reinforce this dynamic, a part of me inwardly proclaims, "Yes, I knew it all along; she is like that." Then I begin to defend myself further against my projected fear of being belittled, and she in desperation continues, "You are being ridiculous, you are making something out of nothing." One could argue that when she says, "You are being ridiculous..." she is belittling me, but it is actually because my defensive, aggressive attitude has finally caused her to react in this manner. Thus, the negative dynamic continues and grows stronger. Over some years, various facial expressions of my wife, or even her bodily postures, can activate my fear of being belittled and produce the same outcome.

Most people remain completely unaware of the unconscious projections that run rampant through their marriage or partnerships, build resentments, and this dynamic of projective identification invariably locks them in an unending struggle. As resentment builds, it is stored away. Resentments can gradually ruin a relationship by destroying the good feelings each person has for the other. This happens as the interactions focus more and more on the negative feelings each holds for the other so that the relationship is poisoned and dies.

Psychologists usually interpret projective identification as a defense mechanism. At a deeper level, I see it as the wounded self unsuccessfully re-creating a past scenario it has been desperate and unable to resolve. In the above real example from my own marriage, a part of me, or an "I" in Gurdjieff's terminology, is hoping my wife is not being sarcastic, belittling, or trying to make me feel ashamed. If she is, I want to stand up for myself and resolve the matter—something I could not do as a small child. However, rather than resolving the situation and healing my wound, I behave in a manner that finally gets her to actually say something belittling.

You can study projective identification most easily with a person close to you. Below are two possible scenarios to study with a partner or someone else that is close to you. The first has to do with a negative emotion, and the second with inner considering, a special form of projective identification. There is no limit to the situations you can find to study projective identification.

Study of Projective Identification

1. When you feel afraid, feel you have been slighted or ignored, and you are engaged in or about to engage in a disagreement with your close partner, recognize you may not be able to change the interaction. Resign yourself to the fact that this is going to be unpleasant, and allow yourself to act in whatever way you will. Then see if a small part of you can notice projective identification as it progresses. See how the fear within you that something unpleasant will happen, or the person will say something you are afraid of, brings about the very situation you feared.

2. If you find yourself slighted, ignored, or feel you are not being sufficiently considered by someone, and you are not immediately interacting with the person whose actions "made you" feel this way, place your attention on your throat and upper chest area. Pay attention to the physical sensations present in these areas. Keep your attention on the sensations. If you notice emotions rising, just let them be and bring your attention back to the sensations in your throat. Understanding and insight will come from remaining with the bodily sensations, not by trying to figure out what is happening.

Note here when I suggest that you pay attention to the sensations, I am not suggesting that you sense. Paying attention to the sensations in your throat area is different from sensing.

CHAPTER 14

SELF-HATE

In this chapter, I will examine the roots of self-hate, where it comes from, and why it is pertinent to the teachings of Gurdjieff. Self-hate is an area of self-knowledge that is overlooked and undervalued; it is very important in understanding our behavior as it seems to be prevalent in so many people. I believe the roots of self-hate lie deep in our psychological history and are directly related to Gurdjieff's concepts of essence and personality.

Over the years that I have studied myself, I have become familiar with a distinct part of myself that hates me; moreover, I have found out this part of me is not unique to me. At first, my interest in self-hatred was motivated by my wish to understand myself. Gradually, I realized if I could understand my own self-hatred, I might better understand my clients. As I moved forward in my study, I also began to wonder how self-hate manifests in the world, among people in conflict and even among countries at war. We understand, generally, that war is a manifestation of hatred; but perhaps it also plays a part in what Gurdjieff refers to as our "periodic-need-to-destroy-the-existence-of-others-like-oneself." [1]

I studied self-hatred in two separate arenas. I first familiarized myself with current psychological thought about causes of self-hatred and how it manifests in clients and in myself. Then, I examined humanity's current and historical conflicts through the lens of self-hatred.

Hatred is anger with so much energy behind it that it seeks to annihilate the object it is focused on. When I work with clients, I deal with their self-hate and the havoc it wreaks on their lives every day. In an earlier chapter, I spoke about the gatekeeper, that part of each of us that dispenses disapproval and negativity toward us and other people by attempting to control what we can and cannot do. When this extreme criticism is directed inward, it may manifest as self-hatred. Mainstream psychology refers to this part of the self as the "inner critic." For me, the term "inner critic" is not really strong enough for what we are speaking of here. It takes the power of a gatekeeper to wield the sword of self-hatred. Self-hatred generates emotions so strong at times they can result in suicide or aggression toward others. Let us look at self-hatred in action.

Recently, a client I'll call "Alan," returned from a visit with his somewhat elderly parents. He described how negative they both were in the ways they treated one another and him at times. When I asked how it had affected him, he replied he also had become very negative. He found himself feeling angry toward his mother, but was unable to express his anger, and instead began to hate himself. It was only after he spoke with his uncle, who told him his mother was never going to change, that he found a little peace. It is interesting to note that when Alan was unable to express his angry feelings directly to his mother, he turned them inward, just as he had as a child. He went on to tell me that upon returning home to his wife, he found he was angry with her, too, and provoked a number of quarrels.

When Alan was a child, he had convinced himself that his parents' continual anger and negativity meant there was something wrong with him. Otherwise, he reasoned, why would they be so constantly critical of him? Part of him was extremely angry at the aggressive way his father treated him and the fact that his mother never stood up for him, but always bowed to her husband's will. Due to his fear of physical harm from his father and without any outlet for his anger, he began to stuff it downward. Eventually, his anger turned inward and he began to hate himself. His unreleased and impermissible anger had nowhere to go, and he began to manifest it in distorted ways. He did poorly in school and got into fights as an unconscious means of getting back at his parents. Through drug use, he gained some temporary release from his increasing self-hatred; drugs allowed him to repress and numb his feelings of rage toward his parents.

Alan was lucky, however. He became interested in the painful feelings he did not understand and eventually came to therapy. Many men carry their self-hatred into the world. They join the military or become police officers, fields where they can release their aggression. Others release theirs through violence against others, becoming criminal offenders.

At least three strands interweave to form self-hate, and they are three of the nine basic affects recognized in psychology. One is the affect shame that we discussed in an earlier chapter. Our society has co-opted our natural shame. Instead of feeling ashamed of treating someone unfairly or of doing something reprehensible, society uses shame as a means to keep people's actions within certain boundaries.

The second affect is the natural affect disgust, experienced as acute dislike or contempt, almost to the point of making us feel we need to vomit. The third is the natural affect anger. These three natural affects are biologically hard-wired in us to allow us to assess and react to the environment appropriately. However, self-hatred changes the focal point of their activity. Instead of experiencing anger, disgust, or shame as a natural reaction to environmental stimuli, the focus turns inward and targets the person himself. The three affects then blend into a neuro-psychosomatic response—self-hate.

Our experiences activate the natural affects shame, disgust, and anger we are born with; because we are unable to disidentify with our experiences, situational content links up with these natural affects. For example, many people are ashamed at being nude in front of others, because our parents have taught us nudity is shameful. We are also taught to feel ashamed if we fail a test or fail in another way, such as losing a job. We are also taught to feel disgust with our behavior if our parents' response was that of disgust to the way we behaved as children.

Natural anger has a definite value, as a response to injustice, for example. However, others' spurious expressions of anger have crowded out natural impulses that should activate anger in us. Our parents and others got angry in response to unpleasant situations. Particularly, they may have become angry with us. Gradually, we imitated our caregivers' angry reactions to various situations or to our behavior, and we began to react as we were taught. In this way, we learned to monitor ourselves so as not to touch others or ourselves in certain ways, not to speak or show any feelings that that might embarrass our custodians. We learned gradually to modify our real feelings and showed only those deemed appropriate.

Shame, disgust, and anger without a natural outlet can turn upon the self and interweave to form self-hate. It is the by-product of these three natural affects that have been distorted, reformatted, and now is turned against the person. The gatekeeper becomes the instrument that determines when we feel ashamed, disgusted, or angry with ourselves. The gatekeeper has a repository of memories that will trigger feelings of shame, self-disgust and self-hatred and anger. If I fail a test, I feel ashamed, disgusted, and angry and blame myself. The gatekeeper keeps the scorecard.

Because we were not taught about the natural affects of anger, shame, and disgust, we were likewise not taught about how they could become corrupted. We remain ignorant of self-hate and how to deal with it. Again, this area of human behavior has been left to academia and psychologists, who for the most part write about the affects in relation to their research or clients, but rarely, if ever, study it in themselves! Is it not time to understand how natural affects work within us through self-observation?

Gurdjieff's division of the psyche into essence and personality is shorthand for saying that our psyche has been distorted. He said personality developed at the expense of essence. This lopsided development has had severe consequences. The essence-personality split and the subsequent lack of the development of essence appear to be two underlying factors in the development of all psychological disorders; the third factor being the woundings due to abuse that children are subject to at the hands of caregivers. Self-hate, which results from the distortion of our natural impulses, is a core component of many psychological disturbances: depression and mood disorders, suicide, anxiety disorders, dissociative identity disorder, bipolar disorder, etc. Ultimately, self-hate may prove to be a prime element in the psychosis that leads to war. In war, self-hate is finally given a "legitimate" outlet. War, or so-called "justifiable murder," represents a perfect release for self-hate. The split psyche, which resulted in the dominance of the personality composed of different "I's" over the undeveloped essence, releases its pent-up anger and self-hate by killing people. Ironically, the self-hating individual often becomes a hero for acting in the "line of duty."

Understanding the reasons for emotional disorders has been the focus of psychology since it earliest years. Many psychoanalysts, such as Melanie Klein, base their theories of psychological disorders on the inadequate caregiving children receive. However, there has been no research or interest in the psychological ramifications of the inadequate development of essence. The concept of essence remains unknown for modern psychology and is found almost exclusively in Gurdjieff's Work. If you remember, I said earlier that essence is that part of us that remains undeveloped, and if it were able to mature could become our individuality.

I propose that the lack of development of our essence and overdevelopment of personality results in a profound experience of loss and subsequent inadequacy many people experience; but they are not in touch with their loss. The development of essence depends on the cultivation of balance in the three centers. It requires learning to think critically for ourselves and verify that which others tell us. It requires self-knowledge. Throughout our development, the need for conscious labor and intentional suffering would have needed to be emphasized and modeled by parents, caregivers, and real teachers. The loss of the development of essence in people lays the seeds for both depression and anger, and without a release mechanism for this anger, many gradually succumb to hopelessness. The powerful emotions of hopelessness and anger are often thwarted and misunderstood by parents when children display them. The child then interiorizes these emotions, and anger then becomes misdirected and turned against the self. As the child matures, part of this anger or rage may become self-hatred.

Some of a person's self-hatred may flow out toward the world and toward others. The angry person, soldier, policeman, fundamentalist, terrorist, all exhibit anger. Anger not expressed outwardly may turn against the self in the form of self-sabotage, drug addiction, self-mutilation, suicide, homicide, or worse. It is not hard to recognize homicide as a means of self-annihilation. Aspects of a person's psyche must be walled off to enable him to repress any natural capacities of empathy, love, and compassion in order to commit murder. Soldiers and others who are forced into a situation where they must kill someone else try unsuccessfully to remain unaffected. However, the incidences of post-traumatic stress disorder in soldiers in every war and in police officers in every culture, are proof enough of the brutalization and psychic injury that takes place when people must kill.

As I discussed above, shame and disgust play an important role in forming self-hate. If caregivers and teachers elicit these affects in a child before the child has developed a sufficiently secure sense of self, then the child easily introjects shame and disgust and begins to feel them toward himself. The child reaches the conclusion that if these adults feel he is shameful and disgusting, they must be right. The child thinks, I should feel that way about myself, since that is who I am.

Self-hate is very different from guilt, a more transient cognitively induced phenomenon that often accompanies or leads to self-hate. Most people experience guilt when they do something their pseudo-conscience thinks is wrong. The guilt may last a short or long time and may or may not result in self-hate. Self-hate represents a wish to hurt oneself, but people usually hold off taking steps because of social taboos. Thus, many of us keep self-hate at arm's length and mask it with coping mechanisms such as addiction or other self-calming behaviors.

Another manifestation of self-hate is seen in abhorrent behavior such as child abuse and domestic violence. These behaviors seem different when viewed from the outside, since people hurt others and not themselves. However, viewed from another perspective, it may be understood as an individual's attempt to punish himself by hurting others. Often, the person who commits rape or child abuse was abused and somehow blames themselves for what happened to them. Through child abuse, rape, or other such actions, a person then perpetuates and justifies his negative self-image. He feels valueless and deserving of pain. The child abuser or rapist is well aware of the destructiveness of his actions, but cannot stop his need to create the pain he endured.

In order to study self-hatred, see if you can notice whether you ever talk to yourself in the following way: "Well, he deserves to have failed, he just didn't think it through," or, "She deserves just what she got with that guy." Most of us have such inner judgments of others. You can be pretty sure if you inwardly criticize others, you probably are judging yourself as well. Judging others and oneself is the gatekeeper's full-time job, and self-hate is one of the gatekeeper's strongest proclivities.

A few years ago, a beautiful, young, straight-A student in Santa Rosa, California, took her own life. Her parents never had a clue she was depressed. She had a great social life, was looking forward to college, and instead of being able to anticipate a rosy future, she jumped off the Golden Gate bridge. How did this come about? Because of unrecognized self-hate. How self-hate influences us and others is an immensely important area of study.

Sometimes the voice of self-hate is subtle, and it may take some time to get to know it. I predict that if you search, you will find self-hating voices in yourself. They criticize your performance and are angry you did not do well enough, look good enough, or failed somehow. These voices have a very long memory and may call up situations that took place years before.

Self-hate continually drains our energy reservoirs. It uses up emotional energy and generates a negative attitude toward oneself and others. However, the study of it does not mean you put a lid on it or change it. Change will come about through your interest in it, through exposing it and learning about it.

The history of how self-hate may have developed in you may be difficult to discern, but I have found it is often associated with our imagined missteps in pursuit of some outer form of self-perfection. Many religions and other methodologies that focus only on outer self-perfection by following a form are filled with self-hating individuals. They themselves have not lived up to the religion's precepts, but they subsequently follow, in a distorted fashion, the precepts that were presented to them and preach the same distortions to their flock.

Nurturing and developing essence comes through exposing your self-hate and hatred of others, and the gatekeepers that foster these emotions. When I help a client expose their self-hatred and gatekeeper, there is gradual thawing of self-hate. I believe this occurs because essence awakens and recognizes that it finally has a chance to breathe and grow, and joy can be experienced. The change is very gradual. Perhaps the client sees herself more fully, not only through black and white lenses. She begins to gravitate toward her inner longings and her values and interests shift. Her understanding grows for her humanness;

essence realizes it is onto something, as if it is sniffing out water in the desert.

This process does not mean resistance falls away and it becomes easy. In fact, resistance may increase, but the person simultaneously develops greater tolerance for difficulty and suffering, which may give her increased stamina in the face of new inner and outer obstacles. Sleeping beauty may begin to awaken as the shroud of self-hatred is thrown off.

Chapter 15

CLOSE RELATIONSHIPS

Nowhere can we find a better place to study and learn about ourselves than in close relationships with a spouse, partner, child or close friend. It is an arena where our true selves and our outer personas get to play out. In order to understand more completely the expectations that are at work in relationships, let us look more carefully in this chapter at the fundamental images that operate in close relationships.

COUPLES

Close relationships in marriage or partnership progress through a number of discrete stages. The beginning stage is often interplay of fantasy and wishful thinking, full of romantic feelings of love, exaltation, wonderful sex, and having someone match us completely as a companion and lover. After the initial stage, we struggle to make the other person fit our pictures of what a partner should be or we begin pushing the other around. Alternatively, one person may become dominant and the other subservient. It may often feel like constant work without reward. The third stage is where some couples get down to the work of relationship, or the relationship becomes so difficult, they give up on each other. Gradually, they begin to feel negative about their partner. They may begin to spend more of their time with other people or at work, substituting other people and activities for intimacy. So it goes for more than fifty percent of couples. The resentment builds until it bursts the relationship or deadens it. If it bursts, the parties go their own way, sometimes finding another mate and beginning the same journey over again.

Within the quicksand of arguments and recriminations, there is a wealth of impressions most people miss. This includes people in the Gurdjieff Work who claim to be working on themselves. Perhaps no one has told them about this treasure of impressions that lie just beneath the surface of their relationship. Perhaps they assume that since their group leader did not mention it, it is not important. However, the study of an intimate relationship increases the possibility that a person's authentic self can escape from the jail of its ego-bound personality. Many people who are in long-term relationships remain filled with unrealistic images about these intimate relationships that cause them to miss real opportunities for self-study.

The first image we are spoon-fed is that by being with someone we love, we will become happy and loving, except for some minor disagreements. The underlying premise of this image and the beliefs it holds is hidden in the word "happy." What is it to be happy and can the other person make us so? Do we feel fulfilled if we are happy? How much money, how many movies, dances, concerts, and great sexual encounters will it take to fill the real needs of my deeper self? In my experience, being "happy" does not satisfy inner life. We can hold to the false belief that we would be happy with another if the other were just "so and so." We think, "I would be happy if only I felt supported, appreciated, and respected. Then I could do what I really want to do—be a great writer, a doctor, a success, more fully myself," etc.

The inability to achieve happiness with a long-term partner is evident in many close relationships. Individuals feel they are starving inside—starving for kindness and caring. People become extremely distraught if they have not found bliss with the other, whose only purpose (in their fantasies) should be to meet their every need. Little arguments, big arguments, a lack of feeling supported or appreciated, the inability to understand the other—all our family baggage and lack of understanding of interpersonal dynamics leads many relationships to stagnate or die. The unconscious beliefs, images, and expectations that revolve around a vague image of what comprises true happiness poison these relationships.

Our relationships are fraught with arguments, acting-out, and pain-inducing behavior that lead to resentments, subsequent failed relationships, and multiple marriages. Relationships may endure, depending only on each partner's ability to contain resentment. Likewise, they may fail if the couple is constantly releasing resentment in the form of arguments, sniping at each other, and acting out. In rare instances, couples can resolve many of their differences. In the majority of cases, however, close relationships cannot handle the buildup of resentment and fighting. Eventually, they succumb. It becomes too painful to remain in such an intolerable atmosphere, wanting intimacy, unable to find it and instead only feeling pain.

Relationships could hold out something different for couples in the Work. Still, many Work couples miss the opportunities presented in their relationships. They too become angry, alienated, have affairs, and break up. In short, they look just about like everyone else. Work has not helped them a bit.

My experience has been that my inner growth does not take place in the happy moments. It is in the difficult times, in the midst of my mechanical suffering that I may get a real look at the unconscious patterns that drive me. However, I get a glimpse of my patterns only if I remember myself and my decision to work. Below are some areas of study that may prove fruitful for those in close relationships, a trove of opportunities for seeing transference, projective identification, and attempts to gatekeep the other.

ATTITUDES TOWARD CHILDREN

Attitudes are habitual patterns of thinking, believing, and feeling, in other words, a way of thinking or an emotional stance. However, I am interested in exploring a more limited meaning of the word "attitude"— that is, one's emotional stance with regard to an object, a person, an activity, or a situation. What controls our attitudes? Where have they come from? What is their relationship to what are called "emotional states," especially, negative feelings? There are no easy answers, because attitudes are complex patterns intricately linked with all three centers— the intellectual, emotional, and physical.

Orage says about attitude: "Whatever the emotion evoked by the object, the attitude is determined by it." [1] In other words, our emotional reactions determine every attitude we develop toward an object, person, group, or situation. Emotional reactions determine attitudes to people, things, and situations. Attitudes become fixed in us and these fixed habits, in turn, will determine our automatic reactions. All of us have a repertoire of attitudes in relation to the major areas of our lives: sex, close relations with family and others, our job, politics, money, education, religion, right and wrong, our past, present and future, the world, life itself, and finally, death.

When faced with difficulty, or when a situation is frustrating or painful, my attitude may be inflexible (that is, my habitual reaction to a certain situation may not be appropriate). For example, a child becomes angry when he is frustrated. Parents' attitudes toward their children usually mirror the way their parents responded to them. Instead of considering what is occurring in the moment, the parent might base his or her attitude on their memory. For example, the parent remembers, "It is not all right to get angry. Anger is bad." What if the situation actually requires a different attitude?

Often children who are acting out are responding negatively to stresses that they are completely unaware of. In such instances, the parent's first response may be to clamp a lid on the child's behavior. In the best case, the parent tries to set limits with appropriate sanctions. In less successful cases, the parent uses an abusive response, such as shaming or even smacking the child. Instead of being interested in the reason for the child's distress, the parent tries to squelch the child's disturbing behavior. Instead of comforting the child, the parent's attitude only communicates, "This is not allowed; I don't like it; it's wrong; it's bad; and it's stressing me out, stop it! I won't put up with it!" In short, the parent tries to overpower the child.

Not surprisingly, not only is the parent's attitude unproductive, but it often ignites an escalation of negative behavior. There was no attempt to understand the child's inner experience; the child is incapable of understanding her stress on her own, and her parent's reaction was not empathetic. The child desperately wants some understanding and love. Instead, she is confronted by a parent who does not understand, seems uninterested, and perhaps is even abusive. What choice does the child have in such a situation? She escalates her behavior, repeats it, or stops it and hates her parent or herself. Further, her parent has now modeled an inflexible attitude toward her daughter's behavior that her daughter eventually may repeat with her own children.

Most people remain unconscious of their attitudes throughout their lives. Since I cannot change what I do not understand or even notice, my attitudes will remain the same. Orage says if we could change our attitudes, we would be well on the way to becoming masters of our fate.[2] If he is right, then how do we change them?

One mistake we make is to try to change either the situation or the other person. Adjusting a situation sometimes may be possible, but changing the other person almost always proves impossible. What I need to change is my attitude toward the situation or the person. In the case of the acting-out child, only parents who are interested in what is happening inside their child have a chance to develop a new attitude toward their child and the situation. Parents must realize that something in their child's behavior is beyond the child's comprehension. Then, if they become interested in what is occurring in their child at a deeper level, they might actually be able to help. Only by developing a new interest in the child's behavior, can the parent open up the relationship, understand how to respond, and resolve the situation. Parents need a new understanding of the situation. Developing an interest in what is happening in your child, while realizing that neither you nor she has the answer, helps you to shift your emotions away from an automatic, repressive attitude toward an attitude of questioning and interest that can help both of you. When a child senses genuine interest from a parent, the effect can be profound. In other words, inner change in one person may actually evoke an inner change in another. Inner change is real change, not just a surface alteration.

Rigid attitudes are contracted and frozen. When your hands become very cold, and you have to manipulate some mechanical object, you find you do not have the flexibility for fine movement. You need to warm your hands up before they become flexible. Similarly, when you are frozen emotionally, it is very difficult to adapt to the moment. Interest is equivalent to warming up. In the case of the child acting out, an element of fear may creep into attitudes and freeze them up, the fear becoming part of the attitude itself. With the acting-out child, the parent may be fearful of not responding appropriately, afraid of not setting boundaries and limits for the child, afraid of spoiling the child, afraid of what people will say or afraid of failing to be a good parent. All this fear and anxiety makes us reactive rather than receptive and responsive. The fear pressures us, leaving us no time to consider the situation more carefully.

By contrast, when we are receptive, more possibilities open to us and we have more time, because we are more open to incoming impressions.

In examining this scenario of how a parent might deal with an acting-out child, we have a good example of what Gurdjieff called the difference between "the reason of knowing" that comes from our head only and "the reason of understanding" that comes from our three centers acting together.[3] Summarizing, I might know my child should not act in a certain way. I might know I should not react as I do to her behavior. I might even have ideas about the reasons for her misbehavior. However, knowing or thinking about the situation with my associative mind is very different from understanding what is happening inside the child. The understanding only comes when I open up to new impressions by engaging my emotional center fully, feeling how I care for the child and want to understand her, looking at her behavior and being curious about it. My response can then be quite different from any automatic reaction that would only be determined by my previous automatic attitude.

Everything that has been said about a parent and child will hold in exactly the same way for any person I am close to. My partner or friend may display difficult behavior that I can either react to automatically, depending only on my limited repertoire of attitudes, or I can become curious about his or her behavior, attempt to step into their shoes, to really understand them. The latter interest may lead to entirely new responses, rather than just reactions by me, and in turn, by my partner.

CHANGING ONE'S ATTITUDE

Prejudices are examples of frozen attitudes that arise in us when we see a person of another race, religion, or personality type or when we face a new situation. The etiology, or causative history, of an attitude may be difficult to find, even though we are affected by it constantly.

Think about your attitude toward homeless people or people of another race, religion, or occupation. For example, if you just think about a military man or a priest, notice how different your attitude to these two individuals might be. Do you get a sense of the incredible effect attitudes have on your life? Attitudes directly influence your emotional center. We are swimming in our sea of attitudes every moment, yet we think we are on land.

It is useful to recognize two important attitudes in yourself: (1) your overall attitude toward your own life in particular; and (2) your attitude toward life in general. When we look at others, it seems easy to recognize an optimist or pessimist. However, it is not so simple to categorize our own over-all attitude toward life. Orage says:

> In every case their dominant attitude is decisive of every subordinate attitude. For instance, if your characteristic attitude towards life is gloomy, even your occasional moods of cheerfulness will be affected; they will in all probability be both intense and brief. . . . All religions and similar systems aim, in short, at inducing in us a useful attitude towards life; an attitude that is, in which we can act freely and usefully as regards our own ends or somebody else's. Some religions and systems, for instance, try to induce an attitude of submission towards life, with the design of making use of us for their own advantage. Others—but very few—aim at evoking an active or creative attitude towards life in us with the objective of enlisting our voluntary co-operation. And all alike proceed by a common method, namely, by changing our imagination of life.[4]

We each have an image about life that delineates a pattern in our emotional center. Our imagination influences our emotional center directly. The links between the imagination, our emotional states, and our attitudes may seem plausible when we think about them. However, to understand them, I must investigate these connections through self-study and see how they influence my life.

A chapter in Orage's book *The Active Mind* is entitled "Life as Gymnastics." In it, Orage speaks of the gymnasium as a symbol of the need for exercise of a special type, from which we can extract what we need from our lives. He says we have degraded the image of the gymnasium. We only see it as a structure to keep the physical body healthy. In ancient Greece, it was not only a place to exercise, but also a forum for lectures and discussions of philosophy, medicine, and literature. In

Germany and Russia, up until the twentieth century, the gymnasium was a preparatory school for university applicants. Thus, the gymnasium was a place of discovery and creativity. Orage says, "Moderns will find what the ancient Greeks found in this image of life—the evocation of creative emotion." [5] I believe he is referring to those of us in the Work as the "Moderns." How might it be if we used our own attitudes as a means of becoming as flexible as a yogi in the gymnasium of life? If we do not examine and exercise our attitudes, somehow making them more flexible, then we become rigid, frozen, and emotionally moribund. Let us look at different areas in our lives to find attitudes for self-study.

MY REQUIREMENTS

Directly related to my attitudes are my habitual "requirements," the unrecognized expectations I have about my life and how others should act toward me. Requirements are habitual attitudes I impose upon others and the world. They are what I feel others owe me and what life itself owes me. Some requirements come from mental pictures I have of myself and sound something like, "I should be respected" or "I should be treated specially." If others do not treat me in accordance with my images, it automatically activates an inner negative pattern. Often I hear people say, "He acts so entitled." It may be relatively easy to see an attitude of entitlement in others' behavior, but my own entitlement is often hidden from view.

The type of entitlement I personally find in myself shows when I register annoyance when I am not served immediately, as I believe I should be. My annoyance often arises in a store when I am not waited on quickly. My entitled attitude is immediately activated when someone says he will do something and doesn't keep his word—I believe he has not considered my feelings. I am annoyed when I see some government agency that is organized inefficiently, causing me to have to expend extra energy due to "their stupidity."

I developed many of my entitled attitudes growing up in New York City. New Yorkers live in such a cauldron of external activity and time pressure that it feels only natural to expect anyone who serves them to be at their beck and call. I am not disparaging New Yorkers specifically; this kind of behavior is characteristic of large, overpopulated metropolitan areas. Unconsciously, however, I developed many of the same requirements and was not aware of them in general until I began to study myself.

Most people carry around a huge suitcase of habitual requirements that are continually activated by life situations. This is an incredibly rich area for self-study. We may easily notice some of our personal requirements in other people, but many others that we have remain invisible unless we know what to look for and develop an interest in them. Unconsciously, most of us feel life owes us a good living doing enjoyable work, that we should be happy and not sad, and that we deserve respect. We should have good friends, good sex, a nice place to live, and we should always be comfortable. When we do not get what we think we deserve, our normal reaction is to be annoyed. However, this is our opportunity! When reality does not fit our pictures, the situation annoys us, someone has not respected us, these are chances to see ourselves. Annoyance is always indicative of identification and is a perfect opportunity for self-study.

Study of Your Requirements

1. During the day, make a list of things that annoy you. Remember, you are working here with the hypothesis that you are a multiplicity, so there is no need to change anything or decide whether what you find is good or bad. You want to see all the elements.

2. Do not analyze what is happening to cause your annoyance. Just note the circumstances and the annoyance.

3. Try to catch yourself as you are being annoyed. Just be interested, allow the annoyance to continue and run its course. Maybe, you can notice the sensations your annoyance brings about in your body.

4. At the end of the day, look at your list. Pick out one of the times when you were annoyed, go back over it in your memory, and intentionally bring it back. Seek out what caused your reaction. It is not important that you were right or wrong; no self-justifying is needed, because no one else will see this list.

5. If you work carefully, you may get a glimpse of a requirement at work within you. Make note of it. Perhaps, keep a small notebook or computer file about what the situation is, the date, and what you find. You will soon find you have a list of the situations in which you were annoyed paired with the requirements that activated these annoyances. This information will be specific to you. It may prove very illuminating to look back on these notes a number of years later and see if your requirements changed as time went by.

You may be surprised that vast periods of your life have been filled with unconscious requirements that conditioned you to react with automatic annoyance, anger, or other unpleasant emotions. This type of investigation is worth so much more than trying to stuff down your negative emotions by not expressing them. When your awareness has illuminated your requirements, the core of your being is changed, informed by the very act of seeing them.

The aim is not to change anything now, but rather to realize that most of your actions in such situations are not actions at all. They are reactions to unknown requirements that are automatically recorded in your memory banks. For now, do not change anything. Again, your aim is not to be good, but to be aware of yourself in life. Awareness comes as a result of impartial, compassionate observation. Gradually, you will develop more ability to choose how you wish to be in front of your life situations.

Once you have developed your own knowledge about your requirements, it is interesting to study your emotional reactions when these feelings of entitlement are not met and what becomes of these emotions; for example, your anger, sadness, disgust, or hatred. We create our grievances. Each of us totes around a laundry list of them, an enormously large, unconscious burden. In summary, the study of our requirements is an area that requires our attention. It is another wall of our prison.

GRIEVANCES

Grievances relate to our feelings of entitlement, to unmet requirements, and to our resentments. As I mentioned previously, most of us have a virtual sack of grievances we carry on our shoulders wherever we go, filled with uncommunicated and unrecognized resentments built up over the years. Very few of us have either an understanding of our burden or the skills to get out from under it.

Bringing this psychological material to consciousness is very important. We may find resentments, grievances, or unresolved grief that we have not been able to access because the emotions are either too powerful or buried too deep to experience. If this powerful negative material remains unexamined, it is like a poison that circulates within the emotional center. To process this material, first you need to realize you are carrying it. Then you need to familiarize yourself with it in order to begin to understand it. Only by understanding it, can it be transmuted and, ideally, integrated into your overall understanding of yourself.

Grievances are usually directed toward people who harmed you or toward situations where you felt there was injustice. Here is a practice to help you unpack your suitcase of resentments and grievances and bring them into the field of your consciousness

Unpacking Practice

1. Make a list of the significant events you remember that have left you with resentments or grievances toward others or toward certain situations.

2. Write a short narrative of what took place.

3. Write down what you feel others did to you and what they were responsible for.

4. Write down your actions and what you can be accountable for.

5. Develop an image that objectively as possible contains the entire experience. Allow yourself to be with that image without any judgment of your feelings.

6. When an image reemerges from time to time that symbolizes the entire situation, stay with the image and the emotions it arouses.

Gradually, by unpacking these experiences, one of two things will happen: (1) new integration takes place; or (2) you become aware of material you cannot integrate by yourself and may need to communicate to another person who can help you.

COMMUNICATION

Have you ever noticed during a discussion with a significant other that communication can often deteriorate as the conversation progresses? Each person either truly misunderstands or simply distorts what he hears. Or else, he or she is incapable of understanding their partner's language. A husband may exaggerate a complaint he has about his wife's behavior, because he is afraid he will not be heard if he does not embellish his complaint. Alternatively, he may want to prove her wrong because he believes she always finds fault with him. His exaggeration, of course, makes it almost impossible for his wife to respond reasonably. She must defend against his exaggerated remarks and verbally attacks him because her feelings are hurt. This is a very common type of argument. However, each person in a close relationship could learn from these miscommunications, if he or she were aware of their underlying dynamics.

Studying Yourself While Communicating with Another

1. Automatic exaggeration: Watch for words like always, never, only, and other black-and-white statements.

2. Automatic defending and attacking: "It feels to me as though I am being criticized." When I feel this way, it provokes my automatic defenses and closes off the truth of what the other person is saying. This defense mechanism never allows in what my partner sees about me or allows the exchange really to affect me. It results in a stalemate, a pattern of verbal parry and thrust that closes off any possibility of intimacy.

3. Automatic intolerance: Notice the intolerance you have for others' differences—she may be too organized or see things in a way you could never agree with, or you think she will never understand you. The ability to tolerate differences is a distinct type of work in

itself and can result in the transformation of your feelings as you learn about your own automatic reactions and self-centeredness.

Fritz Peters was a teenager when he went to France to live at the Prieuré, where he met Gurdjieff. Peters describes an incident that took place after Gurdjieff had returned from an extended trip. A man who had been staying at the Prieuré decided to leave because of his frustration working with others on projects and after getting into an argument with Gurdjieff. This man's personality had been particularly difficult for other members of the group to tolerate. Gurdjieff declared he had hired the man specifically for his obnoxious qualities so that the others could study their reactions to his behavior, and that he might not be able find anyone else as difficult who would serve his purposes so well. The students would miss out on an opportunity Gurdjieff had specially provided for them.[6]

Try to notice your intolerance of certain people you must deal with in your work. What is it about them that triggers adverse reactions in you? How much do you dislike their behaviors?

Notice the Following Types of Reactions in Yourself

1. Automatic hate reactions: Admit to yourself that no matter how nice you may believe you are, there are times when you hate your partner. There is nothing wrong with this at all. The problem lies in your reaction to your own hate, what you do with it—you stuff it. You haven't acknowledged it, you haven't allowed it in, and you don't even admit it exists or fully experience your feelings and observe them impartially. You don't seem able to say, "Oh, how interesting, I actually hate Jane right now!"

2. Facial expressions: Here is an area where your partner can really help you. It took a long time for me to realize that I rolled my eyes when I was frustrated during arguments with my wife. I did it because I felt she just did not understand me and rolled my eyes. She interpreted my rolling eyes as hatred of her, a projection on her part, but she was wrong about my feelings. Rolling my eyes was simply due to my frustration with the situation; however, I had made other facial expressions that showed my hate. In couples

therapy, I have found both partners are almost completely unaware of their own facial expressions when confronting each other and do not realize the magnitude of their effect.

3. Automatic postures during conversation: Notice and become familiar with all your poses/postures when engaging in discussion and argument.

THE IMAGO

The *imago* is a concept from Harville Hendrix's therapy with couples.[7] It is extremely useful for understanding communication, projective identification and transference and the role of the imago. The imago is an unconscious symbolic image that represents a person's parents or caregivers. The imago dynamic utilizes projective identification that results in aggravating preexisting wounds and other fears that exist within each partner's unconscious. Transference is the instantaneous fuel that powers the back-and-forth nature of the couple's interaction. Previous woundings are projected upon the imago, and your partner becomes its living representative. When one partner looks at the other, she is unconsciously seeing, in living color, the imago she has created.

The dynamic interaction of transference and projective identification creates the imago. Understanding the interaction between the imagos that are created can give you greater insight into the automatic reactions that operate in your closest relationship. Negative projection and transference by each partner gradually create a negative dynamic that continues to build resentments. Sometimes the extent of the resentment becomes intolerable and irreparable and eventually may cause the relationship to end. Below is an example illustrating the imago in action.

Dennis and Patricia

Dennis and Patricia have been together fifteen years. They are forty-five and forty-two years old, respectively, and have two children, ages eleven and fourteen. It is Friday evening and Dennis has been looking forward to a relaxing weekend. The children have gone on sleepovers with friends. Patricia is also looking forward to having some relaxing time with Dennis and maybe getting closer to him. She feels he is usually unable to be vulnerable and open up to her. She senses he is stressed from his job, and inwardly, he is holding onto some other things that remain a mystery to her. She is constantly asking him to come closer to her. Dennis views Patricia's longing for closeness and her statements that he seems distant as criticism.

Periodically, Dennis does come closer, because he really loves Patricia, but when he does, she asks for even more communication and intimacy. Dennis then takes her further requests as criticism. He feels she is saying he is not doing enough and withdraws, feeling he can never do anything right with her. He breaks off the intimate and affectionate feelings and verbally attacks her because he feels criticized. Patricia takes his attack as proof there is something wrong, both with her and the relationship, and then she gets depressed. When she gets depressed, Dennis feels anxious, does not know what to do, feels hopeless, and withdraws. So, rather than having a relaxing weekend, Dennis and Patricia wind each other up and bicker throughout the weekend. How did this situation come about? A little background is helpful.

Dennis was an only child and came from a family with very high standards. He felt he could never live up to his parents' ideals, felt he did not measure up. In fact, both his parents criticized him. Gradually, Dennis developed an inner gatekeeper that was constantly dissatisfied with his accomplishments. Even though he was successful in his career, he was never able to relax, never able to feel he was okay.

Patricia grew up in a household of four children. Her mother and father were overwhelmed with their responsibilities. Her father was distant and her mother was somewhat depressed. Patricia longed for personal attention from her father but never received it. When she tried to get some additional attention from her parents, they implied there must be something wrong with her for asking. At times, they even told her she should be more like her sister, who was more independent. They told Patricia she should not be so sensitive and needy. She gradually began to criticize her own needs and felt there must be something essentially wrong with her. As a teenager, her self-esteem plummeted, and she felt depressed and hopeless. Patricia's early life experiences made her long desperately for attention and intimacy when she married. When Dennis was courting her, she had thrived on the attention and love he had shown her and especially on his ability to be intimate and share who he was.

Now, when viewed through the lens of the imago, the difficulties that arise in this relationship are very predictable. Dennis winds up feeling criticized because he views Patricia as an amalgam of both his parents—who never seemed to accept him for who he was. It does not matter how carefully Patricia communicates her needs or desire to be closer, Dennis interprets her communication as follows: "You are telling me I am not doing it right, I need to do more, and I can't provide it, I am inadequate, etc." Dennis' interpretation of Patricia's desire for closeness is further bolstered by his tendency to criticize himself. Any comment of Patricia's that even vaguely resembles his own inner criticism (arising from copying his parents' attitudes toward him) causes him to react violently. Dennis sees Patricia as an external critic, an imago of his rejecting and critical parents. You can also see projective identification in Dennis' projection of the criticizing imago onto Patricia. Gradually, because of their failed interactions, Patricia actually develops the traits of Dennis' hypercritical parents due to her own frustration. It then becomes increasingly difficult for any new type of interaction to take place between them. The possibility for intimacy is dying.

Patricia, for her part, fears she will not get her needs met. She views Dennis as being self-centered and overly sensitive. She cannot help expressing her needs and does not understand why she gets either a withdrawal or verbal attack in reaction to her request for closeness. She does not understand that Dennis always feels she is criticizing him. In the end, she feels depressed (like her mother) and resents Dennis for his behavior and his pulling away. He reminds her of her father. She is re-wounded by the imago that Dennis represents each time they have these interactions. After a while, she feels the best thing to do is give up and not ask for the closeness she desperately craves. She resents Dennis, and at the same time, she feels there is something wrong with her and her needs. Their arguments just reinforce her own feelings that something is wrong with her.

The results of such repeated interactions are that Dennis feels criticized and resentful. He is confused and feels hopeless after many years of such conflicts with Patricia. He views himself as a good provider and yet cannot seem to provide for Patricia's needs. Patricia feels angry and depressed and has lost any hope that the relationship will ever change. Their two children feel the friction between their parents and are confused by it. They don't see their parents' arguments, but they can feel the resentment each has toward the other. They get the mistaken impression that this is what being a normal couple feels like.

RESENTMENT

The unconscious interplay of imagos is typical of a great many couples. Resentment is the result, and the resentment builds with each episode of re-wounding. Results vary. Each partner may harden him- or herself so as not to be affected by the other, or the marriage continues with each partner becoming increasingly negative toward the other. They continue the relationship because they have a home, have accumulated material goods or money, for the children's sake, or out of sheer habit. Often, one partner has an affair to ease the pain. Finally, divorce or separation occurs, the legal or symbolic end of the psychological impasse. Sometimes, the relationship continues simply out of fear of being alone, from lassitude or hopelessness about the possibility of finding a better relationship. The formation of resentment is caused by each individual failing to get their needs met. This is not as simple as it sounds because individuals often do not know what their needs are and have little or no practice in being able to communicate them. In addition, people feel vulnerable when they do communicate their needs, and if these expressed needs are not received in a positive way by their partner, they will rarely make the attempt more than a few times. There are remedies. For people in the Work who are interested in self-knowledge, a better understanding of couples' dynamics might help them to see their relationship more clearly. In that way, they might have more choice in their responses. It might also alleviate the pain that arises from difficult situations that are continually recurring.

Why, more precisely, do many relationships ultimately fail? One reason is the inability of either partner to tolerate the resentments and woundings that the couple's negative dynamics have generated. Other culprits can be the unrecognized self-hate each person projects onto the other or the inability to tolerate each other's differences. Lacking the tools to resolve and understand their differences, partners terminate their relationships. Individuals engaged in the Work may be especially prone to marital discord because they may feel increased stress trying to follow Work practices. From the standpoint of the Work, however, few couples avail themselves of the friction generated in close relationships, either for their own individual growth or the relationship's health. However, it could be otherwise.

In *Beelzebub's Tales to His Grandson*, Gurdjieff speaks about a period in history when astrologers, who were knowledgeable about different "types" of people, directed or advised individuals whom to marry.[8] This type of knowledge is not available to us now; however, with a little more understanding of concepts like the imago, we actually might make use of our close relationships for our own growth and even improve them.

Below, I outline a method you may find useful when a difficult situation arises in your partnership. I also recommend you not shy away from the help of a good couple's therapist. There are even therapists who specialize in working with the imago. Often an intense period of couple's therapy can help partners who are committed to each other. Therapy can help them understand the problematic dynamics of their relationship and bring them closer together. Too many close relationships end only to have each partner find a different partner to begin again. Unfortunately, the new relationship, more often than not, generates a similar pattern of mutual resentment and ends in another failed relationship.

Generally, each partner will recapitulate the patterns of personal wounds from the previous relationship in the new one. Unconsciously, the person hopes the new relationship will finally help him heal his wounds. Rather than healing, however, one often just encounters re-wounding. This is not to suggest the difficulties in every partnership are completely resolvable or that all couples should remain together forever. However, in most cases incredible growth can be made from the close relationship many couples already have.

Even the most difficult relationship can be a source of growth if both people are committed to a common aim. If you are engaged in the Gurdjieff Work, having a partner who shares your interest and aim is a blessing. It will also mean the energies generated by your relationship may be intense. However, if we have some basic understanding of the dynamics involved, we can find incredible opportunities for growth within our relationships.

The recognition of the imago as an unconscious force in relationships is so important that I suggest you read Hendrix's *Getting the Love You Want*. If you can become aware of transference, projective identification, and the imago, you may better be able to use your relationship for your work—even in difficult and painful times. Below, I offer one method I have used to help myself and other couples break the cycle of a negative dynamic.

Learning from Relationship Upsets

When an argument occurs in a close relationship and the two of you have been going at it for a while:

1. Agree to take a time-out break from each other, and agree to come back to the discussion at a specified time. You will need half an hour, minimum.

2. Each person goes somewhere quiet and sits alone with the emotional upset. See if you can stay with your body, noticing the sensations. Also notice the images, thoughts, and feelings that arise in you.

3. Don't be in a rush. Take time to allow the upsetting material to rise up. Then watch the ebb and flow within you. See what happens to your state. Notice how you change as you sit with the upset.

4. Don't try to calm yourself down or change anything, just be with yourself and the upsetting material that arises.

5. If you are inclined to journal, write down any insights or any information you gather after sitting for at least fifteen minutes.

6. Envision yourself going back to meet your partner, having the discussion you deeply wish for and wish you already had. You don't need an exact idea of what either of you will say. Instead, imagine how you wish to be during the exchange.

7. Meet your partner again. Attempt to be gentle with each other and have the new discussion you missed having earlier.

8. Limit the new discussion to no more than thirty minutes. Then, leave the discussion and continue your activities or do something pleasant together.

9. The next day, after following the steps outlined above, discuss with your partner what was different in this second discussion—how you affected her or him and vice versa.

PART V

NEW MATERIAL AND REFLECTIONS

Chapter 16

PARTICIPATION

Man as Machine—The Automaton

> Quite right . . . people are very unlike one another, but
> the real difference between people you do not know and
> cannot see. The difference of which you speak simply does
> not exist. This must be understood. All the people you
> see, all the people you know, all the people you may get
> to know, are machines, actual machines working solely
> under the power of external influences, as you yourself
> said. Machines they are born and machines they die.[1]
>
> —G. I. Gurdjieff

In this chapter, we will explore an important and as yet underutilized
method in Work. I have been practicing it for some time, and it has
proved useful when other ways were inadequate. Perhaps my stumbling
upon it was due to the fact that I wanted to find a way to work that freed
up my attention and was not so intellectual. Or, it just could have been
the fact that I wanted to work in a new, less formulaic manner to help
me confront my realization that almost all activity in my life was automatic, habitual, and took place with or without my being present.

If you study yourself seriously, at some point you may come to the
realization you are almost always acting in an automatic pattern. It
takes a great deal of self-study to honestly see that most of your actions
flow automatically, from one to another, with little or none of what we
call "will" or direction on your part. It may appear that we do things, but
my experience has shown me I rarely do anything. Rather, an "it" accomplishes things automatically, in a semiconscious state, and I am not
there to record it or experience it. Automatic "doing" does not require
me to be present and alive.

I drive into Santa Rosa to work every day, and the same associations come up for me each time I drive there. When I get into the car, certain thoughts are aroused automatically. "It" likes cars, and "it" likes to drive. "It" likes to put its hand on the shift lever, likes to take a certain road, notice the same things, make the same movements, associate about its bodily sensations in almost exactly the same way as yesterday. The situation inside my head is very similar to a moving picture running repeatedly, day after day. There are small variations, but generally, the plotline and action sequences vary little.

Active *participation* coupled with *sensing* is the only method I have found that enables me to view this automatic movie clearly. With participation, I gain new impressions in the midst of my automatic functioning. Participation allows me to become aware of all the impressions that arise from the manifestations of the body. Information comes from the five senses, and the emotions, the intellectual center, sexual urges, and kinesthetic impulses. As I mentioned earlier, the intellectual center by itself is unsuited for real self-study, because it operates at a slower rate than the other two major centers. Self-study requires a simultaneous, objective recording of impressions I receive from all parts of myself—from being alive. The intellectual center's mechanism is simply too cumbersome and cluttered with associations to keep pace with the seamless flow of impressions from our different parts. We need a new way of witnessing and recording these automatic patterns, a method that can keep pace with our incoming impressions. We need an instrument that notices finer, quicker impressions as they occur. By the time you are *thinking* about them, they have *already* occurred

THE ART OF PARTICIPATION

One evening in New York, in 1928, Edwin Wolfe made a statement to Gurdjieff about self-observation. He said, "We feel that there may be something wrong in the way we are doing self-observation. Are we wrong Mr. Gurdjieff?" Gurdjieff replied, "Never you do self-observation. Mind-observation you do. Can even make psychopath." [2] Gurdjieff's warning to Wolfe is partly why I found myself so interested in the concept of participation. Gurdjieff was challenging us to find out why we were *not* doing self-observation.

After working for many years with Nyland's method of self-observation, I was convinced I needed additional practices. Nyland's method directed me to have an objective observation of myself that occurs simultaneously with what I am observing. However, such observation rarely occurs. I almost never could be objective in the way the Nyland method demanded. Something was amiss. I began to search for other methods, and found I could use sensing to try to remain present in the moment (see Chapter 4). Surprisingly, sensing fulfilled many of the requirements of objective self-observation. It proved to be an indirect means of obtaining truthful impressions of myself, a means that was more than just intellectual association. However, I had a hunch still more was possible. Even though sensing is light-years ahead of any type of mental self-observation, I found there were other impressions I could not capture through sensing alone. Sensing, however, did prepare me to receive impressions in a new way. The key was in what is called *participation.*

The concept of "participation" had caught my attention a number of years earlier. King briefly mentions it in *The Oragean Version.*[3] But even there, he only touches on it. If you look carefully, you can find the foundations of participation further back in Orage's writings. I believe its usefulness as an aid to self-study has been overlooked.

It seems a long time since I began experimenting with participation. My first experience began one ordinary day. I was about to cross the street in Sebastopol, the small town in Northern California where I live. I hope you will forgive the personal nature of this description, but I believe it is important to describe what was for me a miraculous experience. What struck me was its unexpectedness; even after years of practicing what I thought was self-observation.

I stood on the sidewalk for a few moments, noticing the beautiful, sunny day. I had an image of my aim. I described it to myself something like this: "All right now, Russell, let's see if you can walk across the street and be present in a new way. Instead of trying to observe yourself, simply ride within your body as if you were a stranger inside a new, unfamiliar vehicle. The vehicle will take you across the street. See if you can simply *participate.* [I meant, 'participate' in the sense of joining in receptively or following along inside the body.] Do not attempt to change or even direct where you are going, but instead, just be a passenger. You won't be completely passive even if you are not directing. You'll be following from the inside." That is a long-winded way of describing the image that appeared just before I crossed.

The result of this experience was startling. I noticed that my body first looked to see if there was any traffic (having been raised in New York City as a child, I still tend to cross in the middle of the block). Then I began to cross. I immediately received new impressions of myself. First, I had impressions of my arms moving and felt little aches inside them. Then, I had impressions of being in my legs. Then, thoughts intruded and something inside me *noticed* I did not lift my feet very much and worried I might trip. Then, I received continual impressions of my entire body, including remembering that I wanted to go to the store on the other side. My only effort was that of simply *being in my body, as if I had never been there before*. I ended up marvelling at the simplicity of this effortless effort. The impressions I received were almost continual. All I actually did was actively remain a receptive participating passenger— an interesting paradox, is it not?

The process of participation requires a type of attention that is neither associative nor focused. It a subtler attention that is relaxed and allows impressions to be noticed as if for the very first time. Impressions are constantly bombarding my organism in the waking-sleeping state of consciousness, but I do not notice what is new in them. Impressions are always new in the moment, but I experience them like a movie seen countless times which now bores me. The new attention which participation asked of me was relaxed and yet expansive. It was similar to a catalyst that enables a process to occur, but is not used up and does not chemically join with any part of it.

From these early steps at participating with my body, I expanded my repertoire. Getting in and out of the car, doing simple arm movements, adjusting my legs when sitting in front of a client in session, small gestures, getting up and down from chairs, and even skiing, all these became arenas for gathering new impressions. I learned to gather impressions that would have been impossible with any intellectual attempt to observe my body or even from sensing alone. Participation goes beyond just receiving objective impressions of the body. It leads to impressions of emotions and thoughts. However, please begin with the body for a sufficient period until you are fully grounded in the practice. Then impressions from other centers come to you as a natural result of the work you started with the body. Impressions from the body are the foundation this area of study requires. As your sensitivity increases, you receive other impressions that, of course, have been being received by the body all along without you noticing.

Since starting my work with participation, I have realized more thoroughly the body's intricate connections and continuous balancing act. The intellectual, emotional, moving, instinctive, and sex centers are in constant interplay. A thought easily activates an emotional state. In turn, the emotions tighten certain muscles, and we are usually unaware of the tension. The tightened muscles then activate another thought, etc. The body balances all these neural cues and the subsequent muscular activity. Gradually, these patterns become automatic, like driving a car.

Participation finally has proved to me there is no way the associative mind can remain present simultaneously with the human mechanism. Observation with the mind alone is simply inadequate. It is wonderful in a controlled environment, in quiet settings, in sitting or walking meditation. However, when we are moving about in our daily lives, almost all the action takes place before the mind sees it. The thinking occurs after the show is over. Ouspensky says the emotions are thirty thousand times faster than the associative mind.[4] I once asked Mrs. Annie Lou Staveley, a truly remarkable pupil of Gurdjieff's, why it was so difficult or almost impossible to observe myself when my body was active. She would not give me a direct answer, prompting me to investigate further. Participation has helped me to answer my own question.

As I also mentioned earlier, any system will resist change. Gurdjieff said we are like a mechanical clock with levers, gears, pulleys, and weights. The gears vary in size from a basketball to an atom, and everything is interconnected. If one part changes its speed, every other part of the mechanism reacts in turn. In other words, the body and psyche are always dynamically in balance. Science bears out Gurdjieff's statement. Modern physiology has shown that the central nervous system is always balancing and synthesizing the activities of every aspect of experience.

One mechanism a system has for maintaining the continual relationship of its parts when confronted by external stimuli is to allow continual micro-adjustments, while the larger framework remains relatively unchanged; this is analogous to the biological concept of *homeostasis*. It is a shame that the word "homeostasis" appears to connote *stasis*, lack of movement. A more descriptive term might be "homeobalancing," meaning the organism is in dynamic balance, rather than remaining at rest. Of course, no simple image of a material object can ever fully capture the interaction of the psyche and soma. However, participation, as I have described it, can capture and record the experience of this miracle in action. Participation allows me to study the vehicle in which my consciousness is a temporary passenger. Participation is at once a simple and sophisticated way of working to remain in the present moment, in spite of my habitual behaviors. As we saw earlier, it is distinct from the functioning of the associative mind.

Furthermore, when I combine sensing with participation, I increase the possibility of nurturing the octave of impressions.[5] The octave of impressions is the third and highest octave that comprises our self-regulating and self-feeding system. Nature does not naturally develop this octave. Only through conscious work with the emotional center can the octave of impressions progress and thereby allow a connection with the higher centers to form. We need some images to illustrate the idea of participation. Here is one that impressed me with its simplicity from King:

> The situation has been likened to learning to drive an automobile. First you simply sit in the front seat and observe how the car is driven; this is comparable to Self-Observation and teaches you how the car is run. Then, but without taking the driver's position, you place your hands upon the wheel and upon the gearshift lever and your feet next to the pedal and participate in the driving of the car. You are not yet controlling it yourself, you are simply participating

in its operation by someone else. This for the moment is enough.[6]

Guidelines for Participation

1. Participation excludes any criticism. Since participation will give you a new viewpoint, criticism of any sort will simply cause you to revert to your old viewpoint and will draw your energy away from your ability to participate.

2. Participation excludes trying to improve the process you are participating in. According to King in *The Oragean Version*, "The mechanical organism must always, and will always, be in some kind of integrated balance or imbalance and there can be no change in its habitual activities without at the same time the inauguration of a corresponding, but unnoticed, alteration somewhere else in it." [7]

3. Participation excludes analysis of any type. Analysis is simply intellectual interference similar to criticism that takes energy away from your ability to participate.

4. Participation requires disidentification. This means I must find the balance between participating intentionally in a process, and at the same time, noticing both the participation and the process. King says the following in *The Oragean Version*:

   > To do this and simultaneously to maintain one's separateness from that in which one voluntarily and deliberately involves oneself, demands a very subtle combination of restrained activity and voluntary passivity which can only be learned and understood through intense concentration and considerable practice. It demands a degree of interior, psychological discrimination that is not soon to be attained but which must be attained.[8]

5. The heart of participation lies in finding the balance between activity and receptivity. My experience is slightly different from that of Orage. He makes the balance sound extremely difficult.

In fact, I have not found it difficult. It reminds me of an ability I used to have, but seem to have lost. As a child, when I was doing something, a part of me was often present in a passive and yet receptive way, simply witnessing my activity. Even when I behaved badly, another part of me often felt it was being dragged along as a spectator for the ride. The balance needed in participation has a lightness that seems natural. I have found this lightness through not straining in any way.

6. In the beginning, participation should cover the same field of inquiry as self-observation—that is, posture, gesture, movement, facial expression, and tone of voice. Also, hearing, the experience of temperature and sense of touch. In short, the senses; but not certain instinctive functions, which I will delineate later in the chapter.

7. You can try participation anytime or anywhere, except when physical safety may require you to remain fully in your habitual moving patterns; that is, you want to be ready to deal with an emergency while you are driving or operating machinery.

The warning I gave in an earlier chapter about breathing is related to King's statement in the second guideline. I have found his admonition correct. If we change anything in one part of the mechanism, somewhere else, something also will change. The rhythms and mechanics of our breathing mechanism are definitely observable. Vipassana meditation begins by placing the attention on breathing. However, our tendency is to unintentionally make small changes in our breathing while we are observing it. We do not know whether these changes might create larger changes, of which we would remain unaware. We have a wealth of other behavior to participate in. I would leave breathing to the body.

Another area where I believe it is unnecessary to try participation with is your heartbeat. The heartbeat, like the breathing, is always adjusting its rhythm to the requirements of the body. We do not know what changes would occur if we unintentionally altered our heart rate. We have a large enough field for studying participation without including the breathing or heartbeat.

Using Habitual Behaviors to Fuel Presence

In participation, two simultaneous actions are occurring: I participate with the body's unconscious, habitual behavior, and I remain radically (that is, fully) receptive to impressions of my existence at the same time. Thus, radical receptivity is simultaneously active, receptive, and engaged. Nothing is changed except my participation.

Almost all activities such as thinking, feeling, moving, or sexual manifestations are habitual; that is, they operate seamlessly, without my awareness. The organism repeats its habitual patterns over and over. I have listed some guidelines—both cognitive and emotional—to prepare you to work with participation. Following these guidelines are some descriptive images that, I hope, will illustrate further this new, but simple, effort.

Further Guidelines

The first task is to verify that you have habitual patterns in all three centers. Do not be discouraged by what you find; rather, become sincerely interested. See if the following hypotheses fit your experiences from your own work:

Hypothesis A: Almost all of your manifestations are habitual and occur without any will on your part.

Hypothesis B: There are exceptions to Hypothesis A, but they are few and far between.

Hypothesis C: You know little about your faculty of attention. For the most part, it is pulled around either by inner or outer impressions, associations, memories or images.

Hypothesis D: Identification. As previously discussed, identification may be described as follows: living without an observing and separate part of yourself that is objectively aware of your existence and manifestations.

Hypothesis E: Disidentification occurs when a separate impartial part of you is aware you exist and witnesses your manifestations. With these definitions and hypotheses in mind, consider that: identification is *not* something to be avoided, it is a primary characteristic aspect of all your centers; you know little about it, and you need to study and understand it in order to free yourself from total slavery to it.

Hypothesis F: You can engage in any activity as fully as possible with the express purpose of participating—*as if you were locked inside a robot, over which you had no control. You just give yourself up to it; that is, you manifest the way it manifests, but yet, you remain present.*

If you remain radically or actively receptive to that small part of yourself that is simply aware, making no attempt to modify your behavior, you may gain new, objective impressions of yourself.

It is very useful in Work to experience participation for a number of reasons. First, participation will allow you to gain impressions you may not be able to experience any other way. Second, participation bypasses the associative mechanism of the intellectual center. Third, we do not realize we are living in three different types of time at every moment: physical, emotional, and intellectual time. In my experience, as we are, nothing can lead us toward the experience of all three strands of time simultaneously, other than participation. Orage says this about time:

> The chief difficulty, however, is our present-day training, which has prejudiced us in favor of time as a mere single sequence; and naturally we think that only a single sequence is possible . . . Now if we assume that each of these three modes (thinking, feeling, bodily sensation) is a thread of time, and that each thread is always being filled with beads, it is evident that we can, at least, treble our time and consequently our life by becoming simultaneously conscious of all three successions of events. In other words, by becoming simultaneously conscious of our physical movements as sensations, our feelings, and our thoughts we should be leading in reality three lives at once, actualizing three possibilities at every moment." 9

IMAGES OF PARTICIPATION

Participation is so subtle I found I needed some images to explain it to myself, and I pass on a few here that I have found very useful in my own work. You may be familiar with Gurdjieff's analogy of a human being as an old-fashioned equipage, consisting of a horse, carriage, passenger, and driver. Gurdjieff says that this is a rather complete image of a human being. With apologies to Gurdjieff, I would like to adapt it somewhat to describe participation.

Image 1. The Passenger: Imagine for a moment that you are a passenger in an old-fashioned horse-drawn carriage. It has been a very long ride; you have become bored and are dozing on and off. Periodically, you wake up a little, look out the window, notice you are still quite far from your destination and decide to go back to sleep. This pattern of waking and dozing goes on for some time. Finally, as you are somewhat refreshed now from napping and almost awake, you prop yourself up and notice the carriage sways from side to side, back and forth, and even jostles and bangs you against the side every once in a while in some pattern you cannot quite understand.

You decide to see if you can avoid being banged against the side of the carriage and try moving along with it as it sways from side to side. Your body senses the swaying of the carriage and somehow knows just the right way to *go along* with this swaying. You *intentionally* go along with the way your body compensates for the swaying. You are not trying to change anything; you just sway *with* the carriage. The word "with" is the key here. What has now changed?

Instead of just being jostled about in the carriage half-awake, you have employed your mind and body, and even your emotions (by wishing), in order to participate in the movement of the carriage. Up until now, you were thrown about by every bump in the road, but now your body matches the swaying of the carriage: you simply participate. You notice how incredibly sensitive your body is, how its sense of balance anticipates and adjusts to the complex rhythms of the carriage. Likewise, if you participate without attempting to alter how your body is moving, you may even awaken the young learner within you that is interested in new impressions and just enjoys *noticing* them.

All right now, if you are up to it, some of my own images:

Image 2. The Robot: Imagine you are locked in the body of a very advanced robot. You are resting or asleep most of the time, and the robot just handles everything for you; but every now and then, you take control and direct. For the most part, though, the robot just does what it wants and knows how to do it. Sometimes its aims and desires match up with your own, and you feel happy. At other times, you are dismayed because you want to do something or act in a particular way and the robot just does the opposite. There are moments when time just seems to flow by and the robot cruises along. Then one day, the robot decides that it is tired of running this vessel and admits it would like some help with the job. You say you would like to try.

The robot is skeptical at first, but agrees that if you could learn to handle the controls, it might let you take over and cruise around where you want to go for a bit. However, before the robot gives you some control, it wants to make sure you know everything there is to know about "roboting." This is the deal: first, you must understand just the robot's movements. This will be your apprenticeship. If you pass this part and simply learn to take part in its movements, you may get impressions of other of the robot's capacities, such as feeling or thinking. Perhaps you will even understand some of the robot's actions. You are very excited, so you agree to the conditions.

"Oops!" the robot says, "There is another part of the agreement." During this apprenticeship, you are not allowed to change anything. No, in fact, your work, which the robot realizes will be very difficult for you since you are just half-awake, will be *only* to participate in the actions of the robot's arms, legs, head, and gestures. No changing is allowed! Just going along with its movements. You are reluctant. You think, "That is just not fair. I want to control this robot if I am going take the trouble to wake up." The robot is very smart and notices your disappointment and your desire to be in control.

The robot explains: "You know, someday you will be able to take over, but only if you follow my advice now. If you really see what I have to go through to balance all the different energies coming to me in the control room, you would have more than a headache; you might go either crazy or just fall back asleep. So, to start with, just work to keep up with me, get impressions from inside of me of what I am doing, and when you stray or fall asleep, come back to my movements and postures. Then, when you can really take over—and I will know when you are ready—I will show you more about what is actually happening in the midst of all the activity." You are excited and decide to participate.

Now, the image I find most complete.

Image 3. The Pilot: You are an eight-year-old girl, flying with your father in a small single-engine plane. He is a pilot for an emergency medical supply firm and flies medical supplies all over the country following disasters. He is taking you on a long flight with him, to the Midwest from San Francisco. Although you have taken short trips with him before, this long trip is very exciting. You have decided you want to be a pilot just like him. The idea of flying planes fascinates you. You watch him move all the different switches and instruments, but what really catches your eye is the yoke. The yoke, you realize, is like the steering wheel of a car. Your dad turns it, pulls and pushes it to make the plane go in the right direction, left, right, up, and down. You are so excited you ask him if you can take the yoke and turn it, push it, and pull it yourself.

Your dad looks at you very seriously. He knows you are sincere and really want to fly, but realizes you are still too young to be able to actually handle the controls. It requires strength and a feel for how the yoke operates. It also requires knowledge of all the forces that impinge on the operation of the plane. After thinking for a few moments, your dad says he is very interested in you flying and he is willing to teach you.

First, though, he wants you to see how he steers the plane and get a feel for the yoke. You are almost too excited now. A plane is different from a car, and there is a yoke just like your father's directly in front of you. You have been watching it move back and forth and left and right ever since your father started taking you along with him, watching it move almost by itself as your father moved the one in front of him. He asks you to grip your yoke by placing your hands on either side of it. He had always said before that you should not touch it, but now he is actually telling you to hold it.

He looks at you seriously and says that first you must feel how he moves the yoke. You are not allowed to turn it. Instead, you have to let him do the pushing, pulling, and turning and feel through your hands how your yoke responds. Your work will be to participate in the movement of the yoke, while letting your father control it. You are so excited that you almost can't breathe. Hesitantly, you put your hands on the yoke. And, for the first time, you are not just watching it move but experiencing its subtle movements as your father guides the plane. You notice you want to change or help or resist the movements of the yoke, *and you have to keep that wish under control or you cannot feel how your dad flies the plane.* This is exciting. You are wide awake. Then, you notice that the plane and everything you see outside the windshield change ever so slightly in relation to the subtle movements you are experiencing as your father moves the yoke.

The human body, its mechanisms, and its capacities are more complex than the associative mind can possibly imagine. However, we have the potential to understand all of this complexity if we are willing to wake up the young learner within us. I have offered these images to get you interested in this incredible vehicle you inhabit. You cannot take over the yoke yet, but you can be the copilot and not just the cargo.

When you work with participation, it is not important how your attention is distracted or how often. Participation takes place totally in the *now.* It is fueled through the experience of impressions you receive of yourself each moment. It does not matter if you forget your aim and are distracted. Simply *come back and participate* in whatever it is you are doing in the new present moment. Put your full attention on it, do not be afraid to get identified with whatever you are doing, engage it, get into it fully—participate!

The body always serves as the foundation for participation. Eventually, after practice in participating with your body, you will begin to notice subtleties—other things that are happening. You will notice a thought and may participate in having that thought. It might be some inner talking or some fleeting emotion. You may notice some emotion arise about the past, a regret or some painful memory. Be willing to participate in that memory, go hand and hand with it, move with it as an ally. Always use the current situation for your work. At this stage, leave yourself be, without changing anything, but work in a participatory way that allows you to use whatever is happening in the moment. Your second chance to participate in the present moment never expires.

The real gift is that you are *present in the moment* by participating in your experience. This presence, built from impressions of your existence, is immediately transformed into energy for self-consciousness. You can feel good or bad about yourself, think about what is happening—but most importantly, continue to participate. You will receive light by making light; receive consciousness by being conscious. Enter fully into anything that you are doing, physical, emotional, intellectual, or even sexual.

For example, as I type this page now, I am fully participating for moments at a time with my fingers that are typing. The moving center is very intelligent. There is no way my associations could ever keep up with my fingers as they type, but by acting as a copilot, I gain impressions of their intelligence. Learn how to be a copilot, be the little girl or boy in the copilot seat, have your hands on the controls, and go along for the ride. You do not get to direct the airplane yet; you are preparing to be the pilot. In order to be a pilot and take over the controls, you need to know how to be fully in the now. Whether we realize it or not, our body is always in the now. It is present each and every moment. You can use its presence to learn.

EXPERIMENTATION

Many aspects of the Work are ripe for experimentation. After I have some mastery of the principles of self-observation, sensing, and participation, I can further expand my possibilities for self-study and practice. I can bring in more areas and even make changes specifically to study their effect upon me. I can take an aim for a day or a week and study my experience. Experimentation need not involve making big changes, either physically or psychologically. Small changes are actually more useful because they increase my sensitivity to myself. It seems paradoxical, but I find that big changes usually produce unknown and short-lived changes in my state, while small changes may produce recognizable experiences of more lasting value.

You can include others who are also working while you are experimenting. Experimentation means changing something about yourself, shifting your actions or responses. Experimentation is mentioned in King's *Oragean Version*.[10] He places it in second place after working with participation. In my opinion, he does not stress participation suffi-ciently before undertaking experimentation. Experimentation could be seen as taking control of the yoke, of oneself. As I have worked with participation, I have found experimentation flows naturally from the experiences of participation.

Beginning Practices in Experimentation

First, ask yourself, what is the purpose of experimentation? The answer may have many facets: to gain new impressions of yourself, to wake up and remember yourself, to experience choosing your actions or how you wish to be. You can experiment in three specific areas, the intellectual, the emotional, and the physical. I have found that the moving center is a good place to start. For example, you can observe your postures and make small changes.

Experiments with Postures and General Body Movements

A simple method

1. When you are in a meeting, take a new sitting position. Maintain it for twenty minutes if you can. You might just sit up straighter or perhaps sit away from the back of your chair. It will require you to direct your body in a new way. Your body will protest after a short period, because it is used to sitting with the smallest amount of effort. This new posture will create friction between the body's wish to make as little effort as possible and your wish to experi-ence yourself.

2. Use the above friction to remain present and notice how your body affects your emotional state; that is, what emotions come about as the result of the friction between habit and newness. Also, see if you can notice a few thoughts.

Another simple practice

1. As you walk down the street, slow down. Make your speed slow enough to be different from the speed of most of the other people on the street, but not so slow as to attract attention.

2. As you walk this way, notice your habitual pull to speed up, to assume your usual pace. Also, notice how the body in some way wants to match the speed of others.

3. Notice your emotions as you walk. Do you feel awkward, ashamed, as if others will notice you? Perhaps there is some uneasiness.

4. Once you have established a slower pace and noticed some of the items in 1 through 3 above, see if you can look around slowly as you walk. For example, look to the sides, look further into the distance, and see if you can notice something you have not seen before.

5. Try to sense your body as you move. Sensing while moving is not as simple as it seems at first.

Experiments with Emotions

Experimentation with the emotions is perhaps the most interesting and difficult area of practice. Even a small change can produce dramatic impressions.

1. You are at a business meeting. You are the type of person who always talks a lot at these meetings. This time, while you are at the meeting, you say almost nothing. Could it be any simpler?

2. Observe your emotional state while you are quiet. See what you feel as you resist the temptation to speak after someone else—to show how much you know or to show your agreement or disagreement. Of course, be intelligent. You do not want to call too much attention to yourself and get yourself fired.

3. Notice whether your body shifts around or how much tension you hold in your face and mouth. Notice your tongue and perhaps even feel it move in your mouth as it rehearses what you want to say.

4. Sense your body and look at others around the room.

5. See if you can notice how everything just flows along, how habitual and automatic the conversation is; and how habitual and automatic you are.

6. How has being quiet affected you emotionally?

Of course, if you are more introverted, you can reverse the above exercise. For those who have a tendency to speak very little in meetings or perhaps to consider very carefully what they say—try speaking more often. Work with not measuring the exactness of what you say. Then, notice your emotional state, perhaps how uneasy this makes you feel.

A More Advanced Emotional Experiment

Here are a few examples of more advanced areas for experimentation. Experimenting is not about producing an effect on others, but is part of a larger inquiry, observing and experiencing the habitual patterns in all three of your major centers, penetrating into the very heart of their mechanisms.

Remember, we need to experience our mechanicality in order to free ourselves from it. Perhaps it is here you may receive glimpses of something nonmechanical, of freedom, of who you might be.

1. Someone is angry with you or feels you made a mistake. Normally, you would defend your position, try and make them see your side of the issue, convince them you are right and they are the one seeing things incorrectly.

2. As an experiment, you decide *not to* defend yourself, but simply listen to the other person. Perhaps you even experiment with agreeing outwardly with him. Notice what it is like to make such a decision and stand in front of another person who is blaming or shaming you, maybe even while you realize he or she is absolutely wrong.

Notice the feelings that come up. Try to allow them and remain inwardly disidentified. This is a very big change and may produce some unusual experiences.

Experiment with Three-Centered Self-Observation

An interesting experiment with self-observation is to see if you can experience all three centers in the observation. One way to do this is to place the emphasis on sensing and then, while sensing, to experience your emotional state and also whatever thoughts you have going on. You may notice that this is not easy and that attempting to do it more diligently does not work either. There is a reason for this of course. Our attention is constantly pulled away by incoming impressions and just maintaining sensing is often all we are capable of doing. However, do not despair.

It is possible through gentle persistence to sense your body and also to notice your emotional state if the emotional center is not overly activated. Therefore, you begin this type of experimentation in this way:

1. When you "feel" emotionally balanced, begin by fully grounding yourself by sensing your entire body.

2. Next, while sensing, notice and experience your emotional state.

3. While sensing and experiencing your emotional state, notice and experience your mental associations. If you practice in this way, you gradually will develop self-observation that is a three-centered experience in that each center is both involved in the process of observation and is also being experienced.

CHAPTER 17

IN THE MIDST OF LIFE

LIFE AS A UNIVERSITY

I have become intrigued in recent years by an odd question, "Where can I find a true university?" We usually think of a university as a degree-granting institution having a campus with large buildings where students study a variety of subjects. UC Berkeley, where I did undergraduate work, certainly had large buildings and granted degrees, but was it a real university? In terms of developing the student's potential or fostering their ability to think for themselves, I don't think so. Perhaps that is no longer the aim of universities. I learned little in my undergraduate work. The emphasis in classes was on memorizing facts whose usefulness (except perhaps in the sciences and engineering) had little applicability to my life. Although I acquired some knowledge there, that knowledge did not increase my understanding of life in any real way.

It has taken me years to realize that, through my inner work, I must create the real university in the midst of the life I am living. I emphasize the word "living." What does "living" mean for me? It means that, in order to be fully alive, my attention must be engaged. I cannot be continually lost in every activity without any realization that I am actually alive in that moment. To be truly alive, intentionally engaged, and participating in my life, a part of me must be aware of being alive in the moment. If I am alive in this moment, then the true university comes into existence. Most of us do not realize this life is their most important university and miss the education that they could receive.

I surprise my clients at times by pointing out there is a great deal for them to learn about themselves in the midst of a painful or difficult period. They want to get through such difficult periods as quickly as possible. Perhaps this desire to mitigate pain was originally a survival instinct, but it is symbolic of my unconscious life—I want to escape as soon as possible—so I can relax and go back to sleep. Clients almost always focus on the end point, where their problem is resolved, rather than on their moment-to-moment experience. Focusing on the goal and missing the process—the moment we are living in—is a habit we learn from others, primarily our parents, teachers, and friends. Then, we perpetuate the habit throughout our lives, unless we begin to notice it.

Graduate school was very different from my previous education because it emphasized experiential learning. Upon first hearing, many ideas seemed strange to me, but became clear later on. I remember being surprised by the most unusual idea that it might actually be necessary during my life to experience betrayal. At first hearing, this idea seemed strange. However, if we do not experience betrayal, then to a certain extent, we remain naive psychologically. On closer reflection, I realized I had been betrayed a number of times in my life. Each time, I had learned quite a lot about myself, as well as learning about the person who betrayed me. Betrayal opens us to darker experiences we need and inures us to the hardships of life on this planet. A true university might include a course that explored the effects of betrayal and other unpleasant experiences.

A true university would resemble Orage's "Gymnasium of Life," where one would tackle difficulties as a means of developing emotional flexibility and strength. Modern life seems to prepare us for just the opposite. It intentionally encourages us to avoid difficulty by making everything more convenient. We get used to making less and less effort, and then, when things go wrong, we seek to blame and punish others for our suffering. Thus, we do not develop flexibility, but rigidity. A true University of Life would require us to delve into our experiences more deeply, take more meaning from our experiences and teach us to be present in them.

In the last few years, I have become more interested in making greater meaning of my experiences. Questions that I ask about my experience include, "Why am I living?" "How come my life has turned out this way?" "How come I met that person?" "What can I learn about this unpleasant or pleasant experience I am having or have had?" "Is there a lesson, myth, or story that underlies my life?" This last question is very interesting to me. I sometimes ask clients to think about it when they are confronted with difficulty. I say, "If the situation you find your-self in were a myth, what would you learn from it?"

Looking at my own life and assisting others explore their lives through therapy, I find dominant themes that always stand out. These themes include continued disappointments, never being satisfied with what is occurring in the moment, repeated loss, feeling you have never lived up to your capacity, betrayals, how you failed others, and unful-filled longings. We can learn a great deal by becoming aware of all this material. I ask clients to review their lives carefully, and confront the questions that arise from such a review. Little details may have more importance than they first realize. I call it making a "life review."

A life review does not have to be complex. Just sit down with pencil and pad or computer.

1. List your life in ten-year periods.

2. Write down memories that stand out during each period.

3. Make a guess or intuit what lessons or learnings have come from each period. Are there mistakes you made that stand out, or conversely, good decisions you can remember?

Your life review may even lead you to an interest in history. I do not mean the ordinary recordation of different peoples, regions, empires, or cultures that abound in common histories. Instead, attempt an overall psychological history of how humanity has come to be in such a pickle—that is, the predicament of being at odds with each other, with nature, and even with ourselves.

THE WILLEM NYLAND GROUP

My experiences with the Nyland Group spanned a period of thirteen years. Nyland lived on the East Coast. He periodically came to Cali-fornia and often stayed for a week, but for the most part, the group was on its own. The group owned property called the "Land."

At the Land, I first began working with Gurdjieff's Movements and was drawn to them immediately. They represented a special type of education for me, where I experienced learning more deeply and differently than my previous education. The Movements were my first encounter with experiential learning. I learned about my inner self while doing the Movements and working with the class. The class, the music, and the difficult leg, arm, and head sequences combined to give me new impressions of myself as I worked to master them.

During the late 1960s and through the 1970s, "Work weekends" were held at the Land. We worked on construction projects, gardening, crafts, and movements. During my first two years in the group, I was still a college student. During this period, I did not own a car, and in order to get to the Land, I sometimes had to hitchhike from Berkeley. I would start hitchhiking at 5:00 a.m. on Saturday morning and often would not arrive until after 2:00 p.m.

After graduating from Berkeley and giving up my job at Kaiser Hospital, I moved to Freestone, a small town about sixty miles northwest of San Francisco and ten miles south of the Land. Freestone had a general store, a nursery, and a volunteer fire department. I lived in a rundown cottage that sat on the edge of a swamp across from the Freestone Nursery. The small swamp insured that the cottage was always dank and moldy, but I bore it because it was so close to the Land. At one point, I was making up to four trips a week to the Land to take part in workdays or meetings.

Over the years, I took on more responsibility and with another experienced group member facilitated a good-sized group in Berkeley. The main impetus of Nyland's work was to transmit basic concepts and rules for correct self-observation and self-study. According to Nyland, the characteristics of correct self-observation were the most important aspect of Gurdjieff's teaching. He saw the aim of Work practices as being the personal creation within oneself of an observing "I," a latent faculty located in the frontal lobes of the brain, birthed and fed through the impressions of oneself gained through correctly conducted self-observation. I list below Nyland's explication of the defining characteristics of an objective, observing "I."

1. The faculty must *observe.*

2. The observation must be objective, no liking or disliking; that is, the "I" must observe impartially.

3. The observation must be simultaneous with what the "I" faculty is observing or what is occurring in the moment.

4. If the characteristics of a person's self-observation lacked any of the above elements, Nyland's interpretation was that it was not true self-observation.

Furthermore, the real "I" that was being born through one's work was not capable of being objective about one's thoughts or emotions. Thus, observations were to be *only* of the physical body and its manifestations. More narrowly, the manifestations of the physical body one might observe were limited to five distinct categories:

1. General bodily movements

2. Postures

3. Gestures

4. Facial expressions

5. Tone of voice

Nyland's justification for maintaining the focus of observation on the physical body was threefold. First, both emotions and thoughts were too subjective (that is, too filled with likes and dislikes for the fledgling "I" to observe). Second, the body was a big, definite object, easy to observe. Third, and most important, Nyland believed the physical body manifested all our emotions and thoughts, and if my "I" could be impartial toward it, then this "I" could also notice and understand the underlying thoughts and emotions contained within the body's manifestations.

In my experience, it is absolutely correct to begin self-observation with the study of the physical manifestations of the body. However, there are certain inherent difficulties in this presentation of self-observation that I will mention shortly.

According to Nyland, these principles of observation are very simple, and yet they are very difficult to achieve in practice. Normal self-observation does not always meet the criteria, because it is filled with likes and dislikes. It is usually associative, using words for description.

"Stringing the beads" is what my wife, Elizabeth, and I refer to as the way individuals learned to adjust their statements in groups. They tailor what they say in meetings; to give themselves a better chance that the group leaders will accept their observations. As a result, the aliveness of meetings can crumble. Many group leaders do not really understand this unconscious phenomenon, and it is important to watch for it. Very often when people are learning to apply Gurdjieff's methods, the language that they use to describe their experience may not completely match up with others' language. It is important for all members of a group to maintain openness to the intention of what the person is trying to communicate, as it takes time to learn how to communicate one's experience clearly.

It is important to recognize the phenomenon of killing group aliveness. I have all too often witnessed the desperate desire of group members to fit in. It is a natural and necessary part of being in any group. However, this need to fit in may be very harmful when it supplants the guiding principle, which is to support each member in finding the truth about themselves. When the need to fit in takes precedent in a Gurdjieff group, theoretically formed to help its members wake up, one senses the group has lost its way and perhaps its purpose.

Certain group members had difficulties following Nyland's method, which was very precise. Others persisted and reaped many rewards. However, this pointed out to me a basic difficulty in applying Gurdjieff's ideas and practices. It is impossible to reduce Gurdjieff's Work to just one approach. For example, if one restricts the parameters of what is and what is not "correct self-observation" too soon for certain individuals, you can end up throwing out the baby with the bathwater (that is, discouraging individuals who need encouragement). Each person brings a trove of valuable material that can inspire the entire group. Through overly critical comments, you can gradually deplete the group's aliveness and confidence. It would be similar to a piano teacher constantly telling their beginning pupil she is not playing the music correctly and is making too many mistakes. Gradually, the student feels she never does it correctly, never will, and gives up. Sometimes, the criticized person rightly assesses that something has gone off course in the group rather than with her, and leaves; but she never fully understands what was amiss.

People are drawn to this Work for a variety of reasons, but two factors are usually paramount: 1) they wish to know the truth about themselves; and 2) they wish to know their purpose in life. They will express their experiences of self-observation, self-remembering, and other Work practices in accordance with their type, sensitivity, education, communication style, and life experience. The exciting part for them is that they can begin to observe themselves and gain self-knowledge, even though their work at first may be sporadic. Through working with others in a group, a participant can begin to see aspects of herself she could not see alone. Self-observation takes time to learn. People need encouragement. They need to be supported and guided in their attempts.

The teacher or group leader guides the student toward an ideal. The ideal will not be reached in the beginning, and it does not have to be. The process is what is important. The student will gather her impressions—with a greater or lesser degree of objectivity—during her journey. All impressions gained during self-observation can be useful, even if the person strays or makes "mistakes." The leader should not discard them, but instead should help the person find her own meaning within the experience. The tendency in Gurdjieff groups to be over-strict in assessing the observations of members comes, perhaps, from some of the written answers that Gurdjieff gave his pupils. It is important to be discerning when giving comments to members and not negative. Let us also realize that group leaders are certainly not Gurdjieff! He changed his methods frequently. If he found that something did not work or produced results not in keeping with his aim, he did not repeat it, but modified it.

I have personally found I cannot perceive my emotions or thoughts solely from the manifestations of the body. The body does not always manifest what is taking place within it cogently. In fact, my body has become quite adept at concealing the manifestations of my emotional and intellectual life, even from me. A completely objective faculty might be able to discern the manifestations of other centers by observing the tensions in various muscles and joints. However, a completely objective "I" does not exist in the beginning. Other aspects of my being cannot come to light through observing the body alone. Likewise, certain aspects of myself will remain obscure if I am only observing with the intellectual center. This center operates more slowly than the other centers and thus is less capable of following flashes of emotion or instinct. Therefore, the real work in the beginning, middle, and even in advanced work, is to be open and compassionate toward my work and learn to encourage and support myself in this work.

GROUP WORK AND SELF-INITIATION

What is self-initiation and is it important? Self-initiation is a state where I am no longer completely dependent on a teacher to wake me up. Instead, I realize the importance of Work and am able to actualize it in my life. I have a permanent center of gravity for my work that is the result of my own efforts. Isn't this exactly what must be the aim for each of us if we really wish to develop ourselves? Ask yourself, would an authentic teacher or religious leader want followers who did not think for themselves and initiate their own evolution? I do not believe Gurdjieff wanted people to imitate his actions, ideas, or emotions. He wanted people to realize their own direction, and gradually have the power to direct their lives from their own real core.

Some leaders simply want to have followers and imitators. They wish to form an organization to perpetuate their own ideas and aggrandize their egos. Not surprisingly, some people love to be followers. It makes them feel secure and superior. They think they have something they can depend on. However, the Work is very different. The Work requires that you self-initiate, but only gradually, through practice. It demands you think deeply for yourself about your experience and not try to fit your experience into a mold. Rather, you must learn to be truthful, even if your experience does not match up or sound exactly like others. Only in this way, can you evolve inwardly. Gurdjieff himself said, "There is not, nor can there be, any outward initiation. In reality only self-initiation, self-presentation exist." [1] In the end, each of us has to create "the way" in ourselves.

Too many groups gravitate toward a place where the leader's authority is unquestioned, a scenario diametrically opposed to self-initiation. Of course, a beginner must learn to use certain basic tools to be able to study him- or herself. However, after a certain period of time, an individual must be able to find that inner part to carry on their work without following a rote pattern. Then, they can bring their experiences back to the group to enliven and sustain it. If sustaining a group means just repeating the same formula over and over, nothing new can occur.

FALSE WORK GROUPS

There are dangers inherent in joining all groups. Even if I am familiar with the purposes of the group, I do not know the aims of all its members. The group dynamic can be coercive, and I may find myself pursuing aims I never could have imagined. Groups that pursue esoteric ideas are no exception. I am including this information so others may beware and take corrective action, if necessary. At the very least, it pays to be vigilant about the tendency of any group to kill the creative urge that originally gave it life. Be alert to this tendency in any group you participate in. Do not abandon your intuition just because others believe the leaders are knowledgeable and hold these leaders out as authorities. Your experience must tell you if, in fact, they have real understanding and authority.

During the 1960s and up till the present, there have existed many pseudo Gurdjieff groups who purport to be following Gurdjieff's ideas. It is extremely important for all those interested in objective knowledge to learn to separate real, essence information of an authentic teaching from distortion and corruption by dysfunctional individuals without a conscience. Sadly, some people who have a deep passion for Work ideas may find themselves in groups where the direction has been completely perverted. This perversion of ideas brings about results that are diametrically opposed to those of an authentic teaching.

There is a plethora of pseudo-Gurdjieffian groups, some of which have many members. Because of their large size, individuals can be easily swayed to join them, even though they have absolutely nothing to do with Gurdjieff's ideas. The false leaders certainly cannot help anyone along their path of evolution and often mislead people so that they become more rigid instead of opening to new experiences. The members delude themselves into believing they are on some evolutionary path, since they are associated with the group. Unconsciously, the individual believes, "I don't really know anything, but if all these people are here, they must know what they are doing; and if I am a member, surely I will become somebody." Alternatively, people become addicted to the surge of energy these large groups generate. They erroneously interpret the "high" they feel to mean some real change has occurred. I have met many people who believe they have a good understanding of Gurdjieff's ideas due to connection with these fake groups, and one has to be on the lookout for such false groups and use intuition to ferret them out. They have done quite a lot of damage.

DIFFICULTIES OF WORKING IN LIFE

As I mentioned earlier, Gurdjieff's method is unique, in that I can practice it in the midst of my ordinary life. In contrast to other spiritual disciplines, I need not withdraw from life; in fact, it is imperative to stay in it. However, some guidelines from my own experience may be useful. I have noticed that any Work practice is more difficult in the following situations: (1) working when I am in the midst of some task at my job; (2) working in the presence of others who are not also studying Gurdjieff's ideas; and (3) working to remain present when my body begins to move. Let us look at each of these three situations in greater detail.

(1) **Working when at my job.** Why is it so difficult to work when I am at my job? A simple answer would be that I am identified. However, this answer does not really give me much useful information. When I am trying to accomplish a task, I focus on completing it. Our culture trains us to accomplish tasks and not be present while doing them. Our educational system trains us to focus our attention on the results only, rather than experiencing our living presence in the moment. In other words, we were taught to be more concerned with finishing a task than enjoying the experience or noticing we are alive in this body as we are doing it. We are taught *how not to be present* by focusing on the future. This continual focus on the future means I am actually taught *never to live my life*. The joy of living is removed and replaced with getting objects, accomplishing tasks, and racking up symbols of success.

(2) **Working in the presence of others.** The greatest difficulty comes from the effect on me of the combined hypnotic trance of others who are not involved in the Work. Their tendency to focus on the future rather than on the moment exaggerates my own inability to remain present. In addition, a constant flow of accidental associations about

the people I am working with creates an unconscious interactive field that draws me away from self-observation. People have parts that are very concerned with how others view them. These parts take over very easily. I am caught up in this shared energy field of internal considering and react in a manner that maintains my sleep.

(3) **When the body begins to move.** If my body is still, and I have become proficient at sensing, then it is not difficult to remain present. However, as soon as I begin to move, it is much more difficult to continue sensing. I have found that, regardless of the degree of my presence, when I begin to engage in large movements, such as lifting or even walking, my experience of sensing becomes diffuse and my awareness disappears.

It may be there is simply insufficient energy available to us to direct our attention to sensing while we are moving. The body is used to taking most of our energy, and we are unused to maintaining our awareness while we are moving. Participation is useful here as it helps us remain present even while moving.

THE HUMAN PREDICAMENT

I want to delve more deeply into Gurdjieff's tale of the role "higher beings" played over the course of human history. These higher beings (of a different nature to humans) try to adjust a calamity that befalls our solar system. Their intention is to ensure the correct development of our solar system, but their actions have terrible consequences.

The story goes that human beings arose on the earth to create a quality of vibrations that will enhance the solar system, specifically to provide for the development of an unexpected new body, the earth's moon. The higher beings make a precautionary adjustment to the psychological functioning of human beings to ensure they do not prematurely realize the insignificance of their individual existence, destroy themselves, and disrupt the normal development of the solar system. The organ Kundabuffer is inserted into their bodies at the base of their spines. Following the insertion of Kundabuffer, everything appears to go along quite well. Once these higher beings determine there is no longer a need for the adjustment and the danger has passed, they remove the organ, and people are allowed to develop normally.

However, the change has resulted in unforeseen consequences (Oh, those externalities!). It seems that although the higher individuals removed Kundabuffer, its consequences remain. Thus, people still perceive reality topsy-turvy, primarily reacting to external stimuli rather than responding from an objectively developed consciousness. They are vain, self-centered, suggestible to anything that gives them pleasure to the point of addiction, and periodically, they engage in reciprocal human slaughter, e.g., war.

It was 1968, when I first read Gurdjieff's tale of the introduction of the organ Kundabuffer. I was in the Panama Canal Zone visiting my father and was suffering from the flu. Try as I have over the years, having the flu in 107-degree heat in Panama's humidity is not something you ever forget. I think I must have been in an altered state when I read Gurdjieff's account of this most incredible adjustment to the human psyche. I have pondered over the years whether it is really true what he says. Could this actually explain why this planet is in such a terrible state? There was something in his writing, a sense of his not caring whether the reader believed it or not, that caused it to penetrate. I sensed what he was saying was true.

I remember feeling incredibly sad when I realized human beings were not fully to blame for their condition. The original cause of our present condition began during the earliest period of our planet, which was also the earliest period of human psychological development. At first, I was infuriated by the idea that higher beings actually played a part in this mistake. I wanted to blame someone for the desperate state the world was in. I was doubly disheartened by Gurdjieff's pronouncement that few people could escape from the general fate caused by the maleficent organ, Kundabuffer.

For a moment, try to imagine what the effect of Kundabuffer on you might be—cut off from the very core of your being—the part that gives you a sense of the purpose and aim of your existence. By analogy, when a person is cut off from his or her natural abilities because of a stroke, severe accident, or old age, he or she will often respond with anger. Anger is one of several automatic reactions to loss. Others are denial, sadness, grief, or acceptance. Many people I have met sense deep down they are not what they could be. They sometimes say, "I am not living up to my potential." In other words, the loss of human capacities manifests itself in negativity about themselves, their future, others, and life in general.

The lopsided development of the human psyche and the insufficient development of essence led me to wonder how people manifest this lack. King says that at any one time there is only a certain amount of negativity present in the world. It is actually a force:

> But negative emotion per se . . . is an objective force of finite proportion existing at a given time and place; for instance there is so much of it—no more and no less— within a given community or within a given nation at any selected time. This force must produce effects; in other words, it must be expressed in the organic symptoms of the human beings composing the given group. Such expression does not diminish the quantity of negative force present which, when the energies of one personal victim have been exhausted in expressing it, moves on to another whose energies can be utilized in the same way.[2]

King may well be correct that negativity as a force is continually preserved as it circulates throughout humanity. If he is right, then it is incumbent on us to understand the nature of our negativity so that we may counter it, or at least consider it. Attempts to meet negative forces without proper understanding will be ineffectual or worse.

Humanity needs to understand the source of its negativity. It is like a storm in the psychological weather pattern of the planet. Unless we know how to handle our boat in the storm, we will end up either crashing on the rocks or sinking to the bottom. War is often the primary way society expresses negativity. Attempts to control the negative manifestations of people or nations using physical force have proven both ineffectual and destructive.

RECLAIMING OUR ESSENTIAL NATURE

As I have mentioned earlier, we have an undeveloped part of us, an essence part that has gone unnourished and that holds the seeds of our individuality. I believe the fundamental cause of war and other destructive activity is the loss of connection to our essence and its under-development. Because essence remains undeveloped, we do not consciously labor or intentionally suffer in order to actualize our true purpose. Loss produces frustration and negativity. Cut off from its essential nature, humanity produces a tidal wave of negativity against itself. With no way to transform such negativity for conscious purposes, this negativity wreaks havoc on its human victims and on the earth itself. We are all familiar with the results: war, atrocities, devastation of the land, displacement, privation, and misery. All of this suffering results from unconsciousness.

On an individual level, if I want to change, to escape the unintended effects of Kundabuffer—the degradation of my psyche, spiritual emptiness, unhappiness, depression, and destructive relationships—then I need to undertake a special kind of work. The Work can restart the curtailment of my essence. Without work on essence, I remain subject to the unconscious, destructive forces that work their way through humanity, from group to group and person to person.

For some, negativity has become the active force in their lives. They join movements that demand change in the most violent and destructive manner. Some even become terrorists. However, if I work to wake up, to remember myself, I have the possibility of making a contribution to the world. With consciousness, I may, in some small way, work for a world of compassion and meaning. I can learn to transmute negative force.

Gurdjieff said we could no longer remove the effects of Kundabuffer through faith, hope, or love, as Jesus exhorted. We are too far gone. Nevertheless, we can still heed the voice of conscience, and we open the door to conscience through conscious labor and intentional suffering. This is the Work.

CHAPTER 18

SUFFERING AND DEATH

In this chapter, we will look at some of the larger more inclusive topics and questions that all of us must eventually face in life. These include suffering, the chaos inherent in life, our slavery to the pressure of life, aging and death, and the possibilities of the continuation of life after the death of the physical body. We will also look at some related topics that at first glance may seem a bit of a sidetrack, but which are actually closely related to the possibility of our development.

CONSCIOUS AND UNCONSCIOUS SUFFERING

In first-world countries, where we have achieved a modicum of financial security, our focus is generally to avoid suffering at all costs, although there are a few exceptions. A mountaineer will suffer pain and diffi-cult conditions to achieve his goal. A creative artist may endure years of deprivation to write a book or become a painter. The academi-cian or researcher may toil painstakingly over tedious material to get published. The terrorist will suffer death willingly. Common to all of them is their willingness to suffer in pursuit of a specific aim, sometimes a very limited one. Some people choose to suffer for mere aggrandize-ment, others out of a belief they are serving their religion or humanity.

How many of us can really say we welcome struggle of any sort? We appreciate the struggle of the mountain climber and great writer, but we focus on their success or product. We enjoy reading about their exploits, but few of us would suffer to achieve what they have. We live vicariously through them and through their stories.

What do we know about suffering anyway? What sort of experi-ences do we connect with the word? A millionaire real estate agent who loses a big sale suffers. A motorcyclist who misses out on the big bike sale suffers. The writer who has seen his work rejected by numerous publishing houses suffers. The cancer victim suffers. The man or woman without a mate suffers. Approximately two-thirds of the people on the earth are malnourished; they suffer in ways we may not be able to imagine. Others suffer every moment from mental and physical debilitation. For some, their emotional suffering may feel as bad to them as starvation. Suffering represents perhaps the majority of human experience. Of course, all other forms of life suffer as well.

Most of us don't realize we experience some form of suffering almost daily. We have lived with suffering our entire lives, and yet it is often invisible. Of course, if we look, we can easily see it in others. We notice their negative reactions, their constant complaining about something or other. Regardless of how beautiful the day is, how healthy they are, how successful they seem to be, they are still negative about the way things are going. Others we see suffer from the victim modality, and feel things never go right for them. They blame others for their situation, blame the world and sometimes, even life itself. Rarely do they look at themselves as the problem. They all are completely immersed in automatic mechanical suffering. Their suffering is usually just a habitual reaction to circumstances. They want to get the suffering over as quickly as possible; they do not know how to use their reactions to suffering for their own inner growth.

In 2000, I took my sixteen-year-old son for his first trip to New York City where I was raised. We visited my old neighborhood on Manhattan's Upper West Side. We went to the World Trade Center and Greenwich Village. We also visited the New York Stock Exchange. Standing in the viewer's area looking down on the trading floor, we watched the stockbrokers below, almost all men, in a frenzy of activity. They were yelling and pushing, all the while glancing up at the big board. Most of their faces were filled with anxiety. Some talked madly on the phone as others stared off blankly into space. It was as if we were watching a huge anthill. All the ants below were running around not understanding what they were doing. Somehow, it seemed they were destroying themselves in their frenzy. It looked as if they were being eaten alive by their anxiety-ridden activity. Yet, I also realized that each of them was perhaps a millionaire, was considered successful, and was often emulated because of his financial success.

As I watched, I realized from their harried expressions and movements they were in emotional pain. It seemed their essential nature was in torment while they bolstered their egos with erroneous values and phantasmal beliefs. Their life force was being used up for no other purpose than the movement of money. They were really suffering emotionally, although they were hardly aware of it. I wondered if they found anything real for themselves, real satisfaction, anything for their own development. As I was leaving the visitor's area, I looked back at them and a final image came to me—I thought I was looking into Hell.

We might say the stockbroker's suffering, whether he realizes it or not, at least provides him with his basic survival needs. However, most people's jobs provide them with basic needs. The degree of suffering I saw on the floor of the New York Stock Exchange seems symbolic to me of our unconscious indifference to our own suffering. Were the perks of wealth and comfort far beyond their needs worth the emotional hell they suffered every minute of their day? The men on the trading floor, considered highly educated, having graduated from the best universities, appeared to be living totally unconscious lives. Money had consumed them. I have watched garbage men at work who appeared to have more presence while going about their jobs on the city streets and even appeared to enjoy what they were doing.

While suffering is an aspect of life that appears inescapable, not all suffering is necessarily negative. Whether we realize it or not, we have used suffering as a learning tool throughout our lives. All real learning contains some aspect of suffering. We forget about this integral part of learning. Our automatic capacity to organize information and situations often gives us the impression of accomplishment without trial and error. We remember only the end product of our efforts. We forget that effort, mistakes, and suffering are intimately bound together as aspects of learning. In special conditions, these three aspects can become the trinity that Gurdjieff calls "conscious labor." The effort represents the active force, the mistakes represent the force of resistance, and suffering may or may not contain the reconciling force, depending on our attitude and how we use it.

In modern culture, we have almost completely lost the benefits of suffering as a learning tool. What would it mean to suffer consciously? It becomes more and more difficult for us to imagine the richness we can derive from suffering that might feed an essential part of our being.

A woman who has prepared her mind and exercised her body may taste the reward suffering brings if she chooses to remain awake while her child is born, not resorting to drugs to make her unconscious or numb her pain. In agrarian societies, where physical work strengthens women and they give birth in a squatting position, it is reported that the pain of childbirth is not so intense, and the mother has a greater opportunity to experience something besides intense physical agony.

It is interesting to look at the work of someone like Mother Teresa in relation to suffering. What is so striking about her and her coworkers? Why is she so revered? Perhaps we intuitively sense she developed the ability to suffer intentionally, in order to fulfill the needs of the children she served. She worked toward a real aim. It required working in the most poverty-stricken area of Calcutta, where suffering was everywhere. It is difficult to imagine her inner world. I imagine she experienced a harmony few of us experience, although it is something we wish we had. However, most people refuse to work to attain harmony. Instead, we hope vaguely that harmony will come if we have enough material goods and leisure time; yet, it eludes most of us.

In many ways, the possession of material objects and the recognition we receive for our personal achievements have become substitutes for the experience of harmony. We may feel harmonious for a short time when we get a new computer, a dress, a car, or a job. However, for almost all of us, the feelings of harmony last but a short while and then dissolve. Enduring harmony depends on engaging in difficult situations and learning to struggle consciously. Struggle does not necessarily always call for extreme efforts, but it requires intelligent effort. Knowing what a difficult situation requires and then being able to engage the situation in a meaningful way can bring real harmony. In my opinion, any attempt to experience harmony that excludes suffering is fantasy. While modern technology has banished most physical hardship from our lives, it has not been able to end all our suffering. That is impossible.

Another symptom of our attempts to avoid suffering is drug addiction. We try to dull our emotional pain through the use of artificial substances; conversely, we use drugs that give us an unearned experience of higher states consciousness.

Our current fascination with technology is also tied to our resistance to making efforts or suffering to achieve an aim. In an attempt to substitute machines to do our work, we actually may increase our angst. We want a computer that corrects our spelling, saves our data, and even picks up the mail for us. Our overarching sense of entitlement means that everything must proceed quickly and automatically. When it doesn't, we get angry and feel as if our rights are being abridged. Just read the letters-to-the-editor section of your newspaper. People cannot tolerate or suffer the inconvenience of delay, and we are not above blaming and shaming others for it. It may take you some time to find examples of this type of behavior in your life, but if you look, you will find it.

CHAOS AND OVERWHELM

Chaos has recently become a topic of scientific interest, particularly to physicists, although most people have heard about it. The study of chaos lies within the province of science rather than the social sciences. We have all experienced chaos in our lives, but when asked what we have learned from it, we falter.

Do you ever feel chaos is about to engulf you? From time to time, I feel I am at war with chaos, a war it seems I am on the verge of losing. For all the chaos theories in the sciences, the most fruitful area of research may have been completely overlooked, that of human experience. Scientific method attempts to limit the influence of subjective and random events in research, and scientists have elevated the scientific method to a religion in their attempt to bypass or erase subjectivity. However, perhaps it is just in subjective experience where we can find a wealth of objective information about chaos.

Anthony Blake summed up some of the recent thinking concerning chaos and order this way: "Chaos is now thought to contain such complexity of order that it appears without order. The psychological phenomena of fragmentation, uncertainty, fleetingness, being at variance with oneself, losing control, confusion, and inconsistency reflect the uncertain reality of existence itself." [1]

A primary capacity that distinguishes us from other animals is our ability to organize our world and to bring awareness to conditions of uncertainty. Other animals can only make small adjustments in response to their environment. Human beings, on the other hand, are capable of complex organization, and we learn quickly to adjust to even major changes in our environment. Our capacities to learn and organize allow us to create works of art, provide service to others, and design the polio vaccine—on the positive side. On the negative side, they also make us capable of producing an atomic bomb or organizing a terror cell, bringing death to thousands.

Humans are three-brained beings—we were given a third brain, our intellectual center. Why? I believe the answer lies in giving us the ability to make use of and manage the hazards, the chaos, and the variability of our existence. We are able not only to adapt to changing conditions, but are given the ability to modify them. Because chaos is an inherently disorganizing force, our organizing capabilities counterbalance it.

We develop our organizing capacity by imitating others. Although it is not automatic at first, the movements, thoughts, and emotional states that we learn are also quickly organized and easily become habitual. We quickly learn to respond to chaos automatically. However, although we reap the benefits of our organizational capacity, it is not really our own—unless we earn the right to own it by becoming conscious of it. Otherwise, it remains a mere mechanism, a mechanical function of our brains. Without bringing in our emotional center, our sense of what is of true value and what is not, this organizational mechanism has no conscience about how we use it. Knowing how to do something—such as how to create an atomic weapon—does not mean we must do it. This is the real meaning of Frankenstein's monster. An objective conscience could help us discriminate between that which is needed and has objective value and that which, although we can make it or do it, is actually injurious for the planet.

Parents and educators teach children ordering, organization, and correlative skills. These skills are crucial to a well-ordered society, and organization becomes part of our survival tool kit. However, what happens when organization breaks down? We don't often notice the breakdown until we feel stressed-out, overwhelmed, have a car accident, hurt our backs lifting incorrectly, or feel confused and unable to make a decision. In short, we are thrown out of our well-ordered world and feel life is out of control. Then we notice the chaos. It is a state most people don't want in their lives. There are, of course, people we all know who appear to try to create chaos in their relationships, their work, and themselves; but these are the exceptions. For the most part, people are scared of chaos.

Bennett said that in the creation of the world, hazard was a necessary phenomenon.[2] In order to have a true creation and not simply produce a machine where only limited repetition of action is possible, the possibility of both success and failure must exist. If it is indeed possible for new experience to arise, it means that existence is elastic and must allow for the unexpected. The world needs spaces where something new can take place. It may be that chaos or hazard represents these spaces required for the evolution of the universe. Thus, the need for constant adjustment in all aspects of life may be the effect of chaos. Because of this need, special beings are required to adjust for the very chaos that makes possible a continuous creative universe. Developed three-brained beings are the necessary adjusters, part of the corrective action that can keep creation flowing properly.

Chaos actually provides us with opportunities that demand creativity and proper use of all our centers to integrate new experiences. We can make great use of chaos in our personal study if we work with all our centers. We first need to study our reactions when confronted by resistance and the unexpected. Which of our centers reacts first? Chaos then becomes a most remarkable teacher, showing us how we do not really understand how things work or how we are. Chaos is evident in our lives, for example, when we misplace things or forget what we told someone. We can also observe chaos when we work with Gurdjieff's practices. We can see it working, for example, in our inability to remember ourselves, even when we set self-remembering as a task.

The study of how we handle chaos can be fascinating. Most of our fears about chaos are unnecessary and habitual. We defend against it in various ways. For example, addictions and other self-calming techniques serve to numb the chaos we experience. However, because chaos is a force of creation, I have found it is crucial to my personal evolution. I especially need to study it since it is a necessary ingredient of the resisting force and will always be present when I work.

EXTERNALITIES

The state of the biosphere is a problem of widespread concern to people everywhere. Millions of people on this planet are struggling to improve their lives, but with only a limited understanding of the roots of the problem. We like to believe the ecology movement is helping us come together as a planet. Clearly, it does make those of us in the first world more aware of our mortality. It shows us we may also face the possibility of scarcity and death from drought, starvation, or being uprooted from our homes. We have developed a false sense of security because of favorable climactic conditions, access to natural resources, and stable governments providing us with economic prosperity and social mobility. However, in the last forty years, we have begun to realize we are poisoning the ecosystem and causing the deaths of countless species. How has this happened?

An important concept from the field of economics is "externality," defined as collateral damage from the unexpected results that arise from planned or invented projects or developments—that is, technological innovation. The death of the ecosystem on a large scale began with the development of the internal combustion engine and the proliferation of electricity. These two developments created externalities that have brought the earth's ecosystem to its knees in under one hundred and fifty years. The recent tsunami in Japan, which caused destruction of a couple of its nuclear reactors and subsequent pollution of the land and the ocean, is one tragic example. Let us look at the development of these technologies. They contain important factors for understanding some of our unconscious behaviors.

The internal combustion engine has given some of the following gifts to civilization: the massive development of transportation, the ability to mine every type of ore and fuel, the ability to multiply mechanical force, and perhaps, most importantly, the large-scale deployment of electrical energy. Externalities, on the other hand, include our total dependence on oil which has led to wars, atmospheric pollution, oil spills, and unrecyclable nuclear waste. Moreover, our oil dependence has led to a global worldview that glorifies economies based on their technological success and their ability to co-opt natural resources from poorer countries.

The ability to generate and harness electricity has made some of the following advances possible: the electric motor and generator, the electric light, communication across great distances at lightning speed, medical diagnostic advances, and the ability to transmit information in the blink of an eye. The externalities of electricity include, but in no way are limited to: addiction to electricity and electronic gadgetry, the use of nonrenewable raw materials that hasten the destruction of natural resources, the concentration of economic and military power in the hands of the few, and too many other negatives to list here.

Most people in industrialized countries recognize their dependence on oil as a major problem. We have also recognized some externalities associated with nuclear reactors—poisonous by-products and meltdowns. However, we ignore to our peril our addiction to electricity—we refuse to recognize the externalities. Our world is imperiled by our addiction to electricity that is a direct result of our attempt to reduce human effort.

The externalities of the internal combustion engine and electricity were unforeseen. In the near future we may be coping with perhaps even greater dangers—the externalities generated by the computer and the increasing saturation of the earth's atmosphere by radio waves. Bennett points out how crucial it is to recognize the difference between our knowledge of science and technology and our understanding of how technology affects us. As mentioned earlier, because we know how to do something, it does not mean we must. How does this idea of externalities relate to the study of Gurdjieff's ideas?

Beelzebub's Tales to His Grandson chronicles the history of our planet. It is, in fact, a book about externalities (that is, unforeseen consequences). It recounts the unforeseen results for humanity of higher beings' decisions. They seemed to have the best intentions for the earth and our solar system, yet the book recounts the disastrous consequences of their efforts—trying to correct one unforeseen externality and producing a host of others. Subsequently, the very actions taken to reduce the possibility of future calamity had just the opposite results. If we can pay careful attention to it, *Beelzebub's Tales to His Grandson* shows us, metaphorically, something about externalities, about the importance of real understanding. For solutions to our present problems, Gurdjieff does not send us to economics, sociology, politics, or religion for answers. Instead, he directs us inward, specifically, towards understanding our own psychology, as well as our potential for development.

Today, the concept and study of "ecopsychology" represents, to some extent, a focus on humanity's relationship to the larger ecosystem. What is lacking, however, is how to place the individual's psychology within this larger framework. External change and technological improvement must be accompanied by human internal change. Without it, we simply continue our march toward planetary destruction. Social, economic, political, and cultural change is predicated on psychological evolution. An individual like Gandhi makes us realize we are not powerless in the face of the problems confronting our country or the world. However, without inner change, our ideals will be of no use. We cannot treat the biosphere well unless we actually realize our function within it. Of foremost importance, we also cannot treat the biosphere properly if we do not treat each other equally well, particularly our children.

A number of my clients are very interested in ecology and are even able to motivate others. Yet they sometimes look at their own work and feel it is insufficient. They focus on the number of people they influence, but marginalize the validity of their own inner work. They focus on outer effect or lack thereof in the world and minimize the psychological importance of their undertaking. The need to make quick changes in the visible world obfuscates the importance of inner change. It is difficult for us to realize that all real change in outer behavior depends first on an inner shift. This is another area of humanity's blindness. Again, we see the world upside-down. No real change can occur without inner change.

THE SLAVERY OF BUSYNESS

I have noticed that, when I am relaxed, I will often quickly add more to my to-do list. After all, I am feeling relaxed and time seems to expand. I do one thing after another until I feel exhausted, with no time left to relax. Does this routine sound familiar to you? I notice it happens to almost all my clients regardless of their place on the economic ladder.

They are all over-burdened by life's requirements, either by responsibilities that are foisted upon them or those they have created.

One of the externalities of modern life is the theft of time. For one thing, we are addicted to electronic aides such as the computer or smartphone, and this addiction magnifies our time burdens. At first, it appears paradoxical that time-saving devices waste our time. However, the computer has made it possible to work everywhere and all the time, to be in immediate contact with anyone almost anywhere in the world—our privacy and leisure time are now constantly invaded by others. Many of us are addicted to surfing the net, mobile texting, emailing, and the stream of constant phone chatter. There is virtually no privacy left. This electronic infiltration resembles a virus that has inhabited and now consumes its host. The host even feels it must do its computer's bidding or it feels out of sorts or out of sync—the host feels sick.

I have to laugh sometimes, but at other times, I'm annoyed. I am on a ski lift at almost eleven thousand feet high in the Sierras overlooking breathtaking Lake Tahoe, and the person at the far end of the lift chair is having an anxious cell phone conversation. A friend recently described a similar scene. She was traveling to see us from Southern California to take part in a day of Movements. While she was waiting for the airport shuttle, eight other people were also waiting, and all of them were texting, talking on, or playing with their cell phones. Only one woman who was holding her baby was not using a phone, but was about to hand her baby off to someone else so she could get to her phone. What happened to waiting patiently, looking around, noticing the sky, feeling the weather or just people-watching, as it used to be called? There is just no time for that kind of loafing anymore, because we need to earn the money to buy the latest new gadget, the new iPhone, the 3D television set, the new laptop.

Restaurants put up signs asking their patrons not to use cell phones, but the signs are ignored. People feel entitled to chat as much as they want, regardless of the situation, with no regard for those around them. Conversations one might expect to be private about love, sexual experience, or personal problems, are all grist for the cell phone mill. All this random chatter continues to diminish our ability to think rationally or consider what we are saying before it comes out of our mouths. We are busy gabbing away; and if we aren't, we feel depressed or that something is missing in our lives. If the busyness of our lives continues to accelerate, we will continue to dilute our experience and move farther from being able to live in the moment. Our busyness exaggerates our tendency to escape the present into obsessional consideration of the future.

Before the age of the computer, we had one thing to do at a time, finish it, and then go on to the next, giving us more of a feel for the flow of a task. If I wanted to write an essay, I might rough it out first on a pad with pencil. Then I could look it over. Finally, if it seemed worthwhile, I might type it out. Now, pad, pencil, paper, eraser, typewriter, correction fluid, and dictionary are no longer part of the process of writing. Instead, I just type something on the word processor. At the material level, it would seem to be an advance, but I propose that something has been lost.

The fewer steps we take to accomplish something, the lazier we become. That is just the way it is. I discover it all the time in myself. I am annoyed if the printer needs a new cartridge; I just don't have the time. I need to get on to other things. Sometimes the only break we get on this carousel is the numbness offered by movies, shopping, alcohol, and other forms of escape. We take a mini-vacation from goal-directed pursuits and lose ourselves. Busyness is numbing and dumbing us down, diluting our inner world. None of this outer frenzy can serve inner growth.

AGING AND DEATH

I mentioned earlier that the study of ecology might help us become more aware of our mortality. The earth has only finite resources. The fragility of our existence is beginning to percolate into human consciousness as world resources dwindle. We also need to realize that the dwindling of resources and the limitation of time applies to us personally.

Nature allots only a limited time in this life for us to work and develop a soul. Nature does not need my individual existence. It is unimportant to nature, except to the degree it is in harmony with Great Nature's more objective aims. Our development is further limited by the amount of our personal energy, by our inability to change our behavior, and the inevitable frailty that occurs as we age. These thoughts are even more sobering to me now than they were when I first thought about them forty years ago.

I became acquainted with the negative results of aging when I was quite young. My parents divorced when I was only four years old and because my mother did not have a job, we had to move in with my grandparents. We lived on the Upper West Side of Manhattan, which had a very high proportion of older people. Being old in a big city is quite different from being old in the country. I like to think that if an older person lives in the country, retirement and old age may more easily become a period of increased creativity and relaxation, doing more of what one enjoys, e.g., gardening, painting, reading, and other hobbies. The possibilities for the aged seem more limited in the city, at least they did at that time.

As a boy, I saw many old men and women sitting on benches in the middle of the great avenue, Broadway. Cars and trucks whizzed by on either side of them. For the most part, they sat silently staring straight ahead. Sometimes a few old women talked with each other. Rarely did they read, but instead sat in heavy coats as if waiting for something. As a boy, I felt they had already died in some way. This was a horrible feeling and I know that it sounds harsh. I remember years later when I read Gurdjieff's Work, and he said that many people we see in large cities are already dead.[3] I knew he was right. I had seen and felt it.

At the end of *Beelzebub's Tales to His Grandson*, Gurdjieff writes about the importance of remembering and staying present to the realization of one's death and the positive role this realization can have as a reminding factor for Work. During periods of trying to keep my own death in front of me, my reactions have ranged from finding that death was truly a motivating factor for my work to having it just depress me. I found that death requires preparation and payment. My body instinctively already knows how to die. My emotional reactions to death create the difficulties. I did not understand how to prepare emotionally. I have found that Work has given me a means to pay both my debt to life and to prepare emotionally for death.

For the vast majority of those under age sixty, death is not their focus, and generally, people try to avoid thoughts of this inevitable experience. When we do have feelings and thoughts about death, they run the gamut from outright denial to the hope of going to heaven if we follow the rules, which perhaps represents another type of denial. The Hindus claim this is just one life among hundreds I will experience: I will be reincarnated, so not to worry. It is important to ask if this is perhaps a form of denial.

GURDJIEFF AND THE DEATH OF THE PHYSICAL BODY

In Chapter 3, I introduced Gurdjieff's concept of "higher being-bodies." Gurdjieff's ideas concerning the continuation of life after death diverge sharply from those we find in organized religion, literature, and history. The universal concepts he presents, however, come from ancient sources. They are based on the principle that I must earn my soul and my immortality; it is not given to me. In other words, I do not now possess an immortal soul. Only with Work can I earn one. Gurdjieff says that through Work alone I can develop higher being-bodies, those that may survive my physical death.

Higher being-bodies can be produced only as the result of special work I initiate during my lifetime. Since they require my physical body and its energies to develop, it is obvious that I cannot develop them after my death. If I maintain my aim of conscious evolution by means of conscious labors and intentional suffering throughout my life, I might be able to continue that aim after my physical body dies—but only if a higher-being body has been, as Gurdjieff says, "coated" within me.

To recap, the two additional bodies I need to develop are composed of finer substances than my physical body.[4] Theosophical and spiritual literature has called the first of these by various names: the "spirit," "astral," or "emotional" body. Gurdjieff's term is the "Kesdjan" body. The second body, that develops with the help of material from the Kesdjan body, is called the "mental," "intellectual," or "soul" body. In *Beelzebub's Tales to His Grandson*, in the chapter, "The Holy Planet 'Purgatory,'" Gurdjieff lays out how, in our present state of waking-sleep, these two higher being-bodies are only a potential for us.[5] They do not exist in us from birth; we must create them. They are actually luxuries for humans.[6] They must be born from material we produce, and this can only happen through Work. We do not really need them to live out our lives on earth. Nature is not interested in the development of these higher being-bodies in individuals. They can only arise at great expense and effort on our part.

At first, the idea that individuals are unimportant to nature seemed alien to me and upset me. Why would nature, so worshiped by the new-age generation not be interested in the spiritual development of human beings? It went against my concept of the beauty and importance of individuality and seemed very undemocratic. However, after thinking about it, what, in fact, is truly individual about any of us? We like to think we are unique, but we need to verify whether we actually are. My own experience has shown me that I may have the potential for individuality, but its development is quite uncertain. I have seen that almost all of what I call my "individuality" is mere mechanics, the repetition of various patterns of behavior, emotions, and thoughts that have developed over my lifetime.

Gurdjieff holds out hope for us to develop as complete beings and, as such, our future might not be completely bleak. He makes a distinction between nature and Great Nature. Great Nature does have a very definite role for the developed man and woman to play, a person who has his or her own "I," who has a real will, and who loves and understands humanity and its purpose. That role is to act not only as fodder for the developing moon, but also to send vibrations upward to further the development of the greater cosmos and unite with the Most Holy Sun Absolute. However, the continuation of each of us as an individual after our deaths depends on our Work now.

Exploring Feelings About Death

- Hold the concept of your own death and the cessation of life within you—just allow it to be there.

- Can you find a way to hold death in a manner that helps you to appreciate your life in the moment?

- Is there a positive side to death you have never considered?

- Can you be interested in your coming death and pay attention to it?

TWO RIVERS—THE DIVISION OF HUMANITY

Bennett divides humanity into two distinct groups: the "psychostatic" and the "psychokinetic." [7] There is a smaller third group he refers to as the "psychotelios" group. This group represents individuals who have completed themselves, but we are not concerned with them here.

The psychostatic group is the general group, composed of all of humanity, where people have fixated on the materiality of life and limited their development to the possibilities offered in their particular culture. The other group, the psychokinetic community, develops within the psychostatic community, but the individuals within it recognize their human potential. They sense the need to develop their abilities to play their part for the greater good. In many ways, Bennett's division resembles Gurdjieff's more abstract description in the last chapter of *Beelzebub's Tales to His Grandson*. Gurdjieff says there that since the beginning of history, humanity has been divided into two rivers.[8] Human beings have a chance to flow into one of the two rivers, either the one that sinks back into the earth or the one that goes on to reach the vast ocean. The communes of the 1960s formed around young people's inner longing for such psychokinetic communities, but they did not last. Missing was a shared cosmology that would tie them to a larger framework—something more enduring than a simple back-to-nature movement or even a consciousness of ecology. More importantly, these groups lacked practical methods for individual inner development.

I believe that to be a member of a psychokinetic community one needs to be a lifelong learner. I must redevelop within myself the capacity to be interested in all of human life and in all that lives. The natural affect interest is perhaps the most important capacity that one can redevelop. In some ways, interest and our capacity for real attention go hand in hand. Interest is the primary motivational force that helps sustain our search. However, the interest must be in what really has objective value for us, the development of our essential potential, of our higher bodies.

One of the questions of our age is how to continue to keep the door open to new interests and continue our self-development and self-study. In many ways, keeping my interests open necessitates membership in a group with such interests. At the least, it requires remaining in contact with others in the psychokinetic community.

MEMORY

One of Gurdjieff's most profound ideas is, as we saw before, the need to remember ourselves. Self-remembering or the state of self-consciousness cannot be reduced to any one definition, but the mere mention of it can remind me how often I forget myself and how unconscious I am most of the time. People go through life without learning much from their experiences because they are not present when experiences take place. They are usually unable to realize any meaning from their experience or even remember it—one of the reasons we seem to need to repeat the same experiences over and over. Yet if we do not stop and pay attention to this repetition, we will miss the knowledge it brings. We might realize we are actually dead during many moments of our lives—that is, in terms of actually experiencing life as we are living it. However, if we remember ourselves, we have the opportunity of experiencing actual moments of being alive. Self-remembering uniquely stimulates our memory. But then, what do we really know about our memory?

If I am honest, I realize I understand very little about my memory. I am usually uninterested in it, so long as it is working properly. After attention, memory is perhaps our most important mental faculty, and yet it remains a mystery, because it is very difficult to study. Academic research into memory is boring and often involves researchers studying the memories of volunteer student subjects. I rarely have heard of a researcher who studied him- or herself. What a novel idea that would be!

It would not generally be acceptable for a researcher to study his or her own memory at the university level because this research would be deemed too subjective. Research on oneself would have to meet the following criteria: (a) one would have to quantify the results; (b) those results would have to be repeatable; and (c) any findings would have to be reviewed by a panel of one's peers, etc. After all, if research is not repeatable and is "subjective," then it is not scientific according to current definition. How then could it be important? The tide may be turning somewhat at the university level, but as my mother used to say,

"It is so slow; will we live long enough to enjoy it?" However, it is true that qualitative research that allows for more subjective experience is gaining acceptance in psychology and some of the other social sciences.

The need for repeatability in scientific research relegates a great deal of university research to the garbage bin of dullness. The experiment's parameters are so restrictive as to squeeze the very life out of experiment. Academia's prejudice against subjective human experience means not only that almost all research will be dull, but also lack applicability to real people. Sadly, few, if any, researchers will ever know or understand anything at all about their own memory.

Memory has been researched more intensively, however, during the last thirty years, due to the aging of the population and resultant increase in Alzheimer's disease and other dementias (memory loss). People are afraid of such diseases; consequently, pharmaceutical companies can make money in designing drugs that may counteract or prevent them. Current research has focused on medications that might reduce the progression of short-term memory loss after the onset of such diseases. Again, psychologists do not bother to study their own intellectual faculty or their own memory. I have seen the effects of memory loss in clients in my private practice, as well as in residents I work with in skilled nursing facilities. It is a frightening experience for the afflicted individual, for his family and friends, and for psychologists and other medical professionals who work with these individuals.

Memory can be a unique and fascinating subject for self-study. In examining my own memory, I see how subtle and difficult it is to study. For example, I sit here typing this manuscript and find that most, if not all, of my memory functions are automatic. My fingers appear to have their own memory of where the keys sit on the keyboard. My posture is also dependent on memory. Every muscle that holds my torso upright depends on a muscular memory that seems to have developed quite a long time ago without my realizing it. That is, I learned to sit this way without being conscious that I was exercising muscular memory. My muscle memory at any waking moment could provide a lifetime of self-study.

A very useful exercise for understanding memory that resides in our other centers is one which Gurdjieff himself suggests. It is to try differentiating the manifestations of my instinctive center from those of my moving center. The work of the instinctive center is automatic from birth onward, and does not require me to learn anything. My heartbeat, respiration, circulation, sensations of temperature and touch, vision, hearing, and smell are all inborn. On the other hand, the outer manifestations of the moving center are referred to as voluntary movements. If I study them carefully, I will see I have learned them. For example, my sitting posture while typing is a learned behavior of my moving center; there are memories being recalled and utilized by my moving center when I sit, even though I remain unaware of them.

Take the time to distinguish which of your manifestations belongs to your moving center and which ones to your instinctive center. You do not need to change anything. Simply assign the manifestation to one or the other center. In this way, you will familiarize your intellectual center with two other centers.

Recently, I have been stopping at moments in the midst of my day and trying to recall what impressions have stood out for me up to that point. The other day, while standing in a checkout line, I was watching an American Indian couple in their forties who seemed to be taking forever. They were involved in a long discussion with the cashier. Behind them, and immediately in front of me, was an older American Indian woman. I found myself annoyed at all three of them because they were taking so long (remember, I am impatient). I had enough inner separation to observe my reactions. I was sufficiently present to gather impressions of my intolerance of people who do not move fast, and I recalled my usual irritability and impatience. However, in this particular situation, I also noticed there were small parts of me that were actually patient. Later that afternoon, I returned to the scene in my memory and looked for what stood out.

It was interesting to find that my memory had recorded many impressions of which my "normal consciousness" was unaware. For example, part of me had noticed the man was wearing orange sunglasses, that he also had some relationship with the older woman directly in front of me, and that his wife was quite beautiful and acted in an unhurried manner. In retrospect, everyone except me appeared unhurried and seemed to be living in the present. His wife had evidently spotted some error in her favor on the bill. She shared this little confidence with her husband right in front of the cashier, but so the cashier would not notice. All these subtle impressions told me a great deal about these two people, things that I hadn't consciously realized at the time. However, I would not have remembered any of these impressions had I not gone back to the experience. Some part of memory had absorbed all these impressions; yet, on the first go-around, I had not noticed the details. Strictly speaking, even though a part of me was present when this experience occurred, my waking-sleeping consciousness took in only a few impressions.

I have realized from reviewing such experiences that I can revisit different memories from my day and mine them for new impressions. By intentionally recalling certain experiences, I can accumulate meaningful material in this way. These memories can provide me with food for understanding myself. Gurdjieff said the number of experiences we have is limited and we need to be economical with them. Looking back over my day to recall memories and make more meaning from them is a means of being more economical. A part of each of us is starving for new impressions, hungry for new meaning, and longing to make new memories. As the poet T. S. Eliot warned, "We had the experience but missed the meaning." [9]

CHAPTER 19

FINAL THOUGHTS

When I first began working with Gurdjieff's ideas, my work did not produce in me any great love for others, but the opposite. I found I was becoming less forgiving and understanding of others and more critical of them. The same was true of my view toward myself. I began to realize my critical view of others closely paralleled my view of myself. Something was wrong here. Applying Gurdjieff's ideas in the ways I had been had accentuated my tendency to criticize myself. I was moving further away from compassionate appreciation and love of humankind. Something in my own work was causing me to contract emotionally rather than become more flexible. A question began peeking out from inside me. I began to ask what is real emotional development through Work really about? I was caught and needed a way out, but in my question, I had found the key.

On the wall at the front of the room in our Movements studio, we have a framed chart. It shows the possible development of humankind as a series of three octaves. The first octave represents the unconscious state of waking-sleeping people. The middle octave represents the possibilities when we work on ourselves. At the topmost point (the ending "Do") of the third and highest octave are the words, "Love of mankind." I have found that for me, the love of humankind represents the highest note of the octave of impressions when I am actually conscious of my existence and purpose. This understanding is one of the greatest gifts I have received from my work.

Love of humankind has come to me in many ways, but primarily through increasing my understanding of my own foibles and predicament. I work with others who are very different from me. They cause friction, and my emotions begin to churn. But my emotions only open up if I am honest about my own reactions to the differences in people and learn to appreciate and value others as much as I value myself. This opportunity to learn from others comes not only from Work situations, but also through many life situations. A great area for self-study for me is working with my reactions during my therapy practice with clients. As I have actually learned about the prison of my mechanicality and unconscious suffering, I have realized that every other person is in a similar prison. This realization has dramatically changed my perspective, my relationship to others, and my experience of them. Compassion has become an important aspect of my work on myself. In some ways, it is a measuring tool—letting me know if I am still on the road or off in a ditch.

Everyone's life contains all the raw material necessary to grow. However, people must develop the capacity to understand themselves as they are, making use of their own, unique raw materials. This is special work. Its ultimate aims can bring a person compassion, objective self-knowledge, and love of humankind. It may seem paradoxical to link self-knowledge with compassion. We might believe that if we were to see the truth about ourselves—our unconsciousness—it would be horrible or unbearable. But I assure you, real impartiality promotes real compassion, and vice versa. Compassion develops our emotional center just as objective self-observation develops consciousness. They are interdependent.

Beelzebub's Tales to His Grandson is a difficult tale to swallow. It can leave one feeling hopeless about the possibility of the regeneration of humanity. However, I do not believe that instilling hopelessness was Gurdjieff's aim. His writings are not meant to increase divisiveness, negativity, lack of compassion or shortsightedness. Rather, as Gurdjieff said, he set out, "To destroy, mercilessly and without any compromise whatever, in the mentation and feelings of the reader, the beliefs and views, by centuries rooted in him, about everything existing in the world." [1] He is telling us we need to really ponder in a new way—about everything. Gurdjieff sees a future for some of us, and impartial understanding and mature compassion are possibilities we can develop and make our own.

In order to develop greater compassion for humanity and ourselves, we must open ourselves to more of Gurdjieff's wisdom, rather than restrict our views to the few ideas of his we find appealing. Each of us can become a researcher of a new type, one who is both the experimenter and the experiment, opening our work in any legitimate and honest way we can, not worrying whether we are being clumsy or do not know enough. Only through participation and active experimentation, can we enlarge our understanding and accomplish our own personal evolution. Self-development does not happen by imitating others' work, especially that of teachers from the past. The task is to take what they have given us and enlarge it through our own work, add to it, keep it alive. This dynamism is what is required to give birth to and nourish Bennett's psychokinetic community that lives within the general mass of humanity.

We need a greater depth of understanding of what is already directly in front of us (that is, our lived experience). The blossoming of the information age has been just that—a plethora of information. It lacks applicability to deepen people's inner lives. We may drown in a sea of information before we get a chance to develop any being, which is measured by our compassion, objective understanding, and the ability to do. This vast flood of information may be our greatest distraction from the real work we need to do.

Inside of us reside forces that developed over centuries of habitual existence. They have been mechanized so that life runs smoothly. We are lulled to sleep while imagining we are awake. These forces so seamlessly blend into our experience that it is difficult to separate out what is real in us. Gurdjieff tried to clarify our predicament. He said that what we consider to be our "unconscious" is actually the seat of our real consciousness. Conversely, the consciousness we present to the world is simply an adaptation to survival in an unnatural world. Because of such a topsy-turvy situation, we need the Work to break us out of the prison of our dysfunction, placing us right-side-up. Then we can take our place in the Real World.

If you learn nothing else from this book, please let it be this: Compassion for yourself is an integral part of self-knowledge and self-observation. For me, compassion was the missing link in the Gurdjieff Work. For some reason, it was left out in our rush to fix ourselves. Without compassion, it is almost impossible for transformation to occur, for us to forgive ourselves, and forgive others. We give lip-service to the importance of forgiveness, but it eludes almost all of us. I have found that compassion is directly related to self-initiation—that is— learning to motivate and power my own work.

Gurdjieff's life and his work are examples of self-initiation. Like him, we need to sort out what in life is really valuable from what is not and strive with all our might toward what is valuable, letting go of the rest. In many ways, discrimination of this kind seems to be the true alchemy— the key to our transformation. A major characteristic of Kundabuffer is that it caused us to accept and be satisfied with the ephemeral in life for what is real, valuable and substantial. This tendency is the basis for many of our misconceptions, dysfunctional relationships, and the major ecological problems we are now experiencing on the planet. How do we change all this? Should it be changed? I leave you with this response from Gurdjieff regarding the possibility of change:

> Whatever they may be speaking about, they ask: Ought it to be like that and how can it be changed, that is, what ought to be done in such a case? As though it were possible to change anything, as though it were possible to do anything. You at least ought to have realized by now how naïve such questions are. Cosmic forces have created this state of affairs and cosmic forces control this state of affairs. And you ask: Can it be left like that or should it be changed! God himself could change nothing. Do you remember what was said about the forty-eight laws? They cannot be changed, but liberation from a considerable portion of them is possible, that is to say, there is a possibility of changing the state of affairs for oneself, it is possible to escape from the general law. You should understand that in this case as well as in all others the general law cannot be changed. But one can change one's own position in relation to this law; one can escape from the general law.[2]

APPENDIX ONE

PRACTICES, EXERCISES AND EXPLORATIONS

APPENDIX TWO

SUMMARY OF PSYCHOLOGICAL DYSREGULATION CAUSED BY KUNDABUFFER

WHAT IS TRAUMA?
- Trauma occurs when an event creates an unresolved impact on an organism.
- Usually we remember at least parts of a traumatic event.
- Sometimes we are unaware of a traumatic event having taken place:
  –Surgeries where a patient is unconscious
  –Trauma so severe that it is blocked by consciousness—near-death experiences

WHAT ARE THE CORE SYMPTOMS OF THE TRAUMATIC RESPONSE?
- Hyperarousal
- Constriction = tensing
- Dissociation = disconnection between consciousness and body = break in felt sense
- Freezing = immobility
- Inability to discharge energy held or repressed

NEW BEHAVIORS CAUSED BY KUNDABUFFER ACCORDING TO GURDJIEFF
- War: aggression, killing in a repeating cycle
- Egoism, self-love, vanity, pride, self-conceit, credulity...
- Suggestibility: "the most terrible for them personally"
- Degradation of genuine sacred being-impulses of Faith, Hope, and Love, due to mixing with properties engendered by Kundabuffer

WHY WAR? THE BUILDING BLOCKS OF AGGRESSIVE BEHAVIOR:

- Stress
- Paranoia and projection
- Anxiety—due to unrecognized fear
- Fear
- Anger or depression
- Emotional and/or mental overwhelm
- Powerlessness—consider terrorism
- Self-hate and automatic hatred of others

PSYCHOLOGICAL RESULTS OF KUNDABUFFER

- Consciousness split in two: Waking-sleeping conscious and subconscious
- Partitioning of the psyche into different "I's"
- Degradation of the human faculty of attention, which originally functioned by the Foolastnitamnian Principle to the Itoklanoz Principle; the result is we die in thirds
- Hypnotic trance gradually induced by seeing life upside down

GURDJIEFF SPLITS THE RESPONSIBILITY FOR OUR PSYCHOLOGICAL PROBLEMS BETWEEN:

- Higher individuals
- Humanity's inability to actualize "being-Partkdolg-duty," that is, conscious labor and intentional suffering, due to all the psychological properties engendered by Kundabuffer having become humanity's "second nature"

RELIGION ARRIVES TO CORRECT FOR KUNDABUFFER

- Unintentional creation of more trauma due to inability to understand traumatic effects already prevalent in humanity
- Dependence on rules and suppression of natural tendencies (that is, sex, etc.)
- Use of aggressive tendencies to solidify power

- Distortion and misuse of natural affects such as shame to control behavior
- Lack of understanding of homeostasis

EXPLOITATION OF "SUGGESTIBILITY" BY RELIGION

- Myth of the soul
- Religion adds to humanity's fantasy of the afterlife without effort
- Escape from suffering becomes an aim
- Fantasy of heaven and hell
- Creation of followers replaces finding true individuality or developing Christ within the individual
- Distorting the natural affect of shame that often results in self-hatred

THE HUMAN BIOLOGICAL AFFECT SYSTEM DISTORTED BY KUNDABUFFER

- Joy
- Interest/excitement*
- Startle
- Anger*
- Fear*
- Shame*
- Sadness
- Disgust
- Dismell

*Extremely dysregulated

NOTES

CHAPTER 1

1. Jacques Lusseyran, *Against the Pollution of the I* (Sandpoint, Idaho: Morning Light Press, 2006), 31.

2. Ibid., 53.

3. G. Gurdjieff, *All and Everything, First Series: Beelzebub's Tales to His Grandson* (New York: Harcourt, Brace and Company, 1950) 1212. The reader should note that Gurdjieff's complete corpus of written work is entitled *All and Everything*, comprised of Ten Books in Three Series:

> FIRST SERIES Three books under the title of *Beelzebub's Tales to His Grandson, An Objectively Impartial Criticism of the Life of Man.*

> SECOND SERIES Three books under the common title of *Meetings with Remarkable Men.*

> THIRD SERIES Four books under the title of *Life Is Real Only Then, When "I Am."*

4. A. R. Orage, *The Active Mind* (London, UK: Janus Press, 1954), 10–11.

5. Simone Weil, *Waiting for God* (New York: HarperCollins, 2001), 57.

6. Ibid., 60.

7. Gurdjieff, *Beelzebub's Tales to His Grandson*, 1106.

CHAPTER 2

1. P. D. Ouspensky, I*n Search of the Miraculous* (New York: Harcourt, Brace & World, Inc., 1949), 105.

2. Ibid., 56.

3. Systems and their resistance to change. Homeostasis: The internal equilibrium of the body, the ultimate gauge of its proper functioning, requires the maintenance of a constant rate of concentration in the blood of certain molecules and ions that are essential to life, as well as maintenance at specified levels of other physical parameters, such as temperature. The equilibrium is maintained despite environmental modifications. This extraordinary property of the body has intrigued

many physiologists. In 1865, Claude Bernard noted, in his Introduction to Experimental Medicine, that the "constancy of the internal milieu was the essential condition to a free life." But it was necessary to find a concept that would make it possible to link together the mechanisms that effected the regulation of the body. The credit for this concept goes to the American physiologist Walter Cannon. In 1932, impressed by what he called "the wisdom of the body," capable of guaranteeing with such efficiency the control of the physiological equilibrium, Cannon coined the word "homeostasis," from two Greek words, meaning to remain the same. Since then, the concept of homeostasis has held a central position in the field of cybernetics. http://pespmc1.vub.ac.be/homeosta.html, accessed Nov. 3, 2010.

4. The idea of a de-centered subjectivity composed of multiple, socially constructed and context-dependent identities began to emerge during the late nineteenth and early twentieth centuries in the writings of a variety of thinkers including, William James (1842–1910), Sigmund Freud (1856–1939), and the critical theorists Max Horkheimer (1895–1973) and Theodor Adorno (1903–1969). These and other thinkers initiated a widespread reevaluation of the philosophy of the subject of multiplicity in the West. During the twentieth century, the "critique of the subject" was debated across a wide array of academic disciplines. Over time, the general idea of a de-centered multiple subject gained increasingly wide acceptance. With this shift, more specific conceptualizations of it, such as mestiza consciousness and multiple identity, emerged to attempt to integrate the multiplicity, diversity, and contradiction into the philosophical understandings of the subject and identity. Such theoretical formulations have generated new philosophical questions that still remain matters of inquiry and debate.

5. C. Daly King, *The Oragean Version* (New York: Business Photo Reproduction, Inc., 1951), 115.

CHAPTER 3

1. Ouspensky, *In Search of the Miraculous*, 150–151.

2. Ibid.

3. Rodney Collin, *The Theory of Conscious Harmony* (Boulder & London: Shambhala, 1984), 70.

4. Ouspensky, *In Search of the Miraculous*, 117-8.

5. Rodney Collin, *The Theory of Celestial Influence* (London: Stuart & Watkins, 1968), 215.

6. Ouspensky, *In Search of the Miraculous*, 77.

7. Ibid., 285.

8. Ibid., 122–140.

9. Ibid., 123.

10. Ibid., 129-30.

11. John G. Bennett, *Talks On Beelzebub's Tales* (High Burton, England: Coombe Springs Press, 1977), 47.

12. Ouspensky, *In Search of the Miraculous*, 40–44.

13. Gurdjieff, *Beelzebub's Tales to His Grandson*, 744–810.

14. Ibid., 767–768, 1106.

15. Gurdjieff, "2nd Meeting, December, 1921," Collections of the Manuscript Division (Washington: Library of Congress).

16. Sitting: A sitting is an exercise that requires the body to be in a relaxed and supported posture. Then the mind is given a period of time to slow down or this slowing down is accomplished by directing the attention.

17. Sensing is the ability to experience the sensitive organizing energy of the human body. *See* Chapter 4.

18. Gurdjieff, *Beelzebub's Tales to His Grandson*, 85-6.

19. Collin, *The Theory of Conscious Harmony*, 71.

CHAPTER 4

1. Wilhelm Reich, *Character Analysis* (New York: Farrar, Straus and Giroux, 1945), 337–346.

2. It might very well be that Carl Gustav Jung's archetypes and his concept of the collective unconscious are aspects of these higher centers.

3. John G. Bennett, *The Masters of Wisdom* (New York: Samuel Weiser Inc., 1977), 20–24.

4. John G. Bennett, *Energies, Material, Vital, Cosmic* (Gloucestershire, UK: Coombe Springs Press, 1964), 15.

5. Neuroplasticity (also known as cortical remapping) refers to the ability of the human brain to change as a result of one's experience—that is, the brain is plastic and malleable. The discovery of this malleability of the brain is rather modern; the previous belief amongst scientists

was that the brain does not change after the critical period of infancy. http://en.wikipedia.org/wiki/Neuroplasticity, accessed, 11/25/10.

6. Ouspensky, *In Search of the Miraculous*, 181.

CHAPTER 5

1. Collin, *The Theory of Conscious Harmony*, 33.

2. Ouspensky, *In Search of the Miraculous*, 80.

3. Ibid., 25.

4. Gurdjieff, *Beelzebub's Tales to His Grandson*, 85-6.

5. Ouspensky, *In Search of the Miraculous*, 138.

6. John G. Bennett, *The Dramatic Universe Volume I* (Gloucestershire, England: Coombe Springs Press, 1966), 474.

7. Hadley Leggett, *Out of LSD? Just 15 Minutes of Sensory Deprivation, Triggers Hallucinations.* www.wired.com/wiredscience/2009/10/hallucinations/ accessed, Nov. 15, 2011.

8. G. I. Gurdjieff, *Man, the Machine*, talk given in London 1922 and Chicago 1924, accessed on Internet January, 2013, http://gurdjieffdominican.com/Gurdjieff_psychology.htm.

9. Gurdjieff, *Beelzebub's Tales to His Grandson*, 1172.

10. Transhumanism.http://en.wikipedia.org/wiki/Transhumanism, accessed, Nov. 3, 2010.

11. G. Gurdjieff, *Beelzebub's Tales to His Grandson*, 1105-1108.

12. Ibid., 88.

13. Ibid., 88, 1233.

14. Maurice Nicoll, *The Mark* (New York: Thomas Nelson & Sons, 1952), 89–99.

15. Gurdjieff, *Beelzebub's Tales to His Grandson*, 362.

16. Ibid., 1055ff.

17. Robert Sapolsky, *Why Zebras Don't Get Ulcers* (New York: W. H. Freeman and Company, 2000), 1–36.

18. Ouspensky, *In Search of the Miraculous*, 154-5.

19. Gurdjieff, *Beelzebub's Tales to His Grandson*, 88.

20. Ibid., 130.

21. Ibid., 445.

22. George Lucas, *Star Wars*, 20th Century Fox, http://en.wikipedia.org/wiki/Star_Wars, accessed Oct. 3, 2010.

CHAPTER 6

1. Ouspensky, *In Search of the Miraculous*, 161–165.

2. Harry Benjamin, *Basic Self-knowledge Based on the Gurdjieff System of Development* (New York: Samuel Weiser, 1980), 52.

3. Abraham H. Maslow, *Religions, Values, and Peak Experiences*, Kappa Delta Pi and 1970 (preface) (The Viking Press, 1964). See also http://en.wikipedia.org/wiki/Peak-experience, accessed Oct. 3, 10. Maslow describes a peak experience as an especially joyous and exciting moment, filled with sudden feelings of intense happiness, well-being, wonder, and awe. It also includes a possible awareness of transcendental unity or knowledge of higher truth. Peak experiences occur as though perceiving the world from an altered and often vastly profound and awe-inspiring perspective. They usually come on suddenly and are often inspired by deep meditation, intense feelings of love, exposure to great art or music, or the overwhelming beauty of nature.

4. Gurdjieff, *Beelzebub's Tales to His Grandson*, 1172.

5. John Godolphin Bennett (8 June 1897–13 December 1974) was a British mathematician, scientist, technologist, industrial research director, and author. He is perhaps best known for his many books on psychology and spirituality, and particularly the teachings of G.I. Gurdjieff. Bennett met Gurdjieff in Istanbul in 1921 and later helped to coordinate the work of Gurdjieff in England after Gurdjieff's arrival in Paris. He also was active in starting the British section of the Subud movement, and cofounded its British headquarters. http://en.wikipedia.org/wiki/John_G._Bennett, accessed October 3, 2010.

6. John Bennett, *What Are We Living For?* (Santa Fe, NM: Bennett Books, 1991), 60–61.

7. Ibid.

8. Ibid., 76–77.

9. Gurdjieff, *Beelzebub's Tales to His Grandson*, 188.

10. Bennett, *What Are We Living For?*, 60–65.

11. Ibid., 64.

12. Ibid.

13. Ibid.

14. Gurdjieff, *Beelzebub's Tales to His Grandson*, 440–444.

15. Ibid., 443.

16. Bennett, *What Are We Living For?*, 70.

17. Ibid.

18. Tom Brown Jr., *The Tracker.* (Berkley: Berkley Publishing Group, 1996).

19. Ouspensky, *In Search of the Miraculous*, 279.

20. Collin, *Theory of Conscious Harmony*, 34.

21. Superego: According to Freud's psychoanalytic theory of personality, the superego is the component of personality composed of the internalized ideals we have acquired from our parents and from society. The superego works to suppress the urges of the id and tries to make the ego behave morally, rather than realistically.

22. Gurdjieff, *Beelzebub's Tales to His Grandson*, 378.

23. Ouspensky, *In Search of the Miraculous*, 155.

24. Ibid., 156.

CHAPTER 7

1. Ouspensky, *In Search of the Miraculous*, 154–55.

2. Gurdjieff, *Beelzebub's Tales to His Grandson*, 538.

3. Ibid., 1164.

4. Ibid., 138, 146–147.

CHAPTER 8

1. G. I. Gurdjieff, *Meetings with Remarkable Men* (New York: E.P. Dutton & Company, 1969), 130–136.

2. The concept of the sovereign learner is a concept developed by Dr. Elizabeth Schreiber. The sovereign learner is that part of us that was active, enthralled, and interested in all aspects of the world and life when we were young. This part depended on the affect interest to fuel it. Gradually, our education, with its wish and glorification of facts and emphasis on rote learning rather than experience, closed this capacity down.

CHAPTER 9

1. John G. Bennett, *Existence. Studies from the Dramatic Universe, No. 2* (Santa Fe, New Mexico: Bennett Books, 2010), 31.

2. Gurdjieff, *Beelzebub's Tales to His Grandson*, 385–386.

3. Ibid.

4. Kurt Lewin, *Forces Behind Food Habits and Methods of Change*, Bulletin of the National Research Council, 1943, 108, 35–65.

5. Ouspensky, *In Search of the Miraculous*, 154–160.

6. Gurdjieff, *Beelzebub's Tales to His Grandson*, 405–410.

7. Nicoll, *The Mark*, 90. Nicoll was a psychiatrist and C.G. Jung's leading exponent in the early 1920s. He met P. D. Ouspensky and then went to the Prieuré to study with Gurdjieff. He wrote a number of books about the Work, including *Psychological Commentaries on the Teaching of Gurdjieff and Ouspensky*, a large compendium of the Work ideas.

8. *Rashomon*: A Japanese crime-mystery film from 1950, directed by Akira Kurosawa, based on two stories by Ryūnosuke Akutagawa.

CHAPTER 10

1. Ouspensky, *In Search of the Miraculous*, 59–60.

2. Gurdjieff, *Views from the Real World* (New York: Penguin Compass, 1984), 128–135.

3. Lusseyran, *Against the Pollution of the I*, 120.

4. Ibid.

5. Gurdjieff, *Beelzebub's Tales to His Grandson*, 417–418.

6. Ibid., 424.

7. Donald L. Nathanson, *Shame and Pride* (New York: W. W. Norton & Company, 1992), 73–147.

8. Gurdjieff, *Beelzebub's Tales to His Grandson*, 424.

9. Carol Collodi, *Pinocchio* (Racine, Wisconsin: Whitman Publishing Co., 1916).

10. Ouspensky, *In Search of the Miraculous*, 254.

11. Kenneth Walker, *A Study of Gurdjieff's Teaching* (London, UK: Jonathon Cape, 1965) 213.

12. Lynn Quirolo. "Transformation in the Fourth Way," Private Paper, 1997.

CHAPTER 11

1. Collin, *Theory of Conscious Harmony*, 55.

2. Ouspensky, *In Search of the Miraculous*, 56.

3. Ibid., 112.

4. Ibid.

5. Robert Johnson, *Transformation: Understanding the Three levels of Masculine Consciousness* (New York: HarperCollins Publishers, 1991), 75.

6. Ouspensky, *In Search of the Miraculous*, 193–194.

7. Dr. Elizabeth Schreiber, private communication.

8. G. I. Gurdjieff, *Meetings with Remarkable Men*, 188-9.

9. Bennett, *What Are We Living For?*, 79.

CHAPTER 12

1. Ouspensky, *In Search of the Miraculous*, 192.

2. Gurdjieff, *Beelzebub's Tales to His Grandson*, 1140–1144.

3. Ivan Pavlov, classical conditioning, http://www.learning-theories.com/classical-conditioning-pavlov.html, accessed Jan. 3, 2011.

4. King, *The Oragean Version*, 177.

5. John G. Bennett, *Noticing* (North Yorks, UK: Coombe Springs Press, 1976) 14.

6. Linda Moore, personal note to author, Mar. 21, 2011.

7. Thomas Moore, *Care of the Soul* (New York: HarperCollins Publishers, 1992), 137–154.

8. Terrence Real , *I Don't Want to Talk About It* (New York: Fireside 1997), 178–179.

9. Ibid., 178.

10. Aaron Kipnis, *Knights Without Armor* (Los Angeles: Jeremy P. Tarcher, 1991), 11–24.

11. Ibid., 29.

12. Benjamin, *Basic Self-knowledge Based on the Gurdjieff System of Development*, 68.

13. Psychological types: see Ouspensky, *In Search of the Miraculous*, 246–247, 254.

14. Rhianon Allen, Arthur S Reber and Emily Reber, *Dictionary of Psychology* (London: Penguin Books, 1985), 387.

CHAPTER 13

1. Rebar, *Dictionary of Psychology*, 810.

2. Ibid.

3. Gurdjieff, *Views from the Real World*, 44.

4. American Psychiatric Association, Diagnostic and Statistical Manual of Mental Disorders (American Psychiatric Association: New York, 2000), 812.

5. Projective identification is a psychological term first introduced by Melanie Klein of the Object Relations school of psychoanalytic thought in 1946. It refers to a psychological process in which one person projects a thought, belief, or emotion onto a second person. In most common definitions of projective identification, there is a second action in which the other person is changed by the projection and begins to behave as though he or she is, in fact, actually characterized by those thoughts or beliefs that the first person has projected. This process generally happens outside the awareness of both parties, although this aspect of the process has been a matter of some argument. What is projected is most often an intolerable, painful, or dangerous idea or belief about the self that the first person cannot accept (that is, "I have behaved wrongly," or "I have a sexual feeling toward . . ."). Or, it may be a valued or esteemed idea that again is difficult for the first person to acknowledge. Projective identification is believed to be a very early or primitive psychological process and is understood to be one of the more primitive defense mechanisms. Yet, it is also thought to be the basis from which more mature psychological processes such as empathy and intuition are formed. *Wikipedia*: http://en.wikipedia.org/wiki/Projective_identification.

CHAPTER 14

1. Gurdjieff, *Beelzebub's Tales to His Grandson*, 318.

CHAPTER 15

1. Orage, *The Active Mind*, 115.

2. Ibid., 115-119.

3. Gurdjieff, *Beelzebub's Tales to His Grandson*, 1168-1169.

> Well then, it is chiefly for this reason that everything which has been newly learned settles in the presences of three-brained beings who have only the Reason-of-knowing and

always remains only simply as information without any kind of cognizance by the whole of their Being.

And therefore new data of every kind, formed and fixed in this way for the three-brained beings who have the Reason-of-knowing, have in respect of their use no significance at all for the welfare of their own subsequent existence. Moreover, the duration of the decrystallisation of this kind of fixed impressions depend on the quantity and the quality of the impulses engendered in the given being. As regards this latter fact ensuing from the already degenerated functioning of the Reason proper to the three-brained beings and which most of your contemporary favorites today already have, one also very rarely used saying of our respected teacher Mullah Nassr Eddin is remembered in me by association and is expressed by the following words: "As soon as anything is needed, it seems that it is filthy and eaten by mice."

Although every kind of what your favorites call knowledge which they have and which has been acquired in the common presences of beings in the said manner, is also subjective, yet it has absolutely nothing in common with what is called "Objective Knowledge."

4. Orage, *The Active Mind*, 118-119.
5. Ibid.
6. Fritz Peters, *My Journey With A Mystic* (Laguna Niguel, California: Tale Weaver Publishing, 1980), 72-78.
7. Harville Hendrix, *Getting the Love Your Want: A Guide for Couples* (New York: Harper & Row, 1990), 25.
8. Gurdjieff, *Beelzebub's Tales to His Grandson*, 286–290, 307.

CHAPTER 16
1. Ouspensky, *In Search of the Miraculous*, 19.
2. Edwin Wolfe, *Episodes with Gurdjieff* (New York, 1973), 11.
3. King, *The Oragean Version*, 109–113.
4. Ouspensky, *In Search of the Miraculous*, 339.

5. Ibid., 181–193.

6. King, *The Oragean Version*, 131.

7. Ibid., 132.

8. Ibid., 132–133.

9. Orage, *The Active Mind*, 54.

10. King, *The Oragean Version*, 116–126.

CHAPTER 17

1. Ouspensky, *In Search of the Miraculous*, 315.

2. King, *The Oragean Version*, 177.

CHAPTER 18

1. Anthony Blake, private communication to the author.

2. John G. Bennett, *The Dramatic Universe Series, 1 Hazard* (Ripon, North Yorks, England: Coombe Springs Press 1976), 14–34.

3. Gurdjieff, *Beelzebub's Tales to His Grandson*, 442–444.

4. Ibid., 755–810, 1106–1109.

5. Ibid., 744–810.

6. Ouspensky, *In Search of the Miraculous*, 41.

7. John G. Bennett, *Needs of a New Age Community* (North Yorkshire, England: Coombe Springs Press, 1977), 27–33.

8. Gurdjieff, *Beelzebub's Tales to His Grandson*, 1227–1232.

9. T. S. Eliot, *Four Quartets* (New York: Harcourt Press, 1943), "Dry Salvages II."

CHAPTER 19

1. Gurdjieff, *Beelzebub's Tales to His Grandson*, v.

2. Ouspensky, *In Search of the Miraculous*, 255.

GLOSSARY

Key

[G] = from Gurdjieff or in Gurdjieff's terminology
[K] = from C. Daly King's *Oragean Version*
[O] = from Ouspensky's *In Search of the Miraculous*
[S] = from Schreiber
Search = *In Search of the Miraculous*
BT = *Beelzebub's Tales to His Grandson, An Objectively Impartial Criticism of the Life of Man*

Active Mentation [G]: Sustained, strong, and realistic thought.
. . . active mentation in a being and the useful results of this mentation are in reality actualized exclusively only with the equal-degree functionings of all his three localizations of the results spiritualized in his presence, called "thinking center," "feeling center," and "moving-motor-center." BT, p. 1172

Active Force (or Affirming or Positive Force); Passive Force (or Denying or Resisting or Receptive Force); Neutralizing Force (or Reconciling) [G]: The elements of Gurdjieff's Law of Three, or Sacred Triamazikamno.

ADD: Attention deficit disorder.

Affects: Shame, anger, disgust, dismell, fear, joy, sadness, interest, and startle. These are hardwired, human biological reactions.

Affirming Force [G]: The first force of the Law of Three.

Air [G]: Second being-food necessary for human sustenance but also containing special active elements. See also Foods.

Alarm Clock [G]: Gurdjieff's term for any stimulus from the outside that will wake us up from the sleeping-waking hypnotic trance we call being awake.

Alzheimer's Disease: Type of dementia wherein the individual gradually loses his cognitive faculties and memory, followed by deterioration of feelings and physical coordination.

Amplification: Expansion of a trait, emotion, sensation, or thought. As a practice, for example, I intentionally increase my manifestation of an emotion to a somewhat greater degree in order to see it more clearly.

Attention: Focusing or concentrating capability. Crucial for any kind of self-observation or self-study.

Authentic-I [S]: Result of data received conceived and nurtured only by the reception of new impressions of myself received by intentionally engaging in self-observation.

Automatic: Our usual state of functioning without consciousness.

Awareness: Mindfulness that something exists.

Being: Inner oneness, degree of harmonization of the centers, as distinct from behavior.

Being Self-Perfection [G]: Harmonization and balancing of the centers with the aim of development of higher being-bodies.

Being-Partkdolg-Duty [G]: The primary means for self-perfecting practiced by three-brained beings on all planets in the universe where such beings exist; also expressed as "conscious labors and intentional sufferings."

Biographical-I [S]: One's identity, built from the experiences of life.

Bobbin-kandelnosts [G]: Devices residing in each center resembling, figuratively, a spool or watch spring upon which are imprinted all the associations of that center. If a person lives only according to the principle of Itoklanoz rather than by the Foolasnitamnian Principle, the associations are activated willy-nilly by internal and external stimuli, and the spool unwinds accordingly. When the Bobbin-kandelnost is fully unwound, the center or brain dies. If the individual has forgotten not to give himself up wholly to the associations from one center only, one brain will use up its material first and die. The other two centers are left alive and the organism is thus severely disabled. Gurdjieff calls it, "dying by thirds."

> Just as the spring of a watch has a winding of a definite duration, so these beings also can associate and experience only as much as the possibilities for experiencing put into them by Nature during the crystallization of those

same Bobbin-kandelnosts in their brains. They can associate and consequently exist just so much, and not a whit
more nor less. BT p. 440.

Bodies [G]: Besides our physical or "planetary" body, we can, with
work, develop two higher bodies within us; but as we are, we do not
work with the proper energy to develop them. They are, the "Kesdjan,"
"astral," or "emotional body" and the "mental" or "soul" body. We must
produce the connections and "coat" these higher bodies intentionally
from finer substances.

> Substances required for the blood of the planetary of the
> being enter into them through their "first-being-food" or,
> as your favourites say, "through food."

> But the substances needed both for coating and for
> perfecting the higher being-body Kesdjan enter their
> common presences through their, as they say, "breathing"
> and through certain what are called "pores" of their skin.

> And the sacred cosmic substances required for the coating
> of the highest being-body, which sacred being-part of
> theirs, as I have already told you, they call soul, can be
> assimilated and correspondingly transformed and coated
> in them, just as in us, exclusively only from the process of
> what is called "Aiessirittoorassnian-contemplation" actu-
> alized in the common presence by the cognized intention
> on the part of all their spiritualized independent parts. BT,
> p. 569.

Buffers [O]: Energy blockages unintentionally created in people, by
themselves and not by nature, through education and the hypnotic
influence of all surrounding life; so that they do not experience the
contradictions among their different "I's."

> "Buffers" lull a man to sleep, give him the agreeable and
> peaceful sensation that all will be well, that no contra-
> dictions exist and that he can sleep in peace. "Buffers"
> are appliances by means of which a man can always be in

the right. "Buffers" help a man not to feel his conscience. Search, p. 155.

Centers [G]: Independent localizations of energy in the body that have their own intelligence and can even act as whole personalities. In various places in *In Search of the Miraculous*, Ouspensky quotes Gurdjieff speaking about the centers ranging in number from three to seven. The instinctive, moving, feeling or emotional, thinking, and sex center are the five lower centers; and the higher emotional, and higher intellectual centers exist in us although we are not in touch with them. Later on in the book, and in *Beelzebub's Tales to His Grandson*, Gurdjieff speaks primarily of just three centers or three brains: the moving/instinctive, the feeling or emotional and the intellectual centers. He distinguishes three-brained beings from two-brained beings (other mammals, birds, and reptiles) and one-brained beings (worms, insects, arachnids, corals, etc.), and says three-brained beings play an active role in the drama of the cosmos. Having three brains or centers means that men and women can manifest the law of three inside themselves.

> Three-brained beings have the possibility personally to perfect themselves, because in them there are localized three centers of their common presence or three brains, upon which afterwards, when the process of Djartklom proceeds in the Omnipresent-Okidanokh, the three holy forces of the sacred Triamazikamno are deposited and they acquire the possibility for their further, this time, independent actualizings. BT, p. 145.

Chaos: Inherent unpredictability of a system.

Classical Conditioning: A method of pairing conditioned stimuli with unconditioned stimuli so that the subject associates one with the other. Example: a father always gives his four-year-old son a big, loving hug as soon as he comes home. The hug is preceded by the front screen door slamming (conditioned stimulus). The son learns to associate this slamming door with his father's wonderful hug (unconditioned stimulus).

Conscience [G]: Universal sense of right and wrong which should govern a person's conduct. Given great emphasis in Gurdjieff's teachings as the "very representative of the Creator" and crucial for our transformation. Through conscience, we can free ourselves from Kundabuffer, which man can no longer do through the practice of Faith Hope or Love (Charity). Conscience is obscured by buffers, including those associated with morality and culture.

> . . . conscience is the fire which alone . . . can create the unity which a man lacks in that state in which he begins to study himself. The concept "conscience" has nothing in common with the concept "morality." Conscience is a general and permanent phenomenon. Conscience is the same for all men and conscience is only possible in the absence of "buffers." Search, p. 156.

Conscious Labor [G]: Intentional work toward an aim while maintaining a sense of one's own presence.

Conscious Labors and Intentional Sufferings [G]: What Gurdjieff called "being-Partkdolg-duty." Gurdjieff does not define them, but simply states they were given to us as the chief means for our self-perfecting and for service to higher purposes.

Conscious Shock [G]: Intentional or artificial action taken to facilitate the start or continuation of an octave, in contrast to mechanical shocks that come about without our own volition.

> The third octave, that is, the octave of impressions, begins through a conscious effort. Search, p. 189.

Consciousness [G]: Properly, the state of being awake and aware of what is going on around you; a state where you yourself exist in the moment. What we ordinarily call "consciousness" is what Gurdjieff called our "waking state," a half-aware state that is continually changing.

> We have only the possibility of consciousness and rare flashes of it. Therefore we cannot define what consciousness is. Search, p. 117.

Countertransference: A therapist's unintentional transference toward a particular client. See also Transference.

Denial: State of mind marked by the refusal or inability to recognize and/or deal with an existing problem.

Denying Force [G]: Second holy force of the Law of Three, also called resisting force, or passive force.

Disidentification: Capacity of separating a part of one's mind from one's thoughts, feelings, or behavior in a given situation.

Enneagram [G]: Symbol showing the interaction of the primordial cosmic laws of three and seven.

Essence [G]: A person's nature before the development of personality; what one is born with.

Evolution and Involution [G]: Two directions of an octave: in the evolutionary octave, energy is boosted up and becomes finer; in the involutionary, energy travels downward, is weakened and becomes coarser.

Experimentation [K]: Advanced practice consisting of making small changes in habits or activities as a means of gaining additional self-knowledge and understanding; as opposed to simply observing.

External Considering [G]: Capacity to put oneself into another's shoes—that is, into the psychological state and/or requirements of another person in a particular situation.

False Personality [G]: Persona or mask each of us develops to adjust to the foreign environment we enter at birth. In many ways, personality is a survival mechanism; but it often has a part added on that is not natural and is unnecessary for survival and interaction with others. This other, false part is born later than personality, and it is usually the result of insecurity.

Foods [G]: Gurdjieff extends the concept of food to include a second kind of food, air, and a third, impressions.

Foolasnitamnian Principle [G]: Way of living proper to three-brained beings, in contrast to the Itoklanoz Principle. The Foolasnitamnian Principle is the natural one and was presumed to again govern three-brained beings on earth after the removal of the organ Kundabuffer.

> The first kind or first principle of being-existence which
> is called Foolasnitamnian is proper to all three-brained

> beings arising on any planet of our Great Universe, and
> the fundamental aim and sense of the existence of these
> beings is that there proceed through them the transmuta-
> tion of cosmic substances necessary for what is called the
> common-cosmic trogoautoegocratic process. BT, p. 130.

Fourth Way [G]: Path proposed by Gurdjieff, distinct from the three traditional ways of the fakir, the monk, and the yogi. The fourth way develops all three of the major centers simultaneously. It is practiced in ordinary life conditions—no withdrawal from ordinary life is necessary or even advisable.

Gatekeeper and Gatekeeping: Individual and collective dynamics that resist and restrict experience. The "gatekeeper" is the personifica-tion of these dynamics.

Hasnamuss [G]: Individual who somehow has managed to develop self-consciousness or higher being-bodies but who lacks conscience, is depraved, takes pleasure in leading others astray, and so on. In partic-ular, the hasnamuss strives to be what he is not.

Hazard: The unpredictable or free nature of existence, which makes possible free choice and acts of intelligence.

Heropass, Merciless Heropass [G]: Passage of time itself.

Higher Being-Body [G]: Soul. See Bodies

Higher Emotional [G]: One of two higher centers that is complete and working within us, but inaccessible in our ordinary state.

> . . . the difference in speed between the speed of our usual
> emotions and the speed of the higher emotional center is
> so great that no connection can take place and we fail to
> hear within us the voices which are speaking and calling to
> us from the higher emotional center. Search, p. 195.

Higher Intellectual [G]: One of two higher centers that is complete and working within us, but only accessible through the higher emotional center.

> In most cases where accidental contact with the higher thinking center takes place a man becomes unconscious. Search, p. 195.

Hydrogens [G]: The basic element or substance of life, when not connected with a particular center. Hydrogens are numbered according to what Gurdjieff called their "density of vibrations," and so can be thought of as higher or lower energies, the higher energies being finer or less dense.

> . . . the term "point of the universe" . . . has a quite definite meaning, namely, a "point" represents a certain combination of hydrogens which is organized in a definite place and fulfills a definite function in one or another system. The concept "point" cannot be replaced by the concept "hydrogen" because "hydrogen" means simply matter not limited by space. A point is always limited in space. At the same time, a "point of the universe" can be designated by the number of the "hydrogen" which predominates in it or is central to it. Search, p. 170.

Hypnosis [G]: Sleep, or waking-sleep, that operates throughout one's ordinary life.

"I": Pronoun used when referring to oneself. The illusion that we have one "I," according to Gurdjieff, arises from the fact that we have the same body and the same or only a few different names throughout our lives. See also Multiplicity of "I's."

Identification [S]: Identification refers to my attachment—that is, an inability to separate my authentic-I from that to which any of my "I's" are attached, be it an idea, belief, image, feeling, sensation, situation, material object, or anything else. State in which a person is only able to experience himself through his attachment at a given moment to whatever has attracted his attention without realizing that he exists separate from whatever has attracted his attention.

> Man is always in a state of identification, only the object of his identification changes. Search, p.150.

Imago: Image a person unconsciously projects onto their partner that represents both of one's parents or other caregivers.

Impressions [G]: Third being-food.

Incarnation: Being in a body.

Inner Considering [G]: Identification with what a person imagines others think of him.

> He always worries other people do not value him enough, are not sufficiently polite and courteous. All this torments him, makes him suspect others and lose an immense amount of energy on guesswork, on suppositions, and develops in him a distrustful and hostile attitude. How somebody looked at him, what somebody thought of him, what somebody said of him – all this acquires for him an immense significance. Search, p. 151.

Instinctive-Moving Center [G]: The part of the human nervous system that controls all involuntary (autonomic nervous system) and also learned movements.

Intellectual Center [G]: The localization (brain) of the intellectual/ cognitive activities of a person.

Intentional Suffering [G]: Consciously putting oneself in an uncomfortable position to fulfill an aim or obligation connected with being-Partkdolg-duty.

Interpersonal: Behaviors and experiences resulting from a relationship between at least two people.

Intrapersonal: Behaviors and experiences taking place within a single individual.

Introjection: Imitation of a psychological or behavioral trait of a parent, caregiver or other, which becomes a permanent aspect of the person's psychological makeup.

Itoklanoz Principle [G] : Living according to the same mechanisms as one- and two-brained beings. Attention being subject to activation and reception of the associations (impressions) of only one center at a time. See also Foolasnitamnian Principle.

Kesdjan body [G]: See Bodies.

Kundabuffer [G]: An inhibiting device that was implanted in humans at some unspecified time long ago, which served to block the development of intelligence. Although it was eventually removed, it still acts on mankind through cultural influences right up to the present day, hindering our ability to perceive reality. This may have been a traumatic event for all of mankind with negative consequences that afflict us all still.

> ... [A] special organ with a property such that, first, they should perceive reality topsy-turvy and, secondly, that every repeated impression from outside should crystallize in them data which would engender factors for evoking in them sensations of "pleasure" and "enjoyment." BT, p. 88.

Kundalini [G]: According to Gurdjieff, a bastardization of the word "Kundabuffer," following the loss of understanding its meaning.

Law of Octaves, Law of Sevenfoldness (Heptaparaparshinokh) [G]: Idea that every process, no matter upon what level it takes place, is governed by a structure analogous to the seven-toned scale. Every completed process is a transition from the initial note "Do" through a series of successive tones to the "Do" of the next octave. The transition is not continuous and requires interventions or shocks at two specific places or "intervals" for it to be completed.

Law of Reciprocal Maintenance [G]: See Reciprocal Maintenance.

Law of Three (Triamazikamno) [G]: Three independent forces—active, passive, and neutralizing, Gurdjieff's second fundamental law of the universe. Nothing can happen nor can there be any real change without the participation of the three independent forces working together.

> ... the second fundamental cosmic law ... consists of three independent forces, that is to say, this sacred law manifests in everything, without exception, and everywhere in the Universe, in three separate independent aspects; and these three aspects exist in the Universe under the following denominations: the first, under the denomination, the Holy-Affirming; the second, the Holy-Denying; and the third, the Holy-Reconciling; and this is also why,

concerning this sacred law and its three independent forces, the said Objective Science has, among its formulations, specially concerning this sacred law, the following: a law which always flows into a consequence and becomes the cause of subsequent consequences, and always functions by three independent and quite opposite characteristic manifestations, latent within it, in properties neither seen nor sensed. BT pp. 138–139.

Level of Being [S]: Degree of completion of the possibilities inherent in the human organism.

Megalocosmos [G]: The whole universe.

Mental Body: The higher mind, in some teachings; in the analogy of the equipage, where the carriage is the physical body; the horse is the astral body; the driver is the mental body; and the master is the causal body.

Mentation [G]: Thinking, in Gurdjieff's terminology; in general, thinking carefully about something.

Metanoia: From the Greek, "to think in a new way." Translated in the Bible as "repentance"; more generally, a transformative change of heart.

Movements: Training exercises and sacred dances developed by Gurdjieff to strengthen the attention and the ability to work with all three centers. They are practiced in a group working in concert and accompanied by music. The Movements were said to be both a spiritual practice and a kind of book where one might learn about the ideas of world creation and world maintenance, if one could read the language.

Multiplicity of "I's": Psychological state of an undeveloped man or woman. Ordinary people, says Gurdjieff, lack unity, or a real "I," but say "I" to every passing thought, feeling, emotion, or association.

Muscular Amnesia: Body's tendency to hold tension in a muscle when the need for that tension has passed.

Noticing: John G. Bennett, *Noticing*, (North Yorks, UK: Coombe Springs Press, 1976), 13-14.

"Noticing is connected with the "I," with the real "I." But because we have nothing prepared that is able to give this a place in us, it is just a moment. It is also fair to say that noticing is something that happens to our essence; but because we cannot remain conscious of ourselves in our essence until very considerable changes have happened, we notice, and then our personality takes over. After the moment of noticing, though very interesting things may happen, they no longer have that extraordinary quality. From that moment onwards, we think, we see, we argue with ourselves, we run away, we avoid things, all the different ways in which the personality can react to a situation."

Objective Consciousness: State of being characterized by presence, awareness, and impartiality.
Obligolnian Strivings [G]: Natural aims toward the development of being that a normal man or woman would pursue over the course of a lifetime.
Octaves [G]: See Law of Octaves.
Organic or Instinctive Shame [G]: See Shame.

Participation [K] [S]: Allowing oneself to be what one is, while being a spectator from the inside of oneself.
Personality: Mechanism built into the psyche in response to the demands of culture and society.
Planetary Body [G]: Physical body.
Pondering: Deeply mulling over an idea or situation, being interested in it and viewing it from many different angles; finding the meaning in the words describing a thing or situation. Ideally, attempting to understand, which requires data from each of the three main centers.
Preconscious: State of awareness just beneath a person's ordinary level of consciousness, where a vague knowledge or understanding may reside. The meaning of what is there is usually missed, although if one were more sensitive, he could, in fact, notice it.

Presence: Truly being here, at least in a physical sense, but implying the whole of oneself.

> . . . each is, in his whole presence, exactly similar in every respect to our Megalocosmos. BT, p. 777.

Prieuré: Large estate near Versailles, France, where Gurdjieff set up his Institute for the Harmonious Development of Man.

Projection: Unconscious denial of one's own individual defects, past situations, or experiences, and instead attribution of such defects to others, such as partners in close relationships, leaders, or other group members. Such attribution colors or influences a person's interactions or views of other people.

Projective Identification: Attribution of a thought, belief, or emotion unacceptable to oneself onto another. More complex than simple projection, since the individual does not fully disavow his own impulses and may even remain aware of them, but believes his own reactions are justifiable as responses to the other person's behavior. In this way, a person, in what can feel like a "magical" way, induces the very feelings in the other that he or she mistakenly attributed to this other person.

Psychostatic and Psychokinetic people: John G. Bennett's division of humanity into three groups: the psychostatic group, those who are not making any attempt to evolve, although they may be powerful and effective in the external world; the psychokinetic group, who are actively involved in work on themselves, but are neither fully awake nor fully asleep and may be uncertain and in need of spiritual guidance; and the psychoteleios group, who have realized their potential.

PTSD: Post-traumatic stress disorder. The reaction to a traumatic, often life-threatening event, which has caused a range of dysfunctional behaviors.

Ray of Creation [O]: Large octave comprising the whole universe of which our solar system is a lower branch.

Real "I" [G]: Result of long work to fully know, understand, and be able to direct one's will.

Reciprocal Maintenance [G]: Process of mutual feeding and support through which all systems and life forms in the Universe maintain their existence.

> In all probability there exists in the World some law of the reciprocal maintenance of everything existing. Obviously our lives serve also for maintaining something great or small in the World. BT, pp. 1094–1095.

Reconciling Force [G]: Third force of the Law of Three.

Reflexivity: The ability to reflect on and engage the patterns of one's behavior, thoughts, emotions, movements, and sensations that shape our lives.

Repression: Pushing down of unacceptable feelings or thoughts, in a manner that we cannot access them in our usual state of waking consciousness.

Robot: Automatic functioning of the man-machine without the presence of one's own "I."

Schadenfreude: German word for exultation in the difficulties of others.

Second conscious shock [G]: Associated with self-remembering and valuation of the Work, needed to complete our transformation; allows for the production of finer energies obtained by making a conscious effort in the moment an impression is received. See also Shocks.

Self-calming [G]: Unconsciously decreasing anxiety through various means, including denial, addiction, distraction, justification, etc.

Self-consciousness: Capacity for awareness of one's being.

Self-observation [G]: Impartial observation of oneself existing in the moment.

Self-remembering [G]: One of the key concepts in Gurdjieff's teaching, the directing of the attention toward myself AND toward something else, either inside or outside the body, without allowing the focus on either to wane. In self-observation, our consciousness is split into an observing "I" and the object of self-observation—taking the body, for example, as a starting point. If, you place your attention on the "I" which is now separated from your body, then your awareness of yourself and this "I" is the act of self-remembering.

> Try to remember yourselves when you observe yourselves and later on tell me the results. Only those results will

have any value that are accompanied by self-remembering. Otherwise, you yourself do not exist in your observations. In which case, what are all your observations worth? Search, p. 118.

Self-study: Practice comprising impartial self-observation to gain truthful knowledge and understanding of oneself.

Sensing [G]: Direct experience of the living energy within our bodies, including those of posture and movement as well as those having to do with the interior processes of the organism.

Sensitive Energy: Energy the body uses to organize and operate itself.

Shame [G]: Instinctive or organic feeling proper to three-brained beings, connected with conscience; in contrast to artificial culturally and socially based pseudo-shame.

Shocks [G]: Interventions in a process where an additional energy or quality is needed to reach completion. There are mechanical shocks that arise without our awareness or intention and conscious shocks that require our active participation.

Sittings: Group work consisting of sitting in quiet surroundings and following certain guidelines that prepare and create energy for Work. Individual work of the same type is also called "sitting."

Somatic: Relating to the body, its abilities, attributes, and actions.

Soul: See Bodies.

Sovereign Learner: A term from Elizabeth Schreiber's work: That part of us that was active as a child, the part that was enthralled and interested in all aspects of the world and life.

Splitting: In psychology, the unconscious failure to integrate the good and bad aspects of another person or oneself into a unified whole.

Superego: That part of the personality in Sigmund Freud's psychoanalytic theory that comprises the ideals and strictures we have acquired from our parents and society. The superego works to suppress the urges of the id and tries to make the ego behave morally, rather than realistically.

Stopping Thoughts: Practice that some may associate with Gurdjieff's Work. It is ill-advised to undertake such a practice.

Subconscious [G]: Gurdjieff's terminology for the unconscious. This is where true consciousness has retreated, due to the unbecoming nature of human beings.

Sublimation: In psychology, situation where an individual takes inner energies that may be taboo in society and transforms them into outward activity of a more socially acceptable nature.

Three-Centered or Three-Brained Beings [G]: See Centers.

Transference: Passing on or displacing an emotion or affective attitude from one person to another person or object.

Transformation [G]: Fundamental change in a human being into what he should be, normally; as Gurdjieff would say, a person "made in the image of God" and an intelligent participant in the evolution of the universe.

> . . . that transformation which should in general proceed in the entirety of a man and give him, from his own conscious mentation, the results he ought to have, which are proper to man and not merely to single- or double-brained animals. BT, p. 25.

Trauma [S]: Unintegrated negative human experience that causes disharmony within the psyche and dysfunctional behavior.

Trogoautoegocratic Process [G]: Universal process of eating and being eaten.

> . . . this system, which maintains everything arisen and existing, was actualized by our Endless Creator in order that what is called the "exchange of substances" or the "Reciprocal-feeding" of everything that exists, might proceed in the Universe and thereby that the merciless "Heropass" might not have its maleficent effect on the Sun Absolute. BT, pp. 136–137.

Unconscious: That part of human consciousness in modern psychology that is unavailable in our waking-sleeping state. See Subconscious.

Understanding [G]: Distinguished from knowledge because it comes from being, from the whole of oneself and all three centers.

Waking-Sleeping State: Second of our four possible degrees of consciousness, when we are awake but not self-conscious.

Way of the Fakir [G]: Path of self-development based on mastery of the human body. Asceticism.

Way of the Monk [G]: Path of self-development based on devotion and feeling, associated with religion. Worship.

Way of the Yogi [G]: Path of self-development based on development and mastery of mental energies. Meditation.

BIBLIOGRAPHY

American Psychiatric Association. *Diagnostic and Statistical Manual of Mental Disorders*. New York: American Psychiatric Association, 2000.

Benjamin, Harry. *Basic Self-knowledge: Based on the Gurdjieff System of Development*. New York: Samuel Weiser, 1980.

Bennett, John G. *The Dramatic Universe, Volume I*. Gloucestershire, UK: Coombe Springs Press, 1966.

_____. *The Dramatic Universe Series, 1 Hazard*. Ripon, UK: Coombe Springs Press 1976.

_____. *Energies, Material, Vital, Cosmic* Gloucestershire, UK: Coombe Springs Press, 1964).

_____. *Existence*. Santa Fe: Bennett Books, 2010.

_____. *The Masters of Wisdom*. New York: Samuel Weiser, 1977.

_____. *Needs of a New Age Community*. North Yorkshire, England: Coombe Springs Press, 1977.

_____. *Noticing*. North Yorks, UK: Coombe Springs Press, 1976.

_____. *Talks On Beelzebub's Tales*. Masham, Ripon, UK: Coombe Springs Press, 1977.

_____. *What Are We Living For?* Santa Fe: Bennett Books, 1991.

Brown Jr., Tom. *The Tracker*. Berkley: Berkley Publishing Group, 1996.

Collin, Rodney. *The Theory of Conscious Harmony*. Boulder: Shambhala, 1984.

_____. *The Theory of Celestial Influence*. London: Stuart and Watkins, 1968.

Eliot, T. S. *Four Quartets*. New York: Harcourt Press, 1943.

Gurdjieff, George I. *All and Everything, First Series: Beelzebub's Tales to His Grandson*. New York: Harcourt, Brace and Company, 1950.

_____. *All and Everything, Second Series: Meetings With Remarkable Men*. New York: E.P. Dutton & Co., 1969.

_____. *Views from the Real World*. New York: Compass, 1984.

Hendrix, Harville. *Getting the Love Your Want: A Guide For Couples.* New York: Harper & Row, 1990.

Johnson, Robert. *Transformation: Understanding the Three levels of Masculine Consciousness.* New York: HarperCollins Publishers, 1991.

King, C. Daly. *The Oragean Version.* New York: Business Photo Reproduction, 1951.

Kipnis, Aaron. *Knights Without Armor.* Los Angeles: Jeremy P. Tarcher, 1991.

Lusseyran, Jacques. *Against the Pollution of the I.* Sandpoint, ID: Morning Light Press, 2006.

Moore, Thomas. *Care of the Soul.* New York: HarperCollins Publishers, 1992.

Nathanson, Donald L. *Shame and Pride.* New York: W. W. Norton & Company, 1992.

Nicoll, Maurice. *The Mark.* Boulder: Shambhala, 1985.

Orage, A. R. *The Active Mind.* London: Janus Press, 1954.

Ouspensky, P. D. *In Search of the Miraculous.* New York: Harcourt, Brace & World, 1949.

_____. *The Fourth Way: A Record of Talks and Answers to Questions Based on the Teaching of G. I. Gurdjieff.* New York: Knopf, 1957.

Peters, Fritz, *My Journey With A Mystic.* Laguna Niguel, California: Tale Weaver Publishing, 1980.

Real, Terrence. *I Don't Want to Talk About It.* New York: Fireside 1997.

Rebar, Arthur S. *Dictionary of Psychology.* London: Penguin Books, 1985.

Reich, Wilhelm. *Character Analysis.* New York: Orgone Institute Press, 1949.

Sapolsky, Robert. *Why Zebras Don't get Ulcers.* New York: W. H. Freeman, 2000.

Seligman, Martin E. P. "The Effectiveness of Psychotherapy," American Psychologist 50, no. 12 (December 1995): 965–974.

Tolle, Eckhart. *The Power of Now*. Novato, California: New World Library, 2001.

Walker, Kenneth. *A Study of Gurdjieff's Teaching*. London, UK: Jonathon Cape, 1965.

Weil, Simone. *Waiting for God*. New York: HarperCollins, 2001.

Wolfe, Edwin. *Episodes with Gurdjieff*. San Francisco: Far West Press, 1974.

Index